Mathematica 4 Standard Add-on Packages

D1069956

Library of Congress Cataloging–in–Publication Data

Mathematica 4.0 standard add-on packages : the official guide to
over a thousand additional functions for use with Mathematica 4 /
Wolfram Research.
Champaign, IL : Wolfram Media, 1999.
    p.   cm.
Includes index.
ISBN 1-5795500–6–1 (hardcover: alk. paper)
ISBN 1-5795500–7–X (paperback: alk. paper)
    1. Mathematica (Computer file) 2. Mathematics—Data processing.
I. Wolfram Research (Firm)
QA76.95.M386   1999
510'.285'5369—21   99-20671
                                                           CIP

For the latest updates and corrections to this book visit:
documents.wolfram.com

Comments on this book will be welcomed at:
comments@wolfram.com

**In publications that refer to the *Mathematica*
system, please cite this book as:** Wolfram Research,
Mathematica 4.0 Standard Add-on Packages
(Wolfram Media, 1999)

WOLFRAM
MEDIA

ISBN 1-57955-006-1 Hardback
ISBN 1-57955-007-X Paperback

Wolfram Media, Inc.
web: www.wolfram–media.com; *email:* info@wolfram–media.com
phone: +1–217–398–9090; *fax:* +1–217–398–9095
mail: 100 Trade Center Drive, Champaign, IL 61820, USA

WOLFRAM
RESEARCH

Wolfram Research, Inc.
web: www.wolfram.com
email: info@wolfram.com
phone: 217–398–0700
fax: 217–398–0747
mail: 100 Trade Center Drive
Champaign, IL 61820–7237
USA

Wolfram Research Europe Ltd.
web: www.wolfram.co.uk
email: info@wolfram.co.uk
phone: +44–(0)1993–883400
fax: +44–(0)1993–883800
mail: 10 Blenheim Office Park
Lower Road, Long Hanborough
Oxfordshire OX8 8LN
UNITED KINGDOM

Wolfram Research Asia Ltd.
web: www.wolfram.co.jp
email: info@wolfram.co.jp
phone: +81–(0)3–5276–0506
fax: +81–(0)3–5276–0509
mail: Izumi Building 8F
3–2–15 Misaki-cho
Chiyoda-ku, Tokyo 101–0061
JAPAN

MATHEMATICA®

Note: All services are also available at wolfram.co.uk and wolfram.co.jp, as well as at wolfram.com.

General information:
info@wolfram.com
www.wolfram.com

**Frequently asked technical
and other questions:**
www.wolfram.com/faq

**User registration and password
requests:**
register@wolfram.com
www.wolfram.com/register
*Institutional and other non-owner users
are also encouraged to register.*

Technical support and bug reports:
support@wolfram.com
www.wolfram.com/support
Support is available only to registered users.

***Mathematica* products:**
orders@wolfram.com
www.wolfram.com/orders
*Order all Wolfram Research products
and upgrades online.*

***Mathematica* books and miscellanea:**
www.wolfram.com/bookstore

***MathSource* Electronic Library:**
www.mathsource.com
ftp.mathsource.com

***MathWire* electronic newsletter:**
www.wolfram.com/mathwire

mathgroup newsgroup:
news: comp.soft-sys.math.mathematica
www.wolfram.com/mathgroup

Suggestions:
suggest@wolfram.com
www.wolfram.com/suggestions

***Mathematica* Archive:**
*Wolfram Research maintains an archive
of Mathematica-related documents.
Publications and other non-proprietary
material are welcome at:*

The *Mathematica* Archive
Wolfram Research, Inc.
100 Trade Center Drive
Champaign, IL 61820–7237, USA
email: archive@wolfram.com
web: www.wolfram.com/archive

Book Credits

Editors: Emily Martin and John Novak • *Contributors:* Victor Adamchik, Jeff Adams, Alexei Bocharov, Philip Boyland, Arun Chandra, Yu He, Jerry Keiper, Rob Knapp, Emily Martin, John Novak, Marko Petkovsek, Steven Skiena, Mark Sofroniou, Adam Strzebonski, Ilan Vardi, Audra Wenzlow, Tom Wickham-Jones and David Withoff • *Typesetters:* Buddy Ritchie, Tony Sarno and Philip Wall • *Editorial Assistants:* Caroline Small and Jan Progen • *Proofreaders:* Rebecca Bigelow, Carol Ordal, Wendy Leung and Angela Latham • *Testers:* Anna Marichev, Larry Calmer and Emily Martin • *Cover designers:* John Bonadies and Linda Kwon • *Book designers:* John Bonadies and André Kuzniarek • *Online version developers:* Chris LaReau, Robby Villegas, Leland Ray and Bill White • *Project manager:* André Kuzniarek • *Manufacturing manager:* Jeanine Bensken

For *Mathematica* software credits, see About Mathematica in the *Mathematica* front end.

Table of Contents

1. Introduction

■ The Standard Add-on Packages

The *Mathematica* system contains a large number of built-in functions. Most versions of *Mathematica* also include a collection of standard add-on packages that define many additional functions in areas such as algebra, calculus, graphics, discrete and numerical mathematics, number theory, and statistics. This book describes those functions.

In addition to the standard add-on packages, there are an immense number of specialized add-ons available for *Mathematica*. Some of these add-ons are distributed by Wolfram Research; for a current listing, see our web site at `www.wolfram.com/addons` or contact Wolfram Research. Many add-ons are also available through the *MathSource* electronic library at `www.wolfram.com/mathsource`.

Algebra	Miscellaneous
Calculus	NumberTheory
DiscreteMath	NumericalMath
Geometry	Statistics
Graphics	Utilities
LinearAlgebra	

Directories of standard add-on packages.

The standard add-on packages are divided into directories, each corresponding to a different topic. This introduction gives examples of the use of packages from each directory. Package functions are described in detail in the topic chapters. Functions that have made the transition from the standard add-on packages to the *Mathematica* kernel in Version 4.0, such as the Fourier, Laplace, and Z transforms, are also noted in the appropriate topic chapters.

<<*dir*`	initialize all packages from directory *dir*
<<*dir*`*package*`	read in a package from the named directory

Reading in standard add-on packages.

Throughout this book, packages are specified with the backquote character (`) used in *Mathematica* as a context mark. The appendices include information on contexts and how to set up *Mathematica* packages.

■ Algebra Packages

Mathematica provides many functions for working with polynomials, and the standard add-on `Algebra` packages extend that capability. There are functions for solving polynomial inequalities, counting and isolating roots of polynomials, and representing polynomials in terms of symmetric and remainder parts. The `Algebra` packages define `PolynomialExtendedGCD` and `PolynomialPowerMod`, adjuncts to the built-in functions `PolynomialGCD` and `PolynomialMod`. This group of packages also provides functions for manipulating quaternions and elements of Galois fields.

This initializes the `Algebra` packages.	*In[1]:=* `<<Algebra\``
Define p to be a fifth-degree polynomial in x.	*In[2]:=* `p = Expand[Product[x-j, {j, 5}]]`
	Out[2]= $-120 + 274 x - 225 x^2 + 85 x^3 - 15 x^4 + x^5$
`InequalitySolve` gives a logical expression representing the solution to this polynomial inequality.	*In[3]:=* `InequalitySolve[p < 0, x]`
	Out[3]= $x < 1 \;\|\| \; 2 < x < 3 \;\|\| \; 4 < x < 5$
`SemialgebraicComponents` gives a point in each connected component of the inequality solution set.	*In[4]:=* `SemialgebraicComponents[p < 0, x]`
	Out[4]= $\left\{0, \dfrac{91}{32}, \dfrac{33}{8}\right\}$
Here `CountRoots` gives the number of roots of p in the interval $(2.5, 4.5)$.	*In[5]:=* `CountRoots[p, {x, 2.5, 4.5}]`
	Out[5]= 2

Quaternion numbers $a + \mathrm{I}\, b + \mathrm{J}\, c + \mathrm{K}\, d$, denoted by `Quaternion[a, b, c, d]`, are an extension of the complex numbers $a + \mathrm{I}\, b$.

Load the function `ListPlotVectorField3D` for visualizing vector fields in three dimensions.	*In[6]:=* `<<Graphics\`PlotField3D\``

Consider a set of 27 quaternions, each with a zero real part. This shows how the nonreal part of a quaternion q from this set maps into the nonreal part of quaternion $\exp(q)$.

```
In[7]:= ListPlotVectorField3D[
          Flatten[
          Table[ {{b, c, d},
            Apply[List, Rest[ Exp[Quaternion[0, b, c, d]] ]]},
            {b, 1, 3}, {c, 1, 3}, {d, 1, 3}], 2],
          VectorHeads->True, ScaleFactor->.5]
```

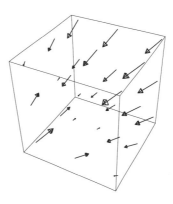

The `FiniteFields` package can be used to explore error-correcting codes for digital transmission and storage, and for other applications of Galois sequences. For example, the Simplex Code based on $GF(2^m)$, a finite field of order 2^m, has efficiency $m/2^m$ and detects 2^{m-2} errors per codeword of length $2^m - 1$.

This gives the Galois sequence for $GF(2^4)$.

```
In[8]:= sequence = First[Transpose[PowerList[GF[2, 4]]]]
Out[8]= {1, 0, 0, 0, 1, 1, 1, 1, 0, 1, 0, 1, 1, 0, 0}
```

This depicts the 15 codewords, each composed of four information bits and 11 check bits. Binary ones appear as white squares and binary zeros appear as black squares.

```
In[9]:= (codewords = Table[RotateRight[sequence, n],
            {n, 0, 14}];
          ListDensityPlot[codewords,
            FrameTicks -> {{4, 15}, Range[15]}])
```

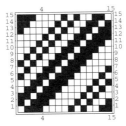

Here are the codewords after transmission through a channel that "flips" each bit with a probability of 0.25. Bits that differ from the original codewords are shaded gray.

```
In[10]:= (received = Map[If[Random[] < .25, Mod[#+1, 2], #]&,
            codewords, {2}];
         delta = Abs[received-codewords];
         ListDensityPlot[Table[If[delta[[i, j]] == 1,
            .5, codewords[[i, j]] ], {i, 15}, {j, 15}],
            FrameTicks -> {{4, 15}, Range[15]}])
```

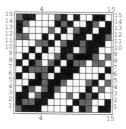

Decoding is accomplished by correlating each received word with the original sequence and finding the position of the peak.

```
In[11]:= decode[x_] := Module[{corr},
           corr = Table[Apply[Plus, (1-2 sequence) *
             RotateLeft[1-2 x, n]], {n, 0, 14}];
           codewords[[ Position[corr, Max[corr]][[1, 1]] ]] ]
```

Three received words were incorrectly decoded. Two words had four bits in error and one had six bits in error.

```
In[12]:= (corrected = Map[decode, received];
         delta = Abs[corrected-codewords];
         ListDensityPlot[Table[If[delta[[i, j]] == 1,
            .5, codewords[[i, j]] ], {i, 15}, {j, 15}],
            FrameTicks -> {{4, 15}, Range[15]}])
```

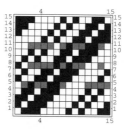

■ Calculus Packages

Mathematica has extensive built-in support for calculus, including integration, differentiation, differential equation solving, and limits. The Calculus packages extend this functionality by providing functions for finding complete integrals of differential equations, computing Padé approximations, and doing vector operations in various three-dimensional coordinate systems. The package VariationalMethods is useful for solving for a function extremizing a definite integral functional, a problem that appears in many areas of physics and engineering.

This causes each `Calculus` package to load as needed.

```
In[1]:= <<Calculus`
```

The function `VariationalBound` can be used to give an upper bound on the first eigenvalue λ_1 associated with the vibrating string problem. Here assume that the string has unit length, density, and tension. The integral $\int_0^1 \phi'(x)^2\, dx$ is minimized over all approximating eigenfunctions $\phi(x)$ having the same form as the specified trial function.

For a vibrating string with a fixed end at $x = 0$, a trial function $\phi(x)$ is picked such that $\phi(0) = 0$. The parameter a is chosen to satisfy a normalization condition.

```
In[2]:= (phitrial = a x^k;
         eq = (Integrate[phitrial^2, {x, 0, 1},
            Assumptions -> {k > 1/2}] == 1);
         phitrial = (phitrial /. Solve[eq, a])[[1]])
```

$$Out[2]= -\sqrt{1+2k}\ x^k$$

The bound is $\lambda_1 \le 2.77$, close to the precise value $\lambda_1 = \pi^2/4$.

```
In[3]:= VariationalBound[D[phi[x], x]^2,
         phi[x], {x, 0, 1}, phitrial, {k}]
```

$$Out[3]= \{2.77254, \{k \to 0.809017\}\}$$

■ Discrete Mathematics Packages

Discrete mathematics is concerned with enumerable mathematical structures, such as are studied in combinatorics, graph theory, and computational geometry. The `DiscreteMath` packages include `Combinatorica`, which provides over 200 functions for the study of combinatorics and graph theory; `ComputationalGeometry`, which provides several important geometric functions useful in nonparametric data analysis; and `RSolve`, for solving recurrence equations.

This causes each `DiscreteMath` package to load as needed.

```
In[1]:= <<DiscreteMath`
```

You can solve recurrence equations directly using `RSolve`.

```
In[2]:= (de = r[n + 2] - 2 * r[n + 1] + r[n] == 2;
         RSolve[{de, r[0] == 1, r[1] == m}, r[n], n])
```

$$Out[2]= \{\{r[n] \to 1 + (-2+m)\,n + n^2\}\}$$

Or you can solve them using the Z transform.

```
In[3]:= ztrans = (ZTransform[de, n, z] /.
         {r[0] -> 1, r[1] -> m})
```

$$Out[3]= -m\,z - z^2 + \text{ZTransform}[r[n], n, z] + z^2\,\text{ZTransform}[r[n], n, z] - 2\,(-z + z\,\text{ZTransform}[r[n], n, z]) ==$$
$$\frac{2z}{-1+z}$$

```
In[4]:= (solve = Solve[ztrans, ZTransform[r[n], n, z]];
         Simplify[InverseZTransform[solve, z, n]])
```

$$Out[4]= \{\{r[n] \to 1 + (-2+m)\,n + n^2\}\}$$

The `Combinatorica` package provides definitions of many graph objects. The five-dimensional hypercube has a three-dimensional cube in each corner of the square.

```
In[5]:= ShowGraph[ Hypercube[5] ]
```

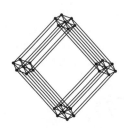

This reads a file of piezometric-head data for the Wolfcamp aquifer in the western United States. The triples give an (x, y) location with respect to an arbitrary origin and the water level in feet above sea level.

```
In[6]:= data = ReadList["wolfcamp.aquifer.data",
          Number, RecordLists->True];
```

The Voronoi polygons are useful in spatial statistics because they define a "region of influence" for each data point. The aquifer water level throughout a polygonal region can be approximated by the measurement at the center of the polygon.

```
In[7]:= (data2D = Map[Drop[#, -1]&, data];
       triangulation = DelaunayTriangulation[data2D];
       {polygonVertices, polygonVal} =
         VoronoiDiagram[data2D, triangulation];
       DiagramPlot[data2D, polygonVertices, polygonVal,
         Axes -> True, AxesLabel -> {x, y},
         AxesOrigin -> {-150, -30},
         LabelPoints -> False, TrimPoints -> 6,
         Ticks -> {Automatic, {-50, 0, 50, 100, 150, 200}}])
```

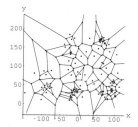

This displays the surface formed by a
linear interpolation between the data
points in the original three-dimensional
set.

```
In[8]:= TriangularSurfacePlot[data, triangulation,
            BoxRatios->{1, 1, .3}, Axes -> True,
            ViewPoint -> {1.3, 2.4, 2.}]
```

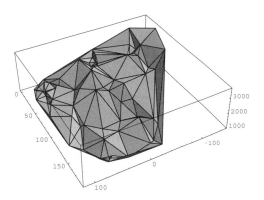

■ Graphics and Geometry Packages

The `Graphics` packages offer log, polar, error, scatter, vector field, surface of revolution, three-dimensional contour, and implicit plots. Functions include maps for visualizing complex functions of complex numbers, and bar and pie charts for visualizing data. *Mathematica*'s built-in graphics are enhanced by arrow, legend, and color directives, and by two-dimensional spline primitives and three-dimensional shape primitives. There are functions for the stellation and geodesation of regular polyhedra, animation of a sequence of graphics, and support for the 3-Script file format. The `Geometry` packages provide functions giving the characteristics of regular polygons and polyhedra and rotation in two and three dimensions.

This causes each `Graphics` package to
be loaded as functions from the
package are needed.

```
In[1]:= <<Graphics`
```

Here is a pie chart of the distribution of certain *Mathematica* users by field.

```
In[2]:=  (styles = Map[Hue, Range[0, 10]/10 .7];
         ShowLegend[
         PieChart[ {29, 20, 16, 16, 5, 4, 3, 2, 1, 1, 4},
           PieStyle -> styles, PieLabels -> Join[
           {"Engineering", "Physical Sciences",
            "Computer Sciences", "Mathematical Sciences"},
           Table["", {7}]], DisplayFunction -> Identity],
         {Transpose[{Drop[styles, 4],
           {"Life Sciences", "Business Finance",
            "Administration", "Social Sciences",
            "Arts Humanities", "Technology", "Other"}
           }], LegendTextSpace -> 5, LegendPosition->{.5, -1},
             LegendShadow->{0, 0}}
         ])
```

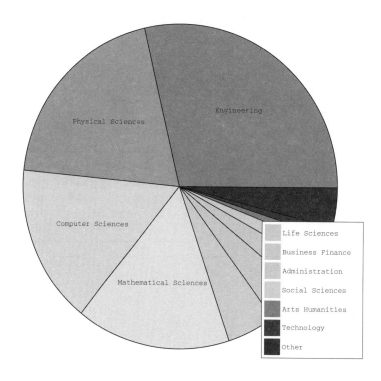

This gives a histogram of the number of primes near four different values of x. The bin widths are proportional to $\log x$ in each case.

```
In[3]:= (t = Map[ (w = 25 Log[#];
          Table[PrimePi[# + j w] - PrimePi[# + (j-1)w],
          {j, -3, 4}])&, 10^(1 + 2Range[4])];
        BarChart3D[t, XSpacing -> .8,
          Ticks -> {{{1, 10^3}, {2, 10^5}, {3, 10^7}, {4, 10^9}},
          None, Automatic}])
```

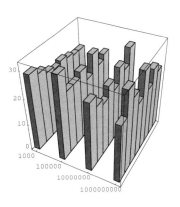

Here scattering cross section (μb) is plotted versus the incident momentum of a particle beam (GeV/c), measured in a laboratory frame of reference. The estimated standard deviation of the cross section at each value of the incident momentum is indicated using error bars.

```
In[4]:= MultipleListPlot[
        Apply[{{#1, #2}, ErrorBar[#3]}&,
        { {4, 367, 17}, {6, 311, 9}, {8, 295, 9}, {10, 268, 7},
          {12, 253, 7}, {15, 239, 6}, {20, 220, 6}, {30, 213, 6},
          {75, 193, 5}, {150, 192, 5} }, 1],
        Frame -> True, SymbolShape -> PlotSymbol[Diamond, .5],
        FrameLabel -> {"incident momentum (GeV/c)",
        "cross section (\[Mu]b)"}]
```

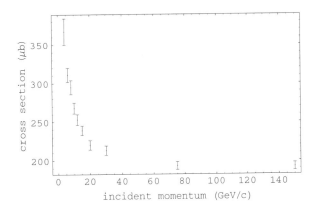

Here is the Wolfcamp aquifer data again, this time displayed as a scatter plot.

```
In[5]:= (data = ReadList["wolfcamp.aquifer.data",
           Number, RecordLists->True];
         ScatterPlot3D[data, BoxRatios->{1, 1, .3}, Axes -> True,
           ViewPoint -> {1.3, 2.4, 2.}])
```

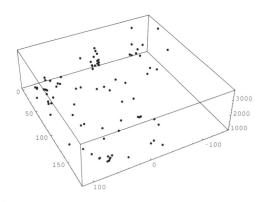

You can visualize the two-parameter gamma probability density function by creating a row of stacked graphics. A function having three parameters can be visualized using a two-dimensional array of stacked graphics.

```
In[6]:= (alphas = {.5, 1., 1.5, 2.};
         betas = {1, 2, 4};
         stacks = MapThread[Append[StackGraphics[#1],
           PlotLabel -> "\[Beta] = "<>ToString[#2]]&,
           {Apply[Plot[Evaluate[PDF[GammaDistribution[#2, #1], x]],
           {x, $MachineEpsilon, 4}, DisplayFunction -> Identity]&,
           Outer[List, betas, alphas], {2}], betas} ];
         Show[GraphicsArray[stacks], PlotLabel ->
           "gamma distribution for \[Alpha] = .5, 1, 1.5, 2"])
```

gamma distribution for α – .5, 1, 1.5, 2

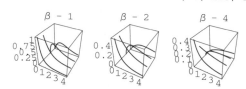

This initializes the Geometry packages.

```
In[7]:= <<Geometry`
```

Here the regular polyhedra are plotted according to number of faces, number of edges, and volume when edges have unit length.

```
In[8]:=  Apply[Show,
           Join[
             Map[Polyhedron[#, {NumberOfFaces[#], NumberOfEdges[#],
               Volume[#]}, .7]&,
               {Tetrahedron, Cube, Octahedron, Dodecahedron,
                Icosahedron}],
             {Axes -> True, AxesLabel -> {"# of faces", "# of edges",
              "volume"},
              Ticks -> {{4, 6, 8, 12, 20}, {6, 12, 12, 30, 30},
                       Automatic}}] ]
```

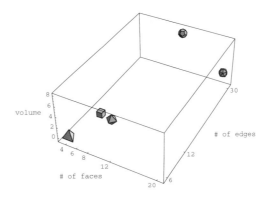

■ Linear Algebra Packages

The LinearAlgebra portion of the standard add-on packages provide functions for producing orthonormal vectors, solving tridiagonal matrix equations, computing the LU factorization or Cholesky decomposition of a matrix, and other sorts of matrix manipulation.

Fast transform algorithms can be expressed as sparse matrix factorizations. This example shows why the fast Fourier transform (FFT) is faster than the discrete Fourier transform (DFT). BlockMatrix from the MatrixManipulation package is used to demonstrate how the DFT matrix factors into smaller blocks.

The discrete Fourier transform of the sequence $\{x_j\}$ is defined by $y_k = \sum_{j=0}^{n-1} \omega_n^{kj} x_j$ where $\omega_n = e^{\frac{2\pi i}{n}}$, or in matrix notation, $y = F_n x$. The essential idea of the FFT is to find an efficient factorization of the matrix F_n.

This initializes the linear algebra packages so that they load as needed.

```
In[9]:=  <<LinearAlgebra`
```

F_4 is the DFT matrix transforming the input sequence x into the output sequence y when the sequence length is 4.

```
In[10]:= MatrixForm[F₄ = Table[ω₄^(jk), {j, 0, 3}, {k, 0, 3}]]
```

$$Out[10]//MatrixForm= \begin{pmatrix} 1 & 1 & 1 & 1 \\ 1 & \omega_4 & \omega_4^2 & \omega_4^3 \\ 1 & \omega_4^2 & \omega_4^4 & \omega_4^6 \\ 1 & \omega_4^3 & \omega_4^6 & \omega_4^9 \end{pmatrix}$$

Define the block matrix P_4 in terms of F_2 and the 2×2 diagonal matrix Ω_2. This factorization can be related to F_4.

```
In[11]:= MatrixForm[P₄ = {{F₂, Ω₂ . F₂}, {F₂, -Ω₂ . F₂}}]
```

$$Out[11]//MatrixForm= \begin{pmatrix} F_2 & \Omega_2 . F_2 \\ F_2 & -\Omega_2 . F_2 \end{pmatrix}$$

Mathematica's typeset output gives a clear depiction of the block structure of P_4.

```
In[12]:= Ω₂ = DiagonalMatrix[{1, ω₄}];
         F₂ = Table[ω₂^(jk), {j, 0, 1}, {k, 0, 1}]; MatrixForm[P₄]
```

$$Out[12]//MatrixForm= \begin{pmatrix} \begin{pmatrix} 1 & 1 \\ 1 & \omega_2 \end{pmatrix} & \begin{pmatrix} 1 & 1 \\ \omega_4 & \omega_2\,\omega_4 \end{pmatrix} \\ \begin{pmatrix} 1 & 1 \\ 1 & \omega_2 \end{pmatrix} & \begin{pmatrix} -1 & -1 \\ -\omega_4 & -\omega_2\,\omega_4 \end{pmatrix} \end{pmatrix}$$

Define I_4 to be the 4×4 identity matrix and let Π_4 be a permutation matrix such that even and odd columns are grouped together. The operation represented by the permutation matrix is referred to as shuffling or twiddling.

```
In[13]:= I₄ = IdentityMatrix[4];
         MatrixForm[Π₄ = I₄[[{1, 3, 2, 4}]]]
```

$$Out[13]//MatrixForm= \begin{pmatrix} 1 & 0 & 0 & 0 \\ 0 & 0 & 1 & 0 \\ 0 & 1 & 0 & 0 \\ 0 & 0 & 0 & 1 \end{pmatrix}$$

BlockMatrix converts P_4, a matrix of submatrices, into a single matrix. This equates the result of applying the DFT to the permutation matrix with the factorization represented by P_4.

```
In[14]:= MatrixForm[F₄ . Π₄] == MatrixForm[BlockMatrix[P₄]]
```

$$Out[14]= \begin{pmatrix} 1 & 1 & 1 & 1 \\ 1 & \omega_4^2 & \omega_4 & \omega_4^3 \\ 1 & \omega_4^4 & \omega_4^2 & \omega_4^6 \\ 1 & \omega_4^6 & \omega_4^3 & \omega_4^9 \end{pmatrix} == \begin{pmatrix} 1 & 1 & 1 & 1 \\ 1 & \omega_2 & \omega_4 & \omega_2\,\omega_4 \\ 1 & 1 & -1 & -1 \\ 1 & \omega_2 & -\omega_4 & -\omega_2\,\omega_4 \end{pmatrix}$$

Substituting the definition of ω_n verifies that the factorization P_4 is equivalent to the DFT matrix F_4 applied to the permutation matrix Π_4.

```
In[15]:= % /. ωₙ_ :> E^(2πI/n)

Out[15]= True
```

Since the inverse of the permutation matrix is its transpose, the DFT matrix F_n may be written as the product of two block matrices and a permutation matrix

$$F_n = P_n \cdot \Pi_n^T = \begin{pmatrix} I_m & \Omega_m \\ I_m & -\Omega_m \end{pmatrix} \cdot \begin{pmatrix} F_m & 0_m \\ 0_m & F_m \end{pmatrix} \cdot \Pi_n^T$$

where 0_m denotes the $m \times m$ zero matrix. Thus, the DFT can be performed using two smaller DFTs, which are combined with a few multiplies and shuffling. This decomposition of F_n into F_m, where $m = \frac{n}{2}$, can be done $\log_2 n$ times. The FFT takes advantage of this decomposition, leading to the $n \log_2 n$ time complexity of the FFT versus the n^2 time complexity of the DFT.

■ Miscellaneous Packages

The packages grouped under Miscellaneous offer a diverse set of functions that are not easily categorized. There are functions for exploring the audio capabilities of *Mathematica* via waveform modulation and musical scales. Other functions provide calendar dates, chemical element data, physical constants, unit conversions, geodetic measurements, and world plots. The package RealOnly is useful for algebra students who have not yet encountered complex numbers.

This loads a package for converting between systems of units.

```
In[1]:= <<Miscellaneous`Units`
```

Consider a particle with uniform acceleration of 5.00 cm/sec² for an interval of ½ hr, with an initial speed of 10.0 ft/sec. This gives the final speed in feet per second.

```
In[2]:= Convert[10.0 Feet/Second + 5.00 Centi Meter/Second^2 1/2 Hour,
            Feet/Second]
```

$$Out[2]= \frac{305.276\, Feet}{Second}$$

The Music package defines a set of equal-tempered pitch/frequency equivalents.

```
In[3]:= <<Miscellaneous`Music`
```

You can use these definitions to construct a minor chord.

```
In[4]:= Play[Sin[2 Pi F3 t] + Sin[2 Pi Aflat3 t] + Sin[2 Pi C4 t],
            {t, 0, .5}]
```

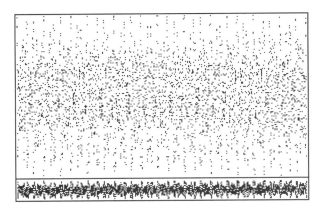

The WorldPlot package can be used to make maps of the continents.

```
In[5]:= <<Miscellaneous`WorldPlot`
```

Here is a plot of Oceania.   *In[6]:=* **WorldPlot[Oceania]**

Basic properties of the chemical   *In[7]:=* **<<Miscellaneous`ChemicalElements`**
elements are provided in the
ChemicalElements package.

This depicts the number of electrons in   *In[8]:=* **ListPlot[Apply[Plus, Map[Last,**
the outermost shell for each chemical   **ElectronConfiguration[Drop[Elements, -2]]], 1]]**
element with a known electron
configuration.

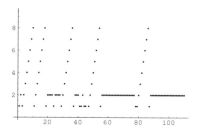

The RealOnly package allows you to   *In[9]:=* **<<Miscellaneous`RealOnly`**
avoid expressing results in terms of
complex numbers. The symbol
Nonreal replaces the result when a
calculation is unable to avoid complex
numbers.

Only one of the solutions to this   *In[10]:=* **Solve[x^3 + x^2 + x + 2. == 0, x]**
equation is real.
                                             Nonreal::warning: Nonreal number encountered.

                                             Out[10]= {{x → -1.35321}, {x → Nonreal}, {x → Nonreal}}

■ Number Theory Packages

Functions relevant to number theory are well represented in *Mathematica* with examples such as
PrimePi, EulerPhi, MoebiusMu, and DivisorSigma. The NumberTheory packages broaden this set of
functions. There are packages for proving primality, exploring the elliptic curve method for integer
factorization, and finding primitive elements of multiple algebraic extensions of rationals. There are

functions for approximating real numbers by rationals and approximating polynomials with real roots by polynomials with integer coefficients. Number theoretic functions such as Ramujan τ and Siegel Θ are also supported.

This causes the `NumberTheory` packages to load as they are needed.

```
In[1]:= <<NumberTheory`
```

Some of the plots in this section require the `Graphics` packages.

```
In[2]:= <<Graphics`
```

The ratios of the integers given by `ProjectiveRationalize` approximate the ratios of the corresponding real numbers 1., 1.73245, 2.71828, and 3.14159 within an error of 10^{-5}.

```
In[3]:= (reals = N[{1, 1/EulerGamma, E, Pi}];
        prec = 5;
        p = ProjectiveRationalize[reals, prec])
```

```
Out[3]= {80435, 139350, 218645, 252694}
```

Several gear ratios can be approximated simultaneously, under the constraint that the smallest gear have fewer than 110 teeth. Here the approximation to $\frac{1}{\pi}$ is 71/223.

```
In[4]:= (While[p[[1]] > 110,
           prec--;
           p = ProjectiveRationalize[reals, prec]];
        p)
```

```
Out[4]= {71, 123, 193, 223}
```

Square-free integers have no factors that are perfect squares. `SquareFreeQ` determines whether an integer is square-free.

Two integers are coprime if their greatest common divisor (GCD) is 1. This shows that there is a positive correlation between the square-free property and coprimality.

```
In[5]:= (sample = Table[Random[Integer, 1000000], {100}];
        xor = Map[(squarefree = SquareFreeQ[#];
            coprime = (GCD[#, Random[Integer, 1000000]] == 1);
            If[Xor[squarefree, coprime], -1, 1])&, sample];
        N[Apply[Plus, xor]/Length[xor]])
```

```
Out[5]= 0.4
```

Every positive integer can be represented as the sum of four squares, but there are relatively few perfect squares. Each of the remaining integers can be minimally represented as a sum of either two or three squares. The number of representations of an integer n as a sum of d squares $r_d(n)$ is given by `SumOfSquaresR[`d`, `n`]`.

This shows the percentage of numbers from 1 to 100 representable as a sum of a minimum of 1, 2, 3, or 4 squares.

```
In[6]:= (squares = Table[
           Which[
                SumOfSquaresR[1, n] != 0, 1,
                SumOfSquaresR[2, n] != 0, 2,
                SumOfSquaresR[3, n] != 0, 3,
                True, 4], {n, 1, 100}];
         PieChart[Map[Count[squares, #]&, Range[4]]])
```

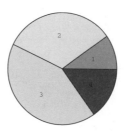

PrimitiveRoot[p] gives a cyclic generator of the multiplicative group mod p, where p is prime. Primitive root arrays are used for wave scattering over a range of frequencies.

This gives the primitive root array for $p = 19$.

```
In[7]:= (p = 19;
         r = PrimitiveRoot[p];
         array = Table[PowerMod[r, n, p], {n, 0, p-2}])
```

```
Out[7]= {1, 2, 4, 8, 16, 13, 7, 14, 9, 18, 17, 15, 11, 3, 6, 12, 5, 10}
```

Here is a depiction of a reflection phase-grating based on the array. The surface is pitted with a sequence of "wells" (shown in white) having depths proportional to the elements of the array.

```
In[8]:= (array5 = Flatten[Table[array, {5}]];
         StackedBarChart[(p-array5), array5,
           BarLabels -> None, BarSpacing -> 0,
           BarStyle -> {GrayLevel[0], GrayLevel[1]},
           AspectRatio ->.1, Ticks -> None])
```

Using a simple model of the complex amplitude of the reflected wave, it can be shown that the spectrum is flat except at zero. This implies that the wave is reflected in all directions except the specular direction.

Equal intensity is scattered into all
diffraction orders except the zero order.

```
In[9]:= (reflected = Map[Exp[I 2 Pi #/p]&, array];
         powerspectrum = Abs[Fourier[reflected]]^2;
         ListPlot[powerspectrum, AxesOrigin -> {0, 0},
           PlotJoined -> True, PlotRange -> All])
```

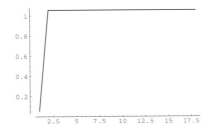

■ Numerical Mathematics Packages

The standard add-on packages for numerical mathematics extend the set of built-in numerical functions, and take advantage of the arbitrary-precision arithmetic that is the foundation of numerical computations in *Mathematica*. The NumericalMath packages provide fitting functions (polynomial, spline, trigonometric), numerical versions of some of the kernel functions (ND, NLimit, NResidue, NSeries), numerical integration functions (CauchyPrincipalValue, ListIntegrate, NIntegrate`, InterpolationFunction), support for numerical solution of differential equations (BesselZeros, Butcher, OrderStar), alternatives to FindRoot using interpolation or interval methods, functions for approximating by a ratio of polynomials, and pedagogical functions for exploring floating-point arithmetic and numerical quadrature.

This initializes the numerical
mathematics packages so that they load
as needed.

```
In[1]:= <<NumericalMath`
```

Here is a set of points that lie
approximately on a circle.

```
In[2]:= (data = Table[(x = Random[Real, {-1, 1}];
           Table[Random[Real, {-.1, .1}], {2}] +
           {x, Sign[.5 - Random[]] Sqrt[1 - x^2]}), {15}];
         ListPlot[data, AspectRatio -> 1,
             Ticks -> {{-1., -.5, .5, 1.}, Automatic}])
```

The points given to `SplineFit` are first sorted according to polar angle. The resulting spline interpolates the points.

```
In[3]:= (data = Map[Last,
            Sort[Map[{Apply[ArcTan, #], #}&, data]]];
       spline = SplineFit[Join[data, {First[data]}], Cubic];
       ParametricPlot[spline[u], {u, 0, 15},
         AspectRatio -> 1, Compiled -> False,
         Ticks -> {{-1., -.5, .5, 1.}, Automatic}])
```

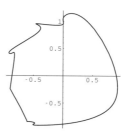

You can use `GeneralMiniMaxApproximation` to approximate the inverse to the Euler gamma function on an interval. This shows the gamma function on $1.5 \le t \le 6$.

```
In[4]:= Plot[Gamma[t], {t, 1.5, 6},
         AxesOrigin -> {1.5, 0}, AspectRatio ->1,
         AxesLabel -> {"t", "Gamma[t]"}]
```

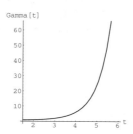

This gives a degree $(2,4)$ rational function that approximates the inverse on $\Gamma(1.5) \le x \le \Gamma(6)$.

```
In[5]:= (gmma = GeneralMiniMaxApproximation[{Gamma[t], t},
         {t, {1.5, 6}, 2, 4}, s];
       inverseGamma = gmma[[2, 1]])
```

$Out[5]=$ $(0.502223186953420 +$
        $2.86068402583854\,s - 4.13444430773448\,s^2)\,/$
        $(1 - 0.524345748809483\,s - 0.860537396694058\,s^2 +$
        $0.00324075015172723\,s^3 - 0.00001505409070277632\,s^4)$

Here is a plot of the approximation. For a minimax approximation, the error is distributed over the interval.

```
In[6]:= (Plot[inverseGamma, {s, Gamma[1.5], Gamma[6]},
            AxesOrigin -> {0, 1.5},
            AspectRatio ->1, AxesLabel -> {"s", "inverseGamma[s]"}])
```

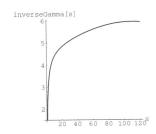

When you want to solve differential equations approximately, there are many considerations to take into account. You must ensure that the numerical solution process is sufficiently accurate (it is consistent with the differential system), that it actually solves the problem in which you are interested (it is convergent), and that any errors do not cause your approximate solution to drift far from the true solution (it is stable). Further, you may wish to ensure that your approximate solution samples (interpolates) the exact solution at specific points. Order stars provide a framework for the study and construction of numerical methods with these desirable properties.

This loads the function Pade for calculating Padé approximations.

```
In[7]:= <<Calculus`Pade`
```

Here the Padé approximation r to f represents the approximate solution of a differential equation, while f represents the exact solution.

```
In[8]:= (f = (z^2*(1 + z^2) + (1 + z/2)*(1 - z - z^3))/
            (z^2*(1 + z^2) + (1 - z/2)*(1 - z - z^3));
          r = Pade[f, {z, 0, 1, 1}])
```

$$Out[8]= \frac{1 + \frac{z}{2}}{1 - \frac{z}{2}}$$

This is an order star plot for analyzing the numerical method represented by the Padé approximation.

In[9]:= `OrderStar[r, f, OrderStarInterpolation->True,`
        `OrderStarLegend->True]`

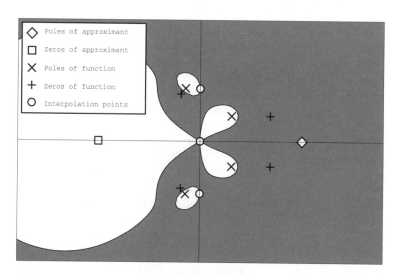

The order star reflects the fact that the order of the approximant at the origin is 2, which is one less than the number of adjoining sectors there. The shaded region gives the region of growth of the approximant over the function and yields information on the accumulation of numerical errors.

■ Statistics Packages

Mathematica users from a wide range of disciplines count on the basic statistical functions provided in the standard add-on packages to do their work. Continuous and discrete univariate and multivariate statistical distributions are supported. There are packages offering descriptive statistics for univariate and multivariate data, data manipulation and smoothing, and classical hypothesis testing and confidence interval estimation. Both linear and nonlinear regression functions permit users to take advantage of an extensive collection of diagnostics.

This causes each `Statistics` package to be loaded as needed.

In[1]:= `<<Statistics`

About 90% of this simulated data derives from a binormal distribution with nearly circular contours located at the origin. The remainder derives from a binormal having highly elliptical contours located in the lower left quadrant.

```
In[2]:= (dist0 = MultinormalDistribution[{0, 0},
            {{1, .1}, {.1, 1}}];
        dist1 = MultinormalDistribution[{-3, -2},
            {{3.2, -2.9}, {-2.9, 2.8}}];
        ListPlot[data = Table[If[Random[] < .9,
                Random[dist0], Random[dist1]], {100}],
            AspectRatio->1, PlotRange -> All])
```

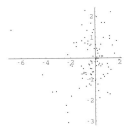

The population distribution is bimodal.

```
In[3]:= ({{xmin, xmax}, {ymin, ymax}} = Map[{Min[#], Max[#]}&,
            Transpose[data]];
        ContourPlot[.9 PDF[dist0, {x, y}] +
         .1 PDF[dist1, {x, y}],
         {x, xmin, xmax}, {y, ymin, ymax},
         ContourShading -> False])
```

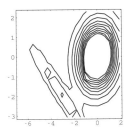

You can visualize the sample distribution by assuming a binormal form and using the sample covariance matrix. But this hides the bimodal nature of the data.

```
In[4]:= (Σ = CovarianceMatrix[data];
         approx = Apply[Plus, Map[
             PDF[MultinormalDistribution[#, Σ], {x, y}]&,
             data]] /
           Length[data];
         ContourPlot[approx, {x, xmin, xmax},
           {y, ymin, ymax}, ContourShading -> False])
```

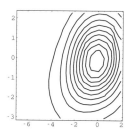

In the previous example, the observations followed a bivariate statistical distribution. You can also simulate data where the value of the independent variable is known with relative certainty, while the measured response is assumed to follow a univariate statistical distribution.

The nonrandom component of the response is a sum of Gaussians, one centered at $x = 3$ and another centered at $x = 18$.

```
In[5]:= (gaussian[μ_, σ_, x_] :=
           PDF[NormalDistribution[μ, σ], x] /
             PDF[NormalDistribution[μ, σ], μ];
         peaks = .6 gaussian[3, 2, x] + 2 gaussian[18, 2, x])
```

$$Out[5]= 2 e^{-\frac{1}{8}(-18+x)^2} + 0.6 e^{-\frac{1}{8}(-3+x)^2}$$

Here is a plot of the data, two Gaussian peaks contaminated by noise (uniformly distributed between 0 and 1.5), perhaps simulating mass spectrometer measurements. From the plot you might guess that there is a peak near $x = 2$ and another near $x = 19$.

```
In[6]:= (data = Table[{x, peaks + Random[Real, 1.5]},
             {x, 1, 30}];
         dataplot = ListPlot[data])
```

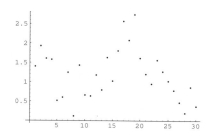

A nonlinear model is chosen: a sum of Gaussians with different locations (μ_1, μ_2) and amplitudes (a_1, a_2), but the same width (σ_3).

```
In[7]:= model = a₁ gaussian[μ₁, σ₃, x] +
           a₂ gaussian[μ₂, σ₃, x]
```

$$Out[7]= e^{-\frac{(x-\mu_1)^2}{2\sigma_3^2}} a_1 + e^{-\frac{(x-\mu_2)^2}{2\sigma_3^2}} a_2$$

A nonlinear model requires good starting values for the parameters to initialize the search for the least-squares estimates. These can be guessed at by looking at the plot. Here is the model at our initial guess for the parameter values.

```
In[8]:= ({{μ10, μ20, a10, a20, σ30} =
         {2, 19, data[[2, 2]], data[[19, 2]], 1};
      model0 = model /. Thread[Rule[
         {μ1, μ2, a1, a2, σ3},
         {μ10, μ20, a10, a20, σ30}]];
      Plot[model0, {x, 1, 30}, PlotRange -> All,
         AxesOrigin -> {0, 0}])
```

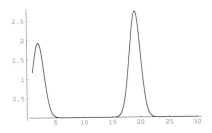

The "true" values for μ_1, μ_2, a_1, and a_2 (3.0, 18.0, 0.6, 2.0) lie within the 95% confidence intervals NonlinearRegress provides for the parameter estimates. The true value for σ_3 (2.0) falls outside the 95% interval.

```
In[9]:= NumberForm[#1, 3]&[
      regress = NonlinearRegress[data,
         model, x, {{μ1, μ10}, {μ2, μ20}, {a1, a10},
         {a2, a20}, {σ3, σ30}}, RegressionReport ->
         {BestFitParameters, ParameterCITable,
         EstimatedVariance, FitCurvatureTable}]]
```

Out[9]//NumberForm=

{BestFitParameters → {μ_1 → -0.641, μ_2 → 18.5,
   a_1 → 1.82, a_2 → 2.01, σ_3 → 5.16}, ParameterCITable →

	Estimate	Asymptotic SE	CI
μ_1	-0.641	2.7	{-6.19, 4.91}
μ_2	18.5	0.57	{17.3, 19.6}
a_1	1.82	0.591	{0.599, 3.03}'
a_2	2.01	0.181	{1.63, 2.38}
σ_3	5.16	0.573	{3.98, 6.34}

EstimatedVariance → 0.194, FitCurvatureTable →

	Curvature
Max Intrinsic	0.35
Max Parameter-Effects	4.35
95. % Confidence Region	0.62

}

Diagnostics provide an evaluation of the least-squares fit. Here the maximum relative intrinsic curvature is smaller than the relative curvature of the 95% confidence region, but not by much. The data analyst should be skeptical about whether the intrinsic form of the chosen model is appropriate. The maximum relative parameter-effects curvature is greater than the 95% threshold, indicating that the model parametrization could be improved.

Recall that the error in the simulated data was uniformly distributed between 0 and 1.5, so there is actually a background constant term of 0.75 unaccounted for in the model. Including the background in the model should yield a better fit.

```
In[10]:= (trueplot = Plot[peaks, {x, 1, 30},
              DisplayFunction -> Identity];
         estimatedplot = Plot[(model /. (BestFitParameters /. regress)),
              {x, 1, 30}, DisplayFunction -> Identity];
         Show[dataplot, trueplot, estimatedplot])
```

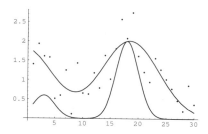

2. Algebra

+■ Algebra `AlgebraicInequalities`

The package provides a function for solving systems of strong polynomial inequalities in one or more unknowns. To be precise, `SemialgebraicComponents[`*ineqs, vars*`]` gives a finite set of solutions of the system of inequalities. That is, within the set of solutions, any solution can be connected by a continuous path to a solution in the finite set. The variable *ineqs* is a list of strong inequalities, where both sides of each inequality are polynomials in variables *vars* with rational coefficients. In other words, `SemialgebraicComponents[`*ineqs, vars*`]` gives at least one point in each connected component of the open semialgebraic set defined by inequalities *ineqs*.

`SemialgebraicComponents[`*ineqs, vars*`]`	give at least one point in each component of the set of solutions of inequalities *ineqs* in the variables *vars*

Solutions of inequalities.

This loads the package.

```
In[1]:= <<Algebra`AlgebraicInequalities`
```

Here is a point from each of the three intervals forming the set of solutions of $x(x^2 - 2)(x^2 - 3) > 0$.

```
In[2]:= SemialgebraicComponents[{x (x^2 - 2) (x^2 - 3) > 0}, x]
```

$$Out[2]= \left\{-\frac{3}{2}, 1, 2\right\}$$

This gives one point in each of the two connected components of the set bounded by the circle $x^2 + y^2 == 4$ and the hyperbola $xy == 1$.

```
In[3]:= SemialgebraicComponents[{x^2 + y^2 < 4, x y > 1}, {x, y}]
```

$$Out[3]= \left\{\left\{-1, -\frac{9}{8}\right\}, \left\{1, \frac{9}{8}\right\}\right\}$$

This proves that the ball $x^2 + (y - 1)^2 + (z - 2)^2 < 1/9$ is contained in the ellipsoid $x^2 + y^2/4 + z^2/9 < 1$.

```
In[4]:= SemialgebraicComponents[{x^2 + y^2/4 + z^2/9 > 1,
            x^2 + (y - 1)^2 + (z - 2)^2 < 1/9},
            {x, y, z}]
```

$$Out[4]= \{\}$$

■ Algebra`FiniteFields`

A field is an algebraic structure obeying the rules of ordinary arithmetic. In particular, a field has binary operations of addition and multiplication, both of which are commutative and associative. A field has two special elements, the additive identity 0, and multiplicative identity 1. This package adds rules to Plus, Times, and Power so that arithmetic on field elements will be defined properly. It also provides low-level utilities for working with finite fields and for formatting finite field elements.

For any finite field there is a fixed prime number p, called the characteristic of the field, such that the sum of p of the 1 field elements gives the 0 field element. A finite field of characteristic p has p^d elements for some positive integer d, which we will loosely call the extension degree. This package represents field elements as polynomials in a single variable. The polynomials have degree at most $d - 1$ and their coefficients are integers reduced mod p.

The internal form of a finite field element is GF[p, *ilist*][*elist*] where GF stands for *Galois field*, p is the prime characteristic of the field, *ilist* is the coefficient list of the irreducible polynomial which defines multiplication in the field, and *elist* is the coefficient list of the polynomial representing the particular element. Because this form can be a bit clumsy, the package provides several shortcuts for entering finite field elements.

GF[p][{k}]	the integer k in the field of integers mod p
GF[p, 1][{k}]	another way of expressing the integer k in the field of integers mod p
GF[p, {0,1}][{k}]	the full form of the integer k in the field of integers mod p
GF[p, d]	a field that is a degree d extension of a prime field isomorphic to Z_p (the integers mod p); an irreducible polynomial is selected automatically
GF[p, *ilist*][*elist*]	the full form of a finite field element, where *ilist* is a list of integers of length $d + 1$ representing the coefficients of an irreducible polynomial, and *elist* is a list of integers of length d giving the coefficients of the polynomial representation of the element

Ways to enter finite field elements.

This loads the package.

In[1]:= **<<Algebra`FiniteFields`**

Add 4 and 5 mod 7. The default output form is subscripted.

In[2]:= **GF[7][{4}] + GF[7][{5}]**

Out[2]= ${\{2\}}_7$

Here is the FullForm of the expression. Note the automatic choice of irreducible polynomial.

In[3]:= **FullForm[%]**

Out[3]//FullForm= GF[7, List[0, 1]] [List[2]]

Here is multiplication in the field of 3^4 == 81 elements.

In[4]:= **GF[3,4][{1,2,1}] GF[3,4][{2,2,2,0}]**

Out[4]= $\{1, 1, 2, 0\}_3$

Field objects are automatically reduced to a canonical form.

In[5]:= **GF[3,4][{1,2,3,4,5}]**

Out[5]= $\{0, 0, 0, 1\}_3$

Since *Mathematica* lists polynomials with the constant term first, the same is done for finite field elements. In this example, the left-hand zero is essential to give the constant term, but the right-hand zero in the input is unnecessary.

In[6]:= **GF[3,4][{0,1,0}]**

Out[6]= $\{0, 1, 0, 0\}_3$

It is nonsense to add elements of different finite fields, so this expression does not evaluate.

In[7]:= **GF[5,1][{1}] + GF[3,4][{1,1,1}]**

Out[7]= $\{1, 1, 1, 0\}_3 + \{1\}_5$

Integers are imported into finite fields.

In[8]:= **1 + GF[3,4][{1,1}]**

Out[8]= $\{2, 1, 0, 0\}_3$

Zero is special. This package makes the assumption that zero is zero, regardless of the field it is in. The main consequence of this is that a field zero is simplified to the integer 0 automatically. Many functions in *Mathematica* work better with this assumption. The assumption is not rigorously correct, but will not produce nonsensical output unless nonsensical input is given.

Field zeros are simplified to the integer 0 after arithmetic.

In[9]:= **{GF[7][{1}] + GF[7][{6}], GF[3,4][{0,0,0}]}**

Out[9]= {0, 0}

The sum of the field zeros from different fields also simplifies to 0.

In[10]:= **GF[7][{0}] + GF[3,4][{0,0,0}]**

Out[10]= $\{0\}_7$

```
SetFieldFormat[f, FormatType -> Subscripted]
                        set the field f to have a Subscripted output (default)
SetFieldFormat[f, FormatType -> FullForm]
                        set the field f to have a FullForm output
SetFieldFormat[f, FormatType -> FunctionOfCoefficients[g]]
                        set the field f to input and output a field element using g as
                        the function name, with the arguments given by the
                        coefficients of the polynomial representation of the field
                        element
SetFieldFormat[f, FormatType -> FunctionOfCode[g]]
                        set the field f to input and output a field element using g as
                        the function name, with the argument given by the integer
                        code specifying the field element
```

Field element formatting.

One may always input or output the FullForm of a finite field element, however the package provides some shortcuts. The elements of a prime field may be written GF[p][{k}] or GF[p, 1][{k}], both of which are interpreted as GF[p, {0,1}][{k}]. In general if $s == p^d$ with p prime and d a positive integer, then GF[s] is interpreted as GF[p, d]. The expression GF[3, 4] stands for a degree 4 extension of the integers mod 3, that is, a field with 81 elements. When this form is used, the package automatically selects an irreducible polynomial, with coefficients given by *ilist* and with the property that GF[p, *ilist*][{0,1}] is a *primitive element* of the field. It is possible to provide your own irreducible polynomial by giving it explicitly, as in GF[3, {1, 1, 1, 1, 2, 1}].

The default OutputForm of a finite field element is a list of integers subscripted by the characteristic of the field. The length of the list is the degree of the field extension over the prime field. If you are working with only one representation of any field, then this will be sufficient to distinguish which field contains a given element.

Since it is possible to have fields of the same size using different irreducible polynomials, it is useful to be able distinguish elements from these fields. It is also convenient to have a more compact way to type finite field elements. The function SetFieldFormat establishes the input and output formats of field elements. You may always input field elements in the ways already described, or ask explicitly for the FullForm of the output.

Note that a field head, such as GF[2, 3] may be assigned to a symbol. The assignment f8 = GF[2, 3] allows you to refer to a specific field element using f8[{1,0,1}].

Give a field with 9 elements a functional format.

In[11]:= **SetFieldFormat[GF[9],**
                        FormatType -> FunctionOfCoefficients[f9]]

Here is some arithmetic with elements from this field.

`In[12]:=  example = {f9[1,2] + f9[2], f9[1,2]^3, 2 f9[2],`
`                 f9[2]/f9[2,2]}`

`Out[12]= {f9[0, 2], f9[2, 1], f9[1], f9[0, 1]}`

Represent each element as an integer in the range 0 to 8, rather than as a sequence of polynomial coefficients.

`In[13]:=  SetFieldFormat[GF[9], FormatType -> FunctionOfCode[f9]]`

Here the arithmetic results are encoded.

`In[14]:=  example`
`Out[14]= {f9[6], f9[5], f9[1], f9[3]}`

This restores the default formatting for this field.

`In[15]:=  SetFieldFormat[GF[9]]`

Characteristic[*f*]	give the characteristic of field *f*
ExtensionDegree[*f*]	give the degree of the extension of field *f* over its base field
FieldSize[*f*]	give the number of elements in field *f*
FieldIrreducible[*f*, *s*]	give the irreducible polynomial which defines multiplication in the field *f*, expressed in terms of the symbol *s*
IrreduciblePolynomial[*s*, *p*, *d*]	find an irreducible polynomial of degree *d* over the integers mod prime *p*, expressed in terms of the symbol *s*

Field parameter functions.

The functions `Characteristic`, `ExtensionDegree`, `FieldSize`, `FieldIrreducible`, and `IrreduciblePolynomial` give important parameters about a finite field.

Characteristic gives the prime characteristic of the field.

`In[16]:=  (fld = GF[81]; Characteristic[fld])`
`Out[16]= 3`

A field extension is a vector space over the base field. ExtensionDegree gives the dimension of this vector space.

`In[17]:=  ExtensionDegree[fld]`
`Out[17]= 4`

FieldSize gives the number of elements in the field.

`In[18]:=  FieldSize[fld]`
`Out[18]= 81`

Here is an identity.

`In[19]:=  FieldSize[fld] == Characteristic[fld]^ExtensionDegree[fld]`
`Out[19]= True`

This gives the irreducible polynomial associated with a field.

`In[20]:=  FieldIrreducible[fld, x]`
`Out[20]= ` $2 + x + x^4$

Successor[*elem*]	give the next element in a canonical ordering of the field elements (this function does not wrap, so the largest element has no successor)
ReduceElement[*elem*]	give a field element in reduced form
ToElementCode[*elem*]	give a nonnegative integer less than the field size that encodes the field element
FromElementCode[*f*, *code*]	give the field element of *f* corresponding to *code*, a nonnegative integer less than the field size
PolynomialToElement[*f*, *poly*]	give the field element of *f* corresponding to *poly*, a polynomial in one variable with integer-valued coefficients
ElementToPolynomial[*elem*, *s*]	give a polynomial in the symbol *s* corresponding to the field element *elem*

Field element manipulation functions.

The functions Successor, ReduceElement, ToElementCode, FromElementCode, PolynomialToElement, and ElementToPolynomial are for working with finite field elements.

This gives the element as a polynomial.   *In[21]:=* **ElementToPolynomial[fld[{1,2,1,2}], x]**

Out[21]= $1 + 2x + x^2 + 2x^3$

PowerListQ[*f*]	give True if a list representing the powers of a primitive element of the field is used to do field arithmetic, False otherwise
FieldExp[*f*, *n*]	give the value of the discrete exponential function associated with the field *f* for integer *n*
FieldInd[*elem*]	give the value of the discrete logarithm function associated with the field for element *elem*
PowerList[*f*]	give a list of the data parts of the nonzero elements of the field *f*, generated by raising a primitive element of the field to integer powers 0, 1, 2, ..., FieldSize[*f*]-1
PowerListToField[*list*]	give the field associated with the specified list of element data parts, where the elements are generated by successive powers of a primitive element

Functions to support fast multiplication and division.

A finite field must have a prime power number of elements. If it has p elements, where p is a prime, then it is isomorphic to the integers mod p. In this case the package does addition, subtraction, multiplication, and positive powers as usual over the integers and reduces the results using Mod. For negative powers the package uses `PowerMod`.

If the field has p^d elements, where $d > 1$, then it is isomorphic to the set of polynomials in some variable having degree less than d and with coefficients in the integers mod p. Addition is polynomial addition except that the coefficients are reduced modulo p. For multiplication the product is also reduced modulo an irreducible (nonfactorable) polynomial over the integers modulo p.

Taking multiplicative inverses is equivalent to finding the extended greatest common divisor modulo p with the irreducible polynomial. In other words, given the field element *elem* and the field's irreducible polynomial *irred*, find polynomials a and b such that `PolynomialGCD[`*elem*`,` *irred*`, Modulus -> `p`]` equals `PolynomialMod[`a *elem* $+ b$ *irred*`, `p`]`. If the result of `PolynomialGCD` is unity, then a is the inverse of *elem*.

There is a faster way to do multiplication and compute inverses, based on the fact that the multiplicative group of any finite field is cyclic. If you have a generator of the group along with a list of the positive powers of the generator in sequence, then multiplication and division can be reduced to adding and subtracting indices of the elements in the list.

The package supports this method of arithmetic by allowing you to either generate a field object from a list representing the powers of a primitive element (`PowerListToField`), or generate a list representing the powers of a primitive element from a field object (`PowerList`). Setting `PowerListQ` to `True` causes field arithmetic to use a list of primitive element powers, by defining the discrete exponential function `FieldExp` and the discrete logarithm function `FieldInd`. The `FieldInd` function is often called the index function for the field. The list of powers will depend on the choice of primitive element and on which irreducible polynomial is used for the field representation. Any element of the field for which `FieldInd[`*elem*`]` is relatively prime to `FieldSize[`*f*`]-1` is also a primitive element of the field.

Field arithmetic using a list of primitive element powers has two disadvantages. It takes time to enter or compute the list, and the list can take considerable memory. In general, if you are doing only a few arithmetic operations, or if you are working in a large field, it is better not to create the list. Note that setting `PowerListQ` to `False` disables this method of doing arithmetic in a particular field, but it does not destroy the computed values of `FieldExp` and `FieldInd`.

This shows that 3 is a primitive element of the integers mod 7. The other primitive element is 5. Since GF[7,1] is a prime field, it is inefficient to use a list of primitive element powers for multiplication.	`In[22]:= PowerList[GF[7,1]]`
	
	`Out[22]= {{1}, {3}, {2}, {6}, {4}, {5}}`

Although using a list of primitive element powers is an inefficient way to do GF[7,1] arithmetic, this enables the method anyway.	`In[23]:= PowerListQ[GF[7,1]] = True`

The position of {6} in PowerList is
one greater than the index given by
FieldInd.

```
In[24]:= FieldInd[GF[7,1][{6}]]
Out[24]= 3
```

FieldExp and FieldInd are inverses.

```
In[25]:= FieldExp[GF[7,1], 3]
Out[25]= {6}₇
```

These definitions for field index and
field exponent are not part of the
conventional definitions, but may be
useful in some applications.

```
In[26]:= {FieldInd[0], FieldExp[GF[7,1], -Infinity]}
Out[26]= {-∞, 0}
```

Some books contain tables equivalent to the list given by PowerList. The function
PowerListToField allows such a list to be used to define a field. The argument of PowerListToField
is a list of $p^d - 1$ d-tuples of integers. The first d-tuple is assumed to give the coefficients of the polynomial representation of the 1 element of the field. This is used to determine whether the coefficients are
listed constant-term-first or constant-term-last. The second d-tuple is assumed to represent a primitive
element of the field. The succeeding d-tuples are assumed to represent successive powers of the
second element. PowerListToField does some elementary error checking to verify that the input list
is valid. If so, PowerListToField computes parameters of the field such as the characteristic and the
irreducible polynomial.

Here is a field of order 9.

```
In[27]:= g9 = PowerListToField[{{1, 0}, {0, 1},
              {1, 2}, {2, 2}, {2, 0}, {0, 2}, {2, 1}, {1, 1}}]
Out[27]= GF[3, {2, 1, 1}]
```

Arithmetic works on fields defined
using PowerListToField.

```
In[28]:= {g9[{1}] + g9[{1,1}], g9[{1,2}] * g9[{2,2}], 1/g9[{0,2}],
          g9[{2,2}]^2}
Out[28]= {{2, 1}₃, {0, 2}₃, {2, 2}₃, {2, 1}₃}
```

The field parameters are computed
automatically.

```
In[29]:= {Characteristic[g9], ExtensionDegree[g9],
              FieldIrreducible[g9,z]}
Out[29]= {3, 2, 2 + z + z²}
```

FieldExp may be used to generate the
list of elements corresponding to the
original list.

```
In[30]:= Table[FieldExp[g9, i], {i, 0, 7}]
Out[30]= {{1, 0}₃, {0, 1}₃, {1, 2}₃, {2, 2}₃, {2, 0}₃, {0, 2}₃, {2, 1}₃,
          {1, 1}₃}
```

This gives the original list consisting of
the data parts of the elements.

```
In[31]:= PowerList[g9]
Out[31]= {{1, 0}, {0, 1}, {1, 2}, {2, 2}, {2, 0}, {0, 2}, {2, 1}, {1, 1}}
```

Compatibility with Other *Mathematica* Functions

Most *Mathematica* functions are not, indeed cannot be, designed to work over arbitrary fields. For
instance, it is nonsensical to integrate an expression containing a finite field object. At best, such
functions will not do anything when given such an expression.

You can generally expect these functions to treat the field object as an unknown symbol. Before using a function on an expression with finite field objects, it is wise to try some test cases first. The types of functions that might reasonably be expected to work are linear algebra and polynomial functions.

Set the format for GF[9].

```
In[32]:= SetFieldFormat[GF[9], FormatType -> FunctionOfCode[f9]]
```

Fractional powers do not work.

```
In[33]:= Power[f9[1], 1/2]
```

$Out[33]= \sqrt{f9[1]}$

Factor fails because it makes the assumption that it is working over the rationals.

```
In[34]:= Factor[Expand[(x + f9[2])(x - f9[2])]]
```

$Out[34]= x^2 + f9[2]$

PolynomialGCD doesn't work either. Use PolynomialExtendedGCD defined in the package instead.

```
In[35]:= PolynomialGCD[x + f9[1], f9[2] x + f9[2]]
```

$Out[35]= 1$

Set the format for GF[3, 4].

```
In[36]:= SetFieldFormat[GF[3,4],
                FormatType -> FunctionOfCoefficients[f81]]
```

PolynomialQuotient and PolynomialRemainder accept polynomials over a field.

```
In[37]:= {PolynomialQuotient[f81[2,2] x^4 + f81[1] x^2 +
             f81[1,1,1], f81[2] x^2 + f81[1,1,1,1], x],
          PolynomialRemainder[f81[2,2] x^4 + f81[1] x^2 +
             f81[1,1,1], f81[2] x^2 + f81[1,1,1,1], x]}
```

$Out[37]= \{x^2\ f81[1, 1] + f81[1, 1, 2, 2], f81[1, 0, 2, 2]\}$

PolynomialMod works on polynomials over the integers, not polynomials over a field. Also note that a polynomial over a field is not automatically sorted from lower power to higher power, because *Mathematica* does not treat GF objects as numbers.

```
In[38]:= PolynomialMod[f81[2,2] x^4 + f81[1] x^2 + f81[1,1,1],
                f81[2] x^2 + f81[1,1,1,1]]
```

$Out[38]= x^2\ f81[1] + f81[1, 1, 1] + x^4\ f81[2, 2]$

Det works on matrices of field elements.

```
In[39]:= (ffmatrix = {{f81[2,1,2], f81[1,1,1]},
                      {f81[1,2,1,2], f81[2]}};
         Det[ffmatrix])
```

$Out[39]= f81[0, 0, 2, 1]$

RowReduce works except that the 1 should be in the field.

```
In[40]:= RowReduce[ffmatrix]
```

$Out[40]= \{\{1, 0\}, \{0, 1\}\}$

Inverse and Dot also work with matrices of field elements.

```
In[41]:= Inverse[ffmatrix] . ffmatrix
```

$Out[41]= \{\{f81[1], 0\}, \{0, f81[1]\}\}$

■ Algebra`Horner`

This package applies Horner's rule to rearrange polynomials in Horner form. This is useful for efficient and stable numerical evaluation. Any polynomial can be rewritten in Horner, or nested, form.

$$p(x) = a_0 x^n + \cdots + a_{n-1} x + a_n$$
$$= (\cdots((a_0 x + a_1) x + a_2) x + \cdots a_{n-1}) x + a_n$$

Assume that x^n can be calculated using only $\log_2(n)$ multiplications for integer n [1]. For a polynomial of degree n, the Horner form requires n multiplications and n additions. The expanded form, however, requires $\sum_{i=1}^{n} \log_2(i) = \log_2(\Gamma(1 + n))$ multiplications, which is already more than twice as expensive for a polynomial of degree 10. Thus, one advantage of Horner form is that the work involved in exponentiation is distributed across addition and multiplication, resulting in savings of some basic arithmetic operations. Another advantage is that Horner form is more stable to evaluate numerically when compared with the expanded form. The reason for this is that each sum and product involve quantities which vary on a more evenly distributed scale.

Horner[*poly*]	put the polynomial *poly* in Horner form
Horner[*poly*, *vars*]	put the polynomial *poly* in Horner form with respect to the variable or list of variables *vars*

Factoring polynomials in Horner or nested form.

The function **Horner** can be used for both univariate and multivariate polynomials. It also works efficiently on both sparse and dense polynomials and fractional exponents.

This loads the package.

```
In[1]:= << Algebra`Horner`
```

By using the Variables function, Horner puts the polynomial into Horner form with respect to the variables identified using Variables.

```
In[2]:= Horner[ 11 x^3 -4 x^2 + 7 x + 2 ]
Out[2]= 2 + x (7 + x (-4 + 11 x))
```

Here the coefficients of the polynomial are symbolic, so it is important to specify the variable x.

```
In[3]:= Horner[ a x^3 + b x^2 + c x + d, x ]
Out[3]= d + x (c + x (b + a x))
```

The exponents of a polynomial do not need to be integers, nor do they need to be of equal increments. The nested polynomial is scaled by the smallest exponent.

```
In[4]:= Horner[ x^(1/3) + x + x^(3/2) ]
```
$$Out[4]= \left(1 + \left(1 + \sqrt{x}\right) x^{2/3}\right) x^{1/3}$$

Exponents must be integers or rational numbers for the expression to be considered a valid polynomial.	`In[5]:= Horner[ 1 + x^a, x ]`
	
	`Horner::fail:`
	                a
	  The expression 1 + x
	    is not a valid polynomial in the variable x
	
	$Out[5]=$ Horner[$1 + x^a$, x]

This constructs a bivariate polynomial.

```
In[6]:= bipoly = Sum[ i j x^i y^j,
                      {i, 0, 2}, {j, 0, 2} ]
```

$Out[6]=$ $x\,y + 2\,x^2\,y + 2\,x\,y^2 + 4\,x^2\,y^2$

Here the polynomial is put in Horner form first with respect to x and then with respect to y.

`In[7]:= Horner[ bipoly, {x, y} ]`

$Out[7]=$ $x\,(y\,(1 + 2\,y) + x\,y\,(2 + 4\,y))$

The factorization that you obtain is dependent upon the ordering of the variables which you specify. In this example, the polynomial is put in Horner form first with respect to y and then with respect to x.

`In[8]:= hornerbipoly = Horner[ bipoly, {y, x} ]`

$Out[8]=$ $y\,(x\,(1 + 2\,x) + x\,(2 + 4\,x)\,y)$

Polynomials are often evaluated using machine-precision floating-point arithmetic. This is an inexact process because there are only finitely many numbers available in the representation. Therefore, different methods of evaluation will give different answers. The following example illustrates how numerical stability of a polynomial can be improved using Horner form. The example also illustrates how the time required for evaluation can be significantly reduced. Timings will be different for different computers, but the relative timings should be similar.

Define the derivative of a Legendre polynomial.

`In[9]:= dpoly[x_] = D[ LegendreP[50, x], x];`

This plots the polynomial and gives the time required for evaluation. Plot uses machine-precision numbers to evaluate the polynomial by default. The plot is not very smooth due to the accumulation of representation errors associated with machine-precision computations.

```
In[10]:= Plot[ Evaluate[ dpoly[x] ], {x, 1, 1.01},
               PlotRange -> All ] //Timing
```

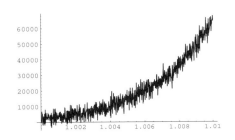

$Out[10]=$ {0.28 Second, -Graphics-}

Here the polynomial is put in Horner form before plotting. The time required to rearrange the polynomial is usually small compared to the time required to render the plot, and the time required to evaluate the polynomial is significantly reduced. The plot reveals that the Horner form of the polynomial is much more stable to evaluate using machine-precision numbers.

```
In[11]:=  Plot[ Evaluate[ Horner[ dpoly[x] ] ], {x, 1, 1.01},
            PlotRange -> All ] //Timing
```

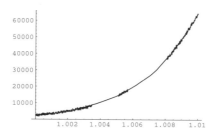

```
Out[11]= {0.12 Second, ▪Graphics▪}
```

High-precision arithmetic can be used to overcome the problem of cancellation. However, high-precision arithmetic is expensive when compared with machine-precision arithmetic. It is preferable to seek alternative strategies, such as structural transformations, whenever possible. For example, the Horner form can be used to reduce the amount of extra precision required to obtain reliable solutions.

Horner[$poly_1/poly_2$]	put the rational function $poly_1/poly_2$ in Horner form by nesting $poly_1$ and $poly_2$
Horner[$poly_1/poly_2,vars_1,vars_2$]	put the rational function $poly_1/poly_2$ in Horner form by nesting $poly_1$ with respect to the variables $vars_1$, and $poly_2$ with respect to the variables $vars_2$

Factoring rational functions in Horner or nested form.

Several types of expressions are detected by Horner, and appropriately nested forms are produced. The following example illustrates how to improve the efficiency of evaluating a rational polynomial approximant to a function.

This loads the package Calculus`Pade`.

```
In[12]:=  << Calculus`Pade`
```

Here is the 3/2 rational Padé approximation to Exp[Log[x]-x].

```
In[13]:=  approx = Pade[ Exp[Log[x]-x], {x, 0, 3, 2}]
```

$$Out[13]= \frac{x - \frac{x^2}{2} + \frac{x^3}{12}}{1 + \frac{x}{2} + \frac{x^2}{12}}$$

This puts the Padé approximation in Horner form. Both the numerator and the denominator are nested, and the variable to use in each is determined automatically.

```
In[14]:=  Horner[ approx ]
```

$$Out[14]= \frac{x \left(1 + \left(-\frac{1}{2} + \frac{x}{12}\right) x\right)}{1 + \left(\frac{1}{2} + \frac{x}{12}\right) x}$$

Expanding the terms illustrates that the Horner form is a nested restructuring of the original expression.

```
In[15]:= Expand[ hornerbipoly - bipoly ] == 0
Out[15]= True
```

We can verify that the nested form is indeed a valid polynomial in the specified variables.

```
In[16]:= PolynomialQ[ hornerbipoly, {x, y} ]
Out[16]= True
```

Nesting polynomials in Horner form is a general technique, but more efficient schemes for evaluating certain polynomials sometimes exist [1]. Additional considerations also arise if polynomials are not dense or computations are to be performed in parallel [2].

References

[1] *The Art of Computer Programming Volume 2: Seminumerical Algorithms*, D. E. Knuth, Second edition, Addison Wesley, London, 1981.

[2] "Optimal Code for Serial and Parallel Computation", R. J. Fateman, *Communications of the ACM*, 12 (12), pp. 694–695, 1969.

■ Algebra`InequalitySolve`

The package provides a function for solving systems of inequalities. `InequalitySolve[`*expr*`, `*x*`]` finds conditions that must be satisfied by real values of x in order for the expression *expr* to be true. The expression should contain logical connectives and polynomial equations and inequalities in the specified variable.

`InequalitySolve[`*expr*`, `*x*`]`	find all real values of x that satisfy the expression containing logical connectives and univariate polynomial equations and inequalities
`InequalitySolve[`*expr*`, {`*x*₁`, `*x*₂`, ... }]`	find all real values of x_i that satisfy the inequalities

Finding solutions to inequalities.

This loads the package.

$In[1]:= $ `<<Algebra`InequalitySolve``

Here is a set of solutions to a polynomial inequality.

$In[2]:= $ `InequalitySolve[x (x^2 - 2) (x^2 - 3) > 0, x]`

$Out[2]= -\sqrt{3} < x < -\sqrt{2} \;||\; 0 < x < \sqrt{2} \;||\; x > \sqrt{3}$

The inequalities may contain absolute values and rational functions.

$In[3]:= $ `InequalitySolve[x/Abs[x - 1] >= 0 && 1/x < x + 1, x]`

$Out[3]= \frac{1}{2}\left(-1+\sqrt{5}\right) < x < 1 \;||\; x > 1$

Multivariate inqualities may also be solved.

$In[4]:= $ `InequalitySolve[x^2 + y^2 < 1 && x < y, {x, y}]`

$Out[4]= -1 < x \le -\frac{1}{\sqrt{2}} \;\&\&\; -\sqrt{1-x^2} < y < \sqrt{1-x^2} \;||\;$

$\qquad -\frac{1}{\sqrt{2}} < x < \frac{1}{\sqrt{2}} \;\&\&\; x < y < \sqrt{1-x^2}$

Here the inequalities contain the exponential function. In general, if inequalities contain nonpolynomial functions of the specified variable, you may get an incorrect result.

$In[5]:= $ `InequalitySolve[Abs[x - 1] <= 5 && E^x <= 3, x]`

`InequalitySolve::npi:`
  `A nonpolynomial equation or inequality encountered. The`
  `solution set may be incorrect.`

$Out[5]= -4 \le x \le Log[3]$

■ Algebra'PolynomialExtendedGCD'

PolynomialExtendedGCD gives the extended greatest common divisor for two univariate polynomials. The *Mathematica* kernel has the functions GCD and ExtendedGCD for integers, and the function PolynomialGCD for multivariate polynomials over the rationals. The function defined in this package works not only for polynomials over the rationals, but also for polynomials over the integers mod prime p, and for polynomials with coefficients in a finite field defined by the package Algebra'FiniteFields'.

In a Euclidean domain, such as addition and multiplication on the integers, or addition and multiplication on univariate polynomials with coefficients in some field, it is possible to write the gcd of two elements as a linear combination of the two elements. The extended gcd gives the coefficients of the linear combination. PolynomialExtendedGCD[$poly_1$, $poly_2$] gives the list $\{gcd, \{r, s\}\}$ where gcd is the greatest common divisor of $poly_1$ and $poly_2$, and r and s are polynomials such that $r\ poly_1 + s\ poly_2 = gcd$.

PolynomialExtendedGCD[$poly_1$, $poly_2$]	give the extended gcd of the two univariate polynomials $poly_1$ and $poly_2$ over the rationals, gaussian rationals, or finite fields
PolynomialExtendedGCD[$poly_1$, $poly_2$, Modulus->p]	give the extended gcd of two univariate polynomials over the integers mod prime p

Polynomial greatest common divisor.

This loads the package.	`In[1]:= <<Algebra'PolynomialExtendedGCD'`
Here is an example over the integers mod 7.	`In[2]:= PolynomialExtendedGCD[x^2 + 2 x + 1,` `            Expand[(x + 1)(x + 2)], Modulus->7]`
	`Out[2]= {1 + x, {6, 1}}`
Here is the same example over the rationals.	`In[3]:= PolynomialExtendedGCD[x^2 + 2 x + 1,` `            Expand[(x + 1)(x + 2)]]`
	`Out[3]= {1 + x, {-1, 1}}`
Load the Algebra'FiniteFields' package.	`In[4]:= <<Algebra'FiniteFields'`

Here is the example over the field GF[7].	`In[5]:= PolynomialExtendedGCD[`
	`            x^2 + GF[7][{2}] x + GF[7][{1}],`
	`            Expand[(x + GF[7][{1}])(x + GF[7][{2}])]]`

	`Out[5]= {{1}₇ + x {1}₇, {{6}₇, {1}₇}}`

Note that the kernel function PolynomialGCD does not work for polynomials over finite fields. Apply First to the result of PolynomialExtendedGCD instead.

```
In[6]:= PolynomialGCD[x^2 + GF[7][{2}] x + GF[7][{1}],
            Expand[(x + GF[7][{1}])(x + GF[7][{2}])]]

Out[6]= 1
```

Here the polynomial coefficients are Gaussian integers.

```
In[7]:= PolynomialExtendedGCD[
          Expand[ ((12+I) z^2 + 7 z + I) (I z + 3)],
          Expand[ ((9+2I) z + (3+I)) ((3I)z + 9)]
        ]
```

$$Out[7]= \left\{-3\,i+z,\right.$$
$$\left\{-\frac{1672}{3469}+\frac{1489\,i}{3469},\ \left(\frac{89}{3469}-\frac{688\,i}{10407}\right)+\left(\frac{1901}{10407}-\frac{2222\,i}{10407}\right)z\right\}\right\}$$

■ Algebra`PolynomialPowerMod`

This package introduces the function `PolynomialPowerMod`, which efficiently computes a power of a polynomial modulo a prime and a polynomial. Support for the `Modulus` option is added to `PolynomialQuotient` and `PolynomialRemainder`. The package also extends the `Modulus` option of `Factor`, `FactorList`, and `PolynomialGCD` to handle large prime moduli.

The factoring algorithm used by the functions in this package is described in D.E. Knuth, *Seminumerical Algorithms*, Addison-Wesley, 1981, Section 4.6.2. You first use the derivative to factor the polynomial f in x into square-free factors. The degree d factorization of f modulo p is obtained by finding the greatest common denominator of f and $x^{p^d} - x$ for $d = 1, 2, ...$. This is computed quickly using repeated squaring. Finally, you use the probabilistic factoring algorithm of Cantor-Zassenhaus to factor the result into irreducible degree d factors.

`PolynomialPowerMod[`$poly_1$`, ` n`, {`$poly_2$`, ` p`}]`
  compute `PolynomialMod[`$poly_1$`^`n`, {`$poly_2$`, ` p`}]` where n is an integer and p is a prime

---

Using `PolynomialPowerMod`.

This loads the package.	`In[1]:= <<Algebra`PolynomialPowerMod``

The package function `PolynomialPowerMod` is more efficient than the built-in function `PolynomialMod` applied to a polynomial raised to a power.	`In[2]:= {Timing[PolynomialPowerMod[1 + x, 200,`
	`        {x^3 + x^2 + 1, Prime[4750]}]][[1]],`
	`      Timing[PolynomialMod[(1 + x)^200,`
	`        {x^3 + x^2 + 1, Prime[4750]}]][[1]]}`
	
	`Out[2]= {0.07 Second, 1.32 Second}`

~ `PolynomialQuotient[`f`, ` g`, ` x`, Modulus -> ` p`]`
  compute `PolynomialMod[PolynomialQuotient[`f,g,x`],`p`]]`

~ `PolynomialRemainder[`f`, ` g`, ` x`, Modulus -> ` p`]`
  compute `PolynomialMod[PolynomialRemainder[`f,g,x`],`p`]]`

`Modulus` option for `PolynomialQuotient` and `PolynomialRemainder`.

Here are two polynomials in x.	`In[3]:= {f, g} = {(1 + x)^3 (1 + x^3), x^2 + 2};`

Using the `Modulus` option of `PolynomialQuotient` is equivalent to applying `PolynomialMod` to the result of `PolynomialQuotient`.	`In[4]:= {PolynomialQuotient[f, g, x, Modulus -> 11],`
	`      PolynomialMod[PolynomialQuotient[f,g,x], 11]}`
	
	`Out[4]= {1 + 7 x + x^2 + 3 x^3 + x^4, 1 + 7 x + x^2 + 3 x^3 + x^4}`

Using the Modulus option of PolynomialRemainder is equivalent to applying PolynomialMod to the result of PolynomialRemainder.

```
In[5]:= {PolynomialRemainder[f, g, x, Modulus -> 11],
            PolynomialMod[PolynomialRemainder[f,g,x],11]}

Out[5]= {10, 10}
```

~ PolynomialGCD[$poly_1$, $poly_2$, ... , Modulus -> p]
  find the greatest common divisor of the polynomials modulo p

~ Factor[$poly$, Modulus -> p]   factor a polynomial modulo p

~ FactorList[$poly$, Modulus -> p]

  give results as lists of factors

Extending PolynomialGCD, Factor, and FactorList to accept large prime moduli.

Using the Modulus option with PolynomialGCD is equivalent to applying PolynomialMod to the result of PolynomialGCD.

```
In[6]:= {PolynomialGCD[x^2-1,x-1, Modulus -> Prime[10^8]],
            PolynomialMod[PolynomialGCD[x^2-1,x-1], Prime[10^8]]}

Out[6]= {2038074742 + x, 2038074742 + x}
```

After loading this package, a polynomial may be factored modulo a large prime.

```
In[7]:= Factor[1 + 2 x^3, Modulus -> Prime[10^7]]

Out[7]= 2 (89712337 + x^3)
```

■ Algebra`Quaternions`

This package implements Hamilton's quaternion algebra. Quaternions have the form $a + bi + cj + dk$ where a, b, c, and d are real numbers. The symbols i, j, and k are multiplied according to the rules $i^2 = j^2 = k^2 = ijk = -1$. Quaternions are an extension of the complex numbers, and work much the same except that their multiplication is not commutative. For instance, $ij = -ji$.

Because of the similarities between quaternions and complex numbers, this package imitates *Mathematica*'s treatment of complex numbers in many ways. To provide a clear distinction between quaternions and complex numbers, all quaternions should be entered using the form `Quaternion[a, b, c, d]` where a, b, c, and d are real numbers. Only limited support is offered to the symbolic form $a + I\,b + J\,c + K\,d$.

`Quaternion[a, b, c, d]`	the quaternion number $a + bi + cj + dk$
`QuaternionQ[w]`	test whether w is a quaternion number
`FromQuaternion[w]`	transform the `Quaternion` object w to the symbolic form $a + I\,b + J\,c + K\,d$
`ToQuaternion[w]`	transform w to a `Quaternion` object if possible

Defining, testing, and transforming quaternions.

This loads the package.

```
In[1]:= <<Algebra`Quaternions`
```

Quaternion objects will not automatically simplify to `Complex` or `Real` numbers.

```
In[2]:= 3 + 2 I + Quaternion[2,0,-6,0] -3 * Quaternion[1,3,-2,0]
Out[2]= Quaternion[2, -7, 0, 0]
```

`FromQuaternion` transforms this `Quaternion` object to an object with head `Complex`.

```
In[3]:= FromQuaternion[%]
Out[3]= 2 - 7 i
```

The primary purpose of this package is to define arithmetic for quaternions. It adds rules to `Plus`, `Minus`, `Times`, `Divide`, and, most importantly, `NonCommutativeMultiply`. It is only legal to use `Times` when multiplying two nonquaternions or a quaternion by a *scalar* (*i.e.*, real) number. When multiplying two quaternions, you must use `NonCommutativeMultiply`.

Addition is done component by component.

```
In[4]:= Quaternion[1,2,3,4] + Quaternion[2,3,4,5]
Out[4]= Quaternion[3, 5, 7, 9]
```

Be sure to use ** rather than * when multiplying quaternions.

```
In[5]:= Quaternion[2,0,-6,3] ** Quaternion[1,3,-2,2]
Out[5]= Quaternion[-16, 0, -1, 25]
```

This multiplication is noncommutative.

```
In[6]:= Quaternion[1,3,-2,2] ** Quaternion[2,0,-6,3]
Out[6]= Quaternion[-16, 12, -19, -11]
```

Be careful with `Divide` since *Mathematica*'s internal rules quickly turn it into `Times`.

```
In[7]:= Quaternion[1,3,-2,0] / Quaternion[1,0,0,0]
Out[7]= Quaternion[1, 0, 0, 0] Quaternion[1, 3, -2, 0]
```

Although quaternions are whole algebraic objects, just as with complex numbers, it is sometimes useful to look at their component parts. These objects form a vector space over the real numbers, with their standard basis being $\{1, i, j, k\}$. You may use standard *Mathematica* techniques for extracting the individual components. However, there are other vector-type parameters such as length and direction which you may want to look at as well.

The projection of a quaternion onto *ijk* space, the nonreal part of the quaternion, is called the *pure quaternion part*. This plays a role similar to the pure imaginary part of a complex number.

`Re[`w`]`	the real part Re w
`Conjugate[`w`]`	the quaternion conjugate w^*
`Abs[`w`]`	the absolute value $|w|$
`AbsIJK[`w`]`	the magnitude of the pure quaternion part of w
`Norm[`w`]`	the sum of the squares of the components of w
`Sign[`w`]`	the sign of the quaternion w
`AdjustedSignIJK[`w`]`	the sign of the pure quaternion part of w, adjusted so its first nonzero component is positive

Component functions of quaternions.

In the conjugate of a quaternion, all the signs of the nonreal components are reversed.

```
In[8]:= q = Conjugate[Quaternion[4,-3,1,-2]]
Out[8]= Quaternion[4, 3, -1, 2]
```

The sign of a quaternion is defined in the same way as the sign of a complex number. It is the "direction" of the quaternion.

```
In[9]:= Sign[q]
```
$$Out[9]= Quaternion\left[2\sqrt{\frac{2}{15}}, \sqrt{\frac{3}{10}}, -\frac{1}{\sqrt{30}}, \sqrt{\frac{2}{15}}\right]$$

This returns a quaternion with norm 1 and real part 0.

```
In[10]:= AdjustedSignIJK[q]
```
$$Out[10]= Quaternion\left[0, \frac{3}{\sqrt{14}}, -\frac{1}{\sqrt{14}}, \sqrt{\frac{2}{7}}\right]$$

This gives the standard Euclidean length.

```
In[11]:= Abs[q]
Out[11]= √30
```

A quaternion with a zero I component will still have a nonzero pure quaternion part.

```
In[12]:= AbsIJK[Quaternion[1,0,2,3]]
Out[12]= √13
```

For a complex number $z = x + iy$, e^z is defined by $e^x(\cos y + i\sin y)$. The package defines e^q in a similar way, using the pure quaternion part of q instead of the pure imaginary part of a complex number. Indeed, it makes analogous definitions for the following elementary functions: Exp, Log, Cos, Sin, Tan, Sec, Csc, Cot, ArcCos, ArcSin, ArcTan, ArcSec, ArcCsc, ArcCot, Cosh, Sinh, Tanh, Sech, Csch, Coth, ArcCosh, ArcSinh, ArcTanh, ArcSech, ArcCsch, and ArcCoth.

The exponential of a quaternion can be quite complicated.

In[13]:= `Exp[Quaternion[2,3,1,6]]`

$$\textit{Out[13]= } \mathtt{Quaternion}\left[e^2 \mathrm{Cos}\left[\sqrt{46}\right], \frac{3\,e^2\,\mathrm{Sin}\left[\sqrt{46}\right]}{\sqrt{46}}, \frac{e^2\,\mathrm{Sin}\left[\sqrt{46}\right]}{\sqrt{46}}, \right.$$

$$\left. 3\sqrt{\frac{2}{23}}\,e^2\,\mathrm{Sin}\left[\sqrt{46}\right]\right]$$

Just as with complex numbers, it is important to beware of branch cuts.

In[14]:= `Sin[Cos[Quaternion[.3,.1,.5,.5]]]`

Out[14]= `Quaternion[0.960163, 0.0114577, 0.0572884, 0.0572884]`

A four-dimensional analog of deMoivre's theorem is used for calculating powers of quaternions.

In[15]:= `Quaternion[1,2,0,1]^2.5`

Out[15]= $\mathtt{Quaternion}\left[-9.0604,\ 2.20741,\ 6.75802 \times 10^{-17},\ 1.1037\right]$

The functions so far have been intended to work with quaternions whose components are arbitrary real numbers. Just as the integers and Gaussian integers are interesting subsets of the reals and complexes, there is a special subset of the quaternions called the quaternion integers. This subset is a little broader than one might expect. It includes not only those quaternions that have all integer components, but also those quaternions that have all components being odd multiples of 1/2. In this subset there are 24 quaternions that have multiplicative inverses. These are the *units* of the algebra. They correspond roughly to $\{1, -1, i, -i\}$ in the Gaussian integers.

Round[w]	the closest integer quaternion to w
OddQ[w]	test whether the quaternion w is odd
EvenQ[w]	test whether the quaternion w is even
IntegerQuaternionQ[w]	test whether the quaternion w is an integer quaternion
UnitQuaternions	the list of 24 units of Hamilton's division algebra
UnitQuaternionQ[w]	test whether w is a unit quaternion

Integer quaternion functions.

Round for quaternions returns a Quaternion in which either all components are integers, or all components are odd multiples of 1/2.

In[16]:= `Round[Quaternion[1/2,3,4,5/2]]`

Out[16]= `Quaternion[0, 3, 4, 2]`

A quaternion is even if its norm is even.

In[17]:= **EvenQ[Quaternion[2,3,4,5]]**

Out[17]= True

A quaternion integer has components that are either all integers or all halves of odd integers.

In[18]:= **IntegerQuaternionQ[Quaternion[3/2,1/2, -1/2,5/2]]**

Out[18]= True

Given a quaternion *q* and a unit quaternion *e*, then *qe* and *eq* are, respectively, right and left *associates* of *q*. It is useful to choose an arbitrary associate and call it the *primary* associate. This package chooses the associate with the largest real component.

LeftAssociates[*w*]	the list of 24 left associates of the quaternion *w*
RightAssociates[*w*]	the list of 24 right associates of the quaternion *w*
PrimaryLeftAssociate[*w*, *side*]	the primary left associate of the quaternion *w*
PrimaryRightAssociate[*w*, *side*]	the primary right associate of the quaternion *w*

The associates of an integer quaternion.

This is the primary left associate of the quaternion.

In[19]:= **PrimaryLeftAssociate[Quaternion[1,4,5,3]]**

Out[19]= Quaternion$\left[\frac{13}{2}, \frac{5}{2}, \frac{3}{2}, \frac{1}{2}\right]$

The primary right associate is often very similar.

In[20]:= **PrimaryRightAssociate[Quaternion[1,4,5,3]]**

Out[20]= Quaternion$\left[\frac{13}{2}, \frac{1}{2}, \frac{5}{2}, \frac{3}{2}\right]$

Quaternion multiplication is noncommutative, so there are two greatest common denominators, one for the left side and one for the right. Since this function depends on the value returned by PrimaryAssociate, the RightGCD and LeftGCD are not unique.

LeftGCD[*w*, *u*]	the greatest common left divisor of *w* and *u*
RightGCD[*w*, *u*]	the greatest common right divisor of *w* and *u*
Mod[*w*,*u*]	*w* modulo *u* (remainder on division of *w* by *u*)

Some integer division functions.

The largest quaternion that divides both of these is Quaternion[1,0,0,0].

In[21]:= **LeftGCD[Quaternion[1,3,4,1], Quaternion[3,4,1,2]]**

Out[21]= Quaternion[1, 0, 0, 0]

The LeftGCD and the RightGCD can be quite different.

```
In[22]:= RightGCD[Quaternion[1,3,4,1], Quaternion[3,4,1,2]]
```

$$Out[22]= \text{Quaternion}\left[\frac{3}{2}, \frac{1}{2}, \frac{1}{2}, -\frac{1}{2}\right]$$

Just as with complex numbers, the quaternion Mod works recursively.

```
In[23]:= Mod[Quaternion[-3,4,1,2],3]
```
```
Out[23]= Quaternion[0, 1, 1, -1]
```

You can specify a quaternion as the modulus.

```
In[24]:= Mod[Quaternion[1,3,4,1], Quaternion[3,4,1,2]]
```
```
Out[24]= Quaternion[1, 1, -1, 0]
```

PrimeQ has the option GaussianIntegers->True that checks to see if a number is prime with respect to the Gaussian integers. This package extends PrimeQ farther to check if a number is prime with respect to the quaternions.

Lagrange proved that every integer can be expressed as a sum of squares of, at most, four integers. Therefore, given an integer n, there is a quaternion q with integer components such that q ** Conjugate[q] == n. So no integer is prime with respect to the quaternions. In fact, a quaternion integer is prime, if and only if, its norm is prime in the usual sense.

PrimeQ[n, Quaternions->True]

         test whether n is a prime with respect to the quaternions

---

An extension of PrimeQ.

19 is a prime with respect to the Gaussian integers.

```
In[25]:= PrimeQ[19, GaussianIntegers->True]
```
```
Out[25]= True
```

It is not a prime with respect to the quaternions. It can be factored into Quaternion[1,4,1,1] and Quaternion[1,-4,-1,-1].

```
In[26]:= PrimeQ[19, Quaternions->True]
```
```
Out[26]= False
```

Quaternion[1,3,0,1] is a prime quaternion.

```
In[27]:= PrimeQ[Quaternion[1,3,0,1], Quaternions->True]
```
```
Out[27]= True
```

■ Algebra`ReIm`

This package extends the class of algebraic identities used by the built-in functions Re, Im, Abs, Conjugate, and Arg, and enables these functions to make more complete use of known properties of symbols and functions. For example, the input Im[z] ^= 0 can be used to declare that z is real, after which Re[z] will evaluate to z. The function RealValued is also included for declaring functions to be real-valued for real arguments.

Some of the functionality provided by this package has been incorporated into the *Mathematica* kernel and may be available without loading the package. In addition, the option GaussianIntegers has been added to several built-in polynomial functions, such as Factor, and is helpful when working with rational expressions containing complex numbers. The function ComplexExpand can also be used for manipulating complex-valued expressions.

This loads the package.	*In[1]:=* **<<Algebra`ReIm`**
Symbols with no special properties are expanded into real and imaginary parts.	*In[2]:=* **Re[1/a]** *Out[2]=* $\dfrac{\mathrm{Re}[a]}{\mathrm{Im}[a]^2 + \mathrm{Re}[a]^2}$
This declares the symbol z to have an imaginary part of zero, and attaches the rule to z.	*In[3]:=* **z /: Im[z] = 0** *Out[3]=* 0
The symbol z is now treated as a real number.	*In[4]:=* **Re[(z + I)^2 + Exp[I z]]** *Out[4]=* $-1 + z^2 + \mathrm{Cos}[z]$
Combinations of real symbols and other expressions can also be handled.	*In[5]:=* **Re[(a + z)^2]** *Out[5]=* $-\mathrm{Im}[a]^2 + (z + \mathrm{Re}[a])^2$

RealValued[f, g, ...]	declare functions to be real for real arguments

The function RealValued.

This declares the symbol x to be real and the functions f and g to be real-valued for real arguments.	*In[6]:=* **Im[x] ^= 0; RealValued[f, g]** *Out[6]=* {f, g}
The imaginary part of this expression is determined using previously declared properties of f, g, and x.	*In[7]:=* **Im[1/(1 - I f[x] g[x])]** *Out[7]=* $\dfrac{f[x]\, g[x]}{1 + f[x]^2\, g[x]^2}$

The rules in this package are based on simple identities that are easy to understand and apply, and you are encouraged to read and modify the package as necessary for your application. If you modify the package, however, or if you use rules involving multiple-valued functions, there are a few issues you should keep in mind.

Many useful identities involving logarithms, roots and other multiple-valued functions are not correct for arbitrary complex arguments. The rules that implement these identities can lead to results that represent unintended branches of the function. If you encounter problems related to branches of multiple-valued functions, the corresponding rules can be modified or removed from the package.

This declares the symbols a and b to be negative.	*In[8]:=* **Negative[a] ^= True; Negative[b] ^= True** *Out[8]=* True
This result corresponds to an analytic continuation of the principal branch of the logarithm function, and was obtained using the rule `Im[Log[a_ b_]] := Im[Log[a] + Log[b]]`. This rule can be modified or removed if the principal branch must be preserved.	*In[9]:=* **Im[Log[a b]]** *Out[9]=* 2π

You should also be careful to avoid infinite recursion when adding rules to this package. For example, the pair of rules `Im[x_]:=x /; Re[x]==0` and `Re[x_]:=x /; Im[x]==0` can lead to infinite recursion, since evaluation of the condition in the rule for `Re[x]` requires evaluation of `Im[x]`, and evaluation of the condition in the rule for `Im[x]` requires evaluation of `Re[x]`.

+■ Algebra`RootIsolation`

This package provides functions for counting and isolating roots of polynomials.

For complex numbers m_1, m_2, and a polynomial f with Gaussian rational coefficients, the function CountRoots gives the number of roots of f in the interval $\{m_1, m_2\}$, multiplicities counted. The interval $\{m_1, m_2\}$ means here the set of all complex z such that

$$(\text{Re}[m_1] < \text{Re}[z] < \text{Re}[m_2] \ \vee \ \text{Re}[m_1] = \text{Re}[z] = \text{Re}[m_2]) \ \wedge$$
$$(\text{Im}[m_1] < \text{Im}[z] < \text{Im}[m_2] \ \vee \ \text{Im}[m_1] = \text{Im}[z] = \text{Im}[m_2])$$

which may be a point, a horizontal or vertical open interval, or an open rectangle.

An interval I is an **isolating interval** for a root a of a polynomial f, if a is the only root of f in I. Isolating roots of a polynomial means finding disjoint isolating intervals for all the roots of the polynomial. The package defines functions for isolating roots of polynomials with rational coefficients.

CountRoots[*poly*, {*x*, m_1, m_2}]	give the number of roots of *poly* in the complex interval $\{m_1, m_2\}$
RealRootIntervals[*poly*]	give disjoint isolating intervals for the real roots of *poly*
RealRootIntervals[{*poly*$_1$, *poly*$_2$, ... }]	give disjoint isolating intervals for the real roots of *poly*$_1$, *poly*$_2$, ...
ComplexRootIntervals[*poly*]	give disjoint isolating intervals for the complex roots of *poly*
ComplexRootIntervals[{*poly*$_1$, *poly*$_2$, ... }]	give disjoint isolating intervals for the complex roots of *poly*$_1$, *poly*$_2$, ...
ContractInterval[*a*, *n*]	give an isolating interval that bounds the value of the algebraic number *a* up to the precision of at least *n* decimal places

Functions for counting and isolating roots of polynomials.

This loads the package.

```
In[1]:= <<Algebra`RootIsolation`
```

This counts roots of f in the open interval (1, 2).

```
In[2]:= f = (x^2 - 2) (x^2 - 3) (x^2 - 4); CountRoots[f, {x, 1, 2}]
Out[2]= 2
```

The polynomial has two roots in the vertical interval as follows: a single root at $\sqrt{-1}$ and a triple root at 0.

```
In[3]:= CountRoots[(x^2+1) x^3, {x, -I, 2 I}]
Out[3]= 4
```

This counts 17th degree roots of unity in the open unit square.

In[4]:= `CountRoots[x^17 - 1, {x, 0, 1 + I}]`

Out[4]= 4

Here are isolating intervals for the real roots of f.

In[5]:= `RealRootIntervals[f]`

Out[5]= $\left\{\{-2, -2\}, \left\{-2, -\frac{3}{2}\right\}, \left\{-\frac{3}{2}, -1\right\}, \left\{1, \frac{3}{2}\right\}, \left\{\frac{3}{2}, 2\right\}, \{2, 2\}\right\}$

The second list shows which interval contains a root of which polynomial.

In[6]:= `RealRootIntervals[{f + 3, f + 5, f + 7}]`

Out[6]= $\left\{\left\{\left\{-\frac{7}{6}, -\frac{8}{7}\right\}, \left\{-\frac{8}{7}, -1\right\}, \{-1, 0\}, \{0, 1\}, \left\{1, \frac{8}{7}\right\}, \left\{\frac{8}{7}, \frac{7}{6}\right\}\right\},\right.$
$\left. \{1, 2, 3, 3, 2, 1\}\right\}$

This gives isolating intervals for all complex roots of f+3.

In[7]:= `ComplexRootIntervals[f + 3]`

Out[7]= $\left\{\{-2, -1\}, \{1, 2\}, \left\{-7 - 7\,\mathbf{i}, -\frac{7}{4}\right\}, \left\{-7, -\frac{7}{4} + 7\,\mathbf{i}\right\},\right.$
$\left. \left\{-\frac{7}{4} - 7\,\mathbf{i}, \frac{7}{2}\right\}, \left\{-\frac{7}{4}, \frac{7}{2} + 7\,\mathbf{i}\right\}\right\}$

Here are isolating intervals for the third and fourth degree roots of unity. The second interval contains a root common to both polynomials.

In[8]:= `ComplexRootIntervals[{x^3 - 1, x^4 - 1}]`

Out[8]= $\left\{\left\{\{-1, -1\}, \{0, 2\},\right.\right.$
$\left\{-\frac{3}{4} - \frac{3\,\mathbf{i}}{2}, -\frac{3}{16} - \frac{3\,\mathbf{i}}{4}\right\}, \left\{-\frac{3}{4} + \frac{3\,\mathbf{i}}{4}, -\frac{3}{16} + \frac{3\,\mathbf{i}}{2}\right\},$
$\left. \left\{-\frac{3}{16} - \frac{3\,\mathbf{i}}{2}, \frac{3}{8} - \frac{3\,\mathbf{i}}{4}\right\}, \left\{-\frac{3}{16} + \frac{3\,\mathbf{i}}{4}, \frac{3}{8} + \frac{3\,\mathbf{i}}{2}\right\}\right\},$
$\left. \{2, \{1, 2\}, 1, 1, 2, 2\}\right\}$

Here is a small interval containing a tenth degree root of unity.

In[9]:= `ContractInterval[Root[x^10 - 1, 5], 10]`

Out[9]= $\left\{-\frac{5308871539}{17179869184} - \frac{65356106147\,\mathbf{i}}{68719476736},\right.$
$\left. -\frac{21235486155}{68719476736} - \frac{32678053073\,\mathbf{i}}{34359738368}\right\}$

See how small the interval is.

In[10]:= `N[%, 20]`

Out[10]= {-0.30901699437526986003 - 0.9510565163072897121 i,
    -0.30901699436071794480 - 0.9510565162927377969 i}

⁺■ Algebra `SymmetricPolynomials`

The package provides functions for generating elementary symmetric polynomials and for representing symmetric polynomials in terms of elementary symmetric polynomials. The Fundamental Theorem of Symmetric Polynomials says that every symmetric polynomial in $x_1, \ldots, x_n$ can be represented as a polynomial in elementary symmetric polynomials as follows:

$$s_1 = x_1 + x_2 + \ldots + x_n$$
$$s_2 = x_1 x_2 + x_1 x_3 + \ldots + x_{n-1} x_n$$
$$\ldots$$
$$s_n = x_1 x_2 \cdot \ldots \cdot x_n$$

When the ordering of variables is fixed, every polynomial can be uniquely represented as a sum of its symmetric part and the remainder as follows:

$$f(x_1, \ldots, x_n) = p(s_1, \ldots, s_n) + q(x_1, \ldots, x_n)$$

The polynomial f is symmetric if and only if the remainder q is zero. The uniqueness of this representation is guaranteed by requiring that q does not contain descending monomials, where a monomial $c x_1^{e_1} \cdot \ldots \cdot x_n^{e_n}$ is called descending iff $e_1 \geq \ldots \geq e_n$.

SymmetricReduction[f, {x_1, ... , x_n}]
　　　　give a pair of polynomials {p, q} in $x_1, \ldots, x_n$, where $f = p + q$, p is the symmetric part, and q is the remainder

SymmetricReduction[f, {x_1, ... , x_n}, {s_1, ... , s_n}]
　　　　give a pair of polynomials {p, q} in $x_1, \ldots, x_n$, where the elementary symmetric polynomials are replaced by $s_1, \ldots, s_n$

SymmetricPolynomial[{x_1, ... , x_n}, k]
　　　　the kth symmetric polynomial in variables $x_1, \ldots, x_n$

Symmetric polynomial functions.

This loads the package.

```
In[1]:= <<Algebra`SymmetricPolynomials`
```

Here is the elementary symmetric polynomial of degree three in four variables.

```
In[2]:= SymmetricPolynomial[{x, y, z, t}, 3]
Out[2]= t x y + t x z + t y z + x y z
```

This gives the polynomial written in terms of elementary symmetric polynomials. The input polynomial is symmetric, so the remainder is zero.

```
In[3]:= SymmetricReduction[(x + y)^2 + (x + z)^2 + (z + y)^2,
            {x, y, z}]
Out[3]= {2 (x + y + z)^2 - 2 (x y + x z + y z), 0}
```

Here the elementary symmetric polynomials in the symmetric part of the input polynomial are replaced with the given variables. The polynomial is not symmetric, so the remainder is not zero.

```
In[4]:= SymmetricReduction[x^5 + y^5 + z^4, {x, y, z}, {s1, s2, s3}]
```

$Out[4]= \left\{ s1^5 - 5 \, s1^3 \, s2 + 5 \, s1 \, s2^2 + 5 \, s1^2 \, s3 - 5 \, s2 \, s3, \, z^4 - z^5 \right\}$

3. Calculus

⁺■ Calculus`DSolveIntegrals`

Most nonlinear partial differential equations do not allow for general solutions. In these cases it is advisable to use the `CompleteIntegral` function that attempts to find a sufficiently representative family of particular solutions called a *complete integral*.

A complete integral of an equation is known to be exhaustive in the sense that solutions of almost all boundary value problems for the equation may then be expressed in quadratures of the complete integral. Thus, the complete integral plays a role similar to that of the Green's function for linear second-order partial differential equations.

`CompleteIntegral[`*eqn*`, `*u*`[`*x,y,*`... ], {`*x,y,*`... }]`   build a complete integral of the differential equation with respect to *u*[*x,y,*...]

Finding the complete integral of an equation.

This loads the package.

In[1]:= `<<Calculus`DSolveIntegrals``

Here B[1] and B[2] are parameters of the solution.

In[2]:= `CompleteIntegral[`
`        Derivative[0, 1][u][x, y] == (u[x, y] +`
`            x^2*Derivative[1, 0][u][x, y]^2)/y,`
`        u[x,y], {x,y}]`

$$Out[2]= \left\{\left\{u[x, y] \to \frac{1}{4}\left((4y - B[1]) B[1] - 2B[1]\,Log[x] - Log[x]^2\right)\right\}\right\}$$

B[*n*] is the default name for the parameters appearing in the result of `CompleteIntegral`. The names of parameters may be selected using the option `IntegralConstants`, just as the names of the undetermined constants in the result of `DSolve` may be selected using the option `DSolveConstants`.

This shows how the names of parameters of the complete integral may be changed. The integral is Example 6.7 from KamkeII.

In[3]:= `CompleteIntegral[-u[x, y] +`
`        (2 + y)*Derivative[0, 1][u][x, y] +`
`        x*Derivative[1, 0][u][x, y] +`
`        3*Derivative[1, 0][u][x, y]^2 == 0,`
`        u[x,y], {x,y}, IntegralConstants->F]`

$$Out[3]= \left\{\left\{u[x, y] \to \frac{1}{12} F[1] (2x + F[1]) + (2 + y) F[2]\right\}\right\}$$

For the needs of advanced users (especially those dealing with analytical mechanics), a function is supported by the package for finding the differential invariants (first integrals or constants of motion) of systems of ordinary differential equations.

```
DifferentialInvariants[{eqn₁, eqn₂, ... }, {u[x], v[x], ... }, x]
```
give a list of differential invariants for the system of
differential equations in terms of variables
$\{u[x], v[x], ...\}$ and x

```
DifferentialInvariants[{eqn₁, eqn₂, ... }, {u, v, ... }, x]
```
give a list of differential invariants for the system of
differential equations in terms of variables $u, v, ...$ and x

Finding the differential invariants for a system of differential equations.

This builds a list of two independent
invariants for a two-dimensional
differential system. The dependence of
u and v on x is suppressed.

```
In[4]:= DifferentialInvariants[
            {u'[x] == -(u[x] (u[x] + v[x])),
             v'[x] == v[x] (u[x] + v[x])},
            {u, v}, x]
```

$$Out[4]= \left\{\sqrt{u\,v}\ x + \text{ArcTan}\left[\frac{u}{\sqrt{u\,v}}\right],\ u\,v\right\}$$

Reference

[KamkeII] E. Kamke, *Differentialgleichungen, Lösungsmethoden und Lösungen, Band 2, Partielle Differentialgleichungen Erster Ordnung fur Eine Gesuchte Funktion*, Academische Verlagsgesellschaft, Leipzig, 1948.

■ Calculus`FourierTransform`

The *Mathematica* kernel provides the functions `FourierTransform` and `InverseFourierTransform` for computing the symbolic Fourier exponential transform and inverse transform. It also provides the functions `FourierSinTransform`, `InverseFourierSinTransform`, `FourierCosTransform`, and `InverseFourierCosTransform` for computing the symbolic Fourier sine and cosine transforms and their inverses. This package provides functions giving numerical approximations to these Fourier transforms. It also provides functions for Fourier series, Fourier coefficients, discrete-time Fourier transforms, and their numerical counterparts. The numerical approximations use *Mathematica*'s numerical integration and summation directly without first trying for an exact solution.

`NFourierTransform[`*expr*`, `*t*`, `ω`]`	find a numerical approximation to the Fourier transform of *expr* evaluated at the numerical value ω, where *expr* is treated as a function of *t*
`NInverseFourierTransform[`*expr*`, `ω`, `*t*`]`	find a numerical approximation to the inverse Fourier transform of *expr* evaluated at the numerical value *t*, where *expr* is treated as a function of ω
`NFourierSinTransform[`*expr*`, `*t*`, `ω`]`	find a numerical approximation to the Fourier sine transform of *expr* evaluated at the numerical value ω, where *expr* is treated as a function of *t*
`NInverseFourierSinTransform[`*expr*`, `ω`, `*t*`]`	find a numerical approximation to the inverse Fourier cosine transform of *expr* evaluated at the numerical value *t*, where *expr* is treated as a function of ω
`NFourierCosTransform[`*expr*`, `*t*`, `ω`]`	find a numerical approximation to the Fourier cosine transform of *expr* evaluated at the numerical value ω, where *expr* is treated as a function of *t*
`NInverseFourierCosTransform[`*expr*`, `ω`, `*t*`]`	find a numerical approximation to the inverse Fourier cosine transform of *expr* evaluated at the numerical value *t*, where *expr* is treated as a function of ω

Finding numerical approximations to Fourier transforms.

This loads the package.	`In[1]:= <<Calculus`FourierTransform``
This gives a numerical approximation to the Fourier transform of $\exp(-t^2)/(1 + |t|)$ with respect to ω at $\omega = 1$.	`In[2]:= NFourierTransform[Exp[-t^2]/(1 + Abs[t]), t, 1]`
	`Out[2]= 0.404024 + 0. i`

In addition to supporting the `NIntegrate` options, the numerical Fourier transform functions support the option `FourierParameters`. This option allows you to choose among the various conventions used for defining Fourier transforms.

setting	Fourier transform	inverse Fourier transform
Mathematica default	$\{0, 1\}$	$\frac{1}{\sqrt{2\pi}} \int_{-\infty}^{\infty} f(t)\, e^{i\omega t}\, dt$
		$\frac{1}{\sqrt{2\pi}} \int_{-\infty}^{\infty} F(\omega)\, e^{-i\omega t}\, d\omega$
general case	$\{a, b\}$	$\sqrt{\frac{|b|}{(2\pi)^{1-a}}} \int_{-\infty}^{\infty} f(t)\, e^{ib\omega t}\, dt$
		$\sqrt{\frac{|b|}{(2\pi)^{1+a}}} \int_{-\infty}^{\infty} F(\omega)\, e^{-ib\omega t}\, d\omega$

Effect of `FourierParameters` setting on Fourier transform.

setting	Fourier sine transform	inverse Fourier sine transform
$\{0, 1\}$	$\sqrt{\frac{2}{\pi}} \int_{0}^{\infty} f(t)\, \sin(\omega t)\, dt$	$\sqrt{\frac{2}{\pi}} \int_{0}^{\infty} F(\omega)\, \sin(\omega t)\, d\omega$
$\{a, b\}$	$2\sqrt{\frac{|b|}{(2\pi)^{1-a}}} \int_{0}^{\infty} f(t)\, \sin(b\omega t)\, dt$	$2\sqrt{\frac{|b|}{(2\pi)^{1+a}}} \int_{0}^{\infty} F(\omega)\, \sin(b\omega t)\, d\omega$

Effect of `FourierParameters` setting on Fourier sine transform.

setting	Fourier cosine transform	inverse Fourier cosine transform
$\{0, 1\}$	$\sqrt{\frac{2}{\pi}} \int_{0}^{\infty} f(t)\, \cos(\omega t)\, dt$	$\sqrt{\frac{2}{\pi}} \int_{0}^{\infty} F(\omega)\, \cos(\omega t)\, d\omega$
$\{a, b\}$	$2\sqrt{\frac{|b|}{(2\pi)^{1-a}}} \int_{0}^{\infty} f(t)\, \cos(b\omega t)\, dt$	$2\sqrt{\frac{|b|}{(2\pi)^{1+a}}} \int_{0}^{\infty} F(\omega)\, \cos(b\omega t)\, d\omega$

Effect of `FourierParameters` setting on Fourier cosine transform.

The Fourier transform is commonly used to transform a problem from the continuous "time domain" into the continuous "frequency domain." The Fourier transform may be viewed as the continuous analog of the Fourier series decomposition, which expresses a periodic function as a superposition of exponential or trigonometric functions. Fourier exponential and trigonometric series decompositions may be computed using the functions FourierSeries and FourierTrigSeries. The coefficients of the exponential series are found using FourierCoefficient and the coefficients of the trigonometric series are found using FourierSinCoefficient and FourierCosCoefficient. If the option setting FourierParameters -> {a, b} is specified, the continuous function of t is treated as having a period of $1/|b|$, instead of the default period of 1.

✦ FourierCoefficient[*expr*, *t*, *n*]	give the nth coefficient in the exponential series expansion of the periodic function of t equal to *expr* on the interval $t = -\frac{1}{2}$ to $t = \frac{1}{2}$
✦ FourierSinCoefficient[*expr*, *t*, *n*]	give the nth coefficient in the sine series expansion
✦ FourierCosCoefficient[*expr*, *t*, *n*]	give the nth coefficient in the cosine series expansion
✦ FourierSeries[*expr*, *t*, *k*]	give the exponential series expansion to order k of the periodic function of t equal to *expr* on the interval $t = -\frac{1}{2}$ to $t = \frac{1}{2}$
~ FourierTrigSeries[*expr*, *t*, *k*]	give the trigonometric series expansion to order k

Computing Fourier coefficients and series.

Here is a plot of the difference between t and the integer closest to t. It is a periodic function with fundamental interval from $-\frac{1}{2}$ to $\frac{1}{2}$.

In[3]:= **rndplt = Plot[t - Round[t], {t, -1.5, 1.5}]**

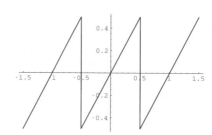

This gives a piece of the Fourier trigonometric series of the difference function. The difference function is odd so its trigonometric series contains only sines.

In[4]:= **FourierTrigSeries[t, t, 3]**

Out[4]= $\dfrac{\text{Sin}[2\pi t]}{\pi} - \dfrac{\text{Sin}[4\pi t]}{2\pi} + \dfrac{\text{Sin}[6\pi t]}{3\pi}$

The plot of the truncated series is similar to that of the function.

In[5]:= **Plot[%, {t, -1.5, 1.5}]**

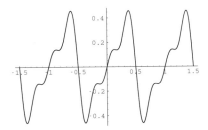

Here are the two plots on the same axes.

In[6]:= **Show[rndplt, %]**

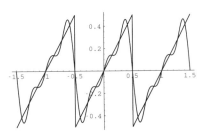

setting	Fourier coefficient
{0, 1}	$\int_{-1/2}^{1/2} f(t)\, e^{2\pi i n t}\, dt$
{a, b}	$\lvert b\rvert^{(1-a)/2} \int_{-1/(2\lvert b\rvert)}^{1/(2\lvert b\rvert)} f(t)\, e^{2\pi i b n t}\, dt$

Effect of `FourierParameters` setting on Fourier exponential coefficients.

setting	Fourier series
{0, 1}	$\sum_{n=-k}^{k} F_n e^{-2\pi i n t}$
{a, b}	$\|b\|^{(1+a)/2} \sum_{n=-k}^{k} F_n e^{-2\pi i b n t}$

Effect of FourierParameters setting on Fourier exponential series.

setting	c_0	c_n
{0, 1}	$\int_{-1/2}^{1/2} f(t)\,dt$	$2 \int_{-1/2}^{1/2} f(t)\, \cos(2\pi n t)\,dt$
{a, b}	$\|b\|^{(1-a)/2} \int_{-1/(2\|b\|)}^{1/(2\|b\|)} f(t)\,dt$	$2\|b\|^{(1-a)/2} \int_{-1/(2\|b\|)}^{1/(2\|b\|)} f(t)\, \cos(2\pi b n t)\,dt$

Effect of FourierParameters setting on Fourier cosine coefficients.

setting	d_n
{0, 1}	$2 \int_{-1/2}^{1/2} f(t)\, \sin(2\pi n t)\,dt$
{a, b}	$2\|b\|^{(1-a)/2} \int_{-1/(2\|b\|)}^{1/(2\|b\|)} f(t)\, \sin(2\pi b n t)\,dt$

Effect of FourierParameters setting on Fourier sine coefficients.

setting	Fourier trigonometric series
{0, 1}	$c_0 + \sum_{n=1}^{k} c_n \cos(2\pi n t) + d_n \sin(2\pi n t)$
{a, b}	$\|b\|^{(1+a)/2}(c_0 + \sum_{n=1}^{k} c_n \cos(2\pi b n t) + d_n \sin(2\pi b n t))$

Effect of FourierParameters setting on Fourier trigonometric series.

In certain circumstances you will not want exact or symbolic coefficients, but numerical approximations to the coefficients. In these cases you can use the numerical versions of the Fourier series functions. The numerical approximation functions accept the FourierParameters option, allowing you to specify the period.

⊹ NFourierCoefficient[*expr, t, n*]

find a numerical approximation to the nth coefficient in the exponential series expansion

⊹ NFourierSinCoefficient[*expr, t, n*]

find a numerical approximation to the nth coefficient in the sine series expansion

⊹ NFourierCosCoefficient[*expr, t, n*]

find a numerical approximation to the nth coefficient in the cosine series expansion

---

⊹   NFourierSeries[*expr, t, k*]   find the exponential series expansion to order k using numerical approximations for the coefficients

⁓ NFourierTrigSeries[*expr, t, k*]

find the trigonometric series expansion to order k using numerical approximations for the coefficients

Finding approximate numerical values for Fourier coefficients and series.

Here is a piece of the trigonometric series of a function that looks like $\sin(\cos(t + \frac{1}{2}))$ on the interval from $-\frac{1}{2}$ to $\frac{1}{2}$. The function elsewhere is obtained by repeating this with period 1.

In[7]:= **NFourierTrigSeries[Sin[Cos[t + 1/2]], t, 3]**

Out[7]= $0.738643 + 0.0370783\, \text{Cos}[2\pi t] - 0.00918056\, \text{Cos}[4\pi t] + 0.0040702\, \text{Cos}[6\pi t] - 0.100338\, \text{Sin}[2\pi t] + 0.0517278\, \text{Sin}[4\pi t] - 0.0346131\, \text{Sin}[6\pi t]$

Here is a plot of the trigonometric polynomial over three periods.

In[8]:= **Plot[%, {t, -1.5, 1.5}]**

The function FourierCoefficient, giving the coefficients of the Fourier exponential series, can be thought of as a transform from the continuous time domain into the discrete frequency domain. Likewise, the (infinite sum) Fourier exponential series can be thought of as an inverse transform from the discrete frequency domain into the continuous time domain. This transform pair is given by FourierCoefficient and InverseFourierCoefficient, and the numerical counterparts are given by NFourierCoefficient and NInverseFourierCoefficient. If the option setting FourierParameters -> {*a*, *b*} is specified, the period of the original function is taken to be $1/|b|$, instead of the default period of 1.

---

* FourierCoefficient[*expr*, *t*, *n*]

         give F_n, a function of integer n and the nth coefficient in the exponential series expansion of the periodic function $f(t)$, equal to *expr* on the interval $t = -\frac{1}{2}$ to $t = \frac{1}{2}$

* InverseFourierCoefficient[*expr*, *n*, *t*]

         give $f(t)$, a periodic function of t, represented by the Fourier exponential series coefficients *expr*, where *expr* is treated as a function of integer n

---

* NFourierCoefficient[*expr*, *t*, *n*]

         find a numerical approximation to the function F_n

* NInverseFourierCoefficient[*expr*, *n*, *t*]

         find a numerical approximation to the function $f(t)$

Continuous-time and discrete-frequency transform pairs: exact and numerical approximations.

Here is a plot of a periodic function of t, with a period of $\frac{2}{3}$.

```
In[9]:= (f = 1 + 2 Cos[3 Pi t] + 2 Cos[6 Pi t];
        Plot[f, {t, -1, 1}])
```

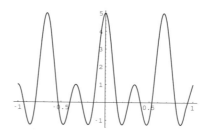

You can use the FourierParameters option to specify the period of the function.

```
In[10]:= Chop[Table[
            NFourierCoefficient[f, t, n,
                FourierParameters -> {0, 3/2},
                AccuracyGoal->8, PrecisionGoal->8],
            {n, -10, 10}]]

Out[10]= {0, 0, 0, 0, 0, 0, 0, 0, 0.816497, 0.816497, 0.816497,
          0.816497, 0.816497, 0, 0, 0, 0, 0, 0, 0, 0}
```

The inverse of the Fourier coefficients gives the original periodic function.

```
In[11]:= (nifc = Chop[Table[
              {t, NInverseFourierCoefficient[If[-2 <= n <= 2, 0.816497, 0],
                 n, t, FourierParameters -> {0, 3/2}]},
              {t, -1, 1, 1/30}]];
          ListPlot[nifc, PlotJoined->True])
```

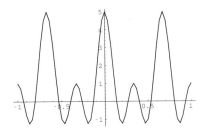

setting	Fourier coefficient	inverse Fourier coefficient
{0, 1}	$\int_{-1/2}^{1/2} f(t)\, e^{2\pi i n t}\, dt$	$\sum_{n=-\infty}^{\infty} F_n\, e^{-2\pi i n t}$
{a, b}	$\|b\|^{(1-a)/2} \int_{-1/(2\|b\|)}^{1/(2\|b\|)} f(t)\, e^{2\pi i b n t}\, dt$	$\|b\|^{(1+a)/2} \sum_{n=-\infty}^{\infty} F_n\, e^{-2\pi i b n t}$

Effect of `FourierParameters` setting on Fourier coefficient.

The Fourier transform from the discrete time domain into the continuous frequency domain is usually termed the discrete-time Fourier transform, or `DTFourierTransform`. The inverse transform from the continuous frequency domain into the discrete time domain is given by `InverseDTFourierTransform`. Just as the Z transform is the discrete analog of the Laplace transform, the discrete-time Fourier transform is the discrete analog of the continuous-time Fourier transform. If the option setting `FourierParameters -> {a, b}` is specified, the period of the discrete-time Fourier transform is taken to be $1/|b|$, instead of the default period of 1.

☞ `DTFourierTransform[`*expr*`, `*n*`, `*omega*`]`

  give $F(\omega)$, a periodic function of ω, equal to the Fourier sum of *expr*, where *expr* is treated as a function of integer n

☞ `InverseDTFourierTransform[`*expr*`, `*omega*`, `*n*`]`

  give f_n, a function of integer n and the inverse Fourier sum of the periodic function $F(\omega)$, where $F(\omega)$ is equal to *expr* on the interval $\omega = -\frac{1}{2}$ to $\omega = \frac{1}{2}$

☞ `NDTFourierTransform[`*expr*`, `*n*`, `*omega*`]`

  find a numerical approximation to the function $F(\omega)$

☞ `NInverseDTFourierTransform[`*expr*`, `*omega*`, `*n*`]`

  find a numerical approximation to the function f_n

Discrete-time and continuous-frequency transform pairs: exact and numerical approximations.

This computes the Fourier transform of a discrete-time rectangular function centered at $n = 0$.

```
In[12]:= dtft = DTFourierTransform[
             Sum[DiscreteDelta[n+j], {j, -1, 1}],
             n, \[Omega]]
```

$$Out[12]= 1 + e^{-2 i \pi \omega} + e^{2 i \pi \omega}$$

Here is a plot of the amplitude spectrum over three periods.

```
In[13]:= Plot[Abs[dtft], {\[Omega], -1.5, 1.5}]
```

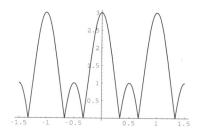

Here is a numerical approximation to the inverse discrete-time Fourier transform, for $n = -5, ..., 5$.

```
In[14]:= Chop[Table[
             NInverseDTFourierTransform[dtft, \[Omega], n,
                AccuracyGoal->8, PrecisionGoal->8],
             {n, -5, 5}]]
```

$$Out[14]= \{0, 0, 0, 0, 1., 1., 1., 0, 0, 0, 0\}$$

The Fourier exponential series and discrete-time Fourier transforms are mathematically equivalent, if one exchanges the roles of time and frequency.

setting	discrete-time Fourier transform	inverse discrete-time Fourier coefficient
{0, 1}	$\sum_{n=-\infty}^{\infty} f_n\, e^{2\pi i n \omega}$	$\int_{-1/2}^{1/2} F(\omega)\, e^{-2\pi i n \omega}\, d\omega$
{a, b}	$\lvert b \rvert^{(1-a)/2} \sum_{n=-\infty}^{\infty} f_n\, e^{2\pi i b n \omega}$	$\lvert b \rvert^{(1+a)/2} \int_{-1/(2\lvert b\rvert)}^{1/(2\lvert b\rvert)} F(\omega)\, e^{-2\pi i b n \omega}\, d\omega$

Effect of `FourierParameters` setting on discrete-time Fourier transform.

■ Calculus`Limit`

This package provides an enhancement to the built-in `Limit`. It allows you to find limits of expressions that contain a wide class of elementary and special functions. This package cannot handle expressions containing hypergeometric, elliptic, and certain other special functions.

The syntax and semantics of the enhanced `Limit` are the same as those of the built-in `Limit`.

`Limit[`*expr*`, x -> `x_0`]`	find the limit of *expr* when x approaches x_0
`Limit[`*expr*`, x -> `x_0`, Direction -> `*d*`]`	find the limit as x approaches x_0 from direction *d*

Finding limits.

This loads the package.

```
In[1]:= <<Calculus`Limit`
```

The package can handle the limit of a combination of expressions having head `Power`.

```
In[2]:= Limit[E^x^x - E^x^(2 x), x->Infinity]
Out[2]= -∞
```

Here the enhanced `Limit` is applied to a combination of logarithmic functions.

```
In[3]:= Limit[(Log[Cot[-x/Log[x]]] - Log[1/x]) /
               Log[Log[x]], x->0]
Out[3]= 1
```

Like the built-in `Limit`, the enhanced `Limit` recognizes the `Direction` option indicating a directional limit.

```
In[4]:= Limit[Exp[Tan[x]/Log[Cos[x]] ],
               x->Pi/2, Direction->-1]
Out[4]= 0
```

This gives the limit of an expression involving the exponential integral function.

```
In[5]:= Limit[E^x ExpIntegralE[2, ArcTan[E^x] - Pi/2] -
               E^x - x, x->Infinity]
Out[5]= 1 - EulerGamma - i π
```

The enhanced `Limit` can handle a combination of logarithmic and polylogarithmic functions.

```
In[6]:= Limit[PolyLog[2, x] + Log[x]^2/2 +
               I Pi Log[x], x ->Infinity]
```
$$Out[6]= \frac{\pi^2}{3}$$

This gives the limit of an expression involving the Riemann zeta function.

```
In[7]:= Limit[Zeta[1+x, v] - 1/x, x->0]
Out[7]= -PolyGamma[0, v]
```

The enhanced `Limit` can find the limit of an expression involving a `PolyGamma` function.

```
In[8]:= Limit[x^2 PolyGamma[2,x], x->Infinity]
Out[8]= -1
```

■ Calculus`Pade`

A rational function is the ratio of polynomials. Because these functions only use the elementary arithmetic operations, they are very easy to evaluate numerically. The polynomial in the denominator allows one to approximate functions that have rational singularities. For these reasons it is frequently useful in numerical work to approximate a given function by a rational function.

There are various methods to perform this approximation. The methods differ in how they interpret the notion of the goodness of the approximation. Each method is useful for certain classes of problems. This package computes Padé approximations and economized rational approximations. The package `NumericalMath`Approximations`` contains functions that perform general rational and minimax approximations.

There is a related class of approximation questions that involve the interpolation or fitting of a set of data points by an approximating function. In this type of situation you can use the built-in functions `Fit`, `InterpolatingPolynomial`, and `Interpolation`. For more information, see the section covering numerical operations on data in *The Mathematica Book*.

`Pade[f, {x, x₀, m, k}]`	give the Padé approximation to f centered at x_0 of degree (m, k)

Padé approximations.

The Padé approximation can be thought of as a generalization of a Taylor polynomial. More precisely, a Padé approximation of degree (m, k) to a function $f(x)$ at a point x_0 is the rational function $\frac{p(x)}{q(x)}$ where $p(x)$ is a polynomial of degree m, $q(x)$ is a polynomial of degree k, and the formal power series of $f(x)q(x) - p(x)$ about the point x_0 begins with the term x^{m+k+1}.

This loads the package.

$In[1]:=$ `<< Calculus`Pade`;`

Here is the Padé approximation of degree $(2, 4)$ to $\cos(x)$ at $x = 0$.

$In[2]:=$ `Pade[Cos[x], {x, 0, 2, 4}]`

$Out[2]=$ $\dfrac{1 - \frac{61\,x^2}{150}}{1 + \frac{7\,x^2}{75} + \frac{x^4}{200}}$

This gives another Padé approximation of the same degree.

$In[3]:=$ `pd = Pade[Exp[x], {x, 1, 2, 4}]`

$Out[3]=$ $\dfrac{e + \frac{1}{3}\,e\,(-1+x) + \frac{1}{30}\,e\,(-1+x)^2}{1 - \frac{2}{3}\,(-1+x) + \frac{1}{5}\,(-1+x)^2 - \frac{1}{30}\,(-1+x)^3 + \frac{1}{360}\,(-1+x)^4}$

The initial terms of this series vanish. This is the property that characterizes the Padé approximation.

$In[4]:=$ `Series[Exp[x] Denominator[pd] -`
              `Numerator[pd], {x, 1, 8}]`

$Out[4]=$ $\dfrac{e\,(x-1)^7}{75600} + \dfrac{e\,(x-1)^8}{120960} + O[x-1]^9$

This plots the difference between the approximation and the true function. Notice that the approximation is very good near the center of expansion, but the error increases very rapidly as you move away.

In[5]:= **Plot[pd - Exp[x], {x, 0, 2}]**

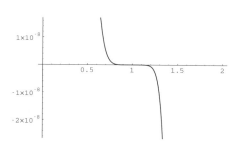

EconomizedRationalApproximation[*f*, {*x*, {*xmin*, *xmax*}, *m*, *k*}]
　　　　　　　　　give the economized rational approximation to *f* that is good in the range *xmin* to *xmax* and has degree (*m*, *k*)

Economized rational approximations.

A Padé approximation is very accurate near the center of expansion, but the error increases rapidly as you get farther away. If one is willing to sacrifice some of the goodness of fit near the center of expansion it is possible to obtain a better fit over the entire interval under consideration. This is what the other types of approximation do.

With an economized rational approximation, the idea is to start with a Padé approximation and perturb it with a Chebyshev polynomial in such a way as to reduce the leading coefficient in the error. This perturbation does cause the vanished terms to reappear. However, the magnitude of the error does not increase very much near the center of expansion and this small increase is compensated for by a decrease in the error farther away. With EconomizedRationalApproximation you specify the interval over which the approximation is to work rather than the center of expansion. In the limit as the length of the interval goes to zero, the economized rational approximation approaches the Padé approximation.

Here is the economized rational approximation of degree (2, 4) of e^x over the interval $0 \le x \le 2$.

In[6]:= **era =**
　　　　　　EconomizedRationalApproximation[Exp[x],
　　　　　　　　　　　　　　　　　　　　{x, {0, 2}, 2, 4}]

$$Out[6]= \frac{\frac{679583\,e}{691200} + \frac{4679\,e\,(-1+x)}{14400} + \frac{23}{720}\,e\,(-1+x)^2}{\frac{679583}{691200} - \frac{9479\,(-1+x)}{14400} + \frac{143}{720}\,(-1+x)^2 - \frac{1}{30}\,(-1+x)^3 + \frac{1}{360}\,(-1+x)^4}$$

This gives the difference between the true function and the economized rational approximation. In general you may even get a small nonvanishing constant term.

In[7]:= **Series[era - Exp[x], {x, 1, 2}]**

$$Out[7]= \frac{e\,(x-1)}{679583} + \frac{1589567\,e\,(x-1)^2}{923666107778} + O[x-1]^3$$

The error has been spread out when compared to the Padé approximation plotted above.

In[8]:= **Plot[era - Exp[x], {x, 0, 2}]**

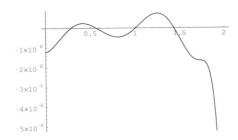

Even though the error at the endpoint $x = 2$ is not particularly small, it is considerably smaller than what Pade gives.

In[9]:= **N[(pd - Exp[x])/(era - Exp[x]) /. x -> 2]**

Out[9]= 7.53512

■ Calculus`VariationalMethods`

The basic problem of the calculus of variations is to determine the function $u(x)$ that extremizes a functional $F = \int_{xmin}^{xmax} f[u(x), u'(x), x] \, dx$. In general, there can be more than one independent variable and the integrand f can depend on several functions and their higher derivatives.

The extremal functions are solutions of the Euler(-Lagrange) equations that are obtained by setting the first variational derivatives of the functional F with respect to each function equal to zero. Since many ordinary and partial differential equations that occur in physics and engineering can be derived as the Euler equations for appropriate functionals, variational methods are of general utility.

`VariationalD[f, u[x], x]`, `VariationalD[f, u[x,y,... ], {x, y,... }]`
> give the first variational derivative of the functional F defined by the integrand f, where f depends on one function u and one independent variable x or several independent variables $x, y, ...$

`VariationalD[f, {u[x,y,... ], v[x,y,... ], ... }, {x,y,... }]`
> give a list of the first variational derivatives of the functional F defined by the integrand f, where f depends on several functions $u, v, ...$ and several independent variables $x, y, ...$

`EulerEquations[f, u[x], x]`, `EulerEquations[f, u[x,y,... ], {x,y,... }]`
> give the Euler equation for the integrand f, where f depends on one function u and one independent variable x or several independent variables $x, y, ...$

`EulerEquations[f, {u[x,y,... ], v[x,y,... ], ... }, {x,y,... }]`
> give a list of the Euler equations for the integrand f, where f depends on several functions $u, v, ...$ and several independent variables $x, y, ...$

First variational derivatives and Euler equations.

`VariationalD` gives the first variational derivatives of a functional F defined by the integrand f. f may depend on several functions $u, v, w, ...$; their derivatives of arbitrary order; and variables $x, y, z, ...$ `EulerEquations` returns the Euler(-Lagrange) equations given the integrand f. Again f may depend on several functions $u, v, w, ...$; their derivatives of arbitrary order; and variables $x, y, z ....$

This loads the package.

In[1]:= `<<Calculus`VariationalMethods``

This is the first variational derivative of $F = \int_{xmin}^{xmax} y(x)\sqrt{1 + y'(x)^2} \, dx$.

In[2]:= `VariationalD[y[x] Sqrt[1+y'[x]^2], y[x], x]`

Out[2]= $\dfrac{1 + y'[x]^2 - y[x] \, y''[x]}{\left(1 + y'[x]^2\right)^{3/2}}$

Here f is the Lagrangian for the simple pendulum and `EulerEquations` gives the pendulum equation.

```
In[3]:= EulerEquations[
            m l^2 theta'[t]^2/2+m g l Cos[theta[t]],
            theta[t], t]
Out[3]= -l m (g Sin[theta[t]] + l theta''[t]) == 0
```

This package defines several coordinates systems as well as the Grad function.

```
In[4]:= <<Calculus`VectorAnalysis`
```

The default coordinate system is set to Cartesian and the coordinates are set to x, y, and z.

```
In[5]:= SetCoordinates[Cartesian[x, y, z]];
```

This generates Laplace's equation.

```
In[6]:= EulerEquations[
            Grad[phi[x,y,z]].Grad[phi[x,y,z]]/2,
            phi[x,y,z], {x,y,z}]
Out[6]= -phi^(0,0,2)[x, y, z] - phi^(0,2,0)[x, y, z] - phi^(2,0,0)[x, y, z] == 0
```

`FirstIntegrals[`f`, `$u[x]$`, `x`]`, `FirstIntegrals[`f`, {`$u[x]$`, `$v[x]$` , ... }, `x`]`	give first integrals when the integrand f is independent of one or more of $\{u[x], v[x], ... \}$, or independent of x
`FirstIntegral[`u`]`	first integral associated with the variable u (appears in the output of `FirstIntegrals`)

First integrals.

When there is only one independent variable x, `FirstIntegrals` gives conserved quantities in the following cases: (1) if f does not depend on a coordinate u explicitly, it is referred to as an ignorable coordinate and the corresponding Euler equation possesses an obvious first integral (a conserved generalized momentum), and (2) if f depends on $u, v, ...$ and their first derivatives only and has no explicit x dependence, `FirstIntegrals` also returns the first integral corresponding to the Hamiltonian.

The Lagrangian for central force motion has an ignorable coordinate ϕ (angular momentum conservation) and is independent of time t (energy conservation). `FirstIntegrals` yields both the first integral corresponding to coordinate ϕ and the first integral corresponding to the Hamiltonian.

```
In[7]:= FirstIntegrals[m(r'[t]^2+r[t]^2 phi'[t]^2)/
            2-U[r], {r[t],phi[t]}, t]
```
$$Out[7]= \left\{FirstIntegral[phi] \to -m\,r[t]^2\,phi'[t],\right.$$
$$\left. FirstIntegral[t] \to \frac{1}{2}\left(2\,U[r] + m\left(r[t]^2\,phi'[t]^2 + r'[t]^2\right)\right)\right\}$$

The Ritz variational principle affords a powerful technique for the approximate solution of (1) eigenvalue problems $\mathbf{A}u = \lambda w u$ where $\mathbf{A}$ is an operator and $w(x, y, ...)$ is a weight function and (2) problems of the form $\mathbf{B}u(x, y, ...) = h(x, y, ...)$ where $\mathbf{B}$ is a positive definite operator and h is given. A judicious choice for the trial function $u_t(x, y, ...)$ that satisfies boundary conditions and depends on variational parameters $\{a, b, ...\}$ must be given in both cases. For (1) `VariationalBound[{`f, g`}, `$u[x, y, ...]$` ],`

$\{\{x, xmin, xmax\}, \{y, ymin, ymax\}, \ldots \}, u_t, \{a, amin, amax\}, \{b, bmin, bmax\}, \ldots]$
extremizes $\left(\int_{xmin}^{xmax} dx \int_{ymin}^{ymax} dy \ldots f \right) / \left(\int_{xmin}^{xmax} dx \int_{ymin}^{ymax} dy \ldots g \right)$ where $f = uAu$ and $g = uwu$. The result is an
upper bound on the corresponding eigenvalue and optimal values for the parameters. For (2)
VariationalBound$[f, u[x, y, \ldots], \{\{x, xmin, xmax\}, \{y, ymin, ymax\}, \ldots \}, u_t, \{a, amin, amax\},$
$\{b, bmin, bmax\}, \ldots]$ extremizes the functional $F = \int_{xmin}^{xmax} dx \int_{ymin}^{ymax} dy \ldots f$ with $f = uBu - 2uh$ and
yields the value of the functional and the optimal parameters. VariationalBound can also be used
to extremize general functionals given appropriate trial functions. NVariationalBound performs the
same functions as VariationalBound numerically. It uses the internal function FindMinimum and has
the same options and input format for parameters.

VariationalBound$[\{f, g\}, u[x, y, \ldots], \{\{x, xmin, xmax\}, \{y, ymin, ymax\}, \ldots \}, u_t,$
$\{a, amin, amax\}, \{b, bmin, bmax\}, \ldots]$

                give an upper bound for the eigenvalue and the optimal
                values of $a, b, \ldots$ in the range $\{\{amin, amax\}, \{bmin, bmax\}, \ldots\}$

VariationalBound$[f, u[x, y, \ldots], \{\{x, xmin, xmax\}, \{y, ymin, ymax\}, \ldots \}, u_t,$
$\{a, amin, amax\}, \{b, bmin, bmax\}, \ldots]$

                give the value of the functional and optimal values of $a, b, \ldots$

NVariationalBound$[\{f, g\}, u[x, y, \ldots], \{\{x, xmin, xmax\}, \{y, ymin, ymax\}, \ldots \}, u_t,$
$\{a, a_0, amin, amax\}, \{b, b_0, bmin, bmax\}, \ldots]$

                evaluate numerically an upper bound for the eigenvalue and
                the optimal values of $a, b, \ldots$ in the range $\{\{amin, amax\},$
                $\{bmin, bmax\}, \ldots\}$ given initial values $a_0, b_0, \ldots$

NVariationalBound$[f, u[x, y, \ldots], \{\{x, xmin, xmax\}, \{y, ymin, ymax\}, \ldots \}, u_t,$
$\{a, a_0, amin, amax\}, \{b, b_0, bmin, bmax\}, \ldots]$

                evaluate numerically the value of the functional and optimal
                values of $a, b, \ldots$ given initial values $a_0, b_0, \ldots$

Ritz variational bounds.

A trial (wave) function for the 2s state of the hydrogen atom with one node at a yields the exact energy in units of Rydbergs. Note that the volume element r^2 is included in functional parameters f and g, and the default range for the parameters is $(-\infty, \infty)$.

```
In[8]:= VariationalBound[{(-u[r] D[r^2 u'[r],r]/r^2-2u[r]^2/r)r^2,
        u[r]^2 r^2},u[r],
        {r,0,Infinity},(a-r)E^(-b r),{a},{b}]

Out[8]= {-0.25, {a → 2., b → 0.5}}
```

The problem of the torsion of a rod of square cross section involves solving $\nabla^2 u = -1$ where u vanishes on the boundary. VariationalBound gives optimal values of parameters for the approximate solution.

```
In[9]:= VariationalBound[-u[x,y](D[u[x,y],{x,2}]+
           D[u[x,y],{y,2}]) -2u[x,y],u[x,y],
        {{x,-a,a},{y,-a,a}},
        (x^2-a^2)(y^2-a^2)(a1+a2(x^2+y^2)),
        {a1},{a2}]
```

$$Out[9]= \left\{-0.561572\,a^4, \left\{a1 \to \frac{0.292193}{a^2}, a2 \to \frac{0.0592283}{a^4}\right\}\right\}$$

The ground state energy of the one-dimensional quantum anharmonic oscillator is determined for the given trial (wave) function by NVariationalBound. Note that the default range for the parameters is $(-\infty, \infty)$ and the initial values are specified.

```
In[10]:= NVariationalBound[
            {u'[x]^2+(x^2+x^4)u[x]^2/4, u[x]^2},
            u[x], {x,-Infinity,Infinity},
            E^(-a x^2)(1+b x^2), {a,0.5},{b,0.1}]
```

$$Out[10]= \{0.804175, \{a \to 0.741361, b \to 0.365558\}\}$$

■ Calculus`VectorAnalysis`

A three-dimensional coordinate system assigns three numbers to each point in space. In defining a coordinate system, you have to make a choice about what to measure and how to measure it. Frequently, physical systems exhibit special symmetries or structures that make a particular coordinate system especially useful. In a mathematically elegant solution to problems related to these systems, often the main step is choosing the correct coordinates.

A variety of tools for doing calculus in various three-dimensional coordinate systems are provided in this package. Because a given symbolic or numeric expression can mean different things in different coordinate systems, *Mathematica* must know what coordinate system you are using and what the coordinate variables are. The initial default coordinate system is `Cartesian`, with coordinate variables `Xx`, `Yy`, and `Zz`. If you frequently work in another system, it may be useful to change the default to that system using `SetCoordinates`.

CoordinateSystem	the name of the default coordinate system
Coordinates[ ]	give the default variables in the default coordinate system
Coordinates[*coordsys*]	give the default variables in the coordinate system *coordsys*
SetCoordinates[*coordsys*]	set the default coordinate system to be *coordsys* with default variables
SetCoordinates[*coordsys*[*vars*]]	set the default coordinate system to be *coordsys* with variables *vars*

Coordinate systems and coordinate variables.

This loads the package.	*In[1]:=* `<<Calculus`VectorAnalysis``
This resets the default coordinate system and variables.	*In[2]:=* `SetCoordinates[Paraboloidal[w1, w2, w3]]`
	Out[2]= `Paraboloidal[w1, w2, w3]`
Here are the new defaults.	*In[3]:=* `{CoordinateSystem, Coordinates[ ]}`
	Out[3]= `{Paraboloidal, {w1, w2, w3}}`

All coordinate systems can be viewed as arising from three one-parameter families of surfaces. The three numbers assigned to each point (*i.e.*, its coordinates) simply tell you to which member of each family the point belongs. Members of these families are called *coordinate surfaces*. In the simplest example, the `Cartesian` system, the coordinate surfaces are members of families of planes parallel to the coordinate planes. In more complicated systems, the coordinate surfaces often belong to families of quadric surfaces such as ellipsoids, hyperboloids or elliptic paraboloids. In certain cases the families of coordinate surfaces depend on parameters such as focal distances or radii. In these cases the coordinate system as a whole depends on the parameters. These parameters are initially given default values and can be reset with `SetCoordinates`.

Bipolar	EllipticCylindrical
Bispherical	OblateSpheroidal
Cartesian	ParabolicCylindrical
ConfocalEllipsoidal	Paraboloidal
ConfocalParaboloidal	ProlateSpheroidal
Conical	Spherical
Cylindrical	Toroidal

Coordinate systems.

There are often conflicting definitions of a particular coordinate system in the literature. When you use a coordinate system with this package, you should look at the definition given below to make sure it is what you want. The easiest way to check the definition of a coordinate system used in the package is to use CoordinatesToCartesian[*pt*, *coordsys*] as described below. This will give you the formulas for the transformation into Cartesian coordinates.

The **Cartesian coordinate system** Cartesian[*x*, *y*, *z*] is the standard rectangular coordinate system in three dimensions.

The **cylindrical coordinate system** Cylindrical[*r*, *theta*, *z*] uses polar coordinates *r* and θ to locate a point in the *x-y* plane and the coordinate *z* for the height of the point above the *x-y* plane.

In the **spherical coordinate system** Spherical[*r*, *theta*, *phi*], the coordinate *r* gives the distance of the point from the origin, the coordinate θ gives the angle measured from the positive *z* axis, and the coordinate ϕ gives the angle measured in the *x-y* plane from the positive *x* axis, counterclockwise as viewed from the positive *z* axis.

In the **parabolic cylindrical coordinate system** ParabolicCylindrical[*u*, *v*, *z*], varying only one of the coordinates *u* and *v* while coordinate *z* is held constant produces opposite facing parabolas. The coordinate *z* specifies distances along the axis of common focus.

In the **paraboloidal coordinate system** Paraboloidal[*u*, *v*, *phi*], varying only one of the coordinates *u* and *v* while coordinate ϕ is held constant produces opposite facing parabolas. The coordinate ϕ specifies rotations about their common bisectors.

The **elliptic cylindrical coordinate system** EllipticCylindrical[*u*, *v*, *z*, *a*], parameterized by *a*, is built around two foci separated by 2*a*. Holding coordinate *u* constant while varying the other coordinates produces a family of confocal ellipses. Fixing coordinate *v* produces a family of confocal hyperbolas. The coordinate *z* specifies distance along the axis of common focus. The default value for parameter *a* is 1.

The **prolate spheroidal coordinate system** ProlateSpheroidal[*xi*, *eta*, *phi*, *a*], parameterized by *a*, is obtained by rotating elliptic cylindrical coordinates about the axis connecting the two foci. The coordinate ϕ specifies the rotation. The default value for parameter *a* is 1.

The **oblate spheroidal coordinate system** OblateSpheroidal[*xi*, *eta*, *phi*, *a*], parameterized by *a*, is obtained by rotating elliptic cylindrical coordinates about an axis perpendicular to the axis connecting the two foci. The coordinate ϕ specifies the rotation. The default value for parameter a is 1.

The **bipolar coordinate system** Bipolar[u, v, z, a], parameterized by a, is built around two foci separated by 2a. Holding coordinate u constant produces a family of circles that pass through both foci. Fixing coordinate v produces a family of degenerate ellipses about one of the foci. The coordinate z specifies distance along the axis of common focus. The default value for parameter a is 1.

The **bispherical coordinate system** Bispherical[u, v, phi, a], parameterized by a, differs from the bipolar system only in that coordinate ϕ measures an azimuthal angle.

The **toroidal coordinate system** Toroidal[u, v, phi, a], parameterized by a, is obtained by rotating bipolar coordinates about an axis perpendicular to the axis connecting the two foci. The coordinate ϕ specifies the rotation. The default value for parameter a is 1.

In the **conical coordinate system** Conical[$lambda$, mu, nu, a, b], parameterized by a and b, the surfaces described by fixing coordinate λ are spheres centered at the origin. Fixing coordinate μ gives cones with apexes at the origin and axes along the z axis, and fixing coordinate v gives cones with apexes at the origin and axes along the y axis. The default values for parameters a and b are 1 and 2, respectively.

In the **confocal ellipsoidal coordinate system** ConfocalEllipsoidal[$lambda$, mu, nu, a, b, c], parameterized by a, b, and c, the surfaces described by fixing coordinate λ are ellipsoids. Fixing coordinate μ gives hyperboloids of one sheet, and fixing coordinate v gives hyperboloids of two sheets. The default values for parameters a, b and c are 3, 2 and 1, respectively.

In the **confocal paraboloidal coordinate system** ConfocalParaboloidal[$lambda$, mu, nu, a, b], parameterized by a and b, the surfaces described by fixing coordinate λ are elliptic paraboloids extending in the negative z direction. Fixing coordinate μ gives hyperbolic paraboloids, and fixing coordinate v gives elliptic paraboloids extending in the positive z direction. The default values for parameters a and b are 2 and 1, respectively.

CoordinateRanges[ ]	give the intervals over which each of the coordinate variables of the default coordinate system may range
Parameters[ ]	give a list of the default parameter values for the default coordinate system
ParameterRanges[ ]	give the intervals over which each of the parameters of the default coordinate system may range

CoordinateRanges[*coordsys*], Parameters[*coordsys*], ParameterRanges[*coordsys*]
give the result for the coordinate system *coordsys*

SetCoordinates[*coordsys*[*vars*, *param*]]
set the default coordinate system to be *coordsys* with variables *vars* and parameter values *param*

The range of coordinate variables and parameters.

This gives the default coordinate variables and their ranges for the Conical system.

```
In[4]:= {Coordinates[Conical],
            CoordinateRanges[Conical]}
```

$Out[4]= \{\{Llambda, Mmu, Nnu\}, \{-\infty < Llambda < \infty, 1 < Mmu^2 < 4, Nnu^2 < 1\}\}$

This means that the Bipolar system has one parameter that must be a positive number. The default value of this parameter is 1.

```
In[5]:= {Parameters[Bipolar],
            ParameterRanges[Bipolar]}
```

$Out[5]= \{\{1\}, 0 < \#1 < \infty\}$

This resets the Bipolar variables and parameter.

```
In[6]:= SetCoordinates[Bipolar[u, v, z, 2]]
```

$Out[6]= Bipolar[u, v, z, 2]$

In the Conical system there are two parameters, and the second must always be larger than the first.

```
In[7]:= {Parameters[Conical],
            ParameterRanges[Conical]}
```

$Out[7]= \{\{1, 2\}, 0 < \#1 < \#2 < \infty\}$

CoordinatesToCartesian[*pt*]	give the Cartesian coordinates of *pt*, where *pt* is given in the default coordinate system
CoordinatesToCartesian[*pt*, *coordsys*]	give the Cartesian coordinates of *pt*, where *pt* is given in the coordinate system *coordsys*
CoordinatesFromCartesian[*pt*]	give the default system coordinates of *pt*, where *pt* is given in Cartesian coordinates
CoordinatesFromCartesian[*pt*, *coordsys*]	give the *coordsys* coordinates of *pt*, where *pt* is given in Cartesian coordinates

Converting to and from Cartesian coordinates.

This gives Cartesian coordinates of the point whose Spherical coordinates are {1, Pi/2, Pi/4}.

$In[8]:=$ **CoordinatesToCartesian[{1, Pi/2, Pi/4},**
         Spherical]

$Out[8]= \left\{ \dfrac{1}{\sqrt{2}}, \dfrac{1}{\sqrt{2}}, 0 \right\}$

You get the general coordinate transformation formula when you give the variables in symbolic form.

$In[9]:=$ **CoordinatesToCartesian[{u, v, phi},**
         Paraboloidal]

$Out[9]= \left\{ u\,v\,Cos[phi],\ u\,v\,Sin[phi],\ \dfrac{1}{2}\,(u^2 - v^2) \right\}$

Here are the formulas for changing from Cartesian to Bispherical coordinates.

$In[10]:=$ **CoordinatesFromCartesian[{x, y, z},**
          Bispherical]

$Out[10]= \left\{ 2\,Re\left[ArcCot\left[\sqrt{x^2 + y^2} - i\,z\right]\right],\ 2\,Im\left[ArcCot\left[\sqrt{x^2 + y^2} - i\,z\right]\right], \right.$
         $\left. ArcTan[x, y] \right\}$

The standard vector product operations, such as the dot and cross product, are usually defined and computed in the Cartesian coordinate system. If you have vectors given in a different coordinate system, you can compute vector products using DotProduct, CrossProduct, and ScalarTripleProduct. These functions convert the given vectors into Cartesian coordinates and then compute the products using the standard definitions.

`DotProduct[`v_1`, `v_2`]`	compute the dot product of the vectors v_1 and v_2 given in default coordinates
`CrossProduct[`v_1`, `v_2`]`	compute the cross product of the vectors given in default coordinates
`ScalarTripleProduct[`v_1`, `v_2`, `v_3`]`	compute the scalar triple product of the vectors given in default coordinates
`DotProduct[`v_1`, `v_2`, `*coordsys*`]`, `CrossProduct[`v_1`, `v_2`, `*coordsys*`]`, etc.	give the result when the vectors are given in the coordinate system *coordsys*

Computing vector products in various coordinate systems.

This sets the default coordinate system to ParabolicCylindrical with default variables.

```
In[11]:= SetCoordinates[ParabolicCylindrical[ ]]
Out[11]= ParabolicCylindrical[Uu, Vv, Zz]
```

This converts the vectors from the default system to Cartesian coordinates and then computes the scalar product.

```
In[12]:= DotProduct[{1.2, 1.1, 0}, {5.4, -2, 1.2}]
Out[12]= -12.8093
```

Viewed geometrically, the scalar triple product gives the volume of the parallelepiped spanned by the three vectors.

```
In[13]:= ScalarTripleProduct[{1, 0, 0}, {0, 1, 0},
              {0, 0, 1}, Cartesian]
Out[13]= 1
```

`ArcLengthFactor[{`f_x`, `f_y`, `f_z`}, `t`]`	give the derivative of the arc length along the curve parameterized by t in the default coordinate system
`ArcLengthFactor[{`f_x`, `f_y`, `f_z`}, `t`, `*coordsys*`]`	give the derivative in the coordinate system *coordsys*

Differential arc length element.

In Cartesian coordinates the differential arc length element is just $(dx^2 + dy^2 + dz^2)^{1/2}$. When you compute an integral along a parameterized curve in another coordinate system, you need to use the form appropriate to the coordinate system. To get the integral along the curve, you must plug the parameterization into the arc length element, compute the appropriate derivatives, and then integrate with respect to the parameter. The function `ArcLengthFactor` takes the parameterization as an argument and returns the formula for the derivative of the arc length along the curve.

This gives the parameterization of an ascending helix.

```
In[14]:= param = {Cos[t], Sin[t], t}
Out[14]= {Cos[t], Sin[t], t}
```

This means that the derivative of the arc length, with respect to t along the helix, is $\sqrt{2}$. If we think of the parameterization as describing the motion of a particle in Cartesian coordinates, this just means that the speed of the particle is $\sqrt{2}$.

```
In[15]:= ArcLengthFactor[
               param, t, Cartesian] //Simplify
Out[15]= √2
```

Here is a scalar-valued function on three space.

```
In[16]:= f[{x_, y_, z_}] := x^2 y^2 z
```

This gives the integral of the function along the helix.

```
In[17]:= Integrate[ f[param] ArcLengthFactor[
               param, t, Cartesian], {t, 0, 2 Pi}] // Simplify
```

$$Out[17]= \frac{\pi^2}{2\sqrt{2}}$$

The derivative of a coordinate transformation is the matrix of its partial derivatives. In the case of three-dimensional coordinate systems this is always a three by three matrix. This matrix is sometimes called the *Jacobian matrix*. The determinant of this matrix is called the *Jacobian determinant* of the transformation, or else just the *Jacobian*. This determinant measures how infinitesimal volumes change under the transformation. For this reason, the Jacobian determinant is the multiplicative factor needed to adjust the differential volume form when you change coordinates.

JacobianMatrix[ ]	give the derivative matrix of the transformation from the default coordinate system to Cartesian coordinates using the default variables
JacobianMatrix[*pt*]	give the derivative at the point *pt*, where *pt* is given in the default system
JacobianMatrix[*coordsys*]	give the derivative of the transformation from the coordinate system *coordsys* to Cartesian coordinates
JacobianMatrix[*pt*, *coordsys*]	give the derivative at the point *pt*, where *pt* is given in the coordinate system *coordsys*
JacobianDeterminant[ ], JacobianDeterminant[*pt*], etc.	give the determinant of the Jacobian matrix
ScaleFactors[ ], ScaleFactors[*pt*], etc.	give a list of the scale factors

The transformation matrix derivative, its determinant, and scale factors.

This is the matrix of partial derivatives of the transformation from Spherical to Cartesian coordinates.

```
In[18]:= JacobianMatrix[Spherical[r, theta, phi]]

Out[18]= {{Cos[phi] Sin[theta], r Cos[phi] Cos[theta],
            -r Sin[phi] Sin[theta]}, {Sin[phi] Sin[theta],
            r Cos[theta] Sin[phi], r Cos[phi] Sin[theta]},
            {Cos[theta], -r Sin[theta], 0}}
```

The determinant of the derivative of the coordinate transformation gives the infinitesimal change in volume.

```
In[19]:= JacobianDeterminant[Spherical[r, theta, phi]]

Out[19]= r^2 Sin[theta]
```

This triple integral computes the integral of the function r^2 over a solid sphere of radius 2 using spherical coordinates. Note that the Jacobian is included in the integrand, because the integral is expressed in Spherical coordinates.

```
In[20]:= Integrate[r^2 JacobianDeterminant[
            Spherical[r, theta, phi]],
            {r, 0, 2}, {theta, 0, Pi},
            {phi, -Pi, Pi}]
```

$$Out[20]= \frac{128\,\pi}{5}$$

Div[*f*]	give the divergence of the vector field *f* in the default coordinate system
Curl[*f*]	give the curl of the vector field *f* in the default coordinate system
Grad[*f*]	give the gradient of the scalar function *f* in the default coordinate system
Laplacian[*f*]	give the Laplacian of the scalar function *f* in the default coordinate system
Biharmonic[*f*]	give the Laplacian of the Laplacian of the scalar function *f* in the default coordinate system
Div[*f*, *coordsys*], Curl[*f*, *coordsys*], etc.	give the result if the coordinate system is *coordsys*

Common differential operations.

As is the case with the vector products discussed above, the common differential operations in three dimensions are defined in terms of Cartesian coordinates. If you are working in another coordinate system and you wish to compute these quantities, you must, in principle, first transform into the Cartesian system and then do the calculation. When you specify the coordinate system in functions like Laplacian, Grad, and so on, this transformation is done automatically.

Here is the usual gradient.

```
In[21]:= Grad[5 x^2 y^3 z^4, Cartesian[x, y, z]]

Out[21]= {10 x y^3 z^4, 15 x^2 y^2 z^4, 20 x^2 y^3 z^3}
```

This gradient is different, because we are treating the function as being in ProlateSpheroidal coordinates with the (nonstandard) variables x, y, and z.

$In[22]:=$ **Grad[5 x^2 y^3 z^4,**
                    ProlateSpheroidal[x, y, z]]

$Out[22]=$ $\left\{ \dfrac{10\,x\,y^3\,z^4}{\sqrt{Sin[y]^2 + Sinh[x]^2}},\ \dfrac{15\,x^2\,y^2\,z^4}{\sqrt{Sin[y]^2 + Sinh[x]^2}}, \right.$

$\left. 20\,x^2\,y^3\,z^3\,Csc[y]\,Csch[x] \right\}$

If you give an unknown function, the result is returned in symbolic form.

$In[23]:=$ **Curl[{f[r, theta, phi], g[r, theta, phi],**
                    h[r, theta, phi]}, Cylindrical[r, theta, phi]]

$Out[23]=$ $\left\{ \dfrac{-r\,g^{(0,0,1)}[r,\ theta,\ phi] + h^{(0,1,0)}[r,\ theta,\ phi]}{r}, \right.$

$f^{(0,0,1)}[r,\ theta,\ phi] - h^{(1,0,0)}[r,\ theta,\ phi],$

$\dfrac{1}{r}\big(g[r,\ theta,\ phi] - f^{(0,1,0)}[r,\ theta,\ phi] +$

$\left. r\,g^{(1,0,0)}[r,\ theta,\ phi]\big) \right\}$

4. Discrete Mathematics

■ DiscreteMath`CombinatorialFunctions`

This package defines the functions `CatalanNumber`, `Hofstadter`, and `Subfactorial` that are used in combinatorial analysis. Several related functions, such as `Factorial`, `Factorial2`, `Binomial`, `Multinomial`, `Pochhammer`, and `Fibonacci` are normally available in *Mathematica* without loading this package.

`CatalanNumber[`n`]`	n^{th} Catalan number
`Hofstadter[`n`]`	Hofstadter's function
`Subfactorial[`n`]`	subfactorial of n

Combinatorial functions.

The **Catalan numbers**, which appear in various tree enumeration problems, are given in terms of binomial coefficients according to $c_n = \frac{1}{n+1}\binom{2n}{n}$.

Hofstadter's function $q(n)$ is defined recursively for positive integers by $q(1) = q(2) = 1$ and $q(n) = q(n - q(n - 1)) + q(n - q(n - 2))$.

`Subfactorial[`n`]` is given by $n! \sum_{k=0}^{n}(-1)^k/k!$.

This loads the package.	`In[1]:= <<DiscreteMath`CombinatorialFunctions``
This is the number of permutations of four objects that leaves none of the objects unchanged.	`In[2]:= Subfactorial[4]` `Out[2]= 9`
This plot demonstrates the chaotic behavior of Hofstadter's function, described in the book *Gödel, Escher, Bach: An Eternal Golden Braid*.	`In[3]:= ListPlot[Table[Hofstadter[n], {n, 1000}]]`

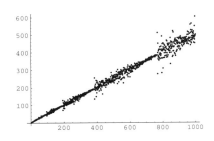

■ DiscreteMath`Combinatorica`

DiscreteMath`Combinatorica` extends *Mathematica* by over 230 functions in combinatorics and graph theory. It includes functions for constructing graphs and other combinatorial objects, computing invariants of these objects, and finally displaying them. This documentation covers only a subset of these functions. The best guide to this package is the book *Implementing Discrete Mathematics: Combinatorics and Graph Theory with Mathematica*, by Steven Skiena, published by Addison-Wesley Publishing Company, 1990.

This loads the package.

```
In[1]:= <<DiscreteMath`Combinatorica`
```

Permutations and Combinations

Permutations and subsets are the most basic combinatorial objects. DiscreteMath`Combinatorica` provides functions for constructing objects both randomly and deterministically, to rank and unrank them, and to compute invariants on them. Here we provide examples of some of these functions in action.

These permutations are generated in minimum change order, where successive permutations differ by exactly one transposition. The built-in generator Permutations constructs permutations in lexicographic order.

```
In[2]:= MinimumChangePermutations[{a,b,c,d}]

Out[2]= {{a, b, c, d}, {b, a, c, d}, {c, a, b, d}, {a, c, b, d},
         {b, c, a, d}, {c, b, a, d}, {d, b, a, c}, {b, d, a, c},
         {a, d, b, c}, {d, a, b, c}, {b, a, d, c}, {a, b, d, c},
         {a, c, d, b}, {c, a, d, b}, {d, a, c, b}, {a, d, c, b},
         {c, d, a, b}, {d, c, a, b}, {d, c, b, a}, {c, d, b, a},
         {b, d, c, a}, {d, b, c, a}, {c, b, d, a}, {b, c, d, a}}
```

The ranking function illustrates that the built-in function Permutations uses lexicographic sequencing.

```
In[3]:= Map[RankPermutation, Permutations[{1,2,3,4}]]

Out[3]= {0, 1, 2, 3, 4, 5, 6, 7, 8, 9, 10, 11, 12, 13, 14, 15, 16, 17,
         18, 19, 20, 21, 22, 23}
```

With $3! = 6$ distinct permutations of three elements, within 20 random permutations we are likely to see all of them. Observe that it is unlikely for the first six permutations to all be distinct.

```
In[4]:= Table[RandomPermutation[3], {20}]

Out[4]= {{1, 3, 2}, {3, 2, 1}, {3, 2, 1}, {3, 1, 2}, {3, 1, 2},
         {3, 2, 1}, {1, 3, 2}, {2, 3, 1}, {3, 2, 1}, {3, 1, 2},
         {1, 2, 3}, {1, 3, 2}, {3, 2, 1}, {3, 2, 1}, {1, 3, 2},
         {3, 1, 2}, {2, 3, 1}, {1, 3, 2}, {3, 1, 2}, {2, 1, 3}}
```

A fixed point of a permutation p is an element in the same position in p as in the inverse of p. Thus, the only fixed point in this permutation is 7.

```
In[5]:= InversePermutation[{4,8,5,2,1,3,7,6}]

Out[5]= {5, 4, 6, 1, 3, 8, 7, 2}
```

The identity permutation consists of n singleton cycles or fixed points.

```
In[6]:= ToCycles[{1,2,3,4,5,6,7,8,9,10}]

Out[6]= {{1}, {2}, {3}, {4}, {5}, {6}, {7}, {8}, {9}, {10}}
```

The classic problem in Polya theory is counting how many different ways necklaces can be made out of k beads, when there are m different types or colors of beads to choose from. When two necklaces are considered the same if they can be obtained only by shifting the beads (as opposed to turning the necklace over), the symmetries are defined by k permutations, each of which is a cyclic shift of the identity permutation. When a variable is specified for the number of colors, a polynomial results.

```
In[7]:= Polya[Table[
             RotateRight[Range[8],i], {i,8}], m]
```

$$Out[7]= \frac{1}{8}\left(4m+2m^2+m^4+m^8\right)$$

The number of inversions in a permutation is equal to that of its inverse.

```
In[8]:= (p=RandomPermutation[50]; {Inversions[p],
         Inversions[InversePermutation[p]]})
Out[8]= {590, 590}
```

Generating subsets incrementally is efficient when the goal is to find the first subset with a given property, since every subset need not be constructed.

```
In[9]:= Table[NthSubset[n,{a,b,c,d}], {n,0,15}]
Out[9]= {{}, {a}, {b}, {a, b}, {c}, {a, c}, {b, c}, {a, b, c},
        {d}, {a, d}, {b, d}, {a, b, d}, {c, d}, {a, c, d}, {b, c, d},
        {a, b, c, d}}
```

In a Gray code, each subset differs in exactly one element from its neighbors. Observe that the last eight subsets all contain 4, while none of the first eight do.

```
In[10]:= GrayCode[{1,2,3,4}]
Out[10]= {{}, {1}, {1, 2}, {2}, {2, 3}, {1, 2, 3}, {1, 3}, {3}, {3, 4},
         {1, 3, 4}, {1, 2, 3, 4}, {2, 3, 4}, {2, 4}, {1, 2, 4}, {1, 4},
         {4}}
```

A k-subset is a subset with exactly k elements in it. Since the lead element is placed in first, the k-subsets are given in lexicographic order.

```
In[11]:= KSubsets[{1,2,3,4,5},3]
Out[11]= {{1, 2, 3}, {1, 2, 4}, {1, 2, 5}, {1, 3, 4}, {1, 3, 5},
         {1, 4, 5}, {2, 3, 4}, {2, 3, 5}, {2, 4, 5}, {3, 4, 5}}
```

Backtrack	NthPermutation
BinarySearch	NthSubset
BinarySubsets	NumberOfDerangements
DerangementQ	NumberOfInvolutions
Derangements	NumberOfPermutationsByCycles
DistinctPermutations	PermutationGroupQ
EquivalenceClasses	PermutationQ
EquivalenceRelationQ	Permute
Equivalences	Polya
Eulerian	RandomHeap
FromCycles	RandomKSubset
FromInversionVector	RandomPermutation
GrayCode	RandomPermutation1
HeapSort	RandomPermutation2
Heapify	RandomSubset
HideCycles	RankPermutation
Index	RankSubset
InversePermutation	RevealCycles
Inversions	Runs
InvolutionQ	SamenessRelation
Josephus	SelectionSort
KSubsets	SignaturePermutation
LexicographicPermutations	StirlingFirst
LexicographicSubsets	StirlingSecond
MinimumChangePermutations	Strings
MultiplicationTable	Subsets
NextKSubset	ToCycles
NextPermutation	ToInversionVector
NextSubset	TransitiveQ

Combinatorica functions for permutations and combinations.

Partitions, Compositions, and Young Tableaux

A partition of a positive integer n is a set of k strictly positive integers that sum up to n. A composition of n is a particular arrangement of non-negative integers that sum up to n. A Young tableaux is a structure of integers $1, ..., n$ where the number of elements in each row is defined by an integer partition of n. Further, the elements of each row and column are in increasing order, and the rows are left justified. These three related combinatorial objects have a host of interesting applications and properties.

Here are the eleven partitions of 6. Observe that they are given in reverse lexicographic order.

```
In[12]:= Partitions[6]
Out[12]= {{6}, {5, 1}, {4, 2}, {4, 1, 1}, {3, 3}, {3, 2, 1},
         {3, 1, 1, 1}, {2, 2, 2}, {2, 2, 1, 1}, {2, 1, 1, 1, 1},
         {1, 1, 1, 1, 1, 1}}
```

Although the number of partitions grows exponentially, it does so more slowly than permutations or subsets, so complete tables can be generated for larger values of *n*.

```
In[13]:= Length[Partitions[20]]
Out[13]= 627
```

Ferrers diagrams represent partitions as patterns of dots. They provide a useful tool for visualizing partitions, because moving the dots around provides a mechanism for proving bijections between classes of partitions. Here we construct a random partition of 100.

```
In[14]:= FerrersDiagram[RandomPartition[100]]
```

Here every composition of 6 into 3 parts is generated exactly once.

```
In[15]:= Compositions[6,3]
Out[15]= {{0, 0, 6}, {0, 1, 5}, {0, 2, 4}, {0, 3, 3}, {0, 4, 2},
         {0, 5, 1}, {0, 6, 0}, {1, 0, 5}, {1, 1, 4}, {1, 2, 3},
         {1, 3, 2}, {1, 4, 1}, {1, 5, 0}, {2, 0, 4}, {2, 1, 3},
         {2, 2, 2}, {2, 3, 1}, {2, 4, 0}, {3, 0, 3}, {3, 1, 2},
         {3, 2, 1}, {3, 3, 0}, {4, 0, 2}, {4, 1, 1}, {4, 2, 0},
         {5, 0, 1}, {5, 1, 0}, {6, 0, 0}}
```

The list of tableaux of shape {3, 2, 1} illustrates the amount of freedom available to tableaux structures. The smallest element is always in the upper left-hand corner, but the largest element is free to be the rightmost position of the last row defined by the *distinct* parts of the partition.

```
In[16]:= Tableaux[{3,2,1}]
Out[16]= {{{1, 4, 6}, {2, 5}, {3}}, {{1, 3, 6}, {2, 5}, {4}},
         {{1, 2, 6}, {3, 5}, {4}}, {{1, 3, 6}, {2, 4}, {5}},
         {{1, 2, 6}, {3, 4}, {5}}, {{1, 4, 5}, {2, 6}, {3}},
         {{1, 3, 5}, {2, 6}, {4}}, {{1, 2, 5}, {3, 6}, {4}},
         {{1, 3, 4}, {2, 6}, {5}}, {{1, 2, 4}, {3, 6}, {5}},
         {{1, 2, 3}, {4, 6}, {5}}, {{1, 3, 5}, {2, 4}, {6}},
         {{1, 2, 5}, {3, 4}, {6}}, {{1, 3, 4}, {2, 5}, {6}},
         {{1, 2, 4}, {3, 5}, {6}}, {{1, 2, 3}, {4, 5}, {6}}}
```

By iterating through the different integer partitions as shapes, all tableaux of a particular size can be constructed.

```
In[17]:= Tableaux[3]
Out[17]= {{{1, 2, 3}}, {{1, 3}, {2}}, {{1, 2}, {3}}, {{1}, {2}, {3}}}
```

The hook length formula can be used to count the number of tableaux for any shape. Using the hook length formula over all partitions of n computes the number of tableaux on n elements.

```
In[18]:= NumberOfTableaux[10]
Out[18]= 9496
```

Each of the 117,123,756,750 tableaux of this shape will be selected with equal likelihood.

```
In[19]:= TableForm[ RandomTableau[{6,5,5,4,3,2}] ]
```

$$
Out[19]//TableForm=
\begin{array}{cccccc}
1 & 4 & 5 & 6 & 10 & 15 \\
2 & 7 & 9 & 14 & 24 & \\
3 & 11 & 18 & 20 & 25 & \\
8 & 16 & 19 & 22 & & \\
12 & 17 & 21 & & & \\
13 & 23 & & & &
\end{array}
$$

A pigeonhole result states that any sequence of $n^2 + 1$ distinct integers must contain either an increasing or a decreasing scattered subsequence of length $n + 1$.

```
In[20]:= LongestIncreasingSubsequence[
             RandomPermutation[50] ]
Out[20]= {2, 6, 9, 11, 20, 25, 30, 34, 36, 39}
```

CatalanNumber	NumberOfCompositions
Compositions	NumberOfPartitions
ConstructTableau	NumberOfTableaux
DeleteFromTableau	PartitionQ
DurfeeSquare	Partitions
EncroachingListSet	RandomComposition
FerrersDiagram	RandomPartition
FirstLexicographicTableau	RandomTableau
InsertIntoTableau	TableauClasses
LastLexicographicTableau	TableauQ
LongestIncreasingSubsequence	TableauxToPermutation
NextComposition	Tableaux
NextPartition	TransposePartition
NextTableau	TransposeTableau

Combinatorica functions for partitions, compositions, and Young tableaux.

Representing Graphs

We define a graph to be a set of vertices with a set of edges, where an edge is defined as a pair of vertices. The representation of graphs takes on different requirements depending upon whether the intended consumer is a person or a machine. Computers digest graphs best as data structures such as adjacency matrices or lists. People prefer a visualization of the structure as a collection of points connected by lines, which implies adding geometric information to the graph.

In the complete graph on five vertices, denoted K_5, each vertex is adjacent to all other vertices. `CompleteGraph[n]` constructs the complete graph on n vertices.

In[21]:= **ShowGraph[CompleteGraph[5]];**

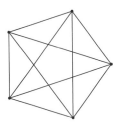

The adjacency matrix of K_5 shows that each vertex is adjacent to all other vertices. The main diagonal consists of zeros, since there are no self-loops in the complete graph, meaning edges from a vertex to itself.

In[22]:= **TableForm[Edges[CompleteGraph[5]]]**

$$Out[22]//TableForm=\begin{matrix} 0 & 1 & 1 & 1 & 1 \\ 1 & 0 & 1 & 1 & 1 \\ 1 & 1 & 0 & 1 & 1 \\ 1 & 1 & 1 & 0 & 1 \\ 1 & 1 & 1 & 1 & 0 \end{matrix}$$

The standard embedding of K_5 consists of five vertices equally spaced on a circle.

In[23]:= **Vertices[CompleteGraph[5]]**

Out[23]= {{0.309017, 0.951057}, {-0.809017, 0.587785}, {-0.809017, -0.587785}, {0.309017, -0.951057}, {1., 0}}

The number of vertices in a graph is termed the order of the graph.

In[24]:= **V[CompleteGraph[5]]**

Out[24]= 5

With an optional argument to specify whether we count directed or undirected edges, M returns the number of edges in a graph.

In[25]:= **{M[CompleteGraph[5]], M[CompleteGraph[5], Directed]}**

Out[25]= {10, 20}

A star is a tree with one vertex of degree $n-1$. Adding any new edge to a star produces a cycle of length 3.

In[26]:= **ShowGraph[AddEdge[Star[10], {1,2}]];**

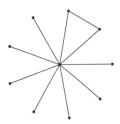

The adjacency list representation of a graph consists of n lists, one list for each vertex v_i, $1 \le i \le n$, which records the vertices to which v_i is adjacent. Each vertex in the complete graph is adjacent to all other vertices.

```
In[27]:= TableForm[ ToAdjacencyLists[CompleteGraph[5]] ]

                    2       3       4       5
                    1       3       4       5
Out[27]//TableForm= 1       2       4       5
                    1       2       3       5
                    1       2       3       4
```

There are $n(n - 1)$ ordered pairs of edges defined by a complete graph of order n.

```
In[28]:= ToOrderedPairs[ CompleteGraph[5] ]

Out[28]= {{1, 2}, {1, 3}, {1, 4}, {1, 5}, {2, 1}, {2, 3}, {2, 4}, {2, 5},
          {3, 1}, {3, 2}, {3, 4}, {3, 5}, {4, 1}, {4, 2}, {4, 3}, {4, 5},
          {5, 1}, {5, 2}, {5, 3}, {5, 4}}
```

An induced subgraph of a graph G is a subset of the vertices of G together with any edges whose endpoints are both in this subset. An induced subgraph that is complete is called a clique. Any subset of the vertices in a complete graph defines a clique.

```
In[29]:= ShowGraph[ InduceSubgraph[CompleteGraph[20],
              RandomSubset[Range[20]]] ];
```

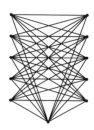

The vertices of a bipartite graph have the property that they can be partitioned into two sets such that no edge connects two vertices of the same set. Contracting an edge in a bipartite graph can ruin its bipartiteness.

```
In[30]:= ShowGraph[ Contract[ CompleteGraph[6,6],{1,7} ] ];
```

A breadth-first search of a graph explores all the vertices adjacent to the current vertex before moving on. A breadth-first traversal of a simple cycle alternates sides as it wraps around the cycle.

```
In[31]:= BreadthFirstTraversal[Cycle[20],1]

Out[31]= {1, 2, 20, 3, 19, 4, 18, 5, 17, 6, 16, 7, 15, 8, 14, 9, 13, 10,
          12, 11}
```

In a depth-first search, the children of the first son of a vertex are explored before visiting his brothers. The depth-first traversal differs from the breadth-first traversal above, in that it proceeds directly around the cycle.

```
In[32]:= DepthFirstTraversal[Cycle[20], 1]
Out[32]= {1, 2, 3, 4, 5, 6, 7, 8, 9, 10, 11, 12, 13, 14, 15, 16, 17, 18,
         19, 20}
```

Different drawings or embeddings of a graph can reveal different aspects of its structure. The default embedding for a grid graph is a ranked embedding from all the vertices on one side. Ranking from the center vertex yields a different but interesting drawing.

```
In[33]:= ShowGraph[
            RankedEmbedding[GridGraph[5,5],{13}]];
```

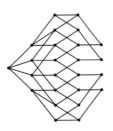

The radial embedding of a tree is guaranteed to be planar, but radial embeddings can be used with any graph. Here we see a radial embedding of a random labeled tree.

```
In[34]:= ShowGraph[ RandomTree[10] ];
```

An interesting general heuristic for drawing graphs models the graph as a system of springs and lets Hooke's law space the vertices. Here it does a good job illustrating the join operation, where each vertex of K_7 is connected to each of two disconnected vertices. In achieving the minimum energy configuration, these two vertices end up on different sides of K_7.

```
In[35]:= ShowGraph[
            SpringEmbedding[
            GraphJoin[EmptyGraph[2], CompleteGraph[7]]]];
```

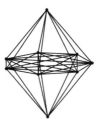

AddEdge	NormalizeVertices
AddVertex	PointsAndLines
BreadthFirstTraversal	PseudographQ
ChangeEdges	RadialEmbedding
ChangeVertices	Radius
CircularVertices	RankGraph
CompleteQ	RankedEmbedding
Contract	ReadGraph
DeleteEdge	RemoveSelfLoops
DeleteVertex	RootedEmbedding
DepthFirstTraversal	RotateVertices
Diameter	ShakeGraph
DilateVertices	ShowGraph
Distribution	ShowLabeledGraph
Eccentricity	SimpleQ
Edges	Spectrum
EmptyQ	SpringEmbedding
FromAdjacencyLists	ToAdjacencyLists
FromOrderedPairs	ToOrderedPairs
FromUnorderedPairs	ToUnorderedPairs
GraphCenter	TranslateVertices
GraphComplement	UndirectedQ
InduceSubgraph	UnweightedQ
M	V
MakeSimple	Vertices
MakeUndirected	WriteGraph

Combinatorica functions for representing graphs.

Generating Graphs

Many graphs consistently prove interesting, in the sense that they are models of important binary relations or have unique graph theoretic properties. Often, these graphs can be parameterized, such as the complete graph on *n* vertices K_n, giving a concise notation for expressing an infinite class of graphs. Start off with several operations that act on graphs to give different graphs and which, together with parameterized graphs, give the means to construct essentially any interesting graph.

The union of two connected graphs has two connected components.

In[36]:= **ShowGraph[GraphUnion[CompleteGraph[3], CompleteGraph[5,5]]];**

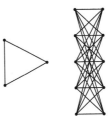

Graph products can be very interesting. The embedding of a product has been designed to show off its structure, and is formed by shrinking the first graph and translating it to the position of each vertex in the second graph.

In[37]:= **ShowGraph[GraphProduct[CompleteGraph[3], CompleteGraph[5]]];**

The line graph $L(G)$ of a graph G has a vertex of $L(G)$ associated with each edge of G and an edge of $L(G)$ if, and only if, the two edges of G share a common vertex.

In[38]:= **ShowGraph[LineGraph[CompleteGraph[5]]];**

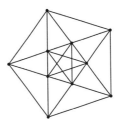

Circulants are graphs whose adjacency matrix can be constructed by rotating a vector *n* times, and include complete graphs and cycles as special cases. Even random circulant graphs have an interesting, regular structure.

```
In[39]:= ShowGraph[
              CirculantGraph[21,
              RandomKSubset[Range[10],3]]];
```

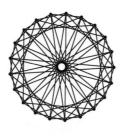

This random graph can be expected to have half the number of edges of a complete graph, even though all labeled graphs occur with equal probability.

```
In[40]:= ShowGraph[ RandomGraph[20,0.5] ];
```

CartesianProduct	GridGraph
CirculantGraph	Hypercube
CodeToLabeledTree	IncidenceMatrix
CompleteGraph	IntervalGraph
Cycle	LabeledTreeToCode
DegreeSequence	LineGraph
EmptyGraph	MakeGraph
ExactRandomGraph	NthPair
ExpandGraph	Path
FunctionalGraph	RandomGraph
GraphDifference	RandomTree
GraphIntersection	RandomVertices
GraphJoin	RealizeDegreeSequence
GraphPower	RegularGraph
GraphProduct	RegularQ
GraphSum	Star
GraphUnion	Turan
GraphicQ	Wheel

Combinatorica functions for generating graphs.

Properties of Graphs

Graph theory is the study of properties or invariants of graphs. Among the properties of interest are such things as connectivity, cycle structure, and chromatic number. Here, we demonstrate how to compute several different graph invariants.

An undirected graph is connected if there exists a path between any pair of vertices. Deleting an edge from a connected graph can disconnect it. Such an edge is called a bridge.

```
In[41]:= ConnectedQ[ DeleteEdge[ Star[10], {1,10} ] ]
Out[41]= False
```

GraphUnion can be used to create disconnected graphs.

```
In[42]:= ConnectedComponents[ GraphUnion[CompleteGraph[3],
            CompleteGraph[4]] ]

Out[42]= {{1, 2, 3}, {4, 5, 6, 7}}
```

An orientation of an undirected graph
G is an assignment of exactly one
direction to each of the edges of G.
This orientation of a wheel directs each
edge in the outer cycle in the same
direction, and completes it by giving
the center an in-degree of $n - 1$ and
out-degree of 1.

```
In[43]:= ShowGraph[ OrientGraph[Wheel[10]],
              Directed];
```

An articulation vertex of a graph G is
a vertex whose deletion disconnects G.
Any graph with no articulation vertices
is said to be biconnected. A graph
with a vertex of degree 1 cannot be
biconnected, since deleting the other
vertex that defines its only edge
disconnects the graph.

```
In[44]:= BiconnectedComponents[
             RealizeDegreeSequence[{4,4,3,3,3,2,1}] ]
Out[44]= {{2, 7}, {1, 2, 3, 4, 5, 6}}
```

The only articulation vertex of a star is
its center, even though its deletion
leaves $n - 1$ connected components.
Deleting a leaf leaves a connected tree.

```
In[45]:= ArticulationVertices[ Star[10] ]
Out[45]= {10}
```

Every edge in a tree is a bridge.

```
In[46]:= Bridges[ RandomTree[10] ]
Out[46]= {{2, 5}, {6, 8}, {7, 8}, {2, 7}, {1, 2}, {3, 4}, {4, 9},
          {4, 10}, {1, 4}}
```

A graph is said to be k-connected if
there does not exist a set of $k - 1$
vertices whose removal disconnects the
graph. The wheel is the basic
triconnected graph.

```
In[47]:= VertexConnectivity[Wheel[5]]
Out[47]= 3
```

A graph is k-edge-connected if there
does not exist a set of $k - 1$ edges
whose removal disconnects the graph.
The edge connectivity of a graph is at
most the minimum degree δ, since
deleting those edges disconnects the
graph. Complete bipartite graphs
realize this bound.

```
In[48]:= EdgeConnectivity[CompleteGraph[3,4]]
Out[48]= 3
```

These two complete bipartite graphs are isomorphic, since the order of the two stages is simply reversed. Here, all isomorphisms are returned.

```
In[49]:= Isomorphism[CompleteGraph[3,2], CompleteGraph[2,3], All]

Out[49]= {{3, 4, 5, 1, 2}, {3, 4, 5, 2, 1}, {3, 5, 4, 1, 2},
          {3, 5, 4, 2, 1}, {4, 3, 5, 1, 2}, {4, 3, 5, 2, 1},
          {4, 5, 3, 1, 2}, {4, 5, 3, 2, 1}, {5, 3, 4, 1, 2},
          {5, 3, 4, 2, 1}, {5, 4, 3, 1, 2}, {5, 4, 3, 2, 1}}
```

A graph is self-complementary if it is isomorphic to its complement. The smallest non-trivial self-complementary graphs are the path on four vertices and the cycle on five.

```
In[50]:= SelfComplementaryQ[ Cycle[5] ] &&
              SelfComplementaryQ[ Path[4] ]

Out[50]= True
```

A directed graph with half the edges is almost certain to contain a cycle. Directed acyclic graphs are often called DAGs.

```
In[51]:= AcyclicQ[
              RandomGraph[7,0.5,Directed], Directed]

Out[51]= False
```

The girth of a graph is the length of its shortest cycle. The girth of a complete graph is 3, since it contains a triangle, the smallest possible cycle.

```
In[52]:= Girth[ CompleteGraph[5] ]

Out[52]= 3
```

An Eulerian cycle is a complete tour of all the edges of a graph. An Eulerian cycle of a bipartite graph bounces back and forth between the stages.

```
In[53]:= EulerianCycle[ CompleteGraph[4,4] ]

Out[53]= {7, 2, 8, 1, 5, 4, 6, 3, 7, 4, 8, 3, 5, 2, 6, 1, 7}
```

A Hamiltonian cycle of a graph G is a cycle that visits every vertex in G exactly once, as opposed to an Eulerian cycle, which visits each edge exactly once. $K_{n,n}$ for $n > 1$ are the only Hamiltonian complete bipartite graphs.

```
In[54]:= HamiltonianCycle[CompleteGraph[3,3], All]

Out[54]= {{1, 4, 2, 5, 3, 6, 1}, {1, 4, 2, 6, 3, 5, 1},
          {1, 4, 3, 5, 2, 6, 1}, {1, 4, 3, 6, 2, 5, 1},
          {1, 5, 2, 4, 3, 6, 1}, {1, 5, 2, 6, 3, 4, 1},
          {1, 5, 3, 4, 2, 6, 1}, {1, 5, 3, 6, 2, 4, 1},
          {1, 6, 2, 4, 3, 5, 1}, {1, 6, 2, 5, 3, 4, 1},
          {1, 6, 3, 4, 2, 5, 1}, {1, 6, 3, 5, 2, 4, 1}}
```

The divisibility relation between integers is reflexive, since each integer divides itself, and anti-symmetric, since x cannot divide y if $x > y$. Finally, it is transitive, as $x \backslash y$ implies $y = c\,x$ for some integer c, so $y \backslash z$ implies $x \backslash z$.

```
In[55]:= ShowLabeledGraph[
              g = MakeGraph[Range[8],(Mod[#1,#2]==0)&] ];
```

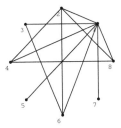

Since the divisibility relation is reflexive, transitive, and anti-symmetric, it is a partial order.

```
In[56]:= PartialOrderQ[g]

Out[56]= True
```

A graph G is transitive if any three vertices x, y, z such that edges $\{x, y\}, \{y, z\} \in G$ imply $\{x, z\} \in G$. The transitive reduction of a graph G is the smallest graph $R(G)$ such that $C(G) = C(R(G))$. The transitive reduction eliminates all implied edges in the divisibility relation, such as $4 \backslash 8$, $1 \backslash 4$, $1 \backslash 6$, and $1 \backslash 8$.

```
In[57]:=  ShowLabeledGraph[TransitiveReduction[g]]
```

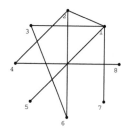

The Hasse diagram clearly shows the lattice structure of the Boolean algebra, the partial order defined by inclusion on the set of subsets.

```
In[58]:=  ShowLabeledGraph[
            HasseDiagram[MakeGraph[Subsets[4],
            ((Intersection[#2,#1]===#1)&&(#1 != #2))&]],
            Subsets[4] ];
```

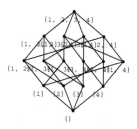

A topological sort is a permutation p of the vertices of a graph such that an edge $\{i, j\}$ implies i appears before j in p. A complete directed acyclic graph defines a total order, so there is only one possible output from TopologicalSort.

```
In[59]:=  TopologicalSort[
            MakeGraph[Range[10],(#1 > #2)&] ]
Out[59]=  {10, 9, 8, 7, 6, 5, 4, 3, 2, 1}
```

Any labeled graph G can be colored in a certain number of ways with exactly k colors $1, ..., k$. This number is determined by the chromatic polynomial of the graph.

```
In[60]:=  ChromaticPolynomial[
            GraphUnion[CompleteGraph[2,2], Cycle[3]], z ]
Out[60]=  -6 z^2 + 21 z^3 - 29 z^4 + 20 z^5 - 7 z^6 + z^7
```

ArticulationVertices	HasseDiagram
Automorphisms	IdenticalQ
BiconnectedComponents	IndependentSetQ
BiconnectedQ	IsomorphicQ
BipartiteQ	Isomorphism
Bridges	IsomorphismQ
ChromaticNumber	MaximumClique
ChromaticPolynomial	MaximumIndependentSet
CliqueQ	MinimumVertexCover
ConnectedComponents	OrientGraph
ConnectedQ	PartialOrderQ
DeBruijnSequence	PerfectQ
DeleteCycle	SelfComplementaryQ
EdgeChromaticNumber	StronglyConnectedComponents
EdgeColoring	TopologicalSort
EdgeConnectivity	TransitiveClosure
Element	TransitiveReduction
EulerianCycle	TravelingSalesman
EulerianQ	TravelingSalesmanBounds
ExtractCycles	TreeQ
FindCycle	TriangleInequalityQ
Girth	TwoColoring
GraphPower	VertexColoring
HamiltonianCycle	VertexConnectivity
HamiltonianQ	VertexCoverQ
Harary	WeaklyConnectedComponents

Combinatorica functions for properties of graphs.

Algorithmic Graph Theory

Finally, there are several invariants of graphs that are of particular interest because of the algorithms that compute them.

The shortest-path spanning tree of a grid graph is defined in terms of Manhattan distance, where the distance between points with coordinates (x, y) and (u, v) is $|x - u| + |y - v|$.

```
In[61]:= ShowGraph[
           ShortestPathSpanningTree[
             GridGraph[5,5],1] ];
```

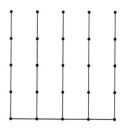

In an unweighted graph, there can be many different shortest paths between any pair of vertices. This path between two opposing corners goes all the way to the right, then all the way to the top.

```
In[62]:= ShortestPath[GridGraph[5,5],1,25]
Out[62]= {1, 2, 3, 4, 5, 10, 15, 20, 25}
```

A minimum spanning tree of a weighted graph is a set of $n - 1$ edges of minimum total weight that form a spanning tree of the graph. Any spanning tree is a minimum spanning tree when the graphs are unweighted.

```
In[63]:= ShowGraph[ MinimumSpanningTree[ CompleteGraph[6,6,6] ] ];
```

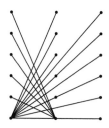

The number of spanning trees of a complete graph is n^{n-2}, as was proved by Cayley.

```
In[64]:= NumberOfSpanningTrees[CompleteGraph[10]]
Out[64]= 100000000
```

The maximum flow through an unweighted complete bipartite graph G is the minimum degree $\delta(G)$.

```
In[65]:= NetworkFlow[ CompleteGraph[4,4], 1, 8]
Out[65]= 4
```

A matching, in a graph G, is a set of edges of G such that no two of them share a vertex in common. A perfect matching of an even cycle consists of alternating edges in the cycle.

```
In[66]:= BipartiteMatching[ Cycle[8] ]
Out[66]= {{1, 2}, {3, 4}, {5, 6}, {7, 8}}
```

Any maximal matching of a K_n is a maximum matching, and perfect if n is even.

```
In[67]:= MaximalMatching[CompleteGraph[8]]
Out[67]= {{1, 2}, {3, 4}, {5, 6}, {7, 8}}
```

Planar graphs are graphs which can be embedded in the plane with no pair of edges crossing. $K_{3,3}$ and K_5 are the basic nonplanar graphs.

```
In[68]:= PlanarQ[CompleteGraph[5]] || PlanarQ[CompleteGraph[3,3]]
Out[68]= False
```

Every planar graph on nine vertices has a nonplanar complement.

```
In[69]:= PlanarQ[ GraphComplement[GridGraph[3,3]] ]
Out[69]= False
```

AllPairsShortestPath	MinimumSpanningTree
BipartiteMatching	NetworkFlowEdges
Cofactor	NetworkFlow
Dijkstra	NumberOfSpanningTrees
FindSet	PathConditionGraph
GraphPower	PlanarQ
InitializeUnionFind	ShortestPathSpanningTree
MaximalMatching	ShortestPath
MaximumAntichain	StableMarriage
MaximumSpanningTree	UnionSet
MinimumChainPartition	

Combinatorica functions for algorithmic graph theory.

Note: For further information about Combinatorica, and to be kept informed about new releases, you may contact the author electronically at skiena@sbcs.sunysb.edu. The latest release of the package and additional files, which may be of interest, are available by anonymous FTP from cs.sunysb.edu.

~■ DiscreteMath`ComputationalGeometry`

Computational geometry is the study of efficient algorithms for solving geometric problems. The nearest neighbor problem involves identifying one point, out of a set of points, that is nearest to the query point according to some measure of distance. The nearest neighborhood problem involves identifying the locus of points lying nearer to the query point than to any other point in the set. This package provides functions for solving these and related problems in the case of planar points and the Euclidean distance metric.

ConvexHull[{{x_1, y_1}, {x_2, y_2}, ... }]	compute the convex hull of a set of points in the plane
DelaunayTriangulation[{{x_1, y_1}, {x_2, y_2}, ... }]	compute the Delaunay triangulation of a set of points in the plane
VoronoiDiagram[{{x_1, y_1}, {x_2, y_2}, ... }]	compute the Voronoi diagram of a set of points in the plane

Computational geometry functions.

The convex hull of a set S is the boundary of the smallest set containing S. The Voronoi diagram of S is the collection of nearest neighborhoods for each of the points in S. For points in the plane, these neighborhoods are polygons. The Delaunay triangulation of S is a triangulation of the points in S such that no triangle contains a point of S in its circumcircle. This is equivalent to connecting the points in S according to whether their neighborhood polygons share a common side.

This loads the package.

```
In[1]:= <<DiscreteMath`ComputationalGeometry`
```

Here is a list of points in the plane.

```
In[2]:= data2D = {{4.4, 14}, {6.7, 15.25},
          {6.9, 12.8}, {2.1, 11.1}, {9.5, 14.9},
          {13.2, 11.9}, {10.3, 12.3}, {6.8, 9.5},
          {3.3, 7.7}, {0.6, 5.1}, {5.3, 2.4},
          {8.45, 4.7}, {11.5, 9.6}, {13.8, 7.3},
          {12.9, 3.1}, {11, 1.1}};
```

This gives the indices of the points lying on the convex hull in counterclockwise order.

```
In[3]:= convexhull = ConvexHull[data2D]
Out[3]= {14, 6, 5, 2, 1, 4, 10, 11, 16, 15}
```

Duplicate points are ignored.

```
In[4]:= ConvexHull[{{0,0}, {1,0}, {0,0}, {2,0},
          {1,1}}]

Out[4]= {4, 5, 1, 2}
```

This gives the counterclockwise vertex adjacency list for each point in the Delaunay triangulation. For example, the entry {1, {4, 3, 2}} indicates that the first point in `data2D` is connected in counterclockwise order to the fourth, third, and second points.

```
In[5]:= (delval =
              DelaunayTriangulation[data2D]) // Shallow[#, {5, 6}]&

Out[5]//Shallow=
   {{1, {4, 3, 2}}, {2, {1, 3, 5}}, {3, {2, 1, 4, 8, 7, 5}},
    {4, {10, 9, 8, 3, 1}}, {5, {2, 3, 7, 6}}, {6, {5, 7, 13, 14}},
    ≪10≫}
```

While `DelaunayTriangulation` need only specify the connections between points, `VoronoiDiagram` must specify both a set of diagram vertices and the connections between those vertices. Another difference between the two functions is that while a triangulation consists of segments, a diagram consists of both segments and rays. For example, in the case of a Voronoi diagram, points in the interior of the convex hull will have nearest neighborhoods that are closed polygons, but the nearest neighborhoods of points on the convex hull will be open polygons.

These considerations make the output of `VoronoiDiagram` more complex than that of `Delaunay` `Triangulation`. The diagram is given as a list of diagram vertices followed by a diagram vertex adjacency list. The finite vertices of the diagram are listed first in the vertex list. The vertices lying at infinity have head `Ray` and are listed last.

This assigns the list of Voronoi diagram vertices to `vorvert` and the Voronoi diagram vertex adjacency list to `vorval`.

```
In[6]:= {vorvert, vorval} = VoronoiDiagram[data2D];
```

The first vertex in `vorvert` is a finite diagram vertex having coordinates {-0.0158537, 8.44146}. The last vertex in `vorvert` is a point at infinity. This point is represented by a `Ray` object having origin {10.5172, 3.46115} and containing {13.95, 0.2}.

```
In[7]:= First[vorvert], Last[vorvert] // Short[#,2]&

Out[7]//Short= {{-0.0158537, 8.44146}, ≪28≫,
                Ray[{10.5172, 3.46115}, {13.95, 0.2}]}
```

Each entry in `vorval` gives the index of a point in `data2D` followed by a counterclockwise list of the Voronoi diagram vertices that comprise the point's nearest neighborhood polygon.

```
In[8]:= vorval // Short

Out[8]//Short= {{1, {4, 7, 21, 22}}, {2, {7, 9, 23, 21}}, ≪13≫,
                {16, {15, 10, 28, 30}}}
```

Here is the Voronoi polygon vertex adjacency list for the first point in `data2D`.

```
In[9]:= vorval[[1,2]]

Out[9]= {4, 7, 21, 22}
```

This selects the coordinates of the polygon vertices from `vorvert`. The first two vertices have head `List`, while the last two have head `Ray`. Thus, the Voronoi polygon associated with the first point in `data2D` is open and is defined by a segment and two rays.

```
In[10]:= vorvert[[%]]

Out[10]= {{4.6927572427572, 11.405744255744}, {5.915335598980,
            13.952782497876}, Ray[{5.915335598980, 13.952782497876},
            {4.30000000000, 16.92500000000}],
            Ray[{4.6927572427572, 11.405744255744},
            {0.350000000000, 14.850000000000}]}
```

VoronoiDiagram[{{x_1, y_1}, {x_2, y_2}, ... }, *delval*]
compute the Voronoi diagram using the Delaunay triangulation vertex adjacency list *delval*

VoronoiDiagram[{{x_1, y_1}, {x_2, y_2}, ... }, *delval*, *convexhull*]
compute the Voronoi diagram using the Delaunay triangulation vertex adjacency list *delval* and the convex hull index list *convexhull*

Computing the Voronoi diagram using the Delaunay triangulation and the convex hull.

This computes the Voronoi diagram of data2D more efficiently by making use of the Delaunay triangulation vertex adjacency list.

In[11]:= **VoronoiDiagram[data2D, delval];**

Here the Voronoi diagram is computed using both the Delaunay triangulation and the convex hull.

In[12]:= **VoronoiDiagram[data2D, delval, convexhull];**

PlanarGraphPlot[{{x_1, y_1}, {x_2, y_2}, ... }]
plot the Delaunay triangulation of the points

PlanarGraphPlot[{{x_1, y_1}, {x_2, y_2}, ... }, *indexlist*]
plot the graph depicted by the counterclockwise list of indices in *indexlist*

PlanarGraphPlot[{{x_1, y_1}, {x_2, y_2}, ... }, *val*]
plot the graph depicted by the vertex adjacency list *val*

DiagramPlot[{{x_1, y_1}, {x_2, y_2}, ... }]
plot the Voronoi diagram of the points

DiagramPlot[{{x_1, y_1}, {x_2, y_2}, ... }, *diagvert*, *diagval*]
plot the diagram depicted by the vertex list *diagvert* and the vertex adjacency list *diagval*

TriangularSurfacePlot[{{x_1, y_1, z_1}, {x_2, y_2, z_2}, ... }]
plot the surface according to the Delaunay triangulation established by projecting the points onto the *x-y* plane

TriangularSurfacePlot[{{x_1, y_1, z_1}, {x_2, y_2, z_2}, ... }, *trival*]
plot the surface according to the triangulation depicted by the vertex adjacency list *trival*

Computational geometry plotting functions.

The default of PlanarGraphPlot is a plot of the Delaunay triangulation of the points.

In[13]:= **PlanarGraphPlot[data2D,
          DefaultFont -> {"Courier", 8.}]**

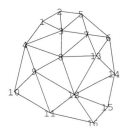

This plots the convex hull of the points.

In[14]:= **PlanarGraphPlot[data2D, convexhull]**

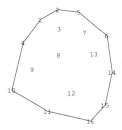

Here is an alternative triangulation.

In[15]:= **trival = Insert[Insert[Delete[delval,
          {{12, 2, 4}, {16, 2, 2}}], 15, {11, 2, 2}],
          11, {15, 2, 3}];**

This plots the triangulation of data2D given by trival.

In[16]:= **PlanarGraphPlot[data2D, trival,
          DefaultFont -> {"Courier", 8.}]**

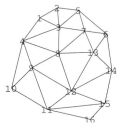

The default of `DiagramPlot` is a plot
of the Voronoi diagram of the points.

In[17]:= **DiagramPlot[data2D]**

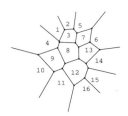

Here is an alternative set of diagram
vertices.

In[18]:= **diagvert = ReplacePart[vorvert,
{-6., 0.}, {27, 2}];**

Here is an alternative diagram vertex
adjacency list.

In[19]:= **diagval = Join[Drop[vorval, -8],
{{9, {1, 6, 8, 3}}, {10, {2, 6, 1,
24, 27}}},
Drop[vorval, 10]];**

This plots the diagram of `data2D` given
by `diagvert` and `diagval`.

In[20]:= **DiagramPlot[data2D, diagvert, diagval]**

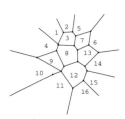

Here is a set of three-dimensional
points having the same x, y coordinates
as data2D.

In[21]:= **data3D = Map[Append[#,
Sqrt[64-(#[[1]]-8)^2-(#[[2]]-8)^2]]&,
data2D];**

The default of `TriangularSurfacePlot` is a plot of the *z* coordinates according to the connectivity established by the Delaunay triangulation of the *x*, *y* coordinates.

In[22]:= **TriangularSurfacePlot[data3D]**

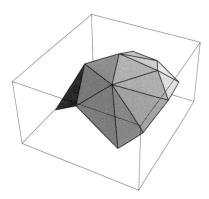

This plots the *z* coordinates according to the connectivity established by the triangulation `trival`.

In[23]:= **TriangularSurfacePlot[data3D, trival]**

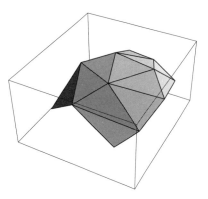

```
ConvexHull[{{x_1, y_1}, {x_2, y_2}, ... }, AllPoints -> False]
                    give the minimum set of points needed to define the convex
                    hull

DelaunayTriangulation[{{x_1, y_1}, {x_2, y_2}, ... }, Hull -> True]
                    give both the Delaunay triangulation vertex adjacency list
                    and the convex hull

PlanarGraphPlot[{{x_1, y_1}, {x_2, y_2}, ... }, LabelPoints -> False]
                    plot the Delaunay triangulation without labels

DiagramPlot[{{x_1, y_1}, {x_2, y_2}, ... }, LabelPoints -> False]
                    plot the Voronoi diagram without labels

DiagramPlot[{{x_1, y_1}, {x_2, y_2}, ... }, TrimPoints -> n]
                    plot the Voronoi diagram with the outermost ray plus (n - 1)
                    of the outermost diagram vertices trimmed
```

Options for computational geometry functions.

This gives the minimum set of points needed to define the convex hull.

```
In[24]:= ConvexHull[{{0,0}, {1,0}, {0,0}, {2,0},
            {1,1}}, AllPoints -> False]

Out[24]= {4, 5, 1}
```

This returns both the Delaunay triangulation and the convex hull.

```
In[25]:= DelaunayTriangulation[data2D,
            Hull -> True] // Shallow

Out[25]//Shallow=
    {{{«2»}, {«2»}, {«2»}, {«2»}, {«2»},
     {«2»}, {«2»}, {«2»}, {«2»}, {«2»}, «6»},
    {2, 1, 4, 10, 11, 16, 15, 14, 6, 5}}
```

Here is a set of random numbers uniformly distributed on $[0, 1] \times [0, 1]$.

```
In[26]:= random = Table[{Random[], Random[]}, {40}];
```

This computes the Voronoi diagram of random.

```
In[27]:= {randvert, randval} =
            VoronoiDiagram[random];
```

The diagram plot is dominated by outlier vertices.

In[28]:= **DiagramPlot[random, randvert, randval, LabelPoints -> False]**

TrimPoints -> 2 means that the diagram is plotted so that both the outermost ray and the outermost vertex are eliminated.

In[29]:= **DiagramPlot[random, randvert, randval, LabelPoints -> False, TrimPoints -> 2]**

The TrimPoints option can be used to magnify the diagram until the points in random fill the plot.

In[30]:= **DiagramPlot[random, randvert, randval, LabelPoints -> False, TrimPoints -> 6]**

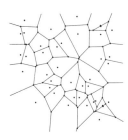

DelaunayTriangulationQ[{{x_1, y_1}, {x_2, y_2}, ... }, *trival*]
    give **True** if the vertex adjacency list *trival* represents a
    Delaunay triangulation of the points, and **False** otherwise

Testing for a Delaunay triangulation.

`delval` is a Delaunay triangulation, so this returns True.

```
In[31]:= DelaunayTriangulationQ[data2D, delval]
Out[31]= True
```

This returns False because `trival` is not a Delaunay triangulation.

```
In[32]:= DelaunayTriangulationQ[data2D, trival]
DelaunayTriangulationQ::inval:
    Triangle {11, 15, 12} is not a valid Delaunay triangle.
Out[32]= False
```

`NearestNeighbor[{`*u* , *v*`}, {{`x_1, y_1`}, {`x_2, y_2`}, ... }]`
    compute the nearest neighbor of the point {*u* , *v*} from the set of points {{x_1, y_1}, {x_2, y_2}, ... }

`NearestNeighbor[{{`u_1, v_1`}, {`u_2, v_2`}, ... }, `*vorvert*, *vorval*`]`
    compute the nearest neighbors of the points {{u_1, v_1}, {u_2, v_2}, ... } given the neighborhood structure depicted by Voronoi diagram vertex list *vorvert* and Voronoi diagram vertex adjacency list *vorval*

Computing the nearest neighbor.

This computes the point in `data2D` nearest to {7.92, 8.92}.

```
In[33]:= neighbor = NearestNeighbor[{7.92, 8.92},
            data2D]
Out[33]= 8
```

If the Voronoi diagram is known, the diagram vertex list and vertex adjacency list can be substituted for the point list for a faster `NearestNeighbor` calculation.

```
In[34]:= NearestNeighbor[{7.92, 8.92},
            vorvert, vorval]
Out[34]= 8
```

This gives the coordinates of the Voronoi polygon containing {7.92, 8.92}.

```
In[35]:= vorvert[[vorval[[neighbor, 2]]]]
Out[35]= {{4.7609125717932, 11.213305679643}, {4.3407539118065,
          9.979089615932}, {6.0923748103187, 6.5731600910470},
          {9.19067656766, 7.63820132013},
          {9.136885245902, 10.166393442623},
          {8.387267080745, 11.103416149068}}
```

For each of the points in `data2D`, the nearest point in `data2D` is the point itself.

```
In[36]:= NearestNeighbor[data2D, vorvert, vorval]
Out[36]= {1, 2, 3, 4, 5, 6, 7, 8, 9, 10, 11, 12, 13, 14, 15, 16}
```

The first half of these points is known to derive from one distribution; the second half is known to derive from another.

```
In[37]:= known = Join[{{5.84, 1.2}, {5.94, 10.99},
            {5.1, 2.82}, {5.8, 1.67}, {5.63, 10.}},
            {{0.31, 5.11}, {7.73, 5.38},
            {10.42, 5.89}, {6.1, 5.1}, {6.92, 5.63}}];
```

Each of these points is believed to derive from one of the two distributions.

```
In[38]:= unknown = {{5.56, 7.48}, {5.1, 1.67},
            {5.17, 4.89}, {0.3, 5.27},
            {6.74, 5.73}, {5.09, 9.07}};
```

This classifies the points in unknown according to the classifications of their nearest neighbors in known.

```
In[39]:= If[# > 5, 2, 1]& /@
            NearestNeighbor[unknown, known]

Out[39]= {2, 1, 2, 2, 2, 1}
```

⊕ **BoundedDiagram[{{a_1, b_1},{a_2, b_2}, ... }, {{x_1, y_1}, {x_2, y_2}, ... }]**
compute the bounded Voronoi diagram of a set of points {x, y}, where the bound is the convex polygon described by the points {a, b}

⊕ **BoundedDiagram[{{a_1, b_1},{a_2, b_2}, ... }, {{x_1, y_1}, {x_2, y_2}, ... }, *delval*]**
compute the bounded Voronoi diagram using the Delaunay triangulation vertex adjacency list *delval*

⊕ **BoundedDiagram[{{a_1, b_1},{a_2, b_2}, ... }, {{x_1, y_1}, {x_2, y_2}, ... }, *delval*, *convexhull*]**
compute the bounded Voronoi diagram using the Delaunay triangulation vertex adjacency list *delval* and the convex hull index list *convexhull*

Computing the bounded Voronoi diagram.

When spatial data is collected within a finite region of the plane, the unbounded Voronoi diagram of the points may not offer an accurate picture of the region of influence of each point. A tile on the periphery of the diagram will be open, indicating an infinite region of influence, when in fact an open tile is simply due to the limited extent of the spatial sampling. It is sometimes useful to intersect the unbounded Voronoi diagram of the data with the boundary of the convex region from which the data was collected. Then each point in the data can be associated with a closed tile or finite region of influence.

BoundedDiagram begins by finding the unbounded Voronoi diagram. It then works counterclockwise around the boundary, integrating bounding polygon vertices into the diagram, and deleting Voronoi diagram vertices falling outside of the boundary. Bounding an open tile of the Voronoi diagram allows one to approximate the true underlying closed tile one would have if the data collection had not been limited to a portion of the plane.

The bounded diagram is represented as two lists: (1) a vertex coordinate list, and (2) a vertex adjacency list, one entry for each point in the original unbounded diagram indicating the associated bounded polygon vertices in counterclockwise order.

Since BoundedDiagram requires the unbounded Voronoi diagram, the computation of the bounded diagram can be made more efficient by providing additional arguments, such as the Delaunay triangulation vertex adjacency list and the convex hull.

These are the coordinates of the rectangular region from which the data2D sample was drawn.

```
In[40]:= b1 = {{0, 1}, {14, 1}, {14, 16}, {0, 16}};
```

This assigns the list of bounded diagram vertices to `diagvert1` and the bounded diagram vertex adjacency list to `diagval1`.

```
In[41]:= {diagvert1, diagval1} = BoundedDiagram[b1, data2D, delval,
            convexhull];
```

Here is a plot of the bounded diagram of data2D given by `diagvert1` and `diagval1`.

```
In[42]:= DiagramPlot[data2D, diagvert1, diagval1]
```

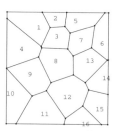

⊹   `TileAreas[ {{`x_1`, `y_1`}, {`x_2`, `y_2`}, ... }, {{`q_1`, `q_2`, ... }, ` *val* `]]`

         find the areas of the tiles centered on {x_i, y_i} and having vertices q_j, as stipulated by the vertex adjacency list *val*

Computing tile areas.

You can make use of Voronoi diagrams to build spatial interaction models, or simply calculate the area of influence of individual tiles.

In an unbounded Voronoi diagram, some of the tiles have infinite area.

```
In[43]:= TileAreas[data2D, diagvert, diagval]
Out[43]= {∞, ∞, 9.29049, ∞, ∞, ∞, 9.79901, 16.8551, 12.6713, ∞, ∞,
          20.8145, 13.2055, ∞, ∞, ∞}
```

In a bounded diagram, each of the tiles has finite area.

```
In[44]:= areas = TileAreas[data2D, diagvert1, diagval1]
Out[44]= {15.7479, 5.41378, 9.29049, 18.5843, 10.2238, 10.6601,
          9.79901, 16.8551, 17.5162, 15.6802, 19.072, 20.8145,
          13.2055, 8.70816, 11.3356, 7.09343}
```

This gives the tile areas scaled by the area of the rectangle from which the sample was drawn.

```
In[45]:= areas/(14 15)
Out[45]= {0.0749898, 0.0257799, 0.0442404, 0.0884965, 0.0486848,
          0.0507625, 0.046662, 0.0802622, 0.0834104, 0.0746675,
          0.0908191, 0.0991167, 0.0628832, 0.0414674, 0.0539793,
          0.0337783}
```

■ DiscreteMath`Permutations`

A permutation is a rule for rearranging a finite collection of elements. In this package, a permutation on n elements is represented by a list containing the first n positive integers. If the integer j is in the ith place in the list, this means that the permutation moves the ith element to the jth place. Thus, for example, {3, 1, 2} represents the permutation that moves 3 to 2, 2 to 1, and 1 to 3.

RandomPermutation[n]	give a random permutation on n elements
Ordering[*list*]	give the permutation that puts the elements in *list* in order
ToCycles[*perm*]	give the cyclic decomposition of *perm*
FromCycles[{cyc_1, cyc_2, ... }]	give the permutation that has the given cyclic decomposition
PermutationQ[*list*]	give True if *list* represents a permutation, and False otherwise

Working with permutations.

A cyclic permutation, or cycle, is a permutation in which any element can be moved to any other element by repeated application of the permutation. All permutations are not cycles, but it is a basic fact that any permutation can be decomposed into a product of cycles. This cyclic decomposition is represented as a list containing the cycles as sublists.

Cycles are represented differently than permutations. If the integer j follows the integer i in the sublist representing the cycle, this means that the cycle moves the ith element to the jth element. The sublist is treated cyclically so the last element is thought of as being before the first. As an example, {{1, 3, 2}, {5, 4}} represents a permutation containing a cycle that sends 1 to 3, 3 to 2, and 2 to 1, and a cycle that switches 4 and 5.

This loads the package.	`In[1]:= <<DiscreteMath`Permutations``
Here is a randomly chosen permutation of 10 elements.	`In[2]:= RandomPermutation[10]` `Out[2]= {1, 9, 3, 10, 8, 6, 2, 7, 5, 4}`
This is the permutation's cyclic decomposition.	`In[3]:= ToCycles[%]` `Out[3]= {{1}, {9, 5, 8, 7, 2}, {3}, {10, 4}, {6}}`
This transforms the cyclic decomposition back into a permutation.	`In[4]:= FromCycles[%]` `Out[4]= {1, 9, 3, 10, 8, 6, 2, 7, 5, 4}`
To transform the given list into one arranged in numerical order, you need to reverse the order of the elements.	`In[5]:= Ordering[{4, 3, 2, 1}]` `Out[5]= {4, 3, 2, 1}`

■ DiscreteMath`RSolve`

A recurrence or difference equation specifies a relationship between different values of an unknown sequence. For example, the equation `a[n] == a[n-1] + a[n-2]` specifies that in the unknown sequence `a[n]`, the sum of the two previous terms gives the next term. There may be many sequences that satisfy a given recurrence equation. If you specify the appropriate initial conditions and the equation is sufficiently well behaved, only one solution sequence will exist. Thus, if you specify the initial conditions `a[0] == a[1] == 1`, the equation above has only one solution, namely, the sequence $1, 1, 2, 3, 5, 8, 13, 21, \ldots$ called Fibonacci numbers.

RSolve[*eqn*, *a*[*n*], *n*]	solve a recurrence equation for *a*[*n*]
RSolve[*eqn*, *a*, *n*]	solve a recurrence equation for the function *a*
RSolve[{*eqn*₁, *eqn*₂, ... }, {*a*₁, *a*₂, ... }, *n*]	
	solve a list of recurrence equations

Solving recurrence equations.

RSolve computes the solution to the given equation using the method of generating functions. The form of the equations given in RSolve is similar to the form used in the built-in DSolve. You can give a single equation, equations with initial conditions, or several equations. The solution is returned in the form of a list of replacement rules.

When initial conditions are specified, the range of integers *n* for which the recurrence equations are valid is inferred from the initial conditions. When initial conditions are not specified, the equations are assumed to be valid for *n* >= 0.

This loads the package.

In[1]:= `<<DiscreteMath`RSolve``

The solution to this recurrence equation is an exponential. The initial value of the solution sequence is left unspecified. The constant `C[1]` may be specified using the option `RSolveConstants`.

In[2]:= `RSolve[a[n+1] == 2 a[n], a[n], n]`

Out[2]= $\{\{a[n] \to 2^n C[1]\}\}$

This specifies an initial value of 5.

In[3]:= `RSolve[{a[n+1] == 2 a[n], a[0] == 5},`
            `a[n], n]`

Out[3]= $\{\{a[n] \to 5\, 2^n\}\}$

This is the recursion relation satisfied by the Fibonacci numbers. The initial conditions specify that the first two terms in the solution should be equal to 1.

In[4]:= `RSolve[{a[n] == a[n-1] + a[n-2],`
            `a[0] == a[1] == 1}, a[n], n]`

Out[4]= $\left\{\left\{a[n] \to \dfrac{2^{1-n}\left(-\left(1-\sqrt{5}\right)^{1+n} + \left(1+\sqrt{5}\right)^{1+n}\right)}{\sqrt{5}}\right\}\right\}$

Here are the first 11 terms in the solution.

```
In[5]:= Table[(a[n] /. %)[[1]], {n, 0, 10}] // Expand

Out[5]= {1, 1, 2, 3, 5, 8, 13, 21, 34, 55, 89}
```

This solves a pair of coupled equations. Notice that it is possible to get the solution in pure-function form, by specifying $\{a, b\}$ rather than $\{a[n], b[n]\}$.

```
In[6]:= RSolve[{a[n+1] - 3 b[n] - 4 a[n] == 1,
                a[n+1] + b[n+1] + b[n] == n,
                a[0] == b[0] == 0},
               {a, b}, n]
```

$$Out[6]= \left\{\left\{a \to \left(\frac{1}{6}\left(-8 - (-2)^{\#1} + 9\, 2^{\#1} - 6\, \#1\right)\&\right),\right.\right.$$
$$\left.\left. b \to \left(\frac{1}{3}\left(2 + (-2)^{\#1} - 3\, 2^{\#1} + 3\, \#1\right)\&\right)\right\}\right\}$$

RSolve can solve any linear constant coefficient equation, as well as systems of such equations. It can also solve two types of linear variable coefficient equations. The first type is a first-order homogeneous equation that has coefficients that are rational functions of n. The second kind of equation is one for which the solution grows slower than $k^n\, n!$ for any constant k and DSolve can solve the associated differential equation.

This is a linear equation with variable coefficients.

```
In[7]:= RSolve[{
               a[0] == a[1] == 2,
               (n+1) (n+2) a[n+2] - 2 (n+1) a[n+1] -
                   3 a[n] == 0},
               a[n], n]
```

$$Out[7]= \left\{\left\{a[n] \to \frac{(-1)^n}{n!} + \frac{3^n}{n!}\right\}\right\}$$

RSolve can also solve nonlinear equations when the nonlinearity comes from a convolution. The solution to this recurrence equation is the sequence of Catalan numbers.

```
In[8]:= RSolve[{c[n+1] == Sum[c[k] c[n-k], {k, 0, n}],
               c[0] == 1}, c[n], n]
```

$$Out[8]= \left\{\left\{c[n] \to \frac{\text{Binomial}[2\,n, n]}{1 + n}\right\}\right\}$$

The function $g(x) = \sum_{n=0}^{\infty} a_n x^n$ is called the generating function of the solution $\{a_n\}$. The exponential generating function of the sequence is the function $h(x) = \sum_{n=0}^{\infty} (a_n/n!)x^n$. For example, e^x is the generating function of the sequence $\{1/n!\}$ and the exponential generating function of the constant sequence $\{1\}$.

PowerSum[*expr*, {*x*, *n*}]	give the generating function of *expr* in terms of *x*, where *expr* is treated as a sequence in *n* and the sum runs from zero to infinity
PowerSum[*expr*, {*x*, *n*, n_0}]	give the generating function of *expr*, where the sum runs from n_0 to infinity
ExponentialPowerSum[*expr*, {*x*, *n*}]	
	give the exponential generating function of *expr*, where the sum runs from zero to infinity
ExponentialPowerSum[*expr*, {*x*, *n*, n_0}]	
	give the exponential generating function of *expr*, where the sum runs from n_0 to infinity

Generating functions of sequences.

This computes $\sum_{n=0}^{\infty} x^n$, which is simply a geometric series.

```
In[9]:= PowerSum[1, {x, n}]
```

$$Out[9]= \frac{1}{1-x}$$

This computes the generating function of the sequence of squares of integers.

```
In[10]:= PowerSum[n^2, {x, n}]
```

$$Out[10]= -\frac{x\,(1+x)}{(-1+x)^3}$$

This confirms that the coefficients of the series expansion of the function are the squares of the integers.

```
In[11]:= CoefficientList[Normal[
              Series[%, {x, 0, 10}]], x]
```

$$Out[11]= \{0, 1, 4, 9, 16, 25, 36, 49, 64, 81, 100\}$$

This exponential generating function is simply the Taylor series for the exponential.

```
In[12]:= ExponentialPowerSum[1, {x, n}]
```

$$Out[12]= e^x$$

Here is the exponential generating function of the sequence of squares of integers.

```
In[13]:= ExponentialPowerSum[n^2, {x, n}]
```

$$Out[13]= e^x\,x\,(1+x)$$

This computes the exponential power sum for a series that has a different form when *n* is odd and even. The function Even is provided in the package. It is equivalent to the built-in EvenQ, except that it does not evaluate when its argument is symbolic.

```
In[14]:= ExponentialPowerSum[
              n^2 + 4 n If[Even[n], 2^n, 3^n] + 1,
              {x, n}]
```

$$Out[14]= e^x + e^x\,x\,(1+x) + 4\left(\frac{3}{2}\,e^{-3x}\,x - e^{-2x}\,x + e^{2x}\,x + \frac{3}{2}\,e^{3x}\,x\right)$$

GeneratingFunction[*eqn*, *a*[*n*], *n*, *x*]
　　　　　　　　give the ordinary generating functions for the solutions *a*[*n*]
　　　　　　　　to the recurrence equation *eqn* in terms of *x*

GeneratingFunction[{*eqn*₁, *eqn*₂, ... }, {*a*₁[*n*], *a*₂[*n*], ... }, *n*, *x*]
　　　　　　　　give the ordinary generating functions for the solutions of a
　　　　　　　　system of equations

ExponentialGeneratingFunction[*eqn*, *a*[*n*], *n*, *x*]
　　　　　　　　give the exponential generating functions for the solutions
　　　　　　　　a[*n*] to the recurrence equation *eqn* in terms of *x*

ExponentialGeneratingFunction[{*eqn*₁, *eqn*₂, ... }, {*a*₁[*n*], *a*₂[*n*], ... }, *n*, *x*]
　　　　　　　　give the exponential generating functions for the solutions of
　　　　　　　　a system of equations

Generating functions for the solutions to recurrence equations.

The solution to the given recurrence equation is the sequence of Fibonacci numbers. Thus, this gives the generating function for this sequence.

```
In[15]:= GeneratingFunction[
             {a[n] == a[n-1] + a[n-2],
              a[0] == a[1] == 1}, a[n], n, x]
```

$$Out[15]= \left\{\left\{-\frac{1}{-1 + x + x^2}\right\}\right\}$$

This recurrence equation gives the sequence of Bernoulli numbers.

```
In[16]:= ExponentialGeneratingFunction[
             Sum[Binomial[n, k] B[k], {k, 0, n}] ==
                 B[n] + If[n==1, 1, 0],
                 B[n], n, x]
```

$$Out[16]= \left\{\left\{\frac{x}{-1 + e^x}\right\}\right\}$$

This computes a list of coefficients in the power series of the generating function just computed and then cancels a factor of *n*! from the *n*th term.

```
In[17]:= CoefficientList[
             Normal[Series[%[[1,1]], {x, 0, 10}]], x] *
                 Table[n!, {n, 0, 10}]
```

$$Out[17]= \left\{1, -\frac{1}{2}, \frac{1}{6}, 0, -\frac{1}{30}, 0, \frac{1}{42}, 0, -\frac{1}{30}, 0, \frac{5}{66}\right\}$$

The resulting list contains Bernoulli numbers.

```
In[18]:= Table[BernoulliB[n], {n, 0, 10}]
```

$$Out[18]= \left\{1, -\frac{1}{2}, \frac{1}{6}, 0, -\frac{1}{30}, 0, \frac{1}{42}, 0, -\frac{1}{30}, 0, \frac{5}{66}\right\}$$

SeriesTerm[*expr*, {*x*, x_0, *n*}]	give the nth coefficient in the power series expansion of *expr* about the point $x = x_0$
SeriesTerm[*expr*, {*x*, x_0, *n*}, Assumptions -> {*cond*}]	make assumptions about parameters such as *n*

Coefficients of power series.

This gives the coefficient of x^{-2} in the power series expansion of $1/(x - 2)x^2$ about $x = 0$.

```
In[19]:= SeriesTerm[1/((x-2) x^2 ), {x, 0, -2}]
```
$$Out[19]= -\frac{1}{2}$$

The coefficient of a series can be computed for a general value of *n*. The default is to assume that $n >= 0$.

```
In[20]:= SeriesTerm[1/(1-x), {x, 0, n}]
```
$$Out[20]= 1$$

Here no assumption is made about *n*.

```
In[21]:= SeriesTerm[1/(1-x), {x, 0, n},
              Assumptions -> {}]
```
$$Out[21]= \text{If}[n \geq 0, 1, 0]$$

Here is another general coefficient where it is assumed that $n >= 0$.

```
In[22]:= SeriesTerm[1/(x - x^3), {x, 0, n}]
```
$$Out[22]= \frac{1}{2} (1 - (-1)^n)$$

When no assumption is made about *n*, the result involves the conditional If.

```
In[23]:= SeriesTerm[1/(x - x^3), {x, 0, n},
              Assumptions -> {}]
```
$$Out[23]= \text{If}[n == -1, 1, 0] + \frac{1}{2} \text{If}[n \geq 0, 1 - (-1)^n, 0]$$

option name	default value	
~ Method	Automatic	which RSolve method to use
+ RSolveConstants	C	which constant to use in RSolve solution

Options for RSolve.

The option Method for RSolve gives the method to be used in solving the given recurrence equation. The default value of Automatic specifies that the method of ordinary generating functions (MethodGF) should be used first. If this fails, the method of exponential generating functions (MethodEGF) is used. MethodGF succeeds when either the solution grows subexponentially and DSolve can solve the associated differential equation, or the equation is homogeneous first order and its coefficients are rational functions of *n*. When neither of these is true, you can often save time by specifying Method -> MethodEGF.

This solution grows faster than exponentially and the equation is inhomogeneous, so `MethodGF` failed.

```
In[24]:= Timing[
             RSolve[{T[0] == 5, 2 T[n]==n T[n-1]+ 3 n!},
                T[n], n]]
```

$$Out[24]= \{1.99\,Second, \{\{T[n] \to (3 + 2^{1-n})\,n!\}\}\}$$

Now `RSolve` uses `MethodEGF` only, so the solution is obtained more quickly.

```
In[25]:= Timing[
             RSolve[{T[0] == 5,2 T[n] == n T[n-1] + 3 n!},
                T[n], n, Method -> MethodEGF]]
```

$$Out[25]= \{0.67\,Second, \{\{T[n] \to (3 + 2^{1-n})\,n!\}\}\}$$

The names of undetermined constants in the result of `RSolve` may be selected using the option `RSolveConstants`. The options `GeneratingFunctionConstants` and `ExponentialGeneratingFunctionConstants` can be used to specify constants in the `GeneratingFunction` and `ExponentialGeneratingFunction` solutions, respectively.

option name	default value	
`GeneratingFunctionConstants`	C	which constant to use in `GeneratingFunction` solution
`ExponentialGeneratingFunctionConstants`	C	which constant to use in `ExponentialGeneratingFunction` solution

Options for `GeneratingFunction` and `ExponentialGeneratingFunction`.

■ DiscreteMath ` Tree `

This package introduces functions for creating, searching, and displaying trees represented as nested lists. Since trees are an efficient, basic tool for storing and manipulating data, the functions defined here are used in several other packages.

A tree is a standard data structure used in computer science and elsewhere for organizing information. Information in a tree is stored in nodes, starting with a root node and ending with terminal nodes called leaves. Nodes are linked to other nodes through branches. Leaves are nodes without any branches. The most common type of tree is the binary tree, in which each node has no more than two branches.

In this package, each node has the form $\{\{expr, n\}, branch_1, branch_2\}$, where *expr* is the information stored at the node, *n* is a sequential number assigned to the node, and $branch_1$ and $branch_2$ are the branches associated with the node. A leaf is represented as $\{\{expr, n\}, \{\}, \{\}\}$ in which the branches are empty lists.

MakeTree[*list*]	create a tree containing the information in *list*
TreeFind[*tree*, *x*]	return the position of the largest element less than or equal to *x* in the list from which *tree* was constructed

Generating and searching trees.

This loads the package.

```
In[1]:= <<DiscreteMath`Tree`
```

Here is a simple tree with three nodes. Node number 2 is the root node and contains the item e2. The first branch is the node {{e1, 1}, {}, {}} and the second branch is the node {{e3, 3}, {}, {}}. Both of these nodes are leaves.

```
In[2]:= MakeTree[{e1, e2, e3}]

Out[2]= {{e2, 2}, {{e1, 1}, {}, {}}, {{e3, 3}, {}, {}}}
```

Here is a tree with real values at the nodes. The root node contains the value 5.46, which is the median of the list. Other nodes are numbered in increasing order.

```
In[3]:= tree = MakeTree[{9.05, 6.48, 8.40, 5.46,
                2.43, 4.46, 2.03}]

Out[3]= {{5.46, 4},
            {{2.43, 2}, {{2.03, 1}, {}, {}}, {{4.46, 3}, {}, {}}},
            {{8.4, 6}, {{6.48, 5}, {}, {}}, {{9.05, 7}, {}, {}}}}
```

This result indicates that node number 5 contains the largest value less than or equal to 6.5. Equivalently, 5 elements in the original list are smaller than 6.5.

```
In[4]:= TreeFind[tree, 6.5]

Out[4]= 5
```

A node number of 0 is returned if all of the nodes are larger than the specified value.

```
In[5]:= TreeFind[tree, 1.0]

Out[5]= 0
```

> | | |
> |---|---|
> | TreePlot[*tree*] | generate a graphical representation of *tree* |
> | ExprPlot[*expr*] | generate a graphical representation of *expr* viewed as a tree |

Graphical representations of trees.

Graphical representations are very useful for understanding the structure of trees. The function TreePlot produces a graphical representation of trees generated by MakeTree. More generally, most *Mathematica* expressions can be thought of as trees, with the head of an expression at each node and the arguments of expressions as branches. The function ExprPlot generates a graphical representation of an expression viewed as a tree.

Here is a graphical representation of a tree with 10 nodes.

In[6]:= **TreePlot[MakeTree[Range[10]]]**

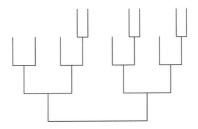

Here is a similar plot of an expression containing nested functions.

In[7]:= **ExprPlot[f[g[x, y, z], g[x, y, h[x, y]],**
        g[x, y]]]

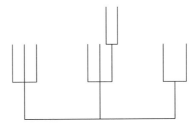

5. Geometry

■ Geometry `Polytopes`

This package contains functions that give geometrical characteristics of regular polygons and regular polyhedra. Polygons and polyhedra are identified by name (Square, Tetrahedron, etc.) in function arguments and in results.

NumberOfVertices[*p*]	number of vertices in polygon *p*
NumberOfEdges[*p*]	number of edges in polygon *p*
NumberOfFaces[*p*]	number of faces in polygon *p*
Vertices[*p*]	list of vertex coordinates for polygon *p*
Area[*p*]	area of polygon *p* when edges have unit length
InscribedRadius[*p*]	radius of the inscribed circle of polygon *p* when edges have unit length
CircumscribedRadius[*p*]	radius of the circumscribed circle of polygon *p* when edges have unit length

Geometrical characteristics of polygons.

Digon	polygon with 2 edges
Triangle	polygon with 3 edges
Square	polygon with 4 edges
Pentagon	polygon with 5 edges
Hexagon	polygon with 6 edges
Heptagon	polygon with 7 edges
Octagon	polygon with 8 edges
Nonagon	polygon with 9 edges
Decagon	polygon with 10 edges
Undecagon	polygon with 11 edges
Dodecagon	polygon with 12 edges

Names of polygons.

The functions `Area`, `InscribedRadius`, and `CircumscribedRadius` give information for a polygon with edges of length 1. The list of coordinates returned by `Vertices` is conventional for the specified polygon and does not necessarily correspond to a polygon with unit edge length.

This loads the package.

```
In[1]:= << Geometry`Polytopes`
```

An octagon has 8 edges.

```
In[2]:= NumberOfEdges[Octagon]
Out[2]= 8
```

This is the area of an octagon when the length of each edge is 1.

```
In[3]:= Area[Octagon]
```
$$Out[3]= 2 \operatorname{Cot}\left[\frac{\pi}{8}\right]$$

These points represent the coordinates of the vertices of an octagon.

```
In[4]:= Vertices[Octagon]
```
$$Out[4]= \left\{\left\{\frac{1}{\sqrt{2}}, \frac{1}{\sqrt{2}}\right\}, \{0, 1\}, \left\{-\frac{1}{\sqrt{2}}, \frac{1}{\sqrt{2}}\right\}, \{-1, 0\}, \right.$$
$$\left.\left\{-\frac{1}{\sqrt{2}}, -\frac{1}{\sqrt{2}}\right\}, \{0, -1\}, \left\{\frac{1}{\sqrt{2}}, -\frac{1}{\sqrt{2}}\right\}, \{1, 0\}\right\}$$

Here is a plot of the vertices of an octagon.

```
In[5]:= Show[Graphics[{PointSize[.05], Point /@ %},
              AspectRatio -> 1]]
```

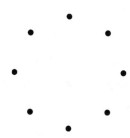

The polyhedra functions Volume, InscribedRadius, and CircumscribedRadius return information for a polyhedron with edges of length 1. The list of coordinates returned by Vertices is conventional for the specified polyhedron and does not necessarily correspond to a polyhedron with unit edge length.

NumberOfVertices[p]	number of vertices in polyhedron p
NumberOfEdges[p]	number of edges in polyhedron p
NumberOfFaces[p]	number of faces in polyhedron p
Vertices[p]	list of vertex coordinates for polyhedron p
Area[p]	area of face of polyhedron p, when edges have unit length
Volume[p]	volume of polyhedron p, when edges have unit length
InscribedRadius[p]	radius of the inscribed sphere of polyhedron p, when edges have unit length
CircumscribedRadius[p]	radius of the circumscribed sphere of polyhedron p, when edges have unit length
Dual[p]	dual of polyhedron p
Schlafli[p]	Schlafli symbol for polyhedron p

Geometrical characteristics of polyhedra.

Tetrahedron	polyhedron with 4 faces
Cube	polyhedron with 6 faces
Octahedron	polyhedron with 8 faces
Dodecahedron	polyhedron with 12 faces
Icosahedron	polyhedron with 20 faces

The five regular polyhedra.

This is the volume of a tetrahedron with edges of length 1.

In[6]:= **Volume[Tetrahedron]**

$$Out[6]= \frac{1}{6\sqrt{2}}$$

These coordinates form the vertices of an octahedron.

In[7]:= **Vertices[Octahedron]**

$$Out[7]= \{\{0, 0, \sqrt{2}\}, \{\sqrt{2}, 0, 0\}, \{0, \sqrt{2}, 0\}, \{0, 0, -\sqrt{2}\}, \\ \{-\sqrt{2}, 0, 0\}, \{0, -\sqrt{2}, 0\}\}$$

■ Geometry `Rotations`

RotationMatrix2D[*theta*]	give the matrix for rotation by angle *theta* in two dimensions
Rotate2D[*vec*, *theta*]	rotate the vector *vec* clockwise by angle *theta*
Rotate2D[*vec*, *theta*, {*x*, *y*}]	rotate about the point {*x*, *y*}

Rotations in two dimensions.

The usual mathematical convention is that angles in the plane are measured counterclockwise from the positive x axis. RotationMatrix2D gives the matrix needed to change coordinates by a rotation in this direction. This means that if this matrix is used to move vectors, they will be rotated in the clockwise direction. As is the case with all built-in *Mathematica* functions, all angles are given in radians.

This loads the package.

```
In[1]:= <<Geometry`Rotations`
```

Here is the matrix for rotation by 60 degrees displayed using MatrixForm.

```
In[2]:= MatrixForm[RotationMatrix2D[ N[Pi/3]] ]
```

$$Out[2]//MatrixForm= \begin{pmatrix} 0.5 & 0.866025 \\ -0.866025 & 0.5 \end{pmatrix}$$

This is a list containing two points in the plane.

```
In[3]:= {a, b} = {{0., 0.}, {0.5, 0.5}}
Out[3]= {{0., 0.}, {0.5, 0.5}}
```

Each point is rotated by 60 degrees about the point {1, 1}.

```
In[4]:= {anew, bnew} =
            {Rotate2D[a, N[Pi/3], {1., 1.}],
             Rotate2D[b, N[Pi/3], {1., 1.}]}
Out[4]= {{-0.366025, 1.36603}, {0.316987, 1.18301}}
```

This shows a line joining the two points before and after the rotation. The point at the center of the rotation is also shown.

```
In[5]:= Show[Graphics[
            {Line[{a, b}], Line[{anew, bnew}],
             {PointSize[.02], Point[{1, 1}]}}],
            AspectRatio->Automatic]
```

RotationMatrix3D[*psi*, *theta*, *phi*]	give the matrix for rotation by the specified Euler angles *psi*, *theta*, and *phi* in three dimensions
Rotate3D[*vec*, *psi*, *theta*, *phi*]	rotate the vector *vec* by the specified Euler angles
Rotate3D[*vec*, *psi*, *theta*, *phi*, {*x*, *y*, *z*}]	rotate about the point {*x*, *y*, *z*}

Rotations in three dimensions.

The rotation given by the Euler angles *psi*, *theta*, and *phi* can be decomposed into a sequence of three successive rotations. The first by angle *psi* about the z axis, the second by angle *theta* about the x axis, and the third about the z axis (again) by angle *phi*. The angle *theta* is restricted to the range 0 to π.

If you give exact arguments, the entries in the matrix are exact.

In[6]:= **RotationMatrix3D[Pi, Pi/3, Pi/4]**

$$Out[6]= \left\{\left\{-\frac{1}{\sqrt{2}}, -\frac{1}{2\sqrt{2}}, \frac{\sqrt{\frac{3}{2}}}{2}\right\}, \left\{\frac{1}{\sqrt{2}}, -\frac{1}{2\sqrt{2}}, \frac{\sqrt{\frac{3}{2}}}{2}\right\}, \left\{0, \frac{\sqrt{3}}{2}, \frac{1}{2}\right\}\right\}$$

To rotate an entire three-dimensional graphics object you need to transform all the coordinates specified in the list of primitives for the object. You can do this using the function RotateShape provided in the package Graphics`Shapes`.

6. Graphics

■ Graphics`Animation`

The ability to view dynamic effects with an animated sequence of graphics is often highly instructive. The effect of motion is produced by displaying a sequence of frames in rapid succession.

A collection of useful routines is supplied in the package Graphics`Animation`. These provide tools for generating sequences of graphical images and displaying them on a variety of computer platforms.

Animate[*grcom*, {*t*, *tmin*, *tmax*, *dt*}]	execute the graphics command *grcom* for the range of values of the parameter *t* using steps of *dt* and animate the resulting sequence
ShowAnimation[{p_1, p_2, p_3, ... }]	animate the sequence of graphics objects, p_i

The basic animation commands.

In this section animations are represented by arrays of the pictures. If you evaluate the *Mathematica* commands on your computer, each image will be displayed in rapid succession giving the appearance of motion.

This loads the package.

In[1]:= **<<Graphics`Animation`**

This gives an animation of sine waves with various frequencies.

In[2]:= **Animate[Plot[Sin[n x], {x, 0, 2 Pi}, Axes -> False], {n, 1, 6, 1}]**

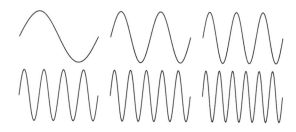

This is an example of the use of ShowAnimation. To ensure the same scale for each image, it is necessary to specify a value for the PlotRange option.

In[4]:= **ShowAnimation[Table[Graphics[Line[{{0, 0}, {Cos[t], Sin[t]}}]], PlotRange -> {{-1, 1}, {-1, 1}}], {t, 0, 2Pi, Pi/8}]]**

In addition to Animate and ShowAnimation, there are a number of other functions in the packages that are designed to make more specific types of pictures.

MoviePlot[*f*[*x*, *t*], {*x*, *xmin*, *xmax*}, {*t*, *tmin*, *tmax*}]
        animate Plot[*f*[*x*, *t*], {*x*, *xmin*, *xmax*}] for the given range of the variable *t*

MoviePlot3D[*f*[*x*, *y*, *t*], {*x*, *xmin*, *xmax*}, {*y*, *ymin*, *ymax*}, {*t*, *tmin*, *tmax*}]
        animate the three-dimensional plots

MovieDensityPlot[*f*[*x*, *y*, *t*], {*x*, *xmin*, *xmax*}, {*y*, *ymin*, *ymax*}, {*t*, *tmin*, *tmax*}]
        animate the density plots

MovieContourPlot[*f*[*x*, *y*, *t*], {*x*, *xmin*, *xmax*}, {*y*, *ymin*, *ymax*}, {*t*, *tmin*, *tmax*}]
        animate the contour plots

MovieParametricPlot[{*f*[*s*, *t*], *g*[*s*, *t*]}, {*s*, *smin*, *smax*}, {*t*, *tmin*, *tmax*}]
        animate the parametric plots

SpinShow[*graphics*]   rotate the three-dimensional graphics object

Animation of various plots.

For the purposes of display, only ten frames are plotted. To show the true proportions of the image, give the option AspectRatio the value Automatic and give explicit ranges for the PlotRange option to ensure that all the images have the same scale.

```
In[5]:= MovieParametricPlot[ {s Cos[2 Pi s + t], s Sin[2 Pi s + t]}, {s,
        0, 4}, {t, 0, 2Pi}, Frames -> 10, Axes -> False, AspectRatio
        -> Automatic, PlotRange -> {{-4, 4}, {-4, 4}}]
```

option name	default value	
SpinOrigin	{0, 0, 1.5}	used with SpinDistance to determine the ViewPoint
SpinDistance	2	used with SpinOrigin to determine the ViewPoint
SpinTilt	{0,0}	specifies Euler angles β and γ to give a tilt to the rotation
SpinRange	{0 Degree, 360 Degree}	the range of angles over which the first Euler angle α will be varied
RotateLights	False	whether the light sources should rotate with the object

Options to SpinShow.

SpinShow works by changing the viewpoint of the image. It generates a ViewPoint by rotating around a sphere of radius SpinDistance and shifting the result by the SpinOrigin. The actual rotation uses the first Euler angle α with initial and final values determined by the settings of the SpinRange. A final amount of freedom is provided by the SpinTilt option that gives the β and γ Euler angles of the rotation, which can give the rotation an amount of wobble.

This gives a parametric plot that will be animated.

```
In[9]:=  g = ParametricPlot3D[
             {x, Cos[t] Sin[x] , Sin[t] Sin[x]},
             {x, -Pi, Pi}, {t, 0, 2Pi},
             Axes -> False, Boxed -> False]
```

This demonstrates the use of SpinShow on the parametric plot. Due to the symmetry of the image we need only animate half a cycle. The animation of the projection of a three-dimensional object often enhances the depth effect.

```
In[10]:= SpinShow[ g, Frames -> 10, SpinRange -> {0 Degree, 180 Degree}
             ]
```

On a computer with a notebook user interface for *Mathematica*, such as a Microsoft Windows, Macintosh, or X Windows-based computer, animations can be initiated by selecting a group of pictures and choosing the appropriate animation command in the front end. The utilities in this package can be used for the production of sequences of images.

■ Graphics`ArgColors`

There are several ways to specify a complex number. The simplest is to give its real and imaginary parts. You can also use polar coordinates and specify the complex number by an angle, called the *argument*, and a length, called the *absolute value* or *norm*. Thus, the complex number z is equal to `Abs[z] Exp[I Arg[z]]`.

The functions `ArgColor`, `ArgShade`, and `ColorCircle` provided in this package are enhanced graphics directives. `ArgColor` and `ArgShade` allow you to specify the color or gray level of graphics elements using the argument of a complex number. `ColorCircle[r]` treats r cyclically, but with a period of 2π instead of 1. It begins with red and runs through the spectrum, blending the high end back into red.

`ArgColor[z]`	give a color value whose hue is proportional to the argument of the complex number z
`ArgShade[z]`	give a gray level
`ColorCircle[r]`	give a color value whose hue is proportional to r
`ColorCircle[r, b]`	give a color value whose hue is proportional to r, with brightness b

Colors and gray levels using the arguments of complex numbers.

This loads the package.

```
In[1]:= <<Graphics`ArgColors`
```

The values of this function are points on the unit circle.

```
In[2]:= un[k_] := Exp[2 Pi I k / 10],
```

For numbers near the negative x axis, `ArgShade` gives a low gray level. The shade grows darker as you move clockwise around the circle.

```
In[3]:= Show[Graphics[Table[
           {ArgShade[un[j]],
            Disk[{Re[un[j]], Im[un[j]]}, 0.2]},
           {j, 10}], AspectRatio -> Automatic]]
```

■ Graphics `Arrow`

In top-level *Mathematica* code, it is possible to create a graphic representing a two-dimensional arrow. However, since such a graphic is in the standard *Mathematica* coordinate system, it does not maintain its aspect ratio when the aspect ratio of the coordinate system is changed. This can lead to a rather odd looking arrow. This package implements a new graphics primitive to generate arrows that can maintain their aspect ratio, and can be quite flexible.

`Arrow[`*start*`, `*finish*`, `*opts*`]`	a graphics primitive that draws an arrow from coordinate *start* to *finish*

The `Arrow` graphics primitive.

The `Arrow` primitive behaves much as built-in `Graphics` primitives. It obeys color directives, and the line of the arrow follows thickness and dashing directives.

This loads the package.

```
In[1]:= <<Graphics`Arrow`
```

Here is a simple example of two arrows in different colors.

```
In[2]:= Show[Graphics[{Arrow[{0, 0},{1, 1}],
            Hue[0], Arrow[{.75, .25},{.25, .75}]}]]
```

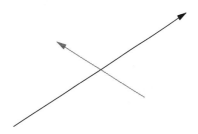

You can even place arrows in options.

```
In[3]:= Plot[Sin[x], {x, 0, 2Pi},
            Epilog -> {Arrow[{4, .25}, {Pi/2, 1}],
                Text["Here", {4, .15}, {0, -1}]}
        ]
```

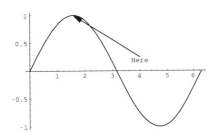

option name	default value	
HeadScaling	Automatic	scaling to use for coordinates in arrowhead; either Automatic, Relative, or Absolute
HeadShape	Automatic	shape of the arrowhead; if Automatic uses a description parameterized by HeadLength, HeadWidth, and HeadCenter
HeadLength	Automatic	length of the arrowhead; varies according to the value of HeadScaling
HeadWidth	.5	width of the arrowhead, expressed as a factor of the length of the arrowhead
HeadCenter	1	location of the center of the base of the arrowhead, expressed as a factor of the length of the arrowhead
ZeroShape	Automatic	shape of an arrow with no length; default is a dot

Options for the Arrow primitive.

There are several options that can be used to adjust the style of the arrowhead. HeadScaling determines the scaling of the coordinate system used in drawing the arrowhead. When it is Automatic, the coordinate system is centered at the tip of the arrow, and is rotated to lie along the arrow (with the negative direction towards the tail of the arrow). It is scaled by the default attributes coordinate scaling, where the distance across the bottom of the graphic is one unit. This allows the arrowheads to be scaled directly to the size of the graphic. When it is Relative, the coordinate system is scaled so that {0,0} is at the head of the arrow, and {0,-1} is at the tail of the arrow. This means that the size of a given arrowhead will vary with the length of the arrow. When HeadScaling is Absolute, the device coordinate scaling is used, centered at the head of the arrow, and rotated along the arrow. In this coordinate system, units are identical to those used by the standard graphics directives AbsoluteDashing and AbsoluteThickness. Whichever coordinate system is being used must be taken into account when specifying a style of arrowhead other than the default.

There are two ways to specify the shape of an arrowhead. One is a parameterized method, used when HeadShape is Automatic. The parameterized arrowhead is based on three values: HeadLength, HeadWidth, and HeadCenter. HeadLength specifies the distance from the tip of the arrowhead to its base. It is measured in the coordinate system given by HeadScaling, that is, if HeadScaling is Relative, the length is a factor of the length of the entire arrow, and if HeadScaling is Absolute, the length is in printer's points. HeadWidth specifies the greatest distance between the sides of the arrowhead, as a factor of the length of the arrowhead. HeadCenter specifies the location of the center of the base of the arrowhead as a factor of the length of the arrowhead. When HeadCenter is 1, the center of the base is as long as the length of the head, so the head is a triangle; when it is 0, the arrow is reduced to a line.

The other way of specifying the shape of an arrowhead is by a list of Graphics primitives. Currently, the routines only understand a subset of the graphics primitives; they are Point, Line, Polygon, and the various style directives. They are drawn in the same coordinate system as specified by the HeadScaling option, so the heads are automatically rotated to be along the length of the arrow, with the origin of the coordinate system at the tip of the arrow.

An arrow whose starting and ending points are identical has no length, and hence no direction. Thus, we usually use a different shape to describe it. The option ZeroShape can be used for this purpose. When it is set to Automatic, the zero length vector is drawn as a point. The coordinate system is left unrotated, because no direction can be determined.

With relative scaling, the size of the arrowhead varies with the length of the arrow.

```
In[4]:= Show[Graphics[
            Table[Arrow[{0, 0}, x {Sin[x], Cos[x]},
                HeadScaling -> Relative],
                {x, 0, 2 Pi, .3}]
        ], PlotRange -> All]
```

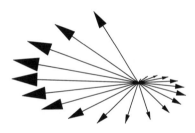

With absolute scaling, all arrowheads are the same size.

```
In[5]:= Show[Graphics[
            Table[Arrow[{0, 0}, x {Sin[x], Cos[x]},
                HeadScaling -> Absolute],
                {x, 0, 2 Pi, .3}]
        ], PlotRange -> All]
```

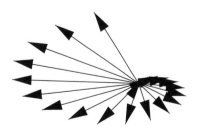

This shows how the shape of the arrowhead can be modified by the parameters HeadCenter and HeadLength.

```
In[6]:= Show[Graphics[
              Table[Arrow[{0,0},{Sin[x], Cos[x]},
                         HeadCenter -> x,
                         HeadLength -> .1],
                  {x,0,1.6,.2}]
              ],
         PlotRange -> {{-.1,1},{-.2,1.1}},
         AspectRatio -> Automatic]
```

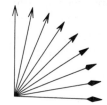

More general objects can be used to describe the head of an arrow. Note that the head is in a special coordinate system rotated along the arrow. The first arrow depicted here has a HeadShape consisting of two triangular polygons. The second arrow depicted has a HeadShape consisting of a cross formed by two intersecting lines.

```
In[7]:= Show[Graphics[{
              Arrow[{0,1},{1,0},
                   HeadScaling -> Relative,
                   HeadShape ->
                            {Polygon[{{0,0},{-.2,.05},{-.2,-.05}}],
                             Polygon[{{-1,0},{-.8,.05},
                                     {-.8,-.05}}]}],
              Arrow[{.25, .25}, {.75,.75},
                   HeadShape -> {Line[{{.1,.1},{-.1,-.1}}],
                        Line[{{.1,-.1},{-.1,.1}}]}]}
              },
         PlotRange ->All]]
```

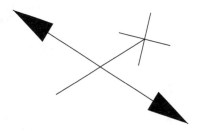

Note that the primary difficulty with the arrows created in this package is that the arrowheads are not involved in the scaling calculations that automatically determine the plot range. It is possible for the head to be inadvertently cut off by a poorly set plot range; in some cases it may be necessary to adjust plot ranges by hand.

■ Graphics ' Colors '

There are many different systems for specifying colors. Different output devices will often use different systems. For example, color displays, which work with emitted or transmitted light, typically use red, green, and blue primary colors. Color printing, on the other hand, which works with reflected light, typically uses cyan, magenta, yellow, and black as primary colors. The built-in *Mathematica* color directives RGBColor, Hue, and CMYKColor handle the most common systems. This package gives color directives using other standard systems. For more information on color output and *Mathematica*, see the section covering color output in *The Mathematica Book*.

CMYColor[c, m, y]	give a color in the CMY (cyan-magenta-yellow) system
YIQColor[y, i, q]	give a color in the YIQ (NTSC video form) system
HLSColor[h, l, s]	give a color in the HLS (hue-lightness-saturation) system
AllColors	list of the names of supported colors

Specifying colors in different systems.

This loads the package.	*In[1]:=* **<<Graphics'Colors'**
This gives the RGBColor that corresponds to the specification given in the YIQColor system.	*In[2]:=* **YIQColor[0.5, -0.1, 0.2]**
	Out[2]= RGBColor[0.53, 0.4, 0.957]

   This package also contains specifications for common colors. These take the form of an assignment of a RGBColor to the name of the color. Thus, for example, Aquamarine is RGBColor[0.498001, 1., 0.831401] and Black is RGBColor[0., 0., 0.].

This gives the specification for orange.	*In[3]:=* **Orange**
	Out[3]= RGBColor[1., 0.5, 0.]

AliceBlue

AlizarinCrimson

Antique

Apricot

Aquamarine

AureolineYellow

Azure

Banana

Beige

Bisque

Black

BlanchedAlmond

Blue

BlueViolet

Brick

Brown

BrownMadder

BrownOchre

Burlywood

BurntSienna

BurntUmber

CadetBlue

CadmiumLemon

CadmiumOrange

CadmiumYellow

Carrot

Cerulean

Chartreuse

Chocolate

ChromeOxideGreen

CinnabarGreen

Cobalt

CobaltGreen

ColdGray

Coral

CornflowerBlue

Cornsilk

Cyan

CyanWhite

DarkGoldenrod

DarkGreen

DarkKhaki

DarkOliveGreen

DarkOrange

DarkOrchid

DarkSeaGreen

DarkSlateBlue

DarkSlateGray

DarkTurquoise

DarkViolet

DeepCadmiumRed

DeepCobaltViolet

DeepMadderLake

DeepNaplesYellow

DeepOchre

DeepPink

DeepSkyBlue

DimGray

DodgerBlue

Eggshell

EmeraldGreen

EnglishRed

Firebrick

Floral

ForestGreen

Gainsboro

GeraniumLake

Ghost

Gold

Goldenrod

GoldOchre

Gray

Colors.

Green	MediumBlue
GreenishUmber	MediumOrchid
GreenYellow	MediumPurple
Honeydew	MediumSeaGreen
HotPink	MediumSlateBlue
IndianRed	MediumSpringGreen
Indigo	MediumTurquoise
Ivory	MediumVioletRed
IvoryBlack	Melon
Khaki	MidnightBlue
LampBlack	Mint
Lavender	MintCream
LavenderBlush	MistyRose
LawnGreen	Moccasin
LemonChiffon	Navajo
LightBeige	Navy
LightBlue	NavyBlue
LightCadmiumRed	Oak
LightCadmiumYellow	OldLace
LightCoral	Olive
LightGoldenrod	OliveDrab
LightGray	Orange
LightPink	OrangeRed
LightSalmon	Orchid
LightSeaGreen	PaleGoldenrod
LightSkyBlue	PaleGreen
LightSlateBlue	PaleTurquoise
LightSlateGray	PaleVioletRed
LightSteelBlue	PapayaWhip
LightViridian	Peach
LightYellow	PeachPuff
LimeGreen	Peacock
Linen	PermanentGreen
Magenta	PermanentRedViolet
ManganeseBlue	Peru
Maroon	Pink
MarsOrange	Plum
MarsYellow	PowderBlue
MediumAquamarine	PrussianBlue

Colors. (continued)

Purple	SteelBlue
Raspberry	TerreVerte
RawSienna	Thistle
RawUmber	Titanium
Red	Tomato
RoseMadder	Turquoise
RosyBrown	TurquoiseBlue
RoyalBlue	Ultramarine
SaddleBrown	UltramarineViolet
Salmon	VanDykeBrown
SandyBrown	VenetianRed
SapGreen	Violet
SeaGreen	VioletRed
Seashell	WarmGray
Sepia	Wheat
Sienna	White
SkyBlue	Yellow
SlateBlue	YellowBrown
SlateGray	YellowGreen
Smoke	YellowOchre
Snow	Zinc
SpringGreen	

Colors. (continued)

■ Graphics`ComplexMap`

To plot the graph of a complex-valued function of a complex variable, four dimensions are required as follows: two for the complex variable and two for the complex function value. One method, to circumvent the need for four-dimensional graphics, is to show how the function transforms sets of lines that lie in the complex plane. Each line will be mapped into some curve in the complex plane and these can be represented in two dimensions.

The functions `CartesianMap` and `PolarMap` defined in this package make pictures of this form. `CartesianMap` shows the image of Cartesian coordinate lines, while `PolarMap` shows the effect on polar coordinate lines.

`CartesianMap[`*f*, {*xmin*, *xmax*}, {*ymin*, *ymax*}`]`	
	plot the image of the Cartesian coordinate lines in the given ranges under *f*
`PolarMap[`*f*, {*rmin*, *rmax*}, {*thetamin*, *thetamax*}`]`	
	plot the image of the polar coordinate lines in the given ranges under *f*

Plotting the image of coordinate lines in the complex plane.

This loads the package.	`In[1]:= <<Graphics`ComplexMap``
We set the option Frame -> True to get frame axes on all our plots.	`In[2]:= SetOptions[Graphics, Frame -> True];`
This shows the Cartesian grid.	`In[3]:= CartesianMap[Identity, { -5, 5}, { -5, 5}]`

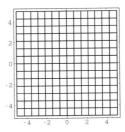

This is the polar coordinate system.

In[4]:= **PolarMap[Identity, { 0, 1}, { 0, 2 Pi}]**

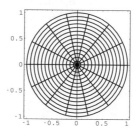

Here is the image of the Cartesian grid under exponentiation.

In[5]:= **CartesianMap[Exp, { -1, 1}, { -2, 2}]**

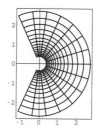

The square root function halves the angle of each complex number. The starting point is moved slightly from -Pi to avoid problems with the branch cut of the square root function.

In[6]:= **PolarMap[Sqrt, { 0, 1}, { -Pi + 0.0001, Pi}]**

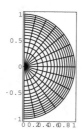

■ Graphics`ContourPlot3D`

You can create standard two-dimensional contour plots using the built-in functions ContourPlot and ListContourPlot. ContourPlot3D is the three-dimensional analog of ContourPlot. ContourPlot[f, {x, $xmin$, $xmax$}, {y, $ymin$, $ymax$}] will plot lines showing particular values of f as a function of x and y. Similarly, ContourPlot3D[f, {x, $xmin$, $xmax$}, {y, $ymin$, $ymax$}, {z, $zmin$, $zmax$}] will plot surfaces showing particular values of f as a function of x, y, and z. ContourPlot3D works by dividing the three-dimensional space into cubes and deciding if the surface intersects each cube. If the surface does intersect a cube, ContourPlot3D will subdivide this cube further, and so on.

ContourPlot3D[f, {x, $xmin$, $xmax$}, {y, $ymin$, $ymax$}, {z, $zmin$, $zmax$}]   generate a three-dimensional contour plot of f as a function of x, y, and z
ListContourPlot3D[{{{f_{111}, f_{112}, ... }, {f_{121}, f_{122}, ... }, ... }, ... }]   generate a three-dimensional contour plot from the three-dimensional array of values f_{zyx}

Making three-dimensional contour plots.

This loads the package.

In[1]:= **<<Graphics`ContourPlot3D`**

This produces a three-dimensional plot of the zero values of the function.

In[2]:= **ContourPlot3D[Cos[Sqrt[x^2 + y^2 + z^2]],**
 {x,-2,2}, {y,0,2}, {z,-2,2}]

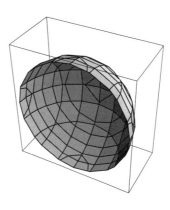

option name	default value	
Contours	{0.}	the list of values for the contours to be plotted
ContourStyle	{}	the list of styles for the contours to be plotted
MaxRecursion	1	the number of levels of recursion used in each cube
PlotPoints	{3,5}	the number of evaluation points to use in each direction

Options for ContourPlot3D.

Each value specified in Contours generates a different surface. ContourStyle colors each surface. To use this option, you must set Lighting -> False. MaxRecursion sets the number of times you subdivide each cube. However, if the surface does not intersect the cube, the cube is not subdivided. With MaxRecursion -> 0 the plot points are chosen from PlotPoints ->x or PlotPoints ->{x, y, z}. If MaxRecursion is greater than 0, recursion takes place. You can give a different number of plot points for the first and subsequent divisions of a cube. PlotPoints ->$\{x_1, x_2\}$ means that x_1 plot points are used first, and then if you subdivide, x_2 plot points are used. PlotPoints ->$\{\{x_1, x_2\}, \{y_1, y_2\}, \{z_1, z_2\}\}$ is also valid. ContourPlot3D and ListContourPlot3D return a Graphics3D object. This means the functions will accept any option that can be specified for a Graphics3D object.

Here is another plot showing a contour value of 0.1.

```
In[3]:= ContourPlot3D[x y z,
            {x,-1,1}, {y,-1,1}, {z,-1,1},
            Contours -> {.1}]
```

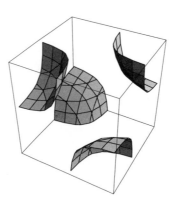

option name	default value	
Contours	{0.}	the list of values for the contours to be plotted
ContourStyle	{}	the list of styles for the contours to be plotted
MeshRange	Automatic	the ranges of x, y, and z

Options for ListContourPlot3D.

ListContourPlot3D takes a three-dimensional data set interpreted as a representation of a function $f(x, y, z)$, where the ranges of x, y, and z are set by the MeshRange option. With the default value of Automatic for MeshRange, the ranges of x, y, and z are specified by the dimensions of the data set.

This defines a three-dimensional array
of data.

```
In[4]:= data = Table[x^2 + 2*y^2 + 3*z^2,
                    {z, -1, 1, .25},
                    {y, -1, 1, .25},
                    {x, -1, 1, .25}];
```

Here is a plot of the contours 1.5 and
3.0 specified by green and red contour
surfaces, respectively.

```
In[5]:= ListContourPlot3D[data,
            MeshRange -> {{-1,1}, {-1,1}, {-1,1}},
            Contours -> {1.5, 3.},
            Lighting -> False, Axes -> True,
            ContourStyle -> {{RGBColor[0,1,0]},
            {RGBColor[1,0,0]}}]
```

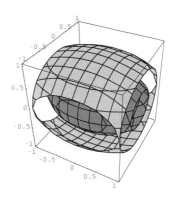

~■ Graphics`FilledPlot`

FilledPlot[*f*, {*x*, *xmin*, *xmax*}]	plot *f* using the variable *x*, with the space between the curve and the horizontal axis filled
FilledPlot[{*f*₁, *f*₂, ... }, {*x*, *xmin*, *xmax*}]	plot the *fᵢ*, filling the space between each successive pair of curves with a different color

Generating filled plots.

This loads the package.

In[1]:= **<< Graphics`FilledPlot`**

Here is a basic fill between the curve and the axis.

In[2]:= **FilledPlot[Sin[x], {x, 0, 2 Pi}]**

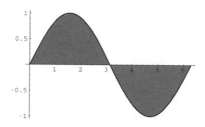

This fills between the first and second curve and the second and third curve.

In[3]:= **FilledPlot[{Sin[x], Cos[x], x^2/18}, {x, 0, 2 Pi}]**

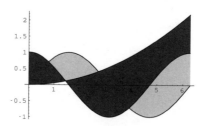

option name	default value	
Fills	Automatic	curves and styles to use for fills
Curves	Back	how to display the curves

Options for FilledPlot.

There are several ways to control the fills in your plots. A specification of
`Fills -> {color₁, color₂, ... }` generates a plot with fills between curve n and $n + 1$ using $color_n$.
A specification of `Fills -> {{{curve₁₁, curve₂₁}, color₁}, ... }` generates a plot with fills between
$curve_{1n}$ and $curve_{2n}$ using $color_n$. The curve specification `Axis` gives the x axis. The option `Curves`
controls how the lines of the curves are to be displayed. Specifying a value of `Back` causes curves to
be covered by subsequent fills. A value of `Front` places all curves in front of the fills and a value of
`None` causes the curves not to be drawn.

This specifies which curves to fill
between and the gray levels of the
filled regions.

```
In[4]:= FilledPlot[{x^2/18, Cos[x], Sin[x]},
            {x, 0, 2 Pi},
            Fills -> {{{1, Axis}, GrayLevel[.8]},
            {{2, 3}, GrayLevel[.3]}},
            Curves -> Front]
```

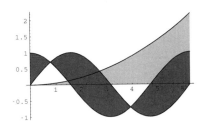

You can use any standard graphics options in `FilledPlot`. The fill is plotted only where the
defining curves exist (*i.e.*, where the functions are real valued).

The function $\sqrt{x^2 - 1}$ is real valued
only for $|x|$ greater than 1, so this is
the only region that is filled.

```
In[5]:= FilledPlot[{Cos[x], Sqrt[x^2 - 1]},
            {x, -1.5, 1.5},
            AspectRatio -> Automatic]
```

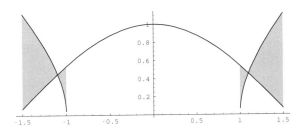

~ FilledListPlot[{y_1, y_2, ... }]	generate a filled plot between the curve given by {1, y_1}, {2, y_2}, ... and the x axis
~ FilledListPlot[{{x_1, y_1}, {x_2, y_2}, ... }]	generate a filled plot between the curve given by the data and the x axis
~ FilledListPlot[$data_1$, $data_2$, ...]	generate a filled plot between the curves specified by the given $data_i$

Generating filled plots from data.

The package also allows you to create filled plots between curves specified by data, rather than equations. FilledListPlot accepts the same options for specifying fills as FilledPlot.

This is a filled plot from data.   *In[6]:=* **FilledListPlot[{1,3,2,5,2}]**

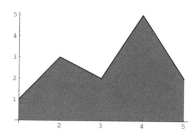

This is a filled plot from data specified   *In[7]:=* **FilledListPlot[{{1.1, 2}, {2.5, 1},**
by x and y coordinates.   **{4.5, 3}, {5.2, 4.2}}]**

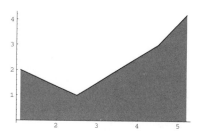

This is a filled plot of multiple data
sets.

```
In[8]:= FilledListPlot[ {1,3,2,5,2},
            {{1.1, 2}, {2.5, 1}, {4.5, 3}, {5.2, 4.2}}
        ]
```

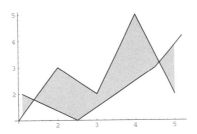

AxesFront -> True	specify that the axes and grid lines are to be drawn in front of the graphic, rather than behind

The AxesFront option.

The FilledPlot package defines a new option for Graphics objects called AxesFront. This is to allow the axes to be drawn over the graphic, so polygons will not obscure the tick marks. By default, the option is set to False; for the FilledPlot functions, it is set to True. Note that because this is a Graphics option, it can be used outside of FilledPlot. Also, when combining a FilledPlot with another graphics object, the usual option precedences will take effect (*i.e.*, if the FilledPlot is drawn after a graphic with the option set to False, the polygons may overlay the axes).

This polygon covers the axes.

```
In[9]:= Show[Graphics[{GrayLevel[.6], Polygon[{{0,0},{1,0},{1,1}}]},
            AxesFront -> False, Axes -> True,
            AxesOrigin -> {.5,.5}]]
```

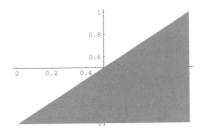

Now the axes are over the polygon.

```
In[10]:= Show[Graphics[{GrayLevel[.6],
                Polygon[{{0,0},{1,0},{1,1}}]},
          AxesFront -> True, Axes -> True,
          AxesOrigin -> {.5,.5}]]
```

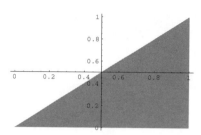

■ Graphics`Graphics`

You can do most standard plots in two dimensions using the built-in functions Plot, ListPlot, and ParametricPlot. In certain situations you may want to display your data or function in a more specialized format, such as a bar chart or a log-log plot. The functions provided in this package may be used to produce such plots.

LogPlot[*f*, {*x*, *xmin*, *xmax*}]	generate a linear-log plot of *f* as a function of *x* from *xmin* to *xmax*
LogLinearPlot[*f*, {*x*, *xmin*, *xmax*}]	generate a log-linear plot of *f*
LogLogPlot[*f*, {*x*, *xmin*, *xmax*}]	generate a log-log plot of *f*
LogListPlot[{{x_1, y_1}, {x_2, y_2}, ... }]	generate a linear-log plot from the points (x_1, y_1), ...
LogLinearListPlot[{{x_1, y_1}, {x_2, y_2}, ... }]	generate a log-linear plot from the points (x_1, y_1), ...
LogLogListPlot[{{x_1, y_1}, {x_2, y_2}, ... }]	generate a log-log plot from the points (x_1, y_1), ...
LogListPlot[{y_1, y_2, ... }], LogLinearListPlot[{y_1, y_2, ... }], LogLogListPlot[{y_1, y_2, ... }]	generate a plot of y_1, y_2, ... at *x* values 1, 2, ...

Log plots.

This loads the package.   *In[1]:=* **<< Graphics`Graphics`**

This gives a log-log plot of x^2.

In[2]:= `LogLogPlot[x^2, {x, 1, 3}]`

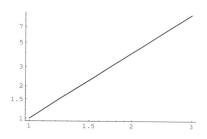

Here, `expdata` is a list of exponential data with a random offset between -1 and 1.

In[3]:= `expdata = Table[`
`        {x, .92 10^(.94 x) + Random[Real,`
`            {-1.0, 1.0}]}, {x, 0.2, 1.2, .1}]`

Out[3]= `{{0.2, 0.530506}, {0.3, 2.02172},`
`        {0.4, 1.90648}, {0.5, 3.45787}, {0.6, 4.08852},`
`        {0.7, 4.35505}, {0.8, 5.68323}, {0.9, 6.23631},`
`        {1., 7.72731}, {1.1, 9.71022}, {1.2, 13.2113}}`

In a log plot, the exponential data appear roughly linear.

In[4]:= `LogListPlot[expdata]`

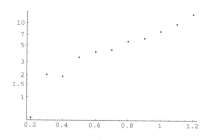

`PolarPlot[f, {t, tmin, tmax}]`	generate a polar plot of radius f as a function of angle t from *tmin* to *tmax*
`PolarPlot[{f`$_1$`, f`$_2$`, ... }, {t, tmin, tmax}]`	generate several polar plots together on the same graph
`PolarListPlot[{r`$_1$`, r`$_2$`, ... }]`	generate a polar plot of radii r_1, r_2, ... at equally spaced angles

Polar plots.

This plots an ellipse and a limacon on the same graph.

In[5]:= `PolarPlot[{4/(2 + Cos[t]), 4 Cos[t] - 2},`
`            {t, 0, 2 Pi}]`

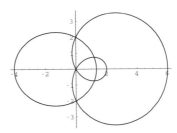

BarChart[*datalist*₁, *datalist*₂, ...]
generate a bar chart of the data sets

GeneralizedBarChart[*datalist*₁, *datalist*₂, ...]
generate a bar chart of the data sets, where the data specify position, height, and width of the bars

StackedBarChart[*datalist*₁, *datalist*₂, ...]
generate a stacked bar chart of the data sets

PercentileBarChart[*datalist*₁, *datalist*₂, ...]
generate a stacked bar chart of the data sets, where the data for each group of bars are scaled so that the absolute values of the heights sum to one

Bar charts.

Graphics`Graphics` has functions for producing a variety of bar charts. Each bar chart function accepts a number of options controlling the style of the charts.

This gives a bar chart comparing two lists of numbers. Note that the lists need not have the same length.

In[6]:= `BarChart[{1, -3, 4, 5, 2, 3}, {3, 6, 4, 3}]`

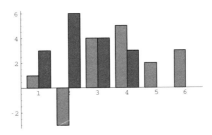

Here the bars are stacked rather than placed side by side.

In[7]:= StackedBarChart[{1, -3, 4, 5, 2, 3},
         {3, 6, 4, 3}]

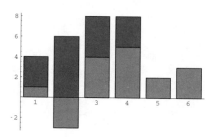

A percentile bar chart scales the stacked bars so that each group has an absolute height of one.

In[8]:= PercentileBarChart[{1, -3, 4, 5, 2, 3},
         {3, 6, 4, 3}]

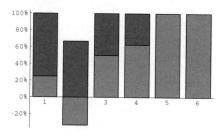

In this chart the bars are explicitly positioned.

In[9]:= GeneralizedBarChart[
         {{1, 3, .2}, {4, 9, 1}, {2.1, -6, .5}},
         {{3, 5, .5}, {1.5, -2, 1}, {-.4, 2, .5}}]

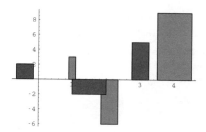

option name	default value	
BarOrientation	Vertical	orientation of bars: Vertical or Horizontal
BarStyle	Automatic	style of bars: describes the style of each bar for a single data set, describes the style of each set for multiple data sets
BarLabels	Automatic	labels to be placed at the group tick mark positions
BarEdges	True	whether edges should be shown with the bars
BarEdgeStyle	Automatic	style for the edges of the bars

Options for any of the bar chart functions.

The bar chart functions accept both special bar chart options and standard graphics options.

This percentile bar chart is created using bar chart options BarStyle and BarOrientation and graphics options Axes and Frame.

```
In[10]:= PercentileBarChart[{1,3,-4,5,3.5,3},
             {-3,2,5,3},
             BarStyle -> {RGBColor[0,1,0],
             RGBColor[1,1,0]},
             BarOrientation -> Horizontal,
             Axes -> False, Frame -> True]
```

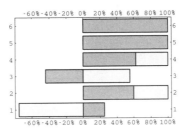

BarValues -> True	label each bar by its value
BarStyle -> *function*	color each bar according to the result obtained by applying function to the bar's height

Options for BarChart and GeneralizedBarChart.

With the functions BarChart and GeneralizedBarChart, BarStyle specifies a function to be applied to the value of a bar, for the purpose of determining the bar's color.

Here the bars are colored according to a BarStyle function that gives one of three different values, depending on bar height.

```
In[11]:= BarChart[{5, 3, 2, -2, 2, 6},
             BarStyle ->
                (Which[
                     # > 4, RGBColor[0,1,0],
                     # < 0, RGBColor[1,0,0],
                     True, RGBColor[1,1,0]]&),
             GridLines -> Automatic
             ]
```

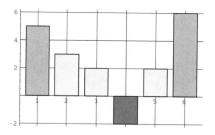

option name	default value	
BarSpacing	Automatic	specify space between each bar, as a fraction of the width of one bar
BarGroupSpacing	Automatic	specify space between each group of bars, as a fraction of the width of one bar (used only in BarChart)

Other bar chart options.

This is an example of using options to create a business chart. Note the use of standard options such as DefaultFont to change the font style.

```
In[12]:= BarChart[{1, 3, 4, 5, 3.5, 3}, {3, 2, 5, 3},
            BarSpacing -> -.3, BarGroupSpacing -> .5,
            BarStyle -> {GrayLevel[.6], Hue[0]},
            BarEdgeStyle ->
                {{Dashing[{.01}],Hue[0]},GrayLevel[0]},
            BarLabels ->
                {"Apr","May","Jun","Jul","Aug","Sep"},
            PlotLabel -> "Projected and Current Profit,
            Tourist Season",
            DefaultFont -> {"Helvetica", 9}
            ]
```

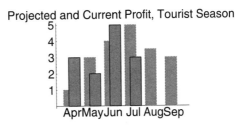

PieChart[*data*]	generate a pie chart of the data

Using PieChart.

PieChart generates a pie chart from a list of positive numbers. Several options are available for controlling the style of the pie.

PieStyle -> *stylelist*	specify styles to be used (cyclically) for the sequence of wedges corresponding to the data points
PieLineStyle -> *linestyle*	specify the style to be used for the lines bordering all wedges
PieLabels -> *lablelist*	labels to be placed (cyclically) on the wedges corresponding to the data points
PieExploded -> All	generate an exploded pie chart
PieExploded -> {*wedge₁*, *wedge₂*, ... }	explode only those wedges indexed by the numbers $wedge_1$, $wedge_2$, ...

Options for PieChart.

The `PieStyle` and `PieLabels` options are applied cyclically if there are not enough styles or labels to correspond with the number of wedges (in the same way that `PlotStyle` works). The `PieLineStyle` option applies equally to all lines in the chart. The `PieExploded` option moves designated wedges away from the center of the chart. The default is `None`, that is, no wedges are moved. You can specify a {*number*, *distance*} pair instead of just the index of a wedge to indicate how far out the wedge should be moved. The wedges are numbered counterclockwise, starting from the middle right.

This combines plots of a pie, an exploded pie, and a partially exploded pie.

```
In[13]:= DisplayTogetherArray[
            PieChart[{.2,.3,.1}],
            PieChart[{.2,.3,.1},
              PieExploded->All],
            PieChart[{.2,.3,.1},
              PieExploded->{{3,.2}}]
          ]
```

A pie may be colored cyclically.

```
In[14]:= PieChart[{.1, .2, .3, .4},
            PieStyle->{
              GrayLevel[.3], GrayLevel[.8]}]
```

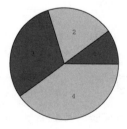

Pie wedges may be labeled.

```
In[15]:= PieChart[{12, 21, 18},
            PieLabels -> {"Joe", "Helen", "Bob"},
            PlotLabel -> "Sales"
         ]
```

DisplayTogether[$plot_1$, $plot_2$, ... , $opts$]	combine the plots that result from the given plot commands in a Graphics object
DisplayTogetherArray[$plotarray$, $opts$]	combine the plots represented by *plotarray* (a nested list of plot commands) in a GraphicsArray object

Displaying plots together.

It is often useful to generate several plots and show them together. The conventional way of doing this is to generate each plot separately with the option DisplayFunction -> Identity and then combine the plots with Show. These functions automate that process. DisplayTogether can be handed any plotting commands that accept DisplayFunction -> Identity as an option. The resulting plots must be able to be combined with Show for this function to be effective. DisplayTogether also accepts options that are suitable for the final output. DisplayTogetherArray accepts the same sort of inputs, but displays them in a GraphicsArray. The input plot commands should be entered in an array whose structure matches that of the desired output array. DisplayTogetherArray accepts options suitable for GraphicsArray.

This is a set of random data following a square law.

```
In[16]:= data = Table[{n/15, (n/15)^2 + 2 + Random[Real,{-.3,.3}]},
            {n, 15}];
```

This fits a linear combination of 1, x, and x^2 to the data.

```
In[17]:= fit = Fit[data, {1, x, x^2}, x]
```

$Out[17]= 1.90847 + 0.644235\,x + 0.452814\,x^2$

This fits a linear combination of 1 and x^3 to the data.

```
In[18]:= altfit = Fit[data, {1,x^3}, x]
```

$Out[18]= 2.13625 + 0.992041\,x^3$

Here the two fitted curves are
combined with a plot of the data.

```
In[19]:=  DisplayTogether[
            Plot[altfit, {x,0,1},
                PlotStyle -> Hue[.6]],
            ListPlot[data,
              PlotStyle -> {Hue[0],
                 PointSize[.03]}],
            Plot[fit, {x,0,1},
              PlotStyle -> {GrayLevel[0],
                 Dashing[{.03}]}]
          ]
```

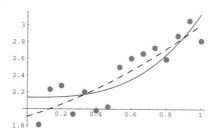

The pie charts previously combined in
a side by side arrangement are
combined here in a different array
arrangement. The structure of the
array in which the chart commands are
input to DisplayTogetherArray is
reflected in the output arrangement of
the charts.

```
In[20]:=  DisplayTogetherArray[
            {{PieChart[{.2,.3,.1}],
              PieChart[{.2,.3,.1},
                 PieExploded -> All]},
            {PieChart[{.2,.3,.1},
                 PieExploded->{{3,.2}}]}
            }
          ]
```

`TextListPlot[{`y_1`, `y_2`, ... }]`	plot y_1, y_2, ... at x values 1, 2, ..., rendering the points as 1, 2, ...
`TextListPlot[{{`x_1`, `y_1`}, {`x_2`, `y_2`}, ... }]`	plot points (x_1, y_1), (x_2, y_2), ..., rendering the points as 1, 2, ...
`TextListPlot[{{`x_1`, `y_1`, `$expr_1$`}, {`x_2`, `y_2`, `$expr_2$`}, ... }]`	plot points (x_1, y_1), (x_2, y_2), ..., rendering the points as $expr_1$, $expr_2$, ...
`LabeledListPlot[{`y_1`, `y_2`, ... }]`	plot y_1, y_2, ... at x values 1, 2, ..., labeling the points as 1, 2, ...
`LabeledListPlot[{{`x_1`, `y_1`}, {`x_2`, `y_2`}, ... }]`	plot points (x_1, y_1), (x_2, y_2), ..., labeling the points as 1, 2, ...
`LabeledListPlot[{{`x_1`, `y_1`, `$expr_1$`}, {`x_2`, `y_2`, `$expr_2$`}, ... }]`	plot points (x_1, y_1), (x_2, y_2), ..., labeling the points as $expr_1$, $expr_2$, ...
`ErrorListPlot[{{`y_1`, `d_1`}, {`y_2`, `d_2`}, ... }]`	generate a list plot with error bars

Variations on `ListPlot`.

`Graphics`Graphics`` also implements a number of `ListPlot` variants. These include some techniques for labeling plots of data, and a function to place error bars on data. The package `Graphics``MultipleListPlot`` has alternatives to these plots and other modifications to the shape of points used in plots of data.

Here the data are defined using the digits of Pi.

```
In[21]:= data = First[RealDigits[N[Pi]]]
Out[21]= {3, 1, 4, 1, 5, 9, 2, 6, 5, 3, 5, 8, 9, 7, 9, 3}
```

The digits of Pi are plotted using the integers 1, 2, 3, ... as plotting symbols.

```
In[22]:= TextListPlot[data]
```

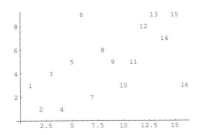

This gives the same plot, except that the integers 1, 2, 3,... serve as labels instead of plotting symbols.

In[23]:= **LabeledListPlot[data]**

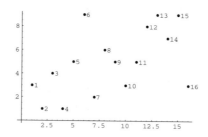

This creates a new list with the magnitude of the error, 1.0, appended to each data pair in expdata.

In[24]:= **erexpdata = Map[Append[#, 1.0]&, expdata]**

Out[24]= {{0.2, 0.530506, 1.}, {0.3, 2.02172, 1.}, {0.4, 1.90648, 1.},
           {0.5, 3.45787, 1.}, {0.6, 4.08852, 1.}, {0.7, 4.35505, 1.},
           {0.8, 5.68323, 1.}, {0.9, 6.23631, 1.}, {1., 7.72731, 1.},
           {1.1, 9.71022, 1.}, {1.2, 13.2113, 1.}}

Here is a plot of the data in expdata with error bars.

In[25]:= **errorp = ErrorListPlot[erexpdata]**

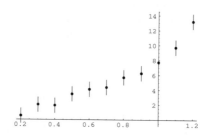

See the package `Graphics`MultipleListPlot`` for another way of plotting error bars that allows multiple data sets and lines between the points, among other features.

✦	Histogram[{x_1, x_2, ... }]	generate a histogram of the raw data
✦	Histogram[{f_1, f_2, ... }, FrequencyData -> True]	
		generate a histogram of the frequency data, where if the category axis cutoffs are given by $c_0, c_1, c_2, ...,$ then f_i is the number of data in the range $c_{j-1} <= x < c_j$

Using `Histogram`.

`Histogram` is used for plotting categorized data frequencies. It gives a bar chart where the width of each bar is proportional to the width of the interval defining the respective category, and the height of the bar is proportional to the frequency with which the data fall in that category. Setting FrequencyData -> True specifies that the data given to Histogram is to be considered not raw data ready for categorization, but frequency data associated with the categories specified by the HistogramCategories option.

This loads a package for generating pseudorandom numbers having a normal distribution.

In[26]:= **Needs["Statistics`NormalDistribution`"]**

Here is a data set normally distributed, with zero mean and unit variance.

In[27]:= **normdata = RandomArray[NormalDistribution[], 100];**

Histogram determines the categories automatically, choosing intervals defined by simple numbers.

In[28]:= **Histogram[normdata]**

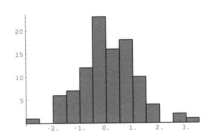

Here is a set of data representing the number of householders in residence for durations of x years, where the categories are $0 <= x < 1$, $1 <= x < 5$, $5 <= x < 10$, $10 <= x < 20$, and $20 <= x < 50$.

In[29]:= **countdata = {6, 39, 30, 27, 24};**

The option HistogramCategories can be used to specify the histogram categories, as defined by a list of cutoffs. Note that when the bar widths are unequal, the bar heights are scaled by the bar widths to give frequency densities.

In[30]:= **Histogram[countdata, FrequencyData->True,**
HistogramCategories -> {0, 1, 5, 10, 20, 50}]

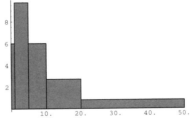

option name	default value	
₊ ApproximateIntervals	Automatic	whether interval boundaries should be approximated by simple numbers; either True, False, or Automatic
₊ FrequencyData	False	whether the data should be considered raw data for which category frequencies are to be found, or whether the data should be considered frequency data for categories specified by HistogramCategories
₊ HistogramCategories	Automatic	specifies the categories in the histogram
₊ HistogramRange	Automatic	specifies the range of data to be included in the histogram
₊ HistogramScale	Automatic	specifies whether the heights of the bars should be scaled so that height measures frequency density or the areas of the bars sum to unity

Special histogram options.

The possible settings for the HistogramCategories option are Automatic, a positive integer n, or a list of cutoffs. If an integer n is specified, then the intervals are taken to be of equal width and to cover the range specified by the HistogramRange option. If ApproximateIntervals -> False, then the histogram will have precisely n categories, but if ApproximateIntervals -> True, the requested number of categories may be adjusted in order to give interval boundaries expressed in terms of simple numbers.

The possible settings for the HistogramRange option are Automatic, which specifies that all data is to be included in the histogram, or {*min*, *max*} which specifies the lower and upper bounds on the data to be included.

The possible settings for the HistogramScale option are Automatic, True, or a positive number m. If Automatic is specified, then the bar heights won't be scaled by the bar widths (yielding frequency densities) unless the bar widths are unequal. Setting HistogramScale -> True will give frequency densities regardless of bar widths, and setting HistogramScale -> m will scale the bar heights so that the areas of the bars sum to m. Setting HistogramScale -> 1 gives a plot approximating the probability density function of the data.

Here `HistogramCategories` specifies the cutoffs used to categorize the normally distributed data. The setting `Ticks -> IntervalCenters` puts ticks at the interval centers, and the setting `HistogramScale -> 1` scales the plot so that the area of the histogram equals unity.

```
In[31]:= Histogram[normdata,
             HistogramCategories ->
             {-3.6, -2.4, -1.4, -.6, 0, .6, 1.4, 2.4, 3.6},
             Ticks -> IntervalCenters, HistogramScale -> 1]
```

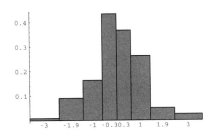

If you plot a histogram of frequency data without specifying the categories, the categories are taken to be of uniform width: $0 <= x < 1$, $1 <= x < 2$, and so on.

```
In[32]:= Histogram[countdata, FrequencyData->True]
```

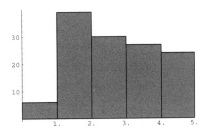

The `Histogram` function accepts special histogram options; special bar chart options, such as `BarEdges`, `BarEdgeStyle`, `BarStyle`, and `BarOrientation`; and standard graphics options like `Ticks`. `Histogram` accepts special `Ticks` settings `IntervalBoundaries` and `IntervalCenters`.

`Ticks -> None`	draw no tick marks
`Ticks -> Automatic`	place tick marks automatically
`Ticks -> IntervalBoundaries`	place ticks at interval boundaries
`Ticks -> IntervalCenters`	place ticks at interval centers
`Ticks -> {xticks, yticks}`	tick mark specifications for each axis

Settings for the `Ticks` option of `Histogram`.

■ Graphics`Graphics3D`

You can do most standard plots in three dimensions using the built-in functions Plot3D, ListPlot3D, and ParametricPlot3D. In certain situations, you may want to display your data in a more specialized format, such as a three-dimensional bar chart or a scatter plot. You may also want special effects, such as shadows or projections. In these cases you can use the functions in this package to produce the appropriate plot.

BarChart3D[{{z_{11}, z_{12}, ... }, {z_{21}, z_{22}, ... }, ... }]
                    make a three-dimensional bar chart using the rectangular array of heights z_{xy}
BarChart3D[{{{z_{11}, $style_{11}$}, {z_{12}, $style_{12}$}, ... }, ... }]
                    use the specified styles

Making three-dimensional bar charts.

This loads the package.

In[1]:= **<<Graphics`Graphics3D`**

This gives a bar chart made from a two-by-three array of bars with integer height.

In[2]:= **BarChart3D[{{1, 2, 3}, {4, 5, 6}}]**

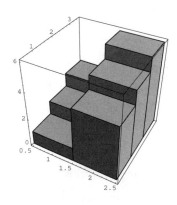

The plot can be redisplayed using any option that can be given for a `Graphics3D` object. This turns off the simulated lighting model and removes the axes and bounding box.

In[3]:= `Show[%, Lighting->False,`
`Boxed->False, Axes->False]`

option name	default value	
XSpacing	0	space between bars in the x direction
YSpacing	0	space between bars in the y direction
SolidBarEdges	True	whether to draw the edges of bars
SolidBarEdgeStyle	GrayLevel[0]	style for edges of bars
SolidBarStyle	GrayLevel[0.5]	style for faces of bars

Options for `BarChart3D`.

`BarChart3D` has the options `XSpacing` and `YSpacing`, which determine the amount of space between bars in the coordinate directions. This must be a number between 0 and 1; the default value is 0. `BarChart3D` returns a `Graphics3D` object. This means you can give any option that can be specified for a `Graphics3D` object. `BarChart3D` has default option settings `Axes -> True` and `BoxRatios -> {1, 1, 1}`.

```
ScatterPlot3D[{{x_1, y_1, z_1}, {x_2, y_2, z_2}, ... }]
                          generate a scatter plot in three dimensions
ScatterPlot3D[{{x_1, y_1, z_1}, {x_2, y_2, z_2}, ... }, PlotJoined -> True]
                          join the points with lines
ListSurfacePlot3D[{{{x_11, y_11, z_11}, {x_12, y_12, z_12}, ... }, ... }]
                          use the array of points in three dimensions to generate
                          vertices in a polygonal mesh
```

Plotting lists of points in three dimensions.

The built-in function ListPlot will take a list of pairs of coordinates and plot them as points in the plane. To plot a list of triples in three dimensions, you can use ScatterPlot3D. To specify a style for the points or curve being displayed, ScatterPlot3D will also accept the PlotStyle option. ListSurfacePlot3D uses an array of points to generate the vertices of polyhedra.

Here is a list of points in three dimensions.

```
In[4]:= lpts = Table[{ t Cos[t],  t Sin[t], t},
                {t, 0, 4Pi, Pi/20}];
```

This produces a scatter plot of the points. They lie on a conical helix.

```
In[5]:= ScatterPlot3D[lpts]
```

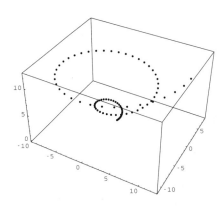

This connects the points with a heavy line.

```
In[6]:= ScatterPlot3D[lpts,
              PlotJoined -> True,
              PlotStyle -> Thickness[0.03]]
```

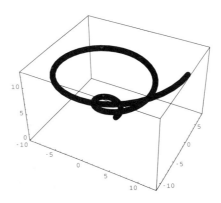

Here is an array of points in three dimensions.

```
In[7]:= apts = Table[{Cos[t] Cos[u], Sin[t] Cos[u],
            Sin[u]}, {t, 0, Pi, Pi/5},
            {u, 0, Pi/2, Pi/10}];
```

The array of points is used to generate vertices in a polygonal mesh. It creates a piece of a sphere.

```
In[8]:= ListSurfacePlot3D[apts]
```

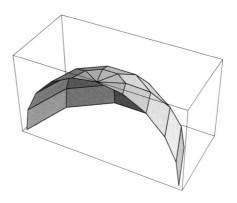

ShadowPlot3D[*f*, {*x*, *xmin*, *xmax*}, {*y*, *ymin*, *ymax*}]
                make a plot of f as a function of x and y, and draw a shadow in the x-y plane

ListShadowPlot3D[{{z_{11}, z_{12}, ... }, {z_{21}, z_{22}, ... }, ... }]
                make a three-dimensional plot of the array of heights z_{xy}, and draw a shadow onto the x-y plane

            Shadow[*g*]   project shadows of the three-dimensional graphics object *g* onto the coordinate planes

Plots with shadows.

ShadowPlot3D and ListShadowPlot3D work exactly like the built-in Plot3D and ListPlot3D, except shadows are drawn.

This puts the shadow in the x-y plane.   *In[9]:=* **ShadowPlot3D[Sin[x y], {x, 0, 3}, {y, 0, 3}]**

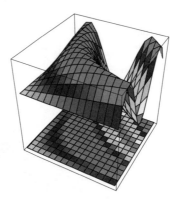

Here is another plot with the shadow moved to the top of the bounding box.

```
In[10]:= ShadowPlot3D[ Exp[-(x^2 + y^2)],
             {x, -2, 2}, {y, -2, 2},
             ShadowPosition -> 1]
```

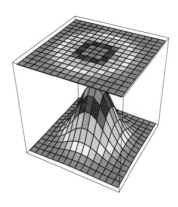

option name	default value	
+ ColorFunction	Hue	function to determine color of surface based on height
SurfaceMesh	True	whether to draw a mesh on the surface
SurfaceMeshStyle	RGBColor[0, 0, 0]	graphics directives to specify the style for the mesh
ShadowMesh	True	whether to draw a mesh on the projection
ShadowMeshStyle	RGBColor[0, 0, 0]	graphics directives to specify the style for the projection
ShadowPosition	-1	whether the projection is above or below the surface

Options for ShadowPlot3D and ListShadowPlot3D.

Shadow has options that determine whether a shadow is drawn in a particular direction. These options are XShadow, YShadow, and ZShadow. The default value for all these options is True. The options XShadowPosition, YShadowPosition, and ZShadowPosition determine whether the projection of the shadow is in the positive or negative coordinate direction. Their default value is -1.

This generates a three-dimensional
graphics object using the built-in
ParametricPlot3D.

In[11]:= **dbell = ParametricPlot3D[**
　　　　　　　{Sin[t], Sin[2t] Sin[u], Sin[2t] Cos[u]},
　　　　　　　{t, -Pi/2, Pi/2}, {u, 0, 2Pi},
　　　　　　　Ticks -> None]

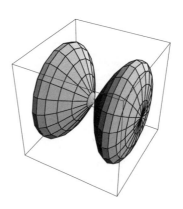

This shows the graphics objects with
projections from the *x* and *y* directions.

In[12]:= **Shadow[dbell, ZShadow -> False]**

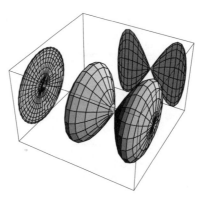

Here is the same object with the *x* shadow moved to the opposite face of the bounding box.

In[13]:= **Shadow[dbell, ZShadow -> False,**
                    XShadowPosition -> 1]

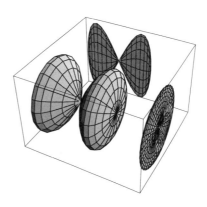

Project[*g*, *pt*]	project the three-dimensional graphics object *g* onto the plane whose normal is the line from the center of *g* to *pt*
Project[*g*, {*e*₁, *e*₂}, *pt*]	project *g* onto the plane spanned by the vectors {e_1, e_2} based at *pt*
Project[*g*, {*e*₁, *e*₂}, *pt*, *origin*]	project in the direction determined by *pt* and *origin*

Projections of three-dimensional graphics objects.

This shows the projection of the dumbbell onto the plane normal to its center and the vector {1, 1, 0}.

In[14]:= **Show[Project[dbell, {1, 1, 0}]]**

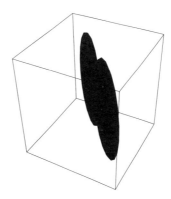

Here is the projection onto another plane.

In[15]:= **Show[Project[dbell, {0, 1, 0}]]**

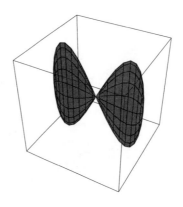

Changing the basis vectors of the projection plane has the effect of rotating it.

In[16]:= **Show[Project[dbell,**
      {{1, 1, 0}, {0, 0, 1}},
      {0, 1, 0}]]

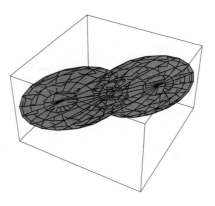

StackGraphics[{g_1, g_2, ... }]	give a Graphics3D object obtained by stacking the two-dimensional graphics objects $g_1, g_2, \ldots$

Stacking graphics.

This generates a list of two-dimensional graphics objects. Setting DisplayFunction->Identity stops Plot from rendering the graphics it produces.

In[17]:= **gtab = Table[**
      Plot[x^n, {x, 0, 5},
        DisplayFunction -> Identity], {n, 5}]

Out[17]= {-Graphics-, -Graphics-, -Graphics-, -Graphics-, -Graphics-}

This shows the graphics stacked in a   *In[18]:=* **Show[StackGraphics[gtab]]**
cube.

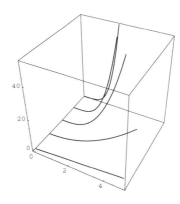

Note that ShadowPlot3D, ListShadowPlot3D, and Shadow all produce *and* display a three-dimensional graphics object. On the other hand, Project and StackGraphics only produce the graphics object. To display the object, you must use Show.

  ✦ Histogram3D[{{x_1, y_1}, {x_2, y_2}, ... }]

                                            generate a histogram of the raw data

  ✦ Histogram3D[{{{f_{11}, f_{12}, f_{13}, ... }, {f_{21}, f_{22}, f_{23}}, ... }, ... }, FrequencyData -> True]

                                            generate a histogram of the frequency data, where if the x-axis cutoffs are given by $c_0, c_1, c_2, ...,$ and the y-axis cutoffs are given by $d_0, d_1, d_2, ...,$ then f_{ij} is the number of data in the range $c_{j-1} <= x < c_j$ and $d_{j-1} <= y < d_j$

Using Histogram3D.

Histogram3D is used for plotting categorized bivariate data frequencies. It gives a solid bar chart where the area of each bar is proportional to the area of the bivariate interval defining the respective category, and the height of the bar is proportional to the frequency with which the data fall in that category. Setting FrequencyData -> True specifies that the data given to Histogram3D is to be considered not raw data ready for categorization, but frequency data for categories specified by HistogramCategories.

This loads a package for generating   *In[19]:=* **Needs["Statistics`MultinormalDistribution`"]**
pseudorandom numbers having a
multinormal distribution.

Here is a data set binormally distributed, with zero mean vector and covariance matrix {{1, .9}, {.9, 1}}.

```
In[20]:=  (binormdist = MultinormalDistribution[{0, 0},
                                                {{1, .9}, {.9, 1}}];
          binormdata = RandomArray[binormdist, 100]);
```

Histogram3D determines the categories automatically, choosing intervals defined by simple numbers.

```
In[21]:=  Histogram3D[binormdata]
```

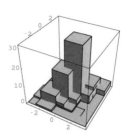

Here is a set of data representing the number of items classified according to bivariate intervals. For example, if the x cutoffs are $c_0, c_1, \ldots$ and the y cutoffs are $d_0, d_1, \ldots$, then there are 4 data counted in the range $c_2 <= x < c_3$ and $d_1 <= y < d_2$.

```
In[22]:=  countdata =
          {{1, 1, 0, 0, 0, 0, 0, 0}, {2, 16, 9, 0, 0, 0, 0, 0},
           {0, 4, 10, 8, 2, 0, 0, 0}, {0, 1, 11, 13, 16, 0, 0, 0},
           {0, 2, 1, 5, 16, 13, 1, 0}, {0, 0, 0, 2, 16, 8, 9, 0},
           {0, 0, 0, 0, 1, 13, 15, 1}, {0, 0, 0, 0, 0, 0, 0, 3}};
```

The option HistogramCategories can be used to specify the histogram categories, as defined by lists of x and y cutoffs.

```
In[23]:=  Histogram3D[countdata, FrequencyData->True,
              HistogramCategories ->
                 {{-3, -2, -1, -.5, 0, .5, 1, 2, 3},
                  {-3, -2, -1, -.5, 0, .5, 1, 2, 3}}]
```

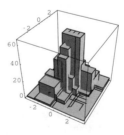

option name	default value	
⊹ ApproximateIntervals	Automatic	whether interval boundaries should be approximated by simple numbers; either True, False, or Automatic
⊹ FrequencyData	False	whether the data should be considered raw data for which category frequencies are to be found, or whether the data should be considered frequency data for categories specified by HistogramCategories
⊹ HistogramCategories	Automatic	specifies the categories in the histogram
⊹ HistogramRange	Automatic	specifies the range of data to be included in the histogram
⊹ HistogramScale	Automatic	specifies whether the heights of the solid bars should be scaled so that height measures frequency density or the volumes of the bars sum to unity

Special histogram options.

The possible settings for the HistogramCategories option are Automatic, a positive integer n, or individual settings for the x and y coordinates $\{hcat_x, hcat_y\}$. If an integer n is specified, then the n bivariate intervals are chosen to cover the range specified by the HistogramRange option. If ApproximateIntervals -> False, then the histogram will have precisely n categories, but if ApproximateIntervals -> True, the requested number of categories may be adjusted in order to give interval boundaries expressed in terms of simple numbers. The individual coordinate settings $hcat_x$ or $hcat_y$ may each be Automatic, a positive integer, or a list of cutoffs.

The possible settings for the HistogramRange option are Automatic or a list $\{hrange_x, hrange_y\}$, where either $hrange_x$ or $hrange_y$ may be set to Automatic or $\{min, max\}$, the latter specifying the lower and upper bounds on the corresponding coordinate of the data to be included in the histogram.

The possible settings for the HistogramScale option are Automatic, True, or a positive number m. If Automatic is specified, then the bar heights won't be scaled by the bar cross-sectional areas (yielding frequency densities) unless the areas are unequal. Setting HistogramScale -> True will give frequency densities regardless of bar areas, and setting HistogramScale -> m will scale the bar heights so that the volumes of the solid bars sum to m. Setting HistogramScale -> 1 gives a plot approximating the probability density function of the data.

Here HistogramCategories specifies the cutoffs used to categorize the binormally distributed data. The setting Ticks -> IntervalBoundaries puts ticks at the interval boundaries, and the setting HistogramScale -> 1 scales the plot so that the volume of the histogram equals unity.

```
In[24]:= Histogram3D[binormdata,
             HistogramCategories ->
             {{-3., -1.5, -.5, 0, .5, 1.5, 3.},
              {-3., -1.5, -.5, 0, .5, 1.5, 3.}},
             Ticks -> IntervalBoundaries, HistogramScale -> 1]
```

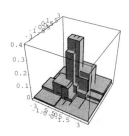

If you plot a bivariate histogram of frequency data without specifying the categories, the categories are taken to have unit area, *i.e.,*
HistogramCategories -> {{0, 1, ... }, {0, 1, ... }}.

```
In[25]:= Histogram3D[countdata, FrequencyData->True]
```

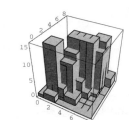

The Histogram3D function accepts special histogram options; special solid bar chart options, such as SolidBarEdges, SolidBarEdgeStyle, and SolidBarStyle; and standard graphics options like Ticks. Histogram3D accepts special Ticks settings IntervalBoundaries and IntervalCenters.

Ticks -> None	draw no tick marks
Ticks -> Automatic	place tick marks automatically
⨍ Ticks -> IntervalBoundaries	place ticks at interval boundaries
⨍ Ticks -> IntervalCenters	place ticks at interval centers
Ticks -> {*xticks*, *yticks*, *zticks*}	tick mark specifications for each axis

Settings for the Ticks option of Histogram3D.

■ Graphics`ImplicitPlot`

There are several ways to specify a curve in the plane. A different plotting function is used for each of these specifications. Graphs of functions are plotted using `Plot`. Curves given parametrically are plotted using `ParametricPlot`. `ImplicitPlot` plots curves that are given implicitly as the solutions to equations.

`ImplicitPlot[`*eqn*`, {`*x*, *xmin*, *xmax*`}]`
               plot the solution to *eqn* using the `Solve` method, with *x* ranging from *xmin* to *xmax*

`ImplicitPlot[`*eqn*`, {`*x*, *xmin*, m_1, m_2, ... , *xmax*`}]`
               plot the solution, avoiding the points m_i

`ImplicitPlot[`*eqn*`, {`*x*, *xmin*, *xmax*`}, {`*y*, *ymin*, *ymax*`}]`
               plot the solution using the `ContourPlot` method

`ImplicitPlot[{`eqn_1, eqn_2, ... `}, `*ranges*, *options*`]`
               plot the solutions to the eqn_i

Plots of curves given implicitly.

There are two methods `ImplicitPlot` can use to plot the solution to the given equations. The method that is used is determined by the form of the variable ranges given. One method uses `Solve` to find solutions to the equation at each point in the *x* range. It carefully avoids dangerous points, plotting to within machine precision of those points, to generate an apparently smooth graph. This is the method used if you just give the range for *x*. The second method treats the equation as a function in three-dimensional space, and generates a contour of the equation cutting through the plane where *z* equals zero. This method is faster than the `Solve` method and handles a greater variety of cases, but may generate rougher graphs, especially around singularities or intersections of the curve. This method is used if you specify a range for both *x* and *y*.

This loads the package.	*In[1]:=* `<< Graphics`ImplicitPlot``
This plots an ellipse using the `Solve` method.	*In[2]:=* `ImplicitPlot[x^2 + 2 y^2 == 3, {x, -2, 2}]`

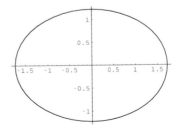

Because range specifications for both x and y are given, the `ContourPlot` method is used.

```
In[3]:= ImplicitPlot[Sin[2 x] + Cos[3 y] == 1,
            {x, -2 Pi, 2 Pi},{y, -2 Pi, 2 Pi},
                PlotPoints->30]
```

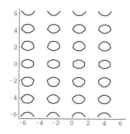

Both methods can accept standard graphics options; the `Solve` method accepts the options of `Plot`, while the `ContourPlot` method accepts `ContourPlot` options.

Here multiple curves are displayed.

```
In[4]:= ImplicitPlot[{(x^2 + y^2)^2 == (x^2 - y^2),
            (x^2 + y^2)^2 == 2 x y}, {x,-2,2},
            PlotStyle->{GrayLevel[0],Dashing[{.03}]}]
```

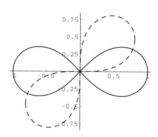

You can find other interesting examples of using a contour plot to do implicit plotting in the book *Exploring Mathematics with Mathematica*, by Theodore Gray and Jerry Glynn (Addison-Wesley, 1991).

■ Graphics ' Legend '

There are two ways to use the functions in this package to place a legend in a graphic; the first can only be used as an option to the built-in function Plot, the second can be applied to any two-dimensional graphic. To use the PlotLegend option to Plot, you simply specify the text for each curve. If there are more curves than text, the text is used cyclically. The second way of placing a legend in a graphic is to use ShowLegend. With ShowLegend you specify the graphic and legend as arguments.

PlotLegend -> {*text*$_1$, *text*$_2$, ... }	option for Plot to place a legend with text for each curve
ShowLegend[*graphic*, *legend*$_1$, *legend*$_2$, ...]	place the *legend*$_i$ in the given graphic
{{{*box*$_1$, *text*$_1$}, ... }, *opts*}	specification of a legend, with color primitives or graphics for the *box*$_i$ and expression suitable for placement in Text primitives in the *text*$_i$
{*colorfunction*, *n*, *minstring*, *maxstring*, *opts*}	specification of a legend with *n* boxes, each colored with the colorfunction; also with optional strings placed by the end boxes

Functions for placing a legend or key in a graphic.

This loads the package.	In[1]:= << Graphics'Legend'

Here are sine and cosine curves with a legend.	In[2]:= Plot[{Sin[x], Cos[x]},
	            {x, -2 Pi, 2 Pi},
	            PlotStyle ->
	                {GrayLevel[0], Dashing[{.03}]},
	            PlotLegend -> {"Sine", "Cosine"}]

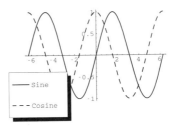

option name	default value	
LegendPosition	{-1, -1}	specify position of legend in relation to graphic, where center of graphic is at {0, 0}
LegendSize	Automatic	give length or {x, y} dimensions in same coordinate system as LegendPosition
LegendShadow	Automatic	None gives no drop shadow for box, {x, y} gives offset for drop shadow
LegendOrientation	Vertical	Horizontal or Vertical, determine the orientation of boxes
LegendLabel	None	label for legend
LegendTextDirection	Automatic	direction text is rotated, as in Text graphics primitive
LegendTextOffset	Automatic	offset of text, as in Text graphics primitive

Options for use with legends.

There are various options that can be used to control the shape and characteristics of a legend. The most important of these is LegendPosition, which places the lower-left corner of a legend box in a position specified by a coordinate system scaled so the center of the graphic is at {0, 0}, and the longest side of the graphic runs from −1 to 1. This same coordinate system is used for LegendSize and LegendShadow.

Here is a density plot with a legend positioned using LegendPosition.

```
In[3]:= ShowLegend[
          DensityPlot[Sin[x y], {x, 0, Pi},
            {y, 0, Pi},
          Mesh -> False, PlotPoints -> 30,
          DisplayFunction -> Identity],
          {GrayLevel[1 - #]&, 10, " 1", "-1",
            LegendPosition -> {1.1, -.4}}]
```

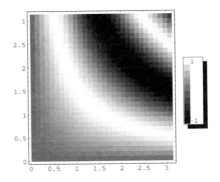

option name	default value	
LegendSpacing	Automatic	space around each key box in the legend, expressed as the ratio of the space to the size of the key box
LegendTextSpace	Automatic	space allocated next to the key boxes for text, expressed as in LegendSpacing
LegendLabelSpace	Automatic	space allocated for the legend label, as in LegendSpacing
LegendBorderSpace	Automatic	space allocated around the entire legend, as in LegendSpacing
LegendBorder	Automatic	style for a border line around the legend box, can only be used if LegendShadow is not None
LegendBackground	Automatic	style for a background to the legend, can only be used if LegendShadow is not None

More options for use with legends.

    Several of the options that determine the amount of blank space around the various elements of a legend accept a number that is the ratio of the size of the space desired to the size of one of the key boxes—the colored boxes that denote a key in the legend. These options include LegendSpacing, LegendTextSpace, LegendLabelSpace, and LegendBorderSpace.

This example uses many of the options
for legends.

```
In[4]:= Plot[{Sin[x], Cos[x]}, {x, 0, 2 Pi},
            PlotStyle -> {GrayLevel[0],
                {GrayLevel[0], Dashing[{.03}]}},
            PlotLegend -> {"sin", "cos"},
            LegendPosition -> {.5, -.7},
            LegendTextSpace -> .5,
            LegendLabel -> "Trig Funcs",
            LegendLabelSpace -> .5,
            LegendOrientation -> Horizontal,
            LegendBackground -> GrayLevel[.5],
            LegendShadow -> {.1, -.2},
            Background -> GrayLevel[.8]]
```

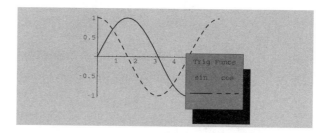

Legend[*legendargs*, *opts*]	give the graphics primitives that describe an individual legend
ShadowBox[*pos*, *size*, *opts*]	give the graphics primitives for a box with a drop shadow

Legend functions that do not display a graphic.

The arguments for Legend are the same as those inside the first set of braces in the description of a legend given in ShowLegend. Using Legend or ShadowBox, you can generate just the graphics primitives of a legend or box with a drop shadow to be used elsewhere in your own graphics.

This represents a box with a shadow.

```
In[5]:= ShadowBox[{0, 0}, {1, 1},
            ShadowBackground -> GrayLevel[.7]]

Out[5]= {GrayLevel[0.7], Rectangle[{0.1, -0.1}, {1.1, 0.9}],
            GrayLevel[1], Rectangle[{0, 0}, {1, 1}], Thickness[0.001],
            GrayLevel[0], Line[{{0, 0}, {1, 0}, {1, 1}, {0, 1}, {0, 0}}]}
```

Here is what the box looks like.   *In[6]:=* **Show[Graphics[%]]**

ShadowOffset -> {*x*, *y*}	give *x* and *y* offset of the shadow from the box
ShadowBackground -> *color*	give the color of the shadow
ShadowForeground -> *color*	give the color of the box with the shadow
ShadowBorder -> *style*	give a graphics primitive or list of primitives denoting the style of the line around the box

Options for ShadowBox.

■ Graphics\`MultipleListPlot\`

MultipleListPlot augments the built-in function ListPlot by providing a convenient way to plot several lists on the same axes, each with a different style of plotting symbol. You can specify error bars with each data point, and a variety of styles for symbol styles exist, including various forms of labeled points.

MultipleListPlot[*list*$_1$, *list*$_2$, ...]	plot the lists of data on the same graph

Plotting several lists.

This loads the package.

```
In[1]:= <<Graphics`MultipleListPlot`
```

Here are some sets of data for use in the examples.

```
In[2]:= (list1 = Table[{x, Sin[2 Pi x]},
                 {x, 0, 1, 0.1}];
         list2 = Table[{x, Cos[2 Pi x]},
                 {x, 0, 1, 0.1}]);
```

This plots the lists on the same graph.

```
In[3]:= MultipleListPlot[list1, list2]
```

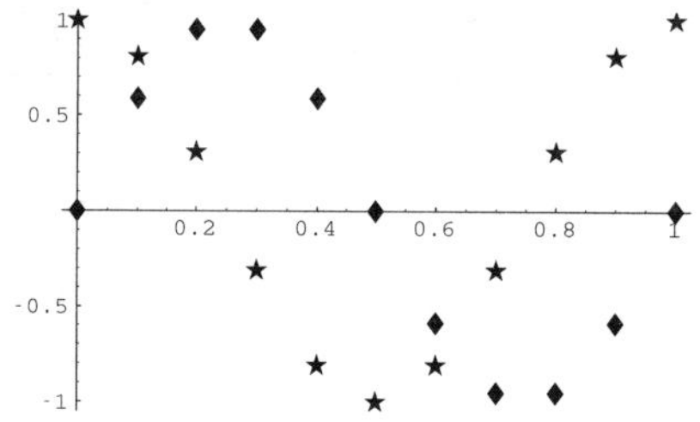

This connects the plotting symbols with lines of different styles.

```
In[4]:= MultipleListPlot[list1, list2,
            PlotJoined -> True]
```

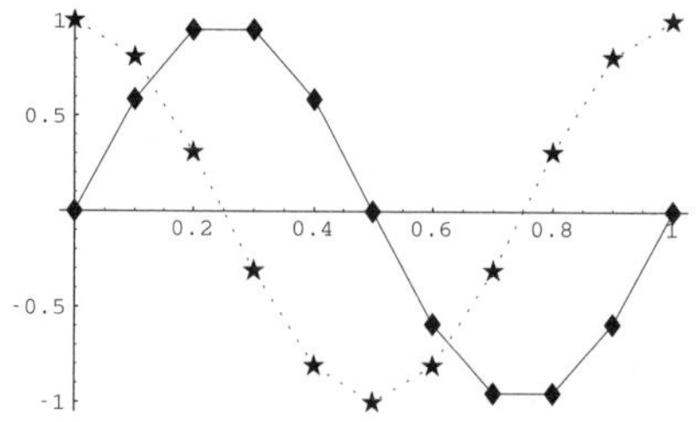

The lines can be drawn for particular lists of data.

`In[5]:= MultipleListPlot[list1, list2,`
`            PlotJoined -> {True, False}]`

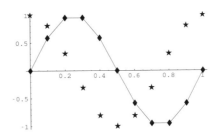

	y	a y value, with the x value determined by the position in the list
	$\{x, y\}$	a point denoted by $\{x, y\}$ coordinates

+	$\{point,$ `ErrorBar[`$yerr$`]`$\}$	a point with an error, where the point may be specified as y or $\{x, y\}$, and the error is $yerr$ in both the positive and negative directions of the y coordinate
+	$\{point,$ `ErrorBar[`$\{negerr, poserr\}$`]`$\}$	a point with different errors in the positive and negative directions
+	$\{point,$ `ErrorBar[`$xerr, yerr$`]`$\}$	a point with errors specified for both the x and y coordinates
+	`ErrorBar[`$\{ymin, ymax\}$`]` or `ErrorBar[`$\{xmin, xmax\}, \{ymin, ymax\}$`]`	
		data given only by a range, where the symbol for the point is drawn at the center of the error bars

Ways to specify a data point in a list of points for `MultipleListPlot`.

There are several ways to specify the points in the data sets. The most basic involve only the locations of the points. If a point is given as a single number, the value is treated as a y value, and the x value is determined by the position of the point in the list of data. If given as a pair $\{x, y\}$, the point is placed at the $\{x, y\}$ coordinates. Each point can be grouped with an error specification, given as an `ErrorBar` object. An `ErrorBar` object can accept a specification of error in the y variable or in both x and y. An error given as a single value indicates the same error in the positive and negative directions; a negative number paired with a positive number indicates a different error in each direction.

This plots a single data set that has points with a variety of error specifications.

```
In[6]:= MultipleListPlot[
        {2,
         {1.5, 3.2},
         {2.5, ErrorBar[0.3]},
         {{4.4, 5.2}, ErrorBar[{-0.5, 0.3}]},
         {{5.5, 2.1}, ErrorBar[{-0.4, 0.3}, {-0.2, 0.5}]} },
        PlotRange -> All,
        Frame -> True]
```

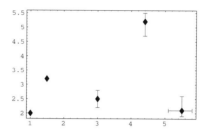

option name	default value	
PlotJoined	False	whether to join points in the data sets; can be a list with one entry for each data set
PlotStyle	Automatic	styles for the lines associated with the data sets
+ SymbolShape	Automatic	shapes for the points in each data set
+ SymbolStyle	Automatic	styles for the points in each data set
+ SymbolLabel	None	labels for the data points
+ PlotLegend	Automatic	if given a list of expressions, draws a legend for the plot with each style labeled by an element of the list
+ ErrorBarFunction	Automatic	a function specifying how to draw error bars

Options for MultipleListPlot.

A variety of characteristics of the plot can be modified by use of options. MultipleListPlot accepts all the usual Graphics and Legend options, as well as the options listed in the preceding table. Legend options are not employed unless PlotLegend is set to a list of labels for the data sets. Most of the options listed in the preceding table, except ErrorBarFunction, cyclically reuse the arguments if given in a list that is not as long as the number of data sets. The default symbol shapes and line styles provide for five data sets before cycling.

The `SymbolShape` option may be set to a list of functions. Each function in the list should accept one argument specifying the location of a data point and should return graphics primitives representing the data point. The `MultipleListPlot` package includes some utilities to make generating these shapes easier, such as `PlotSymbol`, `MakeSymbol`, and `RegularPolygon`. `SymbolShape` can also take `None`, representing no drawn point (for instance, if only a line is desired), and `Label`, where the symbol is a label specified individually for each point by the `SymbolLabel` option.

This uses some options to
`MultipleListPlot`.

```
In[7]:= MultipleListPlot[list1, list2,
            PlotStyle -> {GrayLevel[0], Dashing[{Dot, Dash}]},
            SymbolShape -> {PlotSymbol[Triangle], PlotSymbol[Box]},
            SymbolStyle -> {GrayLevel[0], GrayLevel[.5]}]
```

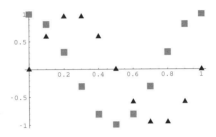

`MultipleListPlot` can automatically generate a legend based on the styles for points and lines. The boxes in the legend are labeled by items from the `PlotLegend` option. All of the standard options to the `Legend` function (detailed in the chapter on the `Graphics `Legend`` package) can be used, including `LegendPosition`, `LegendSize`, `LegendShadow`, and others.

This is a `MultipleListPlot` with a
legend.

```
In[8]:= MultipleListPlot[list1, list2,
            PlotLegend -> {"Sine", "Cosine"},
            PlotJoined -> {False, True}
        ]
```

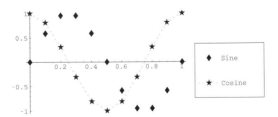

Points can be labeled in a variety of ways. Labels can be placed by each point, or in place of the plotting symbol. Labels can be automatically generated, numbering the data set and the position in that data set. A user-specified function can also be used to automatically generate labels based on the position of the point in the data set.

Here is an example of labeling data
points and using labels for symbols.

```
In[9]:= MultipleListPlot[list1, list2,
            SymbolShape ->
                    {PlotSymbol[Star, Filled -> False], Label},
            SymbolLabel ->
                    {Automatic, {"a", "b", "c", "d", "e"}},
            Frame -> True,
                PlotRange -> All
        ]
```

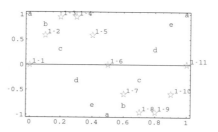

The ErrorBarFunction option can be employed to draw the errors in a different fashion than the standard error bars. For instance, common alternatives are to draw error bars without serifs, or draw the area of the error in a rectangle or ellipse. The user function should take two arguments, where the first is the data point, and the second is an ErrorBar object. The point and error bar will always be completely specified, with the point as {x, y} and the error bar as ErrorBar[*xerr*, *yerr*], no matter what the input form of the data point.

This defines a sample function to use
for drawing the errors.

```
In[10]:= mybarfunc[pt_, ErrorBar[xerr_, yerr_]] :=
            {GrayLevel[0.5],
                Disk[pt, {Max[Abs[xerr]], Max[Abs[yerr]]}]}
```

This plots the error bars as ellipses as
defined by the given function.

```
In[11]:= MultipleListPlot[
            {{{1, 2},      ErrorBar[0.2, 0.4]},
             {{1.5, 3.2},  ErrorBar[0.4, 0.2]},
             {{3, 2.5},    ErrorBar[0.3, 0.1]},
             {{4.4, 5.2},  ErrorBar[.2, {-0.5, 0.3}]},
             {{5.5, 2.1},  ErrorBar[{-0.4, 0.3}, {-0.2, 0.5}]} },
            ErrorBarFunction -> mybarfunc]
```

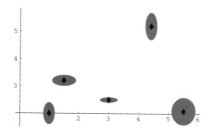

+ PlotSymbol[*type*]	generate a function for a plot symbol of the specified type, where *type* is one of Box, Diamond, Star, or Triangle
+ PlotSymbol[*type*, *size*]	generate a function for a plot symbol of the specified type, with a radius of approximately *size* points
+ PlotSymbol[*type*, Filled -> False]	generate a function for a plot symbol of the specified type, where the symbol is drawn in outline
MakeSymbol[*primitives*]	given a list of graphics primitives, treat the coordinates as offsets from an input point and return a function that can be used to draw a symbol

Specification of some standard plotting symbols.

Some standard plot symbols are supplied for use with the SymbolShape option. These symbols can be drawn with a particular size and can also be drawn in outline. Completely arbitrary symbols can be constructed by applying MakeSymbol to a list of graphics primitives. The coordinates for the symbol are treated as offsets (in the Offset coordinate system) from the data point.

This is an example using some of the ways of creating additional plot symbols.

```
In[12]:= MultipleListPlot[
        Range[7],
        Table[3.5, {7}],
        Sqrt[Range[7]],
      SymbolShape ->
        {PlotSymbol[Triangle],
         MakeSymbol[RegularPolygon[5, 3]],
         MakeSymbol[
           {Line[{{2, 2}, {-2, -2}}],
            Line[{{-2, 2}, {2, -2}}]}]
          ]}
        ]
```

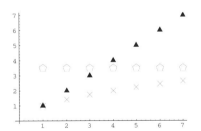

RegularPolygon[*n*]	generate a regular *n*-sided polygon
RegularPolygon[*n*, *rad*]	use radius *rad*
RegularPolygon[*n*, *rad*, *ctr*]	use center *ctr*
RegularPolygon[*n*, *rad*, *ctr*, *tilt*]	
	tilt the *n*-sided polygon counterclockwise by angle *tilt*
RegularPolygon[*n*, *rad*, *ctr*, *tilt*, *k*]	
	connect every *k* vertices

Generating regular polygon symbols.

Additional plotting symbols can be created using the functions MakeSymbol and RegularPolygon. RegularPolygon generates a list of graphics primitives corresponding to shapes based on the regular polyhedra. MakeSymbol is applied to the primitives to create a plotting symbol. As an example, if you give a specification
SymbolShape -> {MakeSymbol[RegularPolygon[*m*]], MakeSymbol[RegularPolygon[*n*]]}, your first list will be plotted using regular *m*-sided polygons, the second list using regular *n*-sided polygons, the third list using *m*-sided polygons again, etc.

This displays a seven-pointed star.

```
In[13]:= Show[Graphics[
              RegularPolygon[7, 2, {0, 0}, 0, 3],
          AspectRatio -> Automatic]]
```

~ Dashing[{Dot, Dash, LongDash, ... }], AbsoluteDashing[{Dot, ... }]	
	specify a dashing pattern as a combination of dots, dashes, and long dashes

Specifying dashing styles.

The MultipleListPlot package enhances the Dashing and AbsoluteDashing styles to allow easy specification of dashing patterns in terms of dots, dashes, and long dashes.

This is a graphic demonstrating some possible dashing patterns.

```
In[14]:= Show[Graphics[MapIndexed[
           {#1, Line[{{0, -First[#2]}, {1, -First[#2]}}]}&,
           {Dashing[{Dot}],
            Dashing[{Dot, Dash}],
            Dashing[{Dot, Dash, Dot, LongDash}],
            Dashing[{Dot, Dot, Dash}]
           }
         ]]]
```

■ Graphics`ParametricPlot3D`

ParametricPlot3D is a built-in function for producing three-dimensional space curves and surfaces, parameterized by one or two coordinates respectively. The option PlotPoints allows you to specify the number of sample points used. This package extends ParametricPlot3D by providing an alternative to the PlotPoints option where the sampling may be specified by giving a step size in each coordinate. The package also introduces PointParametricPlot3D for plotting either one- or two-parameter sets of points in space.

ParametricPlot3D[$\{f_x, f_y, f_z\}$, $\{u, u_0, u_1, du\}$, $\{v, v_0, v_1, dv\}$]	generate a parametric plot of a surface in three dimensions using increments du and dv
PointParametricPlot3D[$\{f_x, f_y, f_z\}$, $\{u, u_0, u_1, du\}$]	plot a one-parameter set of points in three dimensions
PointParametricPlot3D[$\{f_x, f_y, f_z\}$, $\{u, u_0, u_1, du\}$, $\{v, v_0, v_1, dv\}$]	plot a two-parameter set of points

Parametric plots in three dimensions.

This loads the package.

In[1]:= `<<Graphics`ParametricPlot3D``

This gives the plot of a sphere using a mesh of long, thin rectangles.

In[2]:= `ParametricPlot3D[`
`    {Cos[u] Cos[v], Sin[u] Cos[v], Sin[v]},`
`    {u, 0, 2Pi, Pi/20},`
`    {v, -Pi/2, Pi/2, Pi/10}]`

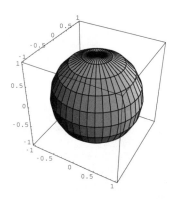

Only a collection of points is shown when you use PointParametricPlot3D.

```
In[3]:= PointParametricPlot3D[
          {Cos[u] Cos[v], Sin[u] Cos[v], Sin[v]},
          {u, 0, 2Pi }, {v, -Pi/2, Pi/2 }]
```

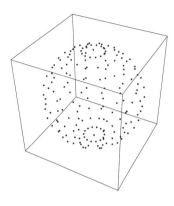

CylindricalPlot3D and SphericalPlot3D plot functions given in cylindrical and spherical coordinates, respectively. The names given to the variables in spherical coordinates vary in the literature. The convention used here is that the angle theta is measured from the positive *z* axis, and the angle phi is measured in the *x-y* plane from the positive *x* axis.

SphericalPlot3D[*r*, {*theta*, *thetamin*, *thetamax*}, {*phi*, *phimin*, *phimax*}]
              generate a plot in three dimensions of *r* as a function of the angles *theta* and *phi*

CylindricalPlot3D[*z*, {*r*, *rmin*, *rmax*}, {*theta*, *thetamin*, *thetamax*}]
              plot *z* as a function of the radius *r* and the angle *theta*

Functions for plotting in three dimensions.

Here is a sphere of radius 2. It is very simple to represent in spherical coordinates.

In[4]:= **SphericalPlot3D[2,**
{theta, 0, Pi}, {phi, 0, 2Pi}]

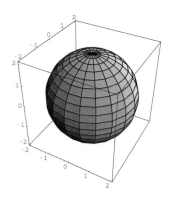

In this plot, the height is given by $(1 + \text{Sin[phi]})r^2$. Polar coordinates are used in the plane.

In[5]:= **CylindricalPlot3D[(1 + Sin[phi]) r^2,**
{r, 0, 1}, {phi, 0, 2Pi}]

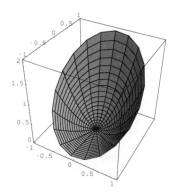

You can use any option that can be
given for Graphics3D.

```
In[6]:= CylindricalPlot3D[ (1 + Sin[phi]) r^2,
           {r, 0, 1}, {phi, 0, 2Pi},
             Boxed -> False, Axes -> False,
             ViewPoint -> {1.5, -0.5, .2}]
```

■ Graphics`PlotField`

Anything that assigns a magnitude and direction at each point gives a vector field. Examples include the electromagnetic field and the velocity field of a fluid. Any ordinary differential equation can be used to define a vector field. These vector fields can be visualized by drawing arrows representing the vectors. The direction of the arrow is equal to the direction of the vector field at its base point. The magnitude of the arrow is proportional to the magnitude of the vector field.

This package plots two-dimensional vector fields. For vector field plots in three dimensions, use the package Graphics`PlotField3D`.

PlotVectorField[{f_x, f_y}, {x, $xmin$, $xmax$}, {y, $ymin$, $ymax$}]	plot the vector field given by the vector-valued function in the range specified
PlotGradientField[f, {x, $xmin$, $xmax$}, {y, $ymin$, $ymax$}]	plot the gradient vector field of the scalar-valued function f
PlotHamiltonianField[f, {x, $xmin$, $xmax$}, {y, $ymin$, $ymax$}]	plot the Hamiltonian vector field of the scalar-valued function f

Plotting vector fields in two dimensions.

This loads the package.	`In[1]:= <<Graphics`PlotField``
The two components of this vector field are given by sin(x) and cos(y).	`In[2]:= PlotVectorField[{Sin[x], Cos[y]}, {x, 0, Pi}, {y, 0, Pi}]`

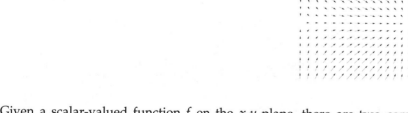

Given a scalar-valued function f on the x-y plane, there are two common ways of constructing a vector field. The function's gradient vector field has first and second components given by $\frac{\partial f}{\partial x}$ and $\frac{\partial f}{\partial y}$, respectively. The two components of the function's Hamiltonian vector field are $\frac{\partial f}{\partial y}$ and $-\frac{\partial f}{\partial x}$. The gradient field gives the direction in which the function is increasing most rapidly. If one treats the function as the Hamiltonian of a mechanical system, the Hamiltonian vector field gives the equations of motion in phase space.

PlotGradientField and PlotHamiltonianField compute formulas for the partial derivatives of the scalar-valued function given as an argument. This means that the functions you give must be such that *Mathematica* can compute their derivatives.

Here is the gradient field of the potential $x^2 + y^2$.

In[3]:= **PlotGradientField[x^2 + y^2,
        {x, -3, 3}, {y, -3, 3}]**

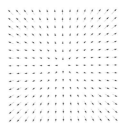

In the plane, the gradient and Hamiltonian vector fields of the same function are always orthogonal.

In[4]:= **PlotHamiltonianField[x^2 + y^2,
        {x, -3, 3}, {y, -3, 3}]**

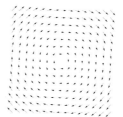

option name	default value	
ScaleFactor	Automatic	linearly rescales the vectors so the longest vector is equal to this value; Automatic fits the vectors in the mesh, None eliminates the rescaling
ScaleFunction	None	a function to use for rescaling the magnitude of vectors
MaxArrowLength	None	length of the largest vector to be drawn, applied after the ScaleFunction but before the ScaleFactor
ColorFunction	None	a function to use for coloring the vectors by their magnitude
PlotPoints	15	the number of evaluation points in each direction

Options for vector field plotting.

This increases the number of sample points in each direction to 20 and draws each vector at half its true magnitude.

```
In[5]:= PlotVectorField[{Sin[x y], Cos[x y]},
        {x, 0, Pi}, {y, 0, Pi},
        PlotPoints -> 20,
        ScaleFunction -> (.5#&),
        ScaleFactor -> None]
```

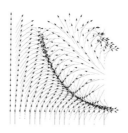

There are a variety of options to control the display of the vectors. Three of them control aspects of the scaling of the vector magnitudes. They are applied in the order ScaleFunction, MaxArrowLength, and ScaleFactor. The ScaleFunction can be a pure function that takes the magnitude of the vector, and returns the new magnitude for that vector. It can also be None, specifying no rescaling by this option. If its application results in a nonnumeric value, the vector is set to zero magnitude. Next, MaxArrowLength eliminates any vectors that are longer than the specified value after the application of the ScaleFunction. It can also be set to None, so no vectors are removed. Finally, the ScaleFactor is applied. It linearly scales the remaining vectors so that the length of the longest one is equal to the specified value. If `ScaleFactor` is set to `Automatic`, then, in the field plotting functions, the longest vector will be sized to the grid increment, so the head of any given vector will not cover the base of any adjacent vector. If it is set to `None`, no rescaling due to this option will occur.

Thus, the `ScaleFunction` option is best used to change the relative magnitudes of the vectors, while the `ScaleFactor` is best used for linear scaling of the vectors when you know the desired length of the longest vector. If you want to perform linear rescaling of the vector lengths without specifying the longest vector, set `ScaleFactor` to `None`, as in the preceding example. `MaxArrowLength` is best for removing unusual outliers, or filtering out all longer vectors so fine changes in the field can be better observed.

All of the two-dimensional vector plots also accept the same options as the `Arrow` primitive; all the arrows in the plot will use these options.

A complex-valued function of a complex argument can be viewed as a vector field on the plane by using the real and complex parts of a complex number to give two coordinates. This is essentially the Polya representation of such a function. However, in the Polya representation the magnitude is scaled using `ScaleFunction -> (Log[# + 1]&)` and the negative of the imaginary part is used.

`PlotPolyaField[f, {x, xmin, xmax}, {y, ymin, ymax}]`   plot the complex-valued function *f* using the Polya representation

Plotting the Polya representation of a complex-valued function.

The complex function $z^4 - 1$ has zeros at the fourth roots of unity, so the magnitude of the vector field is small near these points.

In[6]:= `PlotPolyaField[(x + I y)^4 - 1,`
                `{x, 0, 3}, {y, 0, 3}]`

```
ListPlotVectorField[{{vect₁₁, vect₁₂, ... }, {vect₂₁, vect₂₂, ... }, ... }]
```
make a vector field plot of the rectangular array of vectors
$vect_{xy}$
```
ListPlotVectorField[{{pt₁, vect₁}, {pt₂, vect₂}, ... }]
```
display a list of vectors based at the given points

Vector field plots of lists.

This gives an array of random vectors.

```
In[7]:= varray = Table[
            {Random[Real, {-0.7, 0.7}],
              Random[Real, {-0.7, 0.7}]},
                 {i, 10}, {j, 10}];
```

This displays the array of vectors in a
plot.

```
In[8]:= ListPlotVectorField[varray]
```

This generates a list of vectors as
{*base*, *vector*} pairs.

```
In[9]:= vectors = Table[
            {{Sin[u], Cos[u]}, {u^2 Sin[2u], u^2 Cos[2u]}},
              {u, 0, 2 Pi, Pi/16}];
```

Here are the vectors without any
scaling applied.

```
In[10]:= ListPlotVectorField[
             vectors,
             ScaleFactor -> None,
             Frame -> True
           ]
```

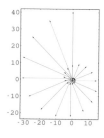

Here are the vectors with the longest vector scaled to a length of 1, and all other vectors scaled proportionately.

```
In[11]:= ListPlotVectorField[
            vectors,
            ScaleFactor -> 1,
            Frame -> True
         ]
```

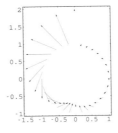

In this plot, the vectors are all scaled by a function that converts their lengths to a constant.

```
In[12]:= ListPlotVectorField[
            vectors,
            ScaleFunction->(.4&),
            Frame -> True]
```

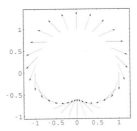

Note that ListPlotVectorField treats the option ScaleFactor -> Automatic the same as ScaleFactor -> None.

■ Graphics `PlotField3D`

This package allows the graphical display of vector fields in three dimensions. The vector field can be represented by lines or arrows that can display direction and magnitude.

PlotVectorField3D[$\{f_x, f_y, f_z\}$, $\{x, xmin, xmax\}$, $\{y, ymin, ymax\}$, $\{z, zmin, zmax\}$]
        plot the vector field given by the vector function in the range specified

PlotGradientField3D[f, $\{x, xmin, xmax\}$, $\{y, ymin, ymax\}$, $\{z, zmin, zmax\}$]
        plot the gradient vector field of the scalar function f

Plotting vector fields in three dimensions.

This loads the package.

In[1]:= **<<Graphics`PlotField3D`**

The components of this vector field are given by y/z, $-x/z$, and 0.

In[2]:= **PlotVectorField3D[{y , -x, 0}/z ,
        {x, -1, 1}, {y, -1, 1}, {z, 1, 3}]**

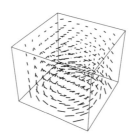

The gradient of a scalar function f is the vector field with components given by $\frac{\partial f}{\partial x}$, $\frac{\partial f}{\partial y}$, and $\frac{\partial f}{\partial z}$, respectively. PlotGradientField computes formulas for the partial derivatives and generates a vector field plot. Thus the function f must be such that *Mathematica* can compute its derivatives.

Here is the gradient field of the scalar function *xyz*.

In[3]:= **PlotGradientField3D[
        x y z, {x, -1, 1}, {y, -1, 1}, {z,-1,1}]**

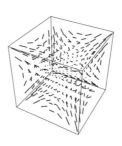

option name	default value	
ScaleFactor	Automatic	the scale of the vectors to the mesh; Max ensures that the largest vector fits in the mesh
ScaleFunction	None	the function to use for rescaling the magnitude of vectors
MaxArrowLength	None	determine the largest vector to be drawn
ColorFunction	None	the colors to use
PlotPoints	7	the number of evaluation points in each direction
VectorHeads	False	whether to draw vectors with heads

Options for vector field plotting.

This sets the number of sample points in each direction to 5 and puts heads on the arrows.

```
In[4]:= PlotVectorField3D[{x , y, z}, {x, 0, 2},
        {y, 0, 2}, {z, 0, 2}, PlotPoints -> 5,
        VectorHeads -> True]
```

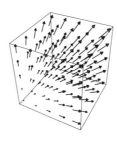

A variable range specification of the form $\{x, xmin, xmax, dx\}$ adjusts the evaluation grid by specifying step sizes of dx in the x direction. An analogous specification in the y and z ranges will adjust the evaluation grid in those directions. You can also adjust the evaluation grid by setting the PlotPoints option.

ListPlotVectorField3D[{{pt_1, $vect_1$}, {pt_2, $vect_2$}, ... }]   plot a list of vectors based at the given points

Vector field plots from lists.

This gives an array of random vectors.

```
In[5]:= array = Flatten[
            Table[ {{i, j, k},
                {Random[Real, {-1, 1}],
                 Random[Real, {-1, 1}],
                 Random[Real, {-1, 1}]}},
                {i, 7}, {j, 7}, {k, 7}], 2];
```

This displays the vectors.

```
In[6]:= ListPlotVectorField3D[array]
```

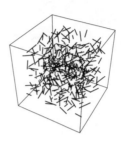

It is often hard to arrange the number of points to have enough samples without making the image overly complex. One way to overcome this is to construct an animation that rotates the whole image.

■ Graphics`Polyhedra`

A Platonic solid is a convex polyhedron whose faces and vertices are all of the same type. There are five such solids. There are also a few nonconvex polyhedra known that have faces and vertices all of the same type. This package contains the graphics primitives necessary for rendering these solids.

Show[Polyhedron[*polyname*]]	display the named polyhedron
Show[Polyhedron[*polyname*, {*x*, *y*, *z*}, *scale*]]	center the polygon at the point {*x*, *y*, *z*} with the size given by *scale*

Displaying the regular polyhedra.

Tetrahedron	Hexahedron
Cube	GreatDodecahedron
Octahedron	SmallStellatedDodecahedron
Dodecahedron	GreatStellatedDodecahedron
Icosahedron	GreatIcosahedron

Polyhedra.

This loads the package.

In[1]:= **<<Graphics`Polyhedra`**

This displays a dodecahedron centered at the origin.

In[2]:= **Show[Polyhedron[Dodecahedron]]**

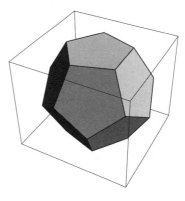

This displays two polyhedra simultaneously. The diameter of the icosahedron is reduced by a factor of 0.7 and its center is moved to the point {3, 3, 3}.

```
In[3]:= Show[
          Polyhedron[GreatStellatedDodecahedron],
          Polyhedron[Icosahedron, {3, 3, 3}, 0.7]
        ]
```

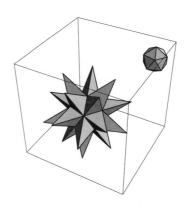

```
Show[Stellate[Polyhedron[polyname]]]
                    display a stellated polyhedron

Show[Stellate[Polyhedron[polyname], ratio]]
                    display a stellated polyhedron with stellation ratio ratio

Show[Geodesate[Polyhedron[polyname], n]]
                    display the projection of the order n regular tessellation of
                    each face of the polyhedron onto the circumscribed sphere

Show[Geodesate[Polyhedron[polyname], n, {x, y, z}, radius]]
                    display the projection of the order n regular tessellation of
                    each face of the polyhedron onto the circumscribed sphere
                    having center {x, y, z} and size radius

Show[Truncate[Polyhedron[polyname]]]
                    display a truncated polyhedron

Show[Truncate[Polyhedron[polyname], ratio]]
                    display a truncated polyhedron with the polygon edges
                    truncated by the ratio ratio

Show[OpenTruncate[Polyhedron[polyname]]]
                    display a truncated polyhedron without the polygons that
                    close the truncated vertices

Show[OpenTruncate[Polyhedron[polyname], ratio]]
                    display a truncated polyhedron with edges truncated by the
                    ratio ratio without the polygons that close the truncated
                    vertices
```

Transformation functions for the regular polyhedra.

The polyhedra are by default centered at the origin with a unit distance from the origin to the midpoint of the edges. Any of the convex solids can be stellated using `Stellate`. This replaces each of the polygon faces by a pyramid with the polygon as its base. The user can also adjust the stellation ratio. Note that ratios less than 1 give concave figures and that the default value of this ratio is 2. `Geodesate` triangulates five-sided or greater polygons before projecting onto the circumscribed sphere. If the order n of the regular tessellation of each face is not given, a default value of 2 is assumed. The default position of the sphere is {0,0,0} with radius 1. `Truncate` and `OpenTruncate` act on every polygon and truncate at each vertex of the polygon. The default value of the truncation ratio is 0.3.

Here is a stellated octahedron with stellation ratio equal to 4.0. This gives very long points.

In[4]:= **Show[Stellate[Polyhedron[Octahedron], 4.0]]**

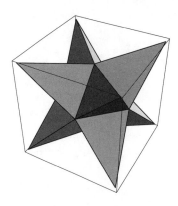

Here is an example of a polyhedron that is triangulated before being projected onto the circumscribed sphere.

In[5]:= **Show[Geodesate[Polyhedron[Dodecahedron], 4]]**

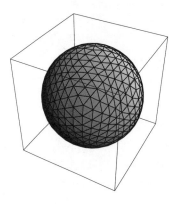

Here is a an example of a polyhedron with edges truncated on each side by 40 percent.

In[6]:= **Show[Truncate[**
 Polyhedron[Dodecahedron], .4]]

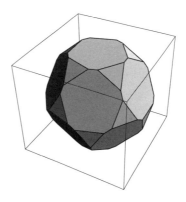

OpenTruncate allows you to view the interior of the truncated polyhedron.

In[7]:= **Show[OpenTruncate[**
 Polyhedron[Dodecahedron], .4]]

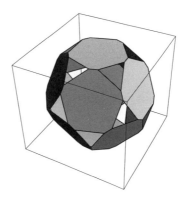

Polyhedron converts the polygon list corresponding to the name of a polyhedron into a Graphics3D object. You can extract the polygon list from the Graphics3D object using First. In addition, Vertices and Faces give you the vertex coordinates and the vertices comprising each face of the polyhedra.

First[Polyhedron[*polyname*]]	give the list of polygons for the named polyhedron
Vertices[*polyname*]	give a list of the coordinates of the vertices of the polyhedron
Faces[*polyname*]	give a list of the vertices associated with each face

Getting face and vertex data.

Here is the list of polygons for the tetrahedron centered at the origin.

In[8]:= **First[Polyhedron[Tetrahedron]]**

Out[8]= {Polygon[{{0., 0., 1.73205}, {0., 1.63299, -0.57735},
            {-1.41421, -0.816497, -0.57735}}], Polygon[
            {{0., 0., 1.73205}, {-1.41421, -0.816497, -0.57735},
            {1.41421, -0.816497, -0.57735}}], Polygon[
            {{0., 0., 1.73205}, {1.41421, -0.816497, -0.57735},
            {0., 1.63299, -0.57735}}], Polygon[
            {{0., 1.63299, -0.57735}, {1.41421, -0.816497, -0.57735},
            {-1.41421, -0.816497, -0.57735}}]}

These are the vertices of the tetrahedron.

In[9]:= **Vertices[Tetrahedron]**

Out[9]= $\left\{ \{0, 0, \sqrt{3}\}, \left\{0, 2\sqrt{\dfrac{2}{3}}, -\dfrac{1}{\sqrt{3}}\right\}, \left\{-\sqrt{2}, -\sqrt{\dfrac{2}{3}}, -\dfrac{1}{\sqrt{3}}\right\}, \right.$

$\left. \left\{\sqrt{2}, -\sqrt{\dfrac{2}{3}}, -\dfrac{1}{\sqrt{3}}\right\} \right\}$

This shows which vertices are associated with which face. For example, the second face has the first, third, and fourth vertices as its corners.

In[10]:= **Faces[Tetrahedron]**

Out[10]= {{1, 2, 3}, {1, 3, 4}, {1, 4, 2}, {2, 4, 3}}

■ Graphics`Shapes`

One of the most powerful aspects of graphics in *Mathematica* is the availability of three-dimensional graphics primitives such as Polygon and Cuboid. You can create three-dimensional graphics objects simply by specifying a list of these primitives. This package provides lists of polygons for some common three-dimensional shapes.

Show[Graphics3D[*shape*]]	display the specified shape

Displaying a three-dimensional shape.

This loads the package.

```
In[1]:= <<Graphics`Shapes`
```

Using Short we can look at a skeleton version of the polygon list for a cone.

```
In[2]:= Short[ Cone[ ], 5]
```

```
Out[2]//Short=
    {Polygon[{{1., 0., -1.},
        {0.951057, 0.309017, -1.}, {0., 0., 1.}}], «18»,
        Polygon[{{0.951057, -0.309017, -1.}, «1», {0., 0., 1.}}]}
```

This displays a torus with default values for all parameters.

```
In[3]:= Show[Graphics3D[ Torus[ ] ]]
```

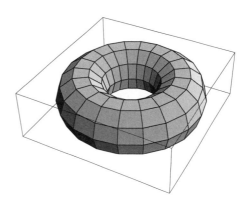

Each of the shapes can take various parameters as arguments. These parameters adjust things such as the radii, height, and size of the polygon mesh. If you do not give any arguments, you get the shape with all default values for the parameters. Thus, for example, Torus[ ] gives a torus with default values for the radius, height, and polygon mesh.

Cylinder[r, h, n]	cylinder with radius r and half height h drawn using n polygons
Cone[r, h, n]	cone with radius r and half height h drawn using n polygons
Torus[r_1, r_2, n, m]	torus with radii r_1 and r_2 drawn using an n by m mesh
Sphere[r, n, m]	sphere with radius r drawn using $n(m-2)+2$ polygons
MoebiusStrip[r_1, r_2, n]	Möbius strip with radii r_1 and r_2 drawn using $2n$ polygons
Helix[r, h, m, n]	helix with radius r, half height h and m turns drawn using an n by m mesh
DoubleHelix[r, h, m, n]	double helix with radius r, half height h and m turns drawn using an n by m mesh

Shapes.

This gives a Möbius strip with a fine mesh.

In[4]:= **Show[Graphics3D[MoebiusStrip[2, 1, 80]]]**

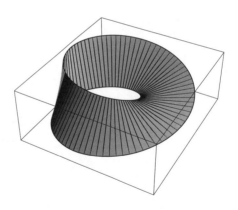

Cone[1, 1, 20]	MoebiusStrip[1, 0.5, 20]
Cylinder[1, 1, 20]	Sphere[1, 20, 15]
DoubleHelix[1, 0.5, 2, 20]	Torus[1, 0.5, 20, 10]
Helix[1, 0.5, 2, 20]	

Shapes with default values of parameters.

You can adjust the position, orientation, and scale of any shape by using `TranslateShape`, `RotateShape`, and `AffineShape`. These functions work by transforming all the coordinates of points given in the polygon list. For example, `RotateShape` multiplies all the coordinates in the polygon list by a specified rotation matrix.

`RotateShape[`*g*`, `*phi*`, `*theta*`, `*psi*`]`	rotate the graphics object *g* by the specified Euler angles
`TranslateShape[`*g*`, {`*x*`, `*y*`, `*z*`}]`	translate the graphics object by the specified vector
`AffineShape[`*g*`, {`*scale*₁`, `*scale*₂`, `*scale*₃`}]`	multiply all coordinates by the respective scale factors

Geometric operations on three-dimensional graphics objects.

This rotates the Möbius strip by the Euler angles Pi/4, Pi/3 and Pi/2.

```
In[5]:= Show[RotateShape[
            Graphics3D[MoebiusStrip[ ] ],
            Pi/4, Pi/3, Pi/2]]
```

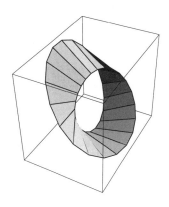

This translates the helix with the smaller radius a distance of 1.5 in the positive *x* direction. The helix with the larger radius has twice as many turns.

```
In[6]:= Show[TranslateShape[
            Graphics3D[ Helix[0.5, 0.5, 2, 20] ],
                {1.5, 0, 0}],
            Graphics3D[ Helix[1, 0.5, 4, 20] ]]
```

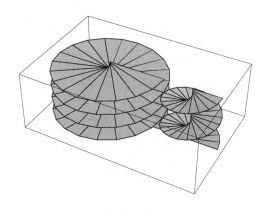

WireFrame[*g*]   show all polygons as transparent

Making polygons appear transparent.

WireFrame as well as TranslateShape, RotateShape, and AffineShape will work on any Graphics3D object that contains the primitives Polygon, Line, and Point.

WireFrame replaces all the polygon specifications by their edges.

```
In[7]:= WireFrame[
            Polygon[{{1, 0, 0}, {0, 1, 0}, {0, 0, 1}}]]
```

Out[7]= -Graphics3D-

This gives a wire frame in the shape of a cone.

In[8]:= **Show[WireFrame[Graphics3D[Cone[ ]]],**
                    Boxed->False]

■ Graphics`Spline`

Spline[*points*, *type*]	a spline curve graphics primitive
Spline[*points*, *type*, *internal*]	an evaluated spline, with information cached for faster rendering

A spline graphics primitive.

This package takes the functions from NumericalMath`SplineFit` and adapts them to a graphics primitive. Currently, three types of splines are supported: Cubic, Bezier, and CompositeBezier. See the documentation for the NumericalMath`SplineFit` package for more information about the various types of splines.

This loads the package.

```
In[1]:= <<Graphics`Spline`
```

Here is a list of points.

```
In[2]:= pts =
        {{0, 0}, {1, 2}, {-1, 3}, {0, 1}, {3, 0}};
```

This is a graph of the cubic Spline primitive combined with other primitives. Here a line of a different color connects the points making up the spline.

```
In[3]:= Show[
        Graphics[{Hue[0], Line[pts], GrayLevel[0],
          Spline[pts, Cubic]}],
        PlotRange -> All]
```

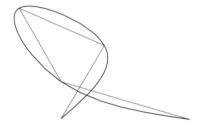

Compare the cubic spline of the previous example to a Bezier spline.

```
In[4]:= Show[
        Graphics[{Hue[0], Line[pts], GrayLevel[0],
          Spline[pts, Bezier]}],
        PlotRange -> All]
```

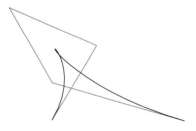

option name	default value	
SplineDots	None	style to render interpolation or control points of curve
SplinePoints	25	initial number of points sampled in default rendering of spline
MaxBend	10.	maximum angle between successive segments when using adaptive rendering
SplineDivision	20.	maximum amount of subdivision to be used in attempting to generate a smooth curve

Options for Spline.

The spline graphics primitive has an option allowing the control points to be shown. By setting the SplineDots option to a style primitive (or list of style primitives), you can control the characteristics of these points. Setting it to None will suppress the display of the points, while setting it to Automatic will place red dots at each point.

Here is a spline with the control points shown.

In[5]:= **Show[Graphics[Spline[pts, CompositeBezier, SplineDots -> Automatic]]]**

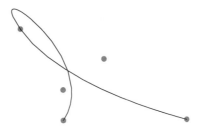

The rendering of the splines uses an adaptive algorithm, similar to that of the Plot function. The initial number of samples taken along the spline is determined by SplinePoints. If the bend between two adjacent segments is greater than MaxBend, additional samples are taken. This process continues up to at most a resolution determined by SplineDivision. If SplineDivision is None, then adaptive methods will not be used; samples will only be taken where determined by SplinePoints. This will be useful on occasion, as the adaptive method is relatively slow.

When rendering a spline in the usual fashion, a Line graphics primitive is generated behind the scenes. It may be useful to incorporate the points of this primitive into other Line and Polygon primitives. In particular, you can create a polygon with a spline along one or more sides.

This represents a Bezier curve.

```
In[6]:= bcurve =
         Spline[
          {{1,0},{1.5,0},{1.5,0.5},
           {2,1.5},{0.7,1.6},{0,1.5},{0,1}},
          Bezier];
```

Here is a polygon with a spline incorporated into one side.

```
In[7]:= Show[
         Graphics[
          Polygon[
           {{0,1},{0,0},{1,0},bcurve}]
         ]]
```

The default method of rendering splines is the adaptive method described above; internally, this generates a *Mathematica* `Line` primitive. In some special cases, however, it is advantageous for *Mathematica* to use special PostScript operators that are not part of the *Mathematica* graphics primitives. For example, a Bezier spline with four points corresponds to the PostScript `curveto` operator.

Advanced users can force *Mathematica* to generate special PostScript code for other kinds of splines by modifying the package function `RenderSpline`. Interested users can see the package itself for an example of this.

■ Graphics`SurfaceOfRevolution`

A surface of revolution is generated by rotating a curve about a given line. `SurfaceOfRevolution` plots the surface of revolution generated by rotating about any axis the graph of a function in the *x-z* plane or a curve described parametrically.

`SurfaceOfRevolution[f, {x, xmin, xmax}]`
  plot the surface of revolution obtained by rotating the curve of *f* in the *x-z* plane between *xmin* and *xmax*

`SurfaceOfRevolution[{`f_x`, `f_z`}, {t, tmin, tmax}]`
  plot the surface of revolution by rotating the curve described parametrically in the *x-z* plane with the variable *t*

`SurfaceOfRevolution[{`f_x`, `f_y`, `f_z`}, {t, tmin, tmax}]`
  plot the surface of revolution by rotating the curve described parametrically in three-dimensional space with the variable *t*

Surface of revolution of a curve.

This loads the package.

`In[1]:=  <<Graphics`SurfaceOfRevolution``

The curve sin(*x*) is rotated about the *z* axis.

`In[2]:=  SurfaceOfRevolution[`
`            Sin[x], {x, 0, 2 Pi}]`

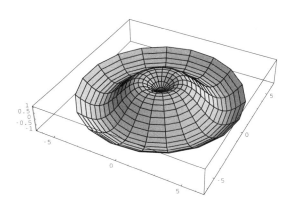

Any options you give are passed
directly to the built-in
ParametricPlot3D.

In[3]:= **SurfaceOfRevolution[Sin[x], {x, 0, 2 Pi},**
ViewVertical -> {1, 0, 0},
Ticks -> {Automatic, Automatic,
{-1., 0, 1.}}]

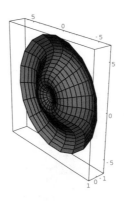

This gives the surface of revolution of
a curve in the *x-z* plane described
parametrically with the variable *u*.

In[4]:= **SurfaceOfRevolution[{1.1 Sin[u], u^2},**
{u, 0, 3 Pi/2}, BoxRatios -> {1, 1, 2}]

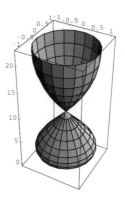

SurfaceOfRevolution[*f*, {*x*, *xmin*, *xmax*}, {*theta*, *thetamin*, *thetamax*}]
plot the surface of revolution obtained by rotating the curve
from angle *thetamin* to angle *thetamax*

Surface of revolution of a curve over a reduced angle.

Here is the same curve rotated from 0 to π.

In[5]:= **SurfaceOfRevolution[{1.1 Sin[u], u^2},**
            {u, 0, 3 Pi/2}, {t, 0, Pi},
            BoxRatios -> {1, 1, 2}]

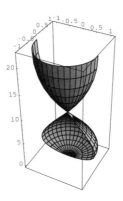

| RevolutionAxis -> {x, z} | rotate about axis connecting the origin to a point in the *x-z* plane |
| RevolutionAxis -> {x, y, z} | rotate about axis connecting the origin to an arbitrary point in three-dimensional space |

Specifying the axis of revolution.

Here is a curve rotated about a different axis in three-dimensional space.

In[6]:= **SurfaceOfRevolution[x^2, {x, 0, 1},**
            RevolutionAxis -> {1, 1, 1}]

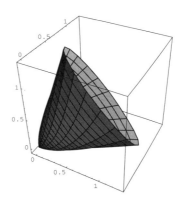

> ```
> ListSurfaceOfRevolution[{point₁, point₂, ... }]
> ```
> generate the surface of revolution of a curve specified by
> points
>
> ```
> ListSurfaceOfRevolution[{point₁, point₂, ... }, {theta, thetamin, thetamax}]
> ```
> generate the surface of revolution over a given range for the
> angle of revolution

Surfaces of revolution from a list of data points.

We can also generate a surface of revolution from a curve specified by a list of data points. The points can lie in the *x-z* plane or in three-dimensional space.

Here is a list of data in the *x-z* plane.

```
In[7]:= dat = Table[{n, n^3}, {n, 0, 1, .1}];
```

This gives the surface of revolution of dat about the axis connecting the origin to point {1, -1, 1} .

```
In[8]:= ListSurfaceOfRevolution[dat, {t, 0, Pi/2},
            RevolutionAxis -> {1, -1, 1},
            PlotRange -> All]
```

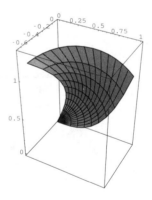

■ Graphics'ThreeScript'

3-Script is a file format for transferring descriptions of three-dimensional graphics objects from *Mathematica* to other programs. All *Mathematica* kernels have the ability to render three-dimensional images into the PostScript page description language. For certain applications, it is desirable to have a description of the image that retains the three-dimensional character that is lost when rendering into PostScript. The package `Graphics'ThreeScript'` supplies a number of utilities for writing suitable *Mathematica* objects into 3-Script format files.

This loads the package.	`In[1]:= <<Graphics'ThreeScript'`
This constructs a `Graphics3D` object.	`In[2]:= obj = Graphics3D[` `        Polygon[{{0,0,0}, {0,1,0}, {0,1,1}}]]`
	`Out[2]= -Graphics3D-`
This writes the 3-Script format into the file `object.ts`. Note that the filename is returned.	`In[3]:= ThreeScript[ "object.ts", obj]` `Out[3]= object.ts`
This shows the contents of the file.	`In[4]:= !!object.ts`

```
% Graphics3D objects

boundingbox

0 0 0

0 1 1

viewpoint

1.3 -2.4 2.

ambientlight

0 0 0

lightsources

1. 0. 1.

1 0 0

1. 1. 1.

0 1 0

0. 1. 1.

0 0 1

polygon

0 0 0

0 1 0

0 1 1
```

The 3-Script format works with all three-dimensional primitives and directives. This includes both `Graphics3D` and `SurfaceGraphics` objects. Note that in the 3-Script format information such as coordinates appears below the command name.

polygon x_1 y_1 z_1 x_2 y_2 z_2 ...	a polygon specified by any number of vertices
line x_1 y_1 z_1 x_2 y_2 z_2 ...	a line that joins a sequence of points
point x y z	a point
mesh m n z_{11} z_{12} ... z_{21} ... z_{mn}	a smooth surface specified by an $m \times n$ array of height values
colormesh m n z_{11} ... z_{mn} r_{11} g_{11} b_{11} ... $b_{(m-1)(n-1)}$	a smooth surface with colors specified for center of each patch
color r g b	objects that follow have the specified RGB color

Standard 3-Script descriptions of three-dimensional objects.

boundingbox *xmin ymin zmin xmax ymax zmax*	ranges of coordinates of objects in the scene
viewpoint *xr yr zr*	default relative position from which to view the scene
ambientlight r g b	isotropic ambient light level
lightsources xd_1 yd_1 zd_1 r_1 g_1 b_1 xd_2 yd_2 zd_2 r_2 g_2 b_2 ...	directions and colors of light sources

3-Script commands used as global directives.

3-Script is used by the *Mathematica* command Live that is available on platforms that support the GL library, such as Silicon Graphics computers. A 3-Script format file is written and this is passed to an external renderer to process. An alternative method you can use to pass a three-dimensional structure, or indeed any *Mathematica* expression into an external program, is to use the *MathLink*® communications protocol.

A complete description of the 3-Script file format is contained in the Wolfram Research technical report, *The 3-Script File Format*, which can be found on MathSource, at http://mathsource.wolfram.com; search the archive for 'threescript'.

■ Graphics'Common'

The Graphics'Common' subdirectory includes a package that is used by Graphics packages to share common symbols. This common package is not meant to be loaded individually. Most users do not need to be aware of it, but if you are writing your own packages using functions defined by a Graphics package, it is wise to check whether a symbol you need is introduced via Graphics'Common'GraphicsCommon'.

*ApproximateIntervals	*HistogramRange
Horizontal	*HistogramScale
*IntervalBoundaries	MaxArrowLength
*IntervalCenters	ScaleFactor
*FrequencyData	ScaleFunction
*HistogramCategories	Vertical

Public symbols introduced by Graphics'Common'GraphicsCommon'.

7. Linear Algebra

■ LinearAlgebra`Cholesky`

There are various ways to decompose a matrix into the product of simpler matrices of special types. These decompositions are frequently useful in numerical matrix calculations. The most general of these decompositions can be computed using the built-in functions QRDecomposition, SchurDecomposition, and SingularValues. The Cholesky decomposition writes a symmetric positive definite matrix as the product of an upper-triangular matrix and its transpose.

CholeskyDecomposition[m]	find the Cholesky decomposition of the symmetric positive definite matrix *m*

Computing the Cholesky decomposition.

A square matrix m is symmetric if it is equal to its transpose. It is positive definite if $v.m.v$ is positive for all nonzero vectors v. Note that a symmetric positive definite matrix must always be real. The Cholesky decomposition gives an upper-triangular matrix u with the property such that m can be written as Transpose[u].u.

This loads the package.

In[1]:= **<<LinearAlgebra`Cholesky`**

Here is the 4 × 4 Hilbert matrix. It is obviously symmetric.

In[2]:= **hil = Table[**
                    1/(i + j - 1), {i, 1, 4}, {j, 1, 4}]

Out[2]= $\{\{1, \frac{1}{2}, \frac{1}{3}, \frac{1}{4}\}, \{\frac{1}{2}, \frac{1}{3}, \frac{1}{4}, \frac{1}{5}\}, \{\frac{1}{3}, \frac{1}{4}, \frac{1}{5}, \frac{1}{6}\},$
$\{\frac{1}{4}, \frac{1}{5}, \frac{1}{6}, \frac{1}{7}\}\}$

All of the eigenvalues of hil are positive reals. This implies that the matrix is positive definite.

In[3]:= **Eigenvalues[N[hil]]**
Out[3]= {1.50021, 0.169141, 0.00673827, 0.0000967023}

Because the entries in hil are fractions, you get an exact result.

In[4]:= **u = CholeskyDecomposition[hil]**

Out[4]= $\{\{1, \frac{1}{2}, \frac{1}{3}, \frac{1}{4}\}, \{0, \frac{1}{2\sqrt{3}}, \frac{1}{2\sqrt{3}}, \frac{3\sqrt{3}}{20}\},$
$\{0, 0, \frac{1}{6\sqrt{5}}, \frac{1}{4\sqrt{5}}\}, \{0, 0, 0, \frac{1}{20\sqrt{7}}\}\}$

The product of u and its transpose gives the original matrix hil.

In[5]:= **MatrixForm[Transpose[u] . u]**

Out[5]//MatrixForm=
$$\begin{pmatrix} 1 & \frac{1}{2} & \frac{1}{3} & \frac{1}{4} \\ \frac{1}{2} & \frac{1}{3} & \frac{1}{4} & \frac{1}{5} \\ \frac{1}{3} & \frac{1}{4} & \frac{1}{5} & \frac{1}{6} \\ \frac{1}{4} & \frac{1}{5} & \frac{1}{6} & \frac{1}{7} \end{pmatrix}$$

■ LinearAlgebra`GaussianElimination`

The *Mathematica* function `LinearSolve` computes the solution to a system of linear equations. There are two distinct steps to this process, and `LinearSolve` does both of them. There are cases where you want to solve several systems of equations with the same left-hand side in each case, but with different right-hand sides. In these cases `LinearSolve` will certainly work, but since the first step of the solution process deals only with the left-hand side, it will be doing much of the work repeatedly. To make matters worse, for large systems, the first step is most of the work anyway.

Because the first step can be seen abstractly as factoring the matrix of coefficients into the product of a lower triangular and an upper triangular matrix, it is often referred to as LU factorization. `LUFactor` performs this factorization and returns a data object with a head of LU. This data object represents the factorization of the original matrix together with information regarding any permutation of the rows that might be necessary to maintain numerical stability in the computation.

The second step in the process is often referred to as back substitution or back-solving. `LUSolve` performs this operation.

`LUFactor[`*mat*`]`	give the LU decomposition along with a pivot list of *mat*
`LUSolve[`*lu*`,` *b*`]`	solve the linear system represented by *lu* and right-hand side *b*
`LU[`*a*`,` *pivots*`]`	data object returned by `LUFactor`, must be given as the first argument to `LUSolve`

Solving a linear system using Gaussian elimination and back substitution.

The data object generated by `LUFactor` is a compact way of storing the information contained in the upper and lower triangular matrices of the factorization. The zeros in the lower part of the upper triangular matrix, the upper part of the lower triangular matrix, and the ones along the diagonal of the lower triangular matrix are not stored explicitly. This allows both the upper and lower triangular matrices to be stored in the space of a single square matrix. The actual storage arrangement is even more complicated than this because the rows usually get permuted in an effort to make the solution process as numerically stable as possible.

This loads the package.

```
In[1]:= <<LinearAlgebra`GaussianElimination`
```

Here is the coefficient matrix of a system.

```
In[2]:= MatrixForm[a = {{5, 3, 0}, {7, 9, 2},
        {-2, -8, -1}}]
```

$$Out[2]//MatrixForm= \begin{pmatrix} 5 & 3 & 0 \\ 7 & 9 & 2 \\ -2 & -8 & -1 \end{pmatrix}$$

This performs the LU factorization.	*In[3]:=* `lu = LUFactor[a]`

$$Out[3]= \text{LU}\left[\left\{\left\{\frac{5}{7}, \frac{12}{19}, -\frac{22}{19}\right\}, \{7, 9, 2\}, \left\{-\frac{2}{7}, -\frac{38}{7}, -\frac{3}{7}\right\}\right\}, \{2, 3, 1\}\right]$$

This is the right-hand side of the system.	*In[4]:=* `b = {6, -3, 7}`
	Out[4]= {6, -3, 7}

LUSolve uses back substitution to get the solution to the system.

In[5]:= `LUSolve[lu, b]`

$$Out[5]= \left\{\frac{75}{44}, -\frac{37}{44}, -\frac{81}{22}\right\}$$

We can also use back substitution to solve a system with a different right-hand side.

In[6]:= `LUSolve[lu, {1,2,3}]`

$$Out[6]= \left\{\frac{31}{44}, -\frac{37}{44}, \frac{51}{22}\right\}$$

This checks that the solution is correct.

In[7]:= `a . % - {1,2,3}`

Out[7]= {0, 0, 0}

The functions LUFactor and LUSolve can be used in the context of other forms of arithmetic such as interval arithmetic or NumericalMath`ComputerArithmetic`.

This converts the coefficient matrix and the right-hand side to have elements that are intervals rather than numbers.

In[8]:= `a = Map[Interval[{#-.01,#+.01}]&, a, {2}]; b = Interval[{#-.01,#+.01}]& /@ b`

Out[8]= {Interval[{5.99, 6.01}], Interval[{-3.01, -2.99}], Interval[{6.99, 7.01}]}

Now we solve the system in the context of interval arithmetic.

In[9]:= `LUSolve[LUFactor[a], b]`

Out[9]= {Interval[{1.59114, 1.82032}], Interval[{-0.875368, -0.804578}], Interval[{-3.89402, -3.48277}]}

This checks the solution.

In[10]:= `N[a . %] - b`

Out[10]= {Interval[{-0.744025, 0.763068}], Interval[{-1.60201, 1.60659}], Interval[{-0.792328, 0.788299}]}

■ LinearAlgebra`MatrixManipulation`

This package includes functions for composing and separating matrices using rows, columns, and submatrices. All of the definitions involve simple combinations of built-in functions. Also included are functions for constructing a variety of special matrices.

AppendColumns[m_1, m_2, ...]	join the columns in matrices m_1, m_2, ...
AppendRows[m_1, m_2, ...]	join the rows in matrices m_1, m_2, ...
BlockMatrix[*blocks*]	join rows and columns of submatrices in *blocks* to form a new matrix

Functions for combining matrices.

This loads the package.

```
In[1]:= << LinearAlgebra`MatrixManipulation`
```

Define a 2 × 2 matrix.

```
In[2]:= a = {{a11, a12}, {a21, a22}}; MatrixForm[a]
```

$$Out[2]//MatrixForm= \begin{pmatrix} a11 & a12 \\ a21 & a22 \end{pmatrix}$$

Define a second matrix.

```
In[3]:= b = {{b11, b12}, {b21, b22}}; MatrixForm[b]
```

$$Out[3]//MatrixForm= \begin{pmatrix} b11 & b12 \\ b21 & b22 \end{pmatrix}$$

This constructs a matrix by combining the columns of the two matrices.

```
In[4]:= AppendColumns[a, b]
```

$$Out[4]= \{\{a11, a12\}, \{a21, a22\}, \{b11, b12\}, \{b21, b22\}\}$$

Here is the same matrix displayed using MatrixForm.

```
In[5]:= MatrixForm[%]
```

$$Out[5]//MatrixForm= \begin{pmatrix} a11 & a12 \\ a21 & a22 \\ b11 & b12 \\ b21 & b22 \end{pmatrix}$$

A matrix can also be constructed by combining the rows of these matrices.

```
In[6]:= AppendRows[a, b] //MatrixForm
```

$$Out[6]//MatrixForm= \begin{pmatrix} a11 & a12 & b11 & b12 \\ a21 & a22 & b21 & b22 \end{pmatrix}$$

Here is a matrix constructed from submatrices a and b.

```
In[7]:= BlockMatrix[{{a, b}, {b, {{0, 0},
            {0, 0}}}}] //MatrixForm
```

$$Out[7]//MatrixForm= \begin{pmatrix} a11 & a12 & b11 & b12 \\ a21 & a22 & b21 & b22 \\ b11 & b12 & 0 & 0 \\ b21 & b22 & 0 & 0 \end{pmatrix}$$

TakeRows[*mat*, *n*]	take the first *n* rows in *mat*
TakeRows[*mat*, -*n*]	take the last *n* rows in *mat*
TakeRows[*mat*, {*m*, *n*}]	take rows *m* through *n* in mat
TakeColumns[*mat*, *n*]	take the first *n* columns in *mat*
TakeColumns[*mat*, -*n*]	take the last *n* columns in *mat*
TakeColumns[*mat*, {*m*, *n*}]	take columns *m* through *n* in *mat*
TakeMatrix[*mat*, *pos*$_1$, *pos*$_2$]	take the submatrix of *mat* between elements at positions *pos*$_1$ and *pos*$_2$
SubMatrix[*mat*, *pos*, *dim*]	take the submatrix of *mat* of dimension *dim* starting at position *pos*

Functions for picking out pieces of matrices.

Here is a 4 × 4 matrix.

In[8]:= **mat = Array[m, {4, 4}]; MatrixForm[mat]**

$$Out[8]//MatrixForm= \begin{pmatrix} m[1, 1] & m[1, 2] & m[1, 3] & m[1, 4] \\ m[2, 1] & m[2, 2] & m[2, 3] & m[2, 4] \\ m[3, 1] & m[3, 2] & m[3, 3] & m[3, 4] \\ m[4, 1] & m[4, 2] & m[4, 3] & m[4, 4] \end{pmatrix}$$

This takes the last two rows of the matrix. The same result is obtained with Take[mat, -2] or mat[[{3, 4}]].

In[9]:= **TakeRows[mat, -2] //MatrixForm**

$$Out[9]//MatrixForm= \begin{pmatrix} m[3, 1] & m[3, 2] & m[3, 3] & m[3, 4] \\ m[4, 1] & m[4, 2] & m[4, 3] & m[4, 4] \end{pmatrix}$$

This takes the second and third columns of the matrix. The same result is obtained with
Take[mat, All, {2, 3}] or
mat[[All, {2, 3}]].

In[10]:= **TakeColumns[mat, {2, 3}] //MatrixForm**

$$Out[10]//MatrixForm= \begin{pmatrix} m[1, 2] & m[1, 3] \\ m[2, 2] & m[2, 3] \\ m[3, 2] & m[3, 3] \\ m[4, 2] & m[4, 3] \end{pmatrix}$$

Here are the first three columns. The same result is obtained with
Take[mat, All, 3] or
mat[[All, {1, 2, 3}]].

In[11]:= **TakeColumns[mat, 3] //MatrixForm**

$$Out[11]//MatrixForm= \begin{pmatrix} m[1, 1] & m[1, 2] & m[1, 3] \\ m[2, 1] & m[2, 2] & m[2, 3] \\ m[3, 1] & m[3, 2] & m[3, 3] \\ m[4, 1] & m[4, 2] & m[4, 3] \end{pmatrix}$$

This takes the submatrix between the element at position {2, 3} and the element at position {4, 4}. The same result is obtained with
Take[mat, {2, 4}, {3, 4}] or
mat[[{2, 3, 4}, {3, 4}]].

In[12]:= **TakeMatrix[mat, {2, 3}, {4, 4}] //MatrixForm**

$$Out[12]//MatrixForm= \begin{pmatrix} m[2, 3] & m[2, 4] \\ m[3, 3] & m[3, 4] \\ m[4, 3] & m[4, 4] \end{pmatrix}$$

Here is the same submatrix, specified as a 3 × 2 matrix starting with the element at position {2, 3}.

$In[13]:=$ **SubMatrix[mat, {2, 3}, {3, 2}] //MatrixForm**

$Out[13]//MatrixForm=$
$$\begin{pmatrix} m[2,\,3] & m[2,\,4] \\ m[3,\,3] & m[3,\,4] \\ m[4,\,3] & m[4,\,4] \end{pmatrix}$$

SquareMatrixQ[*mat*]	test whether mat is a square matrix

Square matrix test.

You can test whether matrices a, b, and mat are square.

$In[14]:=$ **Map[SquareMatrixQ, {a, b, mat}]**

$Out[14]=$ {True, True, True}

UpperDiagonalMatrix[*f*, *n*]	create an $n \times n$ matrix with elements $f[i, j]$ above the diagonal
LowerDiagonalMatrix[*f*, *n*]	create an $n \times n$ matrix with elements $f[i, j]$ below the diagonal
ZeroMatrix[*n*]	create an $n \times n$ matrix of zeros
ZeroMatrix[*m*, *n*]	create an $m \times n$ matrix of zeros
HilbertMatrix[*n*]	create an $n \times n$ Hilbert matrix, with elements given by $1/(i + j - 1)$
HilbertMatrix[*m*, *n*]	create an $m \times n$ Hilbert matrix
HankelMatrix[*n*]	create an $n \times n$ Hankel matrix with the first row and first column given by $1, 2, ...n$
HankelMatrix[*list*]	create a Hankel matrix with the first row and the first column given by *list*

Special matrices.

Here is an upper diagonal matrix with elements f[i, j].

$In[15]:=$ **UpperDiagonalMatrix[f, 3] //MatrixForm**

$Out[15]//MatrixForm=$
$$\begin{pmatrix} f[1,\,1] & f[1,\,2] & f[1,\,3] \\ 0 & f[2,\,2] & f[2,\,3] \\ 0 & 0 & f[3,\,3] \end{pmatrix}$$

Matrix elements can be specified using a pure function.

$In[16]:=$ **LowerDiagonalMatrix[#1 + #2 &, 3] //MatrixForm**

$Out[16]//MatrixForm=$
$$\begin{pmatrix} 2 & 0 & 0 \\ 3 & 4 & 0 \\ 4 & 5 & 6 \end{pmatrix}$$

Here is a 2 × 4 Hilbert matrix.

In[17]:= **HilbertMatrix[2, 4] //MatrixForm**

Out[17]//MatrixForm= $\begin{pmatrix} 1 & \frac{1}{2} & \frac{1}{3} & \frac{1}{4} \\ \frac{1}{2} & \frac{1}{3} & \frac{1}{4} & \frac{1}{5} \end{pmatrix}$

The elements of the Hankel matrix can be given as a list.

In[18]:= **HankelMatrix[{w, x, y, z}] //MatrixForm**

Out[18]//MatrixForm= $\begin{pmatrix} w & x & y & z \\ x & y & z & 0 \\ y & z & 0 & 0 \\ z & 0 & 0 & 0 \end{pmatrix}$

+   `LinearEquationsToMatrices[eqns, vars]`

give a list of the form {*mat*, *vec*}, where *mat* is the matrix of coefficients of the linear equations in the specified variables, and *vec* is the vector of right-hand sides

Creating matrices from a set of linear equations.

This extracts the matrix of coefficients and the vector of right-hand sides from a list of linear equations.

In[19]:= **LinearEquationsToMatrices[**
{a11 x + a12 y == c1,
a21 x + a22 y == c2}, {x, y}]

Out[19]= {{{a11, a12}, {a21, a22}}, {c1, c2}}

+   `PolarDecomposition[mat]`

give a list of the form {*u*, *s*}, where *s* is a positive definite matrix, $u.u^*$ gives the identity matrix, and $u.s = mat$

Polar decomposition of a matrix.

This computes the polar decomposition of a 3 × 3 matrix, then extracts the matrices u and s.

In[20]:= **(mat = {{2., 0, 0}, {3., 4., 0}, {4., 5., 6.}};**
{u, s} = PolarDecomposition[mat])

Out[20]= {{{0.877166, -0.471491, -0.09097}, {0.372767,
0.788031, -0.489951}, {0.302695, 0.395858, 0.86699}},
{{4.08341, 3.00454, 1.81617}, {3.00454, 5.13141, 2.37515},
{1.81617, 2.37515, 5.20194}}}

This gives the identity matrix.

In[21]:= **u . Transpose[Conjugate[u]] // Chop**

Out[21]= {{1., 0, 0}, {0, 1., 0}, {0, 0, 1.}}

This gives the original matrix.

In[22]:= **u . s // Chop**

Out[22]= {{2., 0, 0}, {3., 4., 0}, {4., 5., 6.}}

⁺ LUMatrices[*lu*]	give a list of the form {*l*, *u*}, where *l* and *u* are the lower and upper matrices of the LU decomposition of matrix *mat* and *lu* is the first element of LUDecomposition[*mat*]

LU decomposition of a matrix.

This computes the LU decomposition of a 3 × 3 matrix, returning a combination of the lower and upper triangular matrices, a pivot permutation vector, and a condition number for the matrix.

```
In[23]:= {lu, p, cn} = LUDecomposition[mat]

Out[23]= {{{4., 5., 6.}, {0.5, -2.5, -3.}, {0.75, -0.1, -4.8}},
          {3, 1, 2}, 7.6372}
```

This gives the lower and upper triangular matrices explicitly.

```
In[24]:= {l, u} = LUMatrices[lu]

Out[24]= {{{1., 0., 0.}, {0.5, 1., 0.}, {0.75, -0.1, 1.}},
          {{4., 5., 6.}, {0, -2.5, -3.}, {0, 0, -4.8}}}
```

You need to permute the original matrix to verify the decomposition.

```
In[25]:= mat[[p]] - l.u // Chop

Out[25]= {{0, 0, 0}, {0, 0, 0}, {0, 0, 0}}
```

⊬	VectorNorm[*vec*]	infinity-norm of a vector of approximate numbers
⊬	VectorNorm[*vec*, *p*]	*p*-norm of a vector, $1 <= p < \infty$
⊬	MatrixNorm[*mat*]	infinity-norm of a matrix of approximate numbers
⊬	MatrixNorm[*mat*, *p*]	*p*-norm of a matrix of approximate numbers, where *p* may be 1, 2, or ∞
⊬	InverseMatrixNorm[*mat*]	infinity-norm of the inverse of matrix *mat*
⊬	InverseMatrixNorm[*lu*]	infinity-norm of the inverse of a matrix having LU decomposition *lu*
⊬	InverseMatrixNorm[*mat*, *p*], InverseMatrixNorm[*lu*, *p*]	
		p-norm of the inverse of a matrix
⊬	MatrixConditionNumber[*mat*]	infinity-norm condition number of a matrix of approximate numbers
⊬	MatrixConditionNumber[*mat*, *p*]	
		p-norm condition number of a matrix, where *p* may be 1, 2, or ∞

Vector and matrix norms.

The vector *p*-norm, for a vector $\{v_1, v_2, ...\}$ is given by

$$\left(\sum_i |v_i|^p \right)^{\frac{1}{p}}$$

for $1 <= p < \infty$, and given by Max[$\{v_1, v_2, ... \}$] for $p = \infty$. For a matrix *mat*, the *p*-norm is defined to be the maximum, over all vectors *vec* having a *p*-norm of unity, of the *p*-norm of *mat.vec*. For the norm of the inverse of a matrix, you can explicitly compute the norm of the inverse of *mat*, but asymptotically, it is about three times faster to work with the LU decomposition of *mat*. Hence, either *mat* or the LU decomposition of *mat* may be an argument to InverseMatrixNorm.

This gives the Euclidean or l_2 distance between vectors $\{1, 1, 1\}$ and $\{2, 2, 2\}$.	In[26]:= **VectorNorm[N[{1, 1, 1}-{2, 2, 2}], 2]** Out[26]= 1.73205
This gives the city-block or l_1 distance between the vectors.	In[27]:= **VectorNorm[N[{1, 1, 1}-{2, 2, 2}], 1]** Out[27]= 3.

The l_2 matrix norm may be calculated using MatrixNorm or SingularValues.

```
In[28]:= (mat = N[{{1, 2, 3}, {3, 4, 5}, {6, 7, 8}}];
          {MatrixNorm[mat, 2], Max[SingularValues[mat][[2]]]})

Out[28]= {14.5576, 14.5576}
```

■ LinearAlgebra`Orthogonalization`

For most purposes, the most convenient type of basis for a vector space is orthonormal (*i.e.*, the vectors are unit length and are pairwise orthogonal). The Gram-Schmidt procedure takes an arbitrary basis and generates an orthonormal one. It does this by sequentially processing the list of vectors and generating a vector perpendicular to the previous vectors in the list. For the process to succeed in producing an orthonormal set, the given vectors must be linearly independent. The function GramSchmidt assumes that this is the case. If the given vectors are not linearly independent, indeterminate or zero vectors may be produced.

GramSchmidt[{v_1, v_2, ... }]	generate an orthonormal set from the given list of real vectors
Normalize[*vect*]	normalize *vect*
Projection[*vect$_1$*, *vect$_2$*]	give the orthogonal projection of *vect$_1$* onto *vect$_2$*

Vector operations using the usual inner product.

This loads the package.

In[1]:= <<LinearAlgebra`Orthogonalization`

This applies the Gram-Schmidt procedure to the given list of three-dimensional vectors.

In[2]:= {w1, w2, w3} = GramSchmidt[
        {{3,4,2}, {2,5,2}, {1,2,6}}]

Out[2]= $\{\{\frac{3}{\sqrt{29}}, \frac{4}{\sqrt{29}}, \frac{2}{\sqrt{29}}\}, \{-\frac{32}{\sqrt{1653}}, \frac{25}{\sqrt{1653}}, -\frac{2}{\sqrt{1653}}\},$
$\{-\frac{2}{\sqrt{57}}, -\frac{2}{\sqrt{57}}, \frac{7}{\sqrt{57}}\}\}$

The result is an orthonormal basis, so the dot product of each pair of vectors is zero and each vector has unit length.

In[3]:= { w1 . w2, w2 . w3, w1 . w3,
        w1 . w1, w2 . w2, w3 . w3}

Out[3]= {0, 0, 0, 1, 1, 1}

A vector space is a generalization of the familiar notions of one-, two-, and three-dimensional space. In these familiar spaces we know how to compute lengths of vectors and the angle between two vectors. The usual way of doing this uses the dot product. The length of a vector is simply Sqrt[$v.v$] and two vectors are perpendicular (or orthogonal) if $v.w$ is zero. In a more general vector space, the dot product is replaced by an inner product. By setting the option InnerProduct, you can use GramSchmidt to produce a collection of vectors that are orthonormal with respect to your specified inner product.

> GramSchmidt[{v_1, v_2, ... }, InnerProduct -> *func*]
> generate an orthonormal set using the inner product given by *func*
>
> Normalize[*vect*, InnerProduct -> *func*]]
> normalize *vect* using the inner product given by *func*
>
> Projection[*vect*$_1$, *vect*$_2$, InnerProduct -> *func*]]
> give the orthogonal projection of *vect*$_1$ onto *vect*$_2$ using the inner product given by *func*

Vector operations using a specified inner product.

The function you specify as the InnerProduct can be a pure function of two variables, with the variables given as #1 and #2. For example, the default InnerProduct -> Dot could be expressed as InnerProduct -> (#1.#2&). The parentheses around the formula for the function guarantee that *Mathematica* treats it as a single unit. For more information on pure functions, see *The Mathematica Book*.

The vectors here are functions, and the inner product is the integral of the product of two functions over the interval −1 to 1.

```
In[4]:= GramSchmidt[{1, x, x^2, x^3, x^4},
            InnerProduct ->
                (Integrate[#1 #2,{x,-1,1}]&)] //Simplify
```

$$Out[4]= \left\{ \frac{1}{\sqrt{2}}, \sqrt{\frac{3}{2}}\, x, \frac{1}{2}\sqrt{\frac{5}{2}}\,(-1+3\,x^2), \frac{1}{2}\sqrt{\frac{7}{2}}\, x\,(-3+5\,x^2), \right.$$
$$\left. \frac{3\,(3-30\,x^2+35\,x^4)}{8\sqrt{2}} \right\}$$

Here is the second Legendre polynomial normalized with respect to the same inner product. It is the same as the third element in the basis found using GramSchmidt.

```
In[5]:= Normalize[LegendreP[2,x],
            InnerProduct ->
                (Integrate[#1 #2,{x,-1,1}]&)]
```

$$Out[5]= \sqrt{\frac{5}{2}}\left(-\frac{1}{2} + \frac{3\,x^2}{2} \right)$$

> GramSchmidt[{v_1, v_2, ... }, Normalized -> False]
> generate an orthogonal set, but do not normalize

Generating orthogonal sets without normalizing.

The option Normalized is set to False.

```
In[6]:= {w1, w2} = GramSchmidt[{{3,4,3}, {2,3,6}},
            Normalized -> False]
```

$$Out[6]= \left\{ \{3, 4, 3\}, \left\{ -\frac{20}{17}, -\frac{21}{17}, \frac{48}{17} \right\} \right\}$$

The resulting vectors are orthogonal, but they are not normalized.

```
In[7]:= {w1 . w1, w1 . w2}

Out[7]= {34, 0}
```

∎ LinearAlgebra`Tridiagonal`

There are many numerical techniques for working with matrices of specific forms. Often these routines are far more efficient than the general case. Frequently, the best way to get an efficient general routine is to reduce the problem systematically to a special case that can be solved efficiently.

In addition, special forms of matrices often come up naturally in solving certain classes of problems. One very useful special type of matrix is the `tridiagonal`. In these matrices all elements are zero except for elements on the main, super-, and subdiagonal. More precisely, $m_{i,j} = 0$ if $|i - j| > 1$. Tridiagonal matrices occur in a wide variety of applications, such as the construction of certain splines and the solution of boundary value problems.

`TridiagonalSolve[a, b, c, r]`	solve the matrix equation $m.x = r$ where m is tridiagonal with main, sub-, and superdiagonals given by the lists a, b, and c, respectively

Solving matrix equations with tridiagonal matrices.

This loads the package.

```
In[1]:= <<LinearAlgebra`Tridiagonal`
```

This defines the list that will give the nonzero diagonals of a matrix.

```
In[2]:= {a, b, c} =
           {{7, 1, 11}, {4, 8, 2, 12}, {5, 9, 3}}

Out[2]= {{7, 1, 11}, {4, 8, 2, 12}, {5, 9, 3}}
```

Here is the matrix m constructed from the list.

```
In[3]:= m = Table[Switch[
             j-i, -1, a[[j]], 0, b[[j]], 1,
             c[[j-1]], _, 0], {i, 4}, {j, 4}]

Out[3]= {{4, 5, 0, 0}, {7, 8, 9, 0}, {0, 1, 2, 3}, {0, 0, 11, 12}}
```

This displays the matrix using MatrixForm.

```
In[4]:= MatrixForm[%]
```

$$Out[4]//MatrixForm= \begin{pmatrix} 4 & 5 & 0 & 0 \\ 7 & 8 & 9 & 0 \\ 0 & 1 & 2 & 3 \\ 0 & 0 & 11 & 12 \end{pmatrix}$$

This gives the vector x that solves the equation m.x == {2, 3, 4, 5}.

```
In[5]:= TridiagonalSolve[a, b, c, {2, 3, 4, 5}]
```

$$Out[5]= \left\{-\frac{28}{9}, \frac{26}{9}, \frac{5}{27}, \frac{20}{81}\right\}$$

`TridiagonalSolve` uses Gaussian elimination and back substitution. No pivoting is done. If a pivot happens to be zero, this introduces an `Infinity`. If the matrix is diagonally dominate, which is the case in certain applications, no pivoting is necessary.

You can solve equations containing real and complex numbers as well as symbolic quantities.

```
In[6]:= TridiagonalSolve[
          {2.2, 5.2},
          {4.3, 3.22, 2.1},
          {8.1 + I, 3.4},
          {1, 2.3 I , 3}]
```

Out[6]= {-0.885678 + 0.391313 i, 0.559458 - 0.276803 i,
          0.0432458 + 0.685417 i}

8. Miscellaneous

■ Miscellaneous`Audio`

This package provides functions for the generation of standard waveforms and waveforms with user-specified spectra, the synthesis of amplitude and frequency modulated sinusoids, and a function for reading sound files into *Mathematica*.

The graphic output of *Mathematica*'s sound functions is hardware dependent, so the graphics included in this documentation may differ from those produced by your machine.

Generating Standard Waveforms

Waveform[*type*, *freq*, *dur*]	create a Sound object that is a standard waveform of type *type*, having a fundamental frequency of *freq* hertz, and a duration of *dur* seconds

Creating a standard waveform.

Waveform uses computationally efficient algorithms to create a standard waveform with a theoretically infinite number of overtones.

Sinusoid	Square
Triangle	Sawtooth

Standard waveform definitions.

This loads the package.

```
In[1]:= << Miscellaneous`Audio`
```

Here Waveform returns a Sound object corresponding to a triangle wave having a fundamental of 440 hertz and lasting 0.2 seconds.

```
In[2]:= tri440 = Waveform[Triangle, 440, 0.2]
Out[2]=        -Sound-
```

The Show function allows you to hear the Sound object returned by Waveform.

```
In[3]:= Show[tri440]
Out[3]=        -Sound-
```

```
Waveform[type, freq, dur, Overtones->n]
```
create a standard waveform with *n* overtones

Creating a standard waveform with a specified number of overtones.

By setting the option `Overtones`, you can limit the number of overtones that `Waveform` includes in a sound.

You can generate a square wave that has only eight overtones, then hear the sound with the `Show` function.

```
In[4]:=  Waveform[Square, 880, 0.2,
              Overtones->8] // Show
Out[4]=       -Sound-
```

Here `Table` is used to create a sequence of sawtooth waveform sounds running from ten overtones down to only two.

```
In[5]:=  Table[Waveform[Sawtooth, 880, 0.1,
              Overtones->n], {n, 10, 2, -1}] // Show
Out[5]=       -Sound-
```

When you use the option `Overtones`, the `Waveform` function uses Fourier summation to create the sound. This process is not as computationally efficient as the default algorithm, but generates a cleaner sound with only the specified number of overtones. *Mathematica*'s `SetOptions` function may be used to make Fourier summation the default.

This ensures that `Waveform` will use Fourier summation for the creation of sounds.

```
In[6]:=  SetOptions[Waveform, Overtones->Infinity]
Out[6]=  {DisplayFunction → Identity, Overtones → ∞, PlayRange → All,
          SampleDepth → 8, SampleRate → 8192}
```

This ensures the use of faster algorithms in creating sounds.

```
In[7]:=  SetOptions[Waveform, Overtones->Automatic]
Out[7]=  {DisplayFunction → Identity, Overtones → Automatic,
          PlayRange → All, SampleDepth → 8, SampleRate → 8192}
```

Specifying the Spectrum for a Waveform

```
ListWaveform[{{n₁, a₁}, {n₂, a₂}, ... }, freq, dur]
```
create a Sound object with a fundamental frequency of *freq* lasting for *dur* seconds, with a spectrum in which relative frequency n_i has relative amplitude a_i

---

Creating a waveform with a specified spectrum.

`ListWaveform` allows you to create a waveform with a specific spectrum. The first argument is a list of pairs, in which the first member of each pair is a frequency relative to the fundamental and the second is the frequency's relative amplitude.

For example, you can define a partial list corresponding to an "instrument" in which the partials' frequencies are nonharmonically related and have complicated amplitude relationships. ListWaveform may then be used to generate these relationships at different fundamental frequencies.

This partial list will define the instrument.	`In[8]:= partialList = {{1,1},{1.1,0.1},{1.2,0.9},{1.3,0.2}, {1.4,0.8},{1.5,0.3},{1.6,0.7}, {1.7,0.4},{1.8,0.6},{1.9,0.5}};`
This generates an ascending sequence of six chromatic half-steps, beginning at 440 hertz, all using the same partial list, and each lasting for 0.2 seconds.	`In[9]:= sequence = Table[ListWaveform[partialList, 440 2^(x/12), 0.2], {x,0,5}]` `Out[9]=    {-Sound-, -Sound-, -Sound-, -Sound-, -Sound-, -Sound-}`
Now you can hear one partial list at different fundamental frequencies.	`In[10]:= Show[sequence]` `Out[10]=    -Sound-`

You can create chords with ListWaveform by defining partial lists with amplitude relationships of unity, so that all component frequencies share the same amplitude.

This sequence of relative frequencies defines a major chord. Note that the amplitudes are set at unity, so that the component frequencies are of equal amplitude.	`In[11]:= majorChord = {{1, 1}, {1.26, 1}, {1.5, 1}};`
This creates a major chord based on a fundamental of 493.88 hertz (*i.e.*, the pitch B4).	`In[12]:= ListWaveform[majorChord, 493.88, 0.2] // Show` `Out[12]=    -Sound-`

Amplitude Modulation

Amplitude modulation is a common analog studio technique in which the created sound contains three frequencies: the carrier frequency, and the sum and difference of the carrier and modulating frequencies.

AmplitudeModulation[f_c, f_m, *mi*, *dur*]

create a Sound object that is an amplitude modulated sinusoid, having carrier and modulator frequencies f_c and f_m measured in hertz, a modulation index of *mi*, and a duration of *dur* seconds

---

Amplitude modulation.

The expression used by AmplitudeModulation is given by $(1 + mi \cos(2\pi f_m t)) \cos(2\pi f_c t)$.

When the modulating frequency is subaudio (below 20 hertz), the result of amplitude modulation is what musicians call tremolo.

```
In[13]:= AmplitudeModulation[440, 6, 1, 0.5] //Show
Out[13]=          -Sound-
```

The depth or intensity of the modulation is controlled by the modulation index *mi*. The carrier is said to be overmodulated when *mi* > 1. The best way to understand the effect of *mi* is to try it out with different values, usually between 0.1 and 2.0.

AmplitudeModulation[f_c, f_m, *mi*, *dur*, RingModulation->True]
create a Sound object that is a ring modulated sinusoid

Ring modulation.

If you set the option `RingModulation->True`, the Sound object created by `AmplitudeModulation` will contain only two frequencies: the sum and the difference of the carrier and modulating frequencies. This is called ring modulation, and is given by the expression $mi \cos(2\pi f_m t) \cos(2\pi f_c t)$.

In this example, the output sound contains the frequencies 700 and 300 hertz, the sum and difference of the carrier and modulating frequencies.

```
In[14]:= AmplitudeModulation[200, 500, 1, 0.5,
            RingModulation->True] //Show
Out[14]=          -Sound-
```

Frequency Modulation

Frequency modulation (FM) is a technique used at major universities on workstations and in suburban homes on synthesizers. The ubiquitousness of this technique stems in part from its mathematical simplicity and its ease of implementation in an electronic circuit. The expression for frequency modulation is given by $\sin(2\pi f_c t + \frac{pd}{f_m} \sin(2\pi f_m t))$.

FrequencyModulation[f_c, {f_m, *pd*}, *dur*]
create a Sound object that is a frequency modulated sinusoid, having carrier and modulating frequencies f_c and f_m hertz, peak deviation *pd* hertz, and a duration of *dur* seconds

---

Frequency modulation.

When the modulating frequency is subaudio (below 20 hertz), the result is what musicians call vibrato.

```
In[15]:= FrequencyModulation[660, {7,70}, 0.5] //Show
Out[15]=          -Sound-
```

The modulation index is the ratio of the peak deviation to the modulating frequency. Higher values of the modulation index result in more partials and a brighter sound. Very high values will result in aliasing, and will add low-frequency components to the sound.

This is an example of frequency modulation with a modulation index of 5500/550.

```
In[16]:=  FrequencyModulation[
            440, {550, 5500}, 0.5] //Show
Out[16]=      -Sound-
```

The modulation ratio is the ratio of the modulating frequency to the carrier frequency. If this ratio is an integer greater than zero, the resulting overtones and sidebands will have harmonic relationships to each other, analogous to those of standard orchestral instruments. If the modulation ratio is not integer valued, the resulting overtones and sidebands will have an inharmonic relationship to each other, analogous to percussion instruments and bells. One speaks of a harmonic relationship when the overtones and sidebands have frequencies that coincide with the harmonics of some fundamental, not necessarily the carrier.

FrequencyModulation[f_c, {{f_1, pd_1}, {f_2, pd_2}, ...}, *dur*,
    ModulationType->Cascade]

create a Sound object that is a cascade frequency modulated sinusoid, where pd_i is the peak deviation associated with modulating frequency f_i, both values measured in hertz

Cascade frequency modulation.

Cascade frequency modulation is a type of frequency modulation where the modulating frequency is itself modulated, thus cascading the modulation. The expression for cascade frequency modulation with two modulating frequencies is given by $\sin(2\pi f_c t + \frac{pd_1}{f_{m1}} \sin(2\pi f_{m1} t + \frac{pd_2}{f_{m2}} \sin(2\pi f_{m2} t)))$. This nesting process can be carried out for a list of modulating frequencies of any size.

In this example of cascade frequency modulation, each modulating frequency is given a distinct peak deviation.

```
In[17]:=  FrequencyModulation[880, {{340, 100},
            {550, 50}, {730, 25}}, 0.5,
            ModulationType->Cascade] // Show
Out[17]=      -Sound-
```

FrequencyModulation[f_c, {{f_1, pd_1}, {f_2, pd_2}, ...}, *dur*,
    ModulationType->Parallel]

create a Sound object that is a parallel frequency modulated sinusoid, where pd_i is the peak deviation associated with modulating frequency f_i, both values measured in hertz

Parallel frequency modulation.

In contrast to cascade frequency modulation, parallel frequency modulation is a technique where the carrier frequency is modulated by two or more modulating frequencies that do not modulate each other. The expression for parallel frequency modulation with two modulating frequencies is given by $\sin(2\pi f_c t + \frac{pd_1}{f_{m1}} \sin(2\pi f_{m1} t) + \frac{pd_2}{f_{m2}} \sin(2\pi f_{m2} t))$.

This uses the same values as the example for cascade FM, but generates an instance of parallel FM instead. Note the stronger presence of the higher partials in the resulting sound.

```
In[18]:= FrequencyModulation[880,
            {{340, 100}, {550, 50}, {730, 25}}, 0.5,
            ModulationType->Parallel] // Show

Out[18]=       -Sound-
```

Reading Sound Files from Disk

There are numerous sound file formats used for the storage of sampled sounds. In general, they consist of a header containing information that describes the sound, followed by the sampled sound data. The ReadSoundfile function is capable of reading NeXT/Sun, WAVE, and AIFF sound file formats. ReadSoundfile can read the AIFF format used by SGI, Amiga, and some Apple sound files. It will not work with Apple's SoundDesigner II sound files, due to the fact that data (the sound samples) are kept in the data fork, but format information is kept in the resource fork.

ReadSoundfile["*soundfile*"]	read the specified sound file, and convert the sequence of samples into a list of integers between −32768 and +32767
ReadSoundfile["*soundfile*", PrintHeader->True]	display the header information while reading in the sound file

Reading a sound file into *Mathematica*.

ReadSoundfile lets you read a sampled sound file directly into *Mathematica*. The samples are translated into signed 16-bit integers. If the sound is stereo, ReadSoundfile returns a list of lists for the right and left channels. The returned list can be played with ListPlay or plotted with ListPlot.

This reads the Multimedia sound file chimes.wav, and returns a list of the samples in the file.

```
In[19]:= chimes = ReadSoundfile["chimes.wav",
            PrintHeader->True];

Format: Microsoft PCM WAVE RIFF

Duration: 0.72 seconds

Channels: 1

Sampling rate: 22050

Bits per sample: 8

Data size: 15876 bytes

Number of samples: 15876
```

The list chimes may be played with ListPlay, at the SampleRate displayed by setting PrintHeader->True. Note that the PlayRange is adjusted to account for the 16-bit signed samples.

```
In[20]:= ListPlay[chimes, SampleRate->22050,
            PlayRange->{-2^15,2^15}]

Out[20]=       -Sound-
```

Plot the sound with `ListPlot`. Remember to set `PlotRange` to a range that will accommodate the 16-bit signed amplitudes.

In[21]:= `ListPlot[chimes, PlotRange->{-2^15,2^15}]`

`ReadSoundfile` is capable of reading in sounds that have been mu-law encoded. Mu-law encoding is a logarithmic encoding scheme in which 12 bits of data are stored in 8 bits, resulting in telephone-quality sound. Voice-mail frequently uses some form of mu-law encoding.

Read in the mu-law encoded Sun sound file `bubbles.au`.

In[22]:= `bubbles = ReadSoundfile["bubbles.au",`
`                              PrintHeader->True];`

Format: NeXT/Sun

Duration: 3.90138 seconds

Channels: 1

Sampling rate: 8000

Bits per sample: 8

Data size: 31211 bytes

Number of samples: 31211

Encoding: 8-bit mulaw

Text: bubbling goop

Play the sound with `ListPlay`.

In[23]:= `ListPlay[bubbles, SampleRate->8000,`
`                    PlayRange->{-2^15, 2^15}]`

Out[23]=   -Sound-

In the case of stereo files, the data are returned as a list of two lists: left-channel sample data and right-channel sample data.

This reads in a stereo file.

```
In[24]:= voice = ReadSoundfile["voice.snd",
                   PrintHeader->True] ;

Format: NeXT/Sun
Duration: 0.143492 seconds
Channels: 2
Sampling rate: 22050
Bits per sample: 16
Data size: 25312 bytes
Number of samples: 6328
Text: by Christopher Penrose
```

This plays the stereo sound.

```
In[25]:= ListPlay[voice, SampleRate->22050,
                   PlayRange->{-2^15, 2^15}]

Out[25]=         -Sound-
```

When plotting a stereo sound, remember to add the two lists together; otherwise you will get a plot of the left channel followed by the right channel.

The left and right channels are added together before plotting.

```
In[26]:= ListPlot[Plus @@ voice,
                   PlotRange->{-2^15, 2^15}];
```

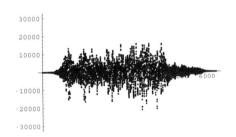

Setting Options DisplayFunction, SampleRate, SampleDepth, and PlayRange

All the sound-generating functions in the `Miscellaneous`Audio`` package use the *Mathematica* `Play` function to do the low-level work of generating sounds. Some options of `Play`, such as `SampleRate`, `SampleDepth`, and `PlayRange`, can significantly change the quality and constitution of the resulting sound. The option `DisplayFunction` affects whether the created `Sound` object will be played immediately after it is returned.

Loading the package will set the options `SampleRate`, `SampleDepth`, and `PlayRange` to their optimum values for your machine. The package also sets `DisplayFunction->Identity`, which causes `Sound` objects to be returned without being played. You can reset these options by using *Mathematica*'s `SetOptions` function, or by specifying them on the command line.

You can create a sound at a specified SampleRate.	`In[27]:= AmplitudeModulation[440, 100, 1, 0.5,`
	`            SampleRate->22050]`
	
	`Out[27]=      -Sound-`

By setting the option `DisplayFunction->$SoundDisplayFunction`, you can hear a sound immediately after it is created by *Mathematica*, without having to use the `Show` function each time. This is most useful when you are experimenting with combinations of arguments and wish to hear the effect they have on the resulting sound.

Now all `Sound` objects returned by `FrequencyModulation` will be played immediately after being returned.	`In[28]:= SetOptions[FrequencyModulation,`
	`         DisplayFunction->$SoundDisplayFunction]`
	
	`Out[28]= {DisplayFunction → (Display[$SoundDisplay, #1]&),`
	`         ModulationType → Standard, PlayRange → All,`
	`         SampleDepth → 8, SampleRate → 8192}`

This assigns a frequency modulated sound to `casfm2` and plays the sound.	`In[29]:= casfm2 = FrequencyModulation[660,{{770, 100},`
	`         {660, 50}, {540, 25}}, 0.5, ModulationType->Cascade]`
	
	`Out[29]=      -Sound-`

You can hear the same function with slightly different values of the modulating frequencies.	`In[30]:= FrequencyModulation[660,{{660, 100},`
	`         {540, 50}, {660, 25}}, 0.5, ModulationType->Cascade]`
	
	`Out[30]=      -Sound-`

Now `FrequencyModulation` will no longer play every `Sound` object it creates.	`In[31]:= SetOptions[FrequencyModulation, DisplayFunction->Identity]`
	
	`Out[31]= {DisplayFunction → Identity, ModulationType → Standard,`
	`         PlayRange → All, SampleDepth → 8, SampleRate → 8192}`

You will be better able to use the sound-generating functions if you are aware of the effect of the various options to `Play`.

`SampleRate` is an option for sound primitives that specifies the number of samples per second to generate for sounds. According to Nyquist's sampling theorem, *n* samples per second are required to accurately represent a waveform having a maximum frequency content of *n*/2 hertz. In other words, your sampling rate must be at least twice the highest frequency you would like to hear. Sampling at a lower rate will result in aliasing, in which frequency components above half the sampling rate are rendered as lower frequency components. Since people register frequencies in the range of 20–20,000 hertz as audio signals, a sampling rate of 40,000 samples per second is the minimum required for the accurate encoding of the entire audio range.

Mathematica allows you to set the `SampleRate` to any positive number. However, the sound that will be created depends upon the sampling rate of your digital-to-analog converter. If the converter's sampling rate is not a multiple of the chosen sampling rate, a software conversion to the converter's sampling rate will automatically take place, and there may be distortions in the resulting sound.

This is a frequency modulated sound at the default `SampleRate`.	`In[32]:= FrequencyModulation[660, {100,100},`
	`            0.5] // Show`
	
	`Out[32]=      -Sound-`

This plays the same sound with `SampleRate->1234`. The additional noise is due to the fact that the digital-to-analog converter's sampling rate is not a multiple of 1234 hertz.

```
In[33]:= FrequencyModulation[660, {100,100}, 0.5,
              SampleRate->1234] // Show

Out[33]=      -Sound-
```

`SampleDepth` (frequently called quantization) is an option for sound primitives which specifies how many bits should be used to encode sound amplitude levels. Setting `SampleDepth->8` gives you 2^8 different amplitude values, and `SampleDepth->16` gives you 2^{16}. You should choose a value for `SampleDepth` that is the best for your hardware.

Here is the pitch A5 using the default setting of `SampleDepth`.

```
In[34]:= Waveform[Sawtooth, 880, 0.5] // Show

Out[34]=      -Sound-
```

On some computers, this `SampleDepth` produces no sound at all. You might get a sound that is simply noisier.

```
In[35]:= Waveform[Sawtooth, 880, 0.5,
              SampleDepth->3] // Show

Out[35]=      -Sound-
```

`PlayRange` is an option for `Play` and related functions which specifies what range of sound amplitude levels should be included. The functions `Waveform` and `FrequencyModulation` set this value to `All`, and the `AmplitudeModulation` function sets it to `{-1,1}`. `PlayRange` in `Play` behaves like `PlotRange` in `Plot`.

Here is a simple plot of a sine waveform.

```
In[36]:= Plot[Sin[x], {x, 0, 2Pi}]
```

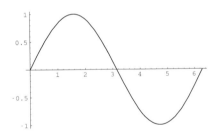

This gives the same plot with a restricted `PlotRange`.

```
In[37]:= Plot[Sin[x], {x, 0, 2Pi},
              PlotRange->{-0.5, 0.5}]
```

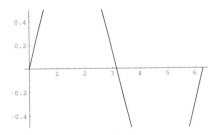

Notice that in the second plot, when the value of the function exceeds the limits specified by `PlotRange`, the value is cut off or clipped. Similarly, if the amplitude of your sound exceeds the setting of `PlayRange`, what you hear will not be a complete representation of your function. This phenomenon is termed waveshaping by composers and distortion by engineers. `PlayRange` should be set sufficiently high so that all generated samples may be represented without distortion.

Playing Sound Objects in Arbitrary Sequences

Since all the sound-generating functions defined in `Miscellaneous`Audio`` return a Sound object, the returned values can be played in sequence with the Show function.

First create three sounds.

```
In[38]:= {s1, s2, s3} =
         {Waveform[Sawtooth, 880, 0.2],
          AmplitudeModulation[440, 530, 1, 0.5],
          FrequencyModulation[660,
               {{300,400},{600,200}},
               0.3, ModulationType->Cascade]}
Out[38]=      {-Sound-, -Sound-, -Sound-}
```

This plays the three Sound objects in reverse sequence.

```
In[39]:= Show[s3, s2, s1]
Out[39]=      -Sound-
```

■ Miscellaneous 'BlackBodyRadiation'

A body that absorbs all radiation incident on it is called an ideal black body. This package provides functions giving the basic properties of black-body radiation at a specified temperature, and a function for plotting black-body spectral distributions.

PeakWavelength[*temp*]	wavelength of the maximum emission of a black body at the specified temperature
TotalPower[*temp*]	total power of a black body at the specified temperature
MaxPower[*temp, band*]	power of a black body at the specified temperature for the specified wavelength band about the peak wavelength

Black-body radiation properties.

This loads the package.

$In[1]:=$ `<<Miscellaneous'BlackBodyRadiation'`

The surface of the sun is about 5000 K. Assuming the sun is a black-body radiator, this gives the wavelength at which its spectrum peaks.

$In[2]:=$ `PeakWavelength[5000 Kelvin]`

$Out[2]= 5.8 \times 10^{-7}$ Meter

This gives the total power radiated by a black body at a temperature of 5000 K.

$In[3]:=$ `TotalPower[5000 Kelvin]`

$$Out[3]= \frac{3.54407 \times 10^{7} \text{ Watt}}{\text{Meter}^2}$$

This gives the radiative power in the wavelength interval of 0.1 μ about the peak wavelength of a black body at a temperature of 5000 K.

$In[4]:=$ `MaxPower[5000 Kelvin, 10^-7 Meter]`

$$Out[4]= \frac{4.01792 \times 10^{6} \text{ Watt}}{\text{Meter}^2}$$

BlackBodyProfile[*temp*$_1$, *temp*$_2$, ...]	plot the black-body spectral distribution profiles at the specified temperatures

Plotting black-body profiles.

This gives the spectral distribution of radiation from a black body for three different temperatures.

`In[5]:=` **BlackBodyProfile[4000 Kelvin, 5000 Kelvin, 6000 Kelvin,**
       PlotRange -> {{0, 2 10^(-6)}, {0, 1.1 10^14}}]

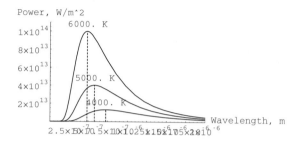

■ Miscellaneous 'Calendar'

This package provides a unified treatment of the basic calendar operations. The main idea is to treat the calendar as a generalized number system, so that days, weeks, months, and years are thought of as generalizing the digits of a number in a given base. A detailed analysis of how this is done is given in the third chapter of *Computational Recreations in Mathematica*, by Ilan Vardi (Addison-Wesley, 1991). The key to the implementation is *Mathematica*'s ability to work consistently with general objects.

DayOfWeek[{*year*, *month*, *day*}]	give the day of the week on which the given date occurred
DaysBetween[{*year*₁, *month*₁, *day*₁}, {*year*₂, *month*₂, *day*₂}]	give the number of days between the given dates
DaysPlus[{*year*, *month*, *day*}, *n*]	give the date *n* days after the given date

Calendar computations using the standard calendar.

This loads the package.

`In[1]:= <<Miscellaneous'Calendar'`

The basic calendar utility is finding the day of the week.

`In[2]:= DayOfWeek[{1988, 6, 23}]`

`Out[2]= Thursday`

This computes the number of days between the given dates. The year 1900 was not a leap year.

`In[3]:= DaysBetween[{1900, 1, 1}, {1901, 1, 1}]`

`Out[3]= 365`

January 2, 1901 is 366 days after January 1, 1900.

`In[4]:= DaysPlus[{1900, 1, 1}, 366]`

`Out[4]= {1901, 1, 2}`

DayOfWeek[{*year*, *month*, *day*}, Calendar -> *cal*]
                    give the day of the week on which the given date occurred
                    using the calendar system *cal*

DaysBetween[{*year*₁, *month*₁, *day*₁}, {*year*₂, *month*₂, *day*₂}, Calendar -> *cal*]
                    give the number of days between the given dates using the
                    calendar system *cal*

DaysPlus[{*year*, *month*, *day*}, *n*, Calendar -> *cal*]
                    give the date *n* days after the given date using the calendar
                    system *cal*

CalendarChange[{*year*, *month*, *day*}, *cal*₁, *cal*₂]
                    convert the date given in *cal*₁ into a date given in *cal*₂

Calendar computations using specified systems.

The Gregorian calendar has been in use in the Western world since 1582 by Roman Catholic countries, and since 1752 by English-speaking countries. The Gregorian calendar counts leap years every year divisible by 4, except for centuries not divisible by 400, which are not leap years.

The calendar used before the Gregorian calendar was the Julian calendar. This system counts *every* year divisible by 4 as a leap year. At present there is a disparity of 13 days between the calendars. The changeover between these two calendars was done by omitting a number of days, therefore one must account for this in computations.

The default calendar used in this package is the one used by England and her former colonies (*e.g.*, the United States). It uses the Gregorian calendar for dates starting with September 14, 1752, and the Julian calendar for dates up to September 2, 1752. If you do not specify a system, this is the calendar used by DayOfWeek, DaysBetween, and DaysPlus.

The Julian calendar is valid to March 1, year 4, but not before then since the year 4 was *not* a leap year.

The Islamic calendar is used mainly to keep track of Islamic holy days. It is a purely lunar calendar and a year has either 354 or 355 days. The months do not correspond to the solar year and migrate over the solar year following a 30-year cycle. The Islamic calendar began on the Hejira, which was July 16, 622, in the Julian calendar.

In the Julian calendar, the year beginning a century not divisible by 400 is a leap year.

```
In[5]:= DaysBetween[{1900, 1, 1}, {1901, 1, 1},
                      Calendar -> Julian]

Out[5]= 366
```

The Gregorian calendar is 13 days ahead of the Julian calendar.

```
In[6]:= CalendarChange[{1992, 2, 29},
                        Gregorian, Julian]

Out[6]= {1992, 2, 16}
```

Here is a conversion into the Islamic system.

```
In[7]:= CalendarChange[{1992, 2, 29},
            Gregorian, Islamic]

Out[7]= {1412, 8, 25}
```

This gives the first day in the Islamic system, the date of the Hejira. The date is given in the Julian calendar because the Gregorian calendar was not used before 1582.

```
In[8]:= CalendarChange[{1,1,1}, Islamic, Julian]

Out[8]= {622, 7, 16}
```

EasterSunday[*year*]	give the date of Easter Sunday in the Gregorian system
EasterSundayGreekOrthodox[*year*]	give the date of Easter Sunday according to the Greek Orthodox Church using the Gregorian system
JewishNewYear[*year*]	give the date of the Jewish New Year occurring in Gregorian years between 1900 and 2099

Dates of holidays.

In 1945, Easter Sunday was on April 1.

```
In[9]:= EasterSunday[1945]

Out[9]= {1945, 4, 1}
```

This uses the pre-Gregorian computation, but the result is given as a Gregorian date.

```
In[10]:= EasterSundayGreekOrthodox[1984]

Out[10]= {1984, 4, 22}
```

This gives the date of the Jewish New Year in the Gregorian year 1997.

```
In[11]:= JewishNewYear[1997]

Out[11]= {1997, 10, 2}
```

~■ Miscellaneous`ChemicalElements`

Abbreviation[*element*]	give the standard abbreviation
AtomicNumber[*element*]	give the atomic number of *element*
AtomicWeight[*element*]	give the atomic weight
StableIsotopes[*element*]	give a list of the stable isotopes of *element*
Elements	list of the names of the chemical elements

Basic properties of the chemical elements.

This loads the package.

```
In[1]:= <<Miscellaneous`ChemicalElements`
```

This gives the atomic weight of tungsten using the data in the package.

```
In[2]:= AtomicWeight[Tungsten]
Out[2]= 183.84
```

If you ask for the atomic weight of an unstable element, *Mathematica* issues a warning message.

```
In[3]:= AtomicWeight[Plutonium]
AtomicWeight::unstable:
    No stable isotope of Plutonium exists.
Out[3]= 244
```

This switches off the warning message.

```
In[4]:= Off[AtomicWeight::unstable]
```

Here is a plot of the ratio of atomic
weight to atomic number.

```
In[5]:= ListPlot[Map[
            AtomicWeight[#]/AtomicNumber[#]&,
            Drop[Elements, -1]],
          PlotJoined -> True]
```

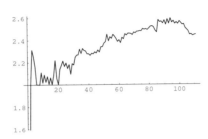

`MeltingPoint[`*element*`]`	give the melting point in degrees Kelvin
`BoilingPoint[`*element*`]`	give the boiling point in degrees Kelvin
`HeatOfFusion[`*element*`]`	give the heat of fusion in kilojoules per mole
`HeatOfVaporization[`*element*`]`	give the heat of vaporization in kilojoules per mole
`Density[`*element*`]`	give the density in kilograms per cubic meter
`ThermalConductivity[`*element*`]`	give the thermal conductivity in watts per meter per Kelvin

Physical properties of chemical elements.

The densities given are usually for the elements at 298 Kelvin. A message is generated if the density given is for another temperature or for a special form of the element. The thermal conductivities are for the specified elements at 300 Kelvin unless a message is returned giving an exception.

This gives the heat of fusion of
nitrogen.

```
In[6]:= HeatOfFusion[Nitrogen]
```

$$Out[6]= \frac{0.72\,\text{Joule Kilo}}{\text{Mole}}$$

When you ask for the density,
Mathematica warns you that this
density is taken at a temperature of 21
Kelvin. The standard used for most
other elements is 298 Kelvin.

```
In[7]:= Density[Nitrogen]
```

`Density::temp: Density is for Nitrogen at 21 Kelvin.`

$$Out[7]= \frac{1026.\,\text{Kilogram}}{\text{Meter}^3}$$

This thermal conductivity is for the gaseous state.

In[8]:= **ThermalConductivity[Nitrogen]**

ThermalConductivity::form:
    Thermal conductivity is for the gaseous form of
      Nitrogen.

Out[8]= $\dfrac{0.02598\,\mathrm{Watt}}{\mathrm{Kelvin\,Meter}}$

ElectronConfiguration[*element*]	give a list of the electron configuration
ElectronConfigurationFormat[*element*]	give a list of the electron configuration including orbital labels

Electronic structure of chemical elements.

When you use ElectronConfiguration to get the electronic configuration of an element, the result is a list using the standard order of listing of subshells 1*s*, 2*s*, 2*p*, 3*s*,.... Each shell is grouped into a sublist. ElectronConfigurationFormat returns the number of electrons in each subshell along with the label for the subshell.

This gives the electronic configuration as a list in the standard format.

In[9]:= **ElectronConfiguration[Actinium]**

Out[9]= {{2}, {2, 6}, {2, 6, 10}, {2, 6, 10, 14}, {2, 6, 10}, {2, 6, 1}, {2}}

This includes the orbital labels in the list.

In[10]:= **ElectronConfigurationFormat[Actinium]**

Out[10]= $1s^2\ 2s^2 2p^6\ 3s^2 3p^6 3d^{10}\ 4s^2 4p^6 4d^{10} 4f^{14}\ 5s^2 5p^6 5d^{10}\ 6s^2 6p^6 6d^1\ 7s^2$

IonizationPotential[*element*]	give the ionization potential of the specified element
SpecificHeat[*element*]	give the specific heat of the specified element

Ionization potential and specific heat of chemical elements.

This gives the specific heat of potassium.

In[11]:= **SpecificHeat[Potassium]**

Out[11]= $\dfrac{0.757\,\mathrm{Joule\,Kelvin}}{\mathrm{Gram}}$

This gives the ionization potential of helium.

In[12]:= **IonizationPotential[Helium]**

Out[12]= 24.587 ElectronVolt

Here is a plot of the ionization potential against the atomic number of the elements.

```
In[13]:= (Off[IonizationPotential::unknown];  Off[Graphics::gptn];
            ListPlot[ IonizationPotential[Elements]/ElectronVolt,
              PlotJoined -> True, PlotRange -> All])
```

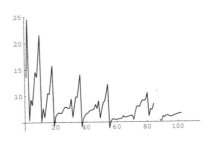

SolarSystemAbundance[*element*]	give the relative abundance of the specified element in the solar system
EarthCrustAbundance[*element*]	give the relative abundance of the specified element in the Earth's crust
EarthOceanAbundance[*element*]	give the relative abundance of the specified element in the Earth's ocean

Abundances of the chemical elements.

This gives the ten most abundant elements in the Solar System.

```
In[14]:= (Off[SolarSystemAbundance::unknown];
            Take[Reverse[Sort[
                  Map[{ SolarSystemAbundance[#] /. Unknown->0, #}&, Elements]
            ]], 10])

Out[14]= {{0.91, Hydrogen}, {0.089, Helium}, {0.00078, Oxygen},
            {0.00033, Carbon}, {0.000112, Neon}, {0.000102, Nitrogen},
            {0.000035, Magnesium}, {0.0000326, Sulfur},
            {0.0000326, Silicon}, {0.0000294, Iron}}
```

~■ Miscellaneous ` CityData `

Mathematica's programming capabilities allow you to create powerful customized tools. In this package, one approach to a sample database is used. This database, containing information about cities, is expandable and can be used with other functions.

CityData[*city, datatype*]	give data from the "field" *datatype* about the named city
CityData[*city*]	give a list of "fieldnames" and their corresponding values for *city*
CityData[*datatype*]	give a list of the cities in the database with information in this "field"

Accessing the `CityData` database.

The database currently contains only position location for a number of cities around the world. Positions are stored as latitudes and longitudes in a *{degree, minute, second}* or *{degree, minute}* format.

This loads the package.	`In[1]:= << Miscellaneous`CityData``
This gives the latitude and longitude of Montreal.	`In[2]:= CityData["Montreal", CityPosition]`
	`Out[2]= {{45, 30}, {-73, -36}}`
This returns the information in the database about Washington.	`In[3]:= CityData["Washington"]`
	`Out[3]= {{CityPosition, {{38, 53, 42}, {-77, -2, -12}}}}`

```
Abidjan, Ivory Coast        Andorre-la-Vella, Andorra
Abu Dhabi, UAE              Ankara, Turkey
Accra, Ghana               Antananarivo, Madagascar
Addis Ababa, Ethiopia      Apia, Western Samoa
Aden, Yemen                Ashkhabad, Turkmenistan
Agana, USA, GU             Asmera, Eritrea
Algiers, Algeria           Asuncion, Paraguay
Alma Alta, Kazakhstan      Athens, Greece
Amman, Jordan              Atlanta, USA, GA
Amsterdam, Netherlands     Baghdad, Iraq
Anchorage, USA, AK         Baku, Azerbaijan
```

Cities defined in `Miscellaneous`CityData``.

Bamako, Mali
Bandar Seri Begawan, Brunei
Bangkok, Thailand
Bangui, Central African Republic
Banjul, The Gambia
Basse-Terre, Guadeloupe
Basseterre, St. Christopher-
    Nevis
Beijing, China
Beirut, Lebanon
Belgrade, Yugoslavia
Belmopan, Belize
Beograd, Serbia
Berlin, Germany
Bern, Switzerland
Bishkek, Kirghizia
Bissau, Guinea-Bissau
Bogota, Colombia
Bombay, India
Bonn, Germany
Boston, USA, MA
Brasilia, Brazil
Bratislava, Slovak Republic
Brazzaville, Congo
Bridgetown, Barbados
Brussels, Belgium
Bucharest, Romania
Budapest, Hungary
Buenos Aires, Argentina
Bujumbura, Burundi
Cairo, Egypt
Calcutta, India
Canberra, Australia
Cape Town, South Africa
Caracas, Venezuela
Cardiff, United Kingdom
Castries, St. Lucia
Cayenne, French Guiana
Charlotte Amalie, USA, VI

Chicago, USA, IL
Colombo, Sri Lanka
Conakry, Guinea
Copenhagen, Denmark
Cupertino, USA, CA
Dacca, Bangladesh
Dakar, Sengal
Dallas, USA, TX
Damascus, Syria
Dar es Salaam, Tanzania
Denver, USA, CO
Djakarta, Indonesia
Djibouti, Djibouti
Doha, Qatar
Domaneab, Nauru
Dublin, Ireland
Dushanbe, Tajikistan
Edinburgh, United Kingdom
El Aaiun, Western Sahara
Fort-de-France, Martinique
Freetown, Sierra Leone
Funafuti, Tuvalu
Gaborone, Botswana
Geneva, Switzerland
Georgetown, Cayman Islands
Georgetown, Guyana
Gibraltar
Godthab, Greenland
Guatemala City, Guatemala
Hamilton, Bermuda
Hanoi, Vietnam
Harare, Zimbabwe
Havana, Cuba
Helsinki, Finland
Hong Kong
Honiara, Solomon Islands
Honolulu, USA, HI
Islamabad, Pakistan
Istanbul, Turkey

Cities defined in Miscellaneous'CityData'. (continued)

Jerusalem, Israel	Mecca, Saudi Arabia
Kabul, Afghanistan	Mexico City, Mexico
Kampala, Uganda	Miami, USA, FL
Karachi, Pakistan	Minneapolis, USA, MN
Katmandu, Nepal	Minsk, Belorussia
Khartoum, Sudan	Mogadisho, Somalia
Kiev, Ukraine	Monaco
Kigali, Rwanda	Monrovia, Liberia
Kingston, Jamaica	Montevideo, Uruguay
Kingstown, St. Vincent-Grenadines	Montreal, Canada
Kinshasa, Zaire	Moroni, Comoros
Kishinev, Moldavia	Moscow, Russia
Kolonia, USA, FM	Muscat, Oman
Koror, Belau	Nairobi, Kenya
Kuala Lumpur, Malaysia	Nassau, Bahamas
Kuwait City, Kuwait	Ndjamena, Chad
Lagos, Nigeria	New Delhi, India
La Paz, Bolivia	New York, USA, NY
Las Palmas, Canary Islands	Niamey, Niger
Libreville, Gabon	Nicosia, Cyprus
Lilongwe, Malawi	Nouakchott, Mauritania
Lima, Peru	Noumea, New Caledonia
Lisbon, Portugal	Nuku'alofa, Tonga
Ljubljana, Slovenia	Nukunonu, Tokelau
Lome, Togo	Oranjestad, Aruba
London, United Kingdom	Osaka, Japan
Los Angeles, USA, CA	Oslo, Norway
Luanda, Angola	Ottawa, Canada
Lusaka, Zambia	Ouagadougou, Burkina Faso
Luxembourg, Luxembourg	Pago Pago, American Samoa
Madrid, Spain	Panama City, Panama
Malabo, Equatorial Guinea	Paramaribo, Surinam
Male, Maldives	Paris, France
Managua, Nicaragua	Peking, China
Manama, Bahrain	Perth, Australia
Manila, Philippines	Philadelphia, USA, PA
Maputo, Mozambique	Phnom Penh, Cambodia
Maseru, Lesotho	Plymouth, Montserrat
Mbabane, Swaziland	Ponta Delgada, Azores

Cities defined in `Miscellaneous`CityData`. (continued)

Port-au-Prince, Haiti
Portland, USA, OR
Port Louis, Mauritius
Port Moresby, Papua New Guinea
Port of Spain, Trinidad and
    Tobago
Porto-Novo, Benin
Port Vila, Vanuatu
Prague, Czech Republic
Praia, Cape Verde Islands
Pretoria, South Africa
Pyongyang, North Korea
Quito, Ecuador
Rabat, Morocco
Rangoon, Burma
Reykjavik, Iceland
Riga, Latvia
Rio de Janeiro, Brazil
Riyadh, Saudi Arabia
Road Town, United Kingdom,
    Virgin Islands
Rome, Italy
Roseau, Dominica
Saint Louis, USA, MO
Salt Lake City, USA, UT
Sana, Yemen
San Diego, USA, CA
San Francisco, USA, CA
San Jose, Costa Rica
San Juan, USA, PR
San Marino, San Marino
San Salvador, El Salvador
Santiago, Chile
Santo Domingo, Dominican Republic
Sao Paulo, Brazil
Sao Tome, Sao Tome and Principe
Sarajevo, Bosnia-Herzogovina
Seoul, South Korea
Shanghai, China
Singapore, Singapore
Skopje, Macedonia
Sofia, Bulgaria

Stanley, Falkland Islands
St. Denis, Reunion
St. George's, Grenada
St. John's, Antigua and Barbuda
Stockholm, Sweden
St. Peterburg, Russia
Sucre, Bolivia
Suva, Fiji
Sydney, Australia
Taipei, Taiwan
Tallinn, Estonia
Tarawa, Kiribati
Tashkent, Uzbekistan
Tblisi, Georgia
Tegucigalpa, Honduras
Tehran, Iran
The Valley, Anguilla
Thimphu, Bhutan
Tianjin, China
Tirana, Albania
Tokyo, Japan
Torshavn, Faroe Islands
Tripoli, Libya
Tunis, Tunisia
Ulan Bator, Mongolia
Vaduz, Liechtenstein
Valletta, Malta
Vancouver, Canada
Vatican City
Victoria, Seychelles
Vienna, Austria
Vientiane, Laos
Vilnius, Lithuania
Warsaw, Poland
Washington, USA, DC
Wellington, New Zealand
Willemstad, Netherlands Antilles
Windhoek, Namibia
Yaounde, Cameroon
Yerevan, Armenia
Zagreb, Croatia
Zurich, Switzerland

Cities defined in Miscellaneous'CityData'. (continued)

You can give a more precise name for a city using the form {*cityname*, *countryname*}, with more precise indicators such as state names following, if necessary. The database also checks the spelling of your request. If there is no matching name, but a name that is close, that name will be suggested to you.

This city is in the database under the name Rome.

```
In[4]:= CityData["Roma", CityPosition]

CityData::alternates:
   Requested city not in database.  Possible alternatives:
      {{Rome, Italy}}

Out[4]= CityData[Roma, CityPosition]
```

CityDistance["*city*$_1$", "*city*$_2$"]	give the distance between the cities in kilometers
CityDistance["*city*$_1$", "*city*$_2$", CityDistanceMethod -> *method*]	give the distance using the specified method, a pure function of two arguments representing the positions of the cities

The CityDistance function.

The function CityDistance uses the positions in the database to determine the distance between two cities. The default method of computing distance is SphericalDistance from the package Miscellaneous`Geodesy`.

This gives the distance between Washington and Montreal.

```
In[5]:= CityDistance["Washington", "Montreal"]//N
Out[5]= 786.915
```

$CityFields	the symbol that holds the names of the data fields in the database
CityPosition	the field in the database that holds position information

Controlling information in the database.

The database is quite expandable; you can add additional cities and additional information for each city.

This places position information for Champaign, Illinois, into the database.

```
In[6]:= CityPosition[{"Champaign", "USA", "IL"}] =
           {{40, 7, 5}, {-88, -14, -48}};
```

Here is the position of Champaign.

```
In[7]:= CityData["Champaign", CityPosition]
Out[7]= {{40, 7, 5}, {-88, -14, -48}}
```

This adds a new field to the database to hold population information.

```
In[8]:= AppendTo[$CityFields, CityPopulation];
```

Here is the population for Washington.   *In[9]:=* **CityPopulation[{"Washington", "USA", "DC"}] = 638000;**

This accesses all data about   *In[10]:=* **CityData["Washington"]**
Washington in the database.
                                         Out[10]= {{CityPosition, {{38, 53, 42}, {-77, -2, -12}}},
                                                    {CityPopulation, 638000}}

■ Miscellaneous 'Geodesy'

Geodesy is the branch of science that deals with such topics as determining positions and areas over large parts of the Earth, the shape and size of the Earth, and the variations in the Earth's gravitational and magnetic fields. The primary functions in this package are used for determining the distance between two points.

SphericalDistance[pos_1, pos_2]	calculate the distance between the pos_i using a spherical model
SpheroidalDistance[pos_1, pos_2]	calculate the distance between the pos_i using a spheroidal model

Finding the distance between two points on a sphere.

Each position can be given in degrees as a latitude-longitude pair. A coordinate can also be expressed in the form {*degrees*, *minutes*, *seconds*}. A negative value for a coordinate indicates that the coordinate is South latitude or West longitude. Distances are returned in kilometers as the default.

This loads the package.	*In[1]:=* **<< Miscellaneous`Geodesy`**
This gives the distance between 0 lat., 0 long., and 45 N. lat., 45 E. long., using a spherical model.	*In[2]:=* **SphericalDistance[{0, 0}, {45, 45}] //N** *Out[2]=* 6671.7
Here is the distance between the same points using a spheroidal model.	*In[3]:=* **SpheroidalDistance[{0, 0}, {45, 45}] //N** *Out[3]=* 6662.47
This is the difference between the two models.	*In[4]:=* **% - %%** *Out[4]=* -9.23014

The spherical model is based on an exact formula, while the spheroidal model is an approximation algorithm that is fairly good for distances of less than 10,000 kilometers. Because of the nature of this approximation, all computation with SpheroidalDistance is done with machine-precision numbers.

Radius -> *radius*	specify the radius of the sphere in the spherical model
SemimajorAxis -> *length*	specify the length of the semimajor axis in the spheroidal model
Eccentricity -> *value*	specify the value of the eccentricity in the spheroidal model

Options to control the size of the shape in the models.

The distances between points can be modified by using different values for the radius of the sphere, or the length of the semimajor axis and the eccentricity of the spheroid using the options Radius,

SemimajorAxis, and Eccentricity, respectively. The default values for these options are those for the Earth from the WGS-84 standard, in kilometers.

`ToAuthalicRadius[`*semimajor*`, `*eccentricity*`]`	compute radius of authalic sphere given spheroid's semimajor axis and eccentricity
`GeodeticToAuthalic[{`*lat*`, `*long*`}, `*eccentricity*`]`	compute coordinates of corresponding point on authalic sphere given latitude and longitude of point on spheroid with specified eccentricity
`ToDegrees[{`*deg*`, `*min*`, `*sec*`}]`	convert coordinate in degree-minute-second format to degrees
`ToDMS[`*deg*`]`	convert coordinate in degrees to degree-minute-second format

Conversions between models and coordinate systems.

The simplest way to convert to the sphere from the spheroid is to use the authalic sphere. This sphere has the same surface area as the reference spheroid.

Here is a comparison of the two shapes, with an ellipse whose eccentricity is much larger than the Earth, for effect.

```
In[5]:= Show[Graphics[{
          Circle[{0, 0}, ToAuthalicRadius[1, .6]],
            Dashing[{.03}],
          Circle[{0, 0}, {1, Sqrt[1 - (.6)^2]} ]}],
              AspectRatio -> Automatic]
```

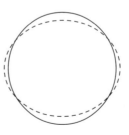

Note that the eccentricity used in the above diagram was .6. The actual eccentricity of the Earth's spheroid is approximately .081.

■ Miscellaneous ` Music `

The functions defined in Miscellaneous ` Music ` allow you to make conversions between cents and hertz, and play scales in one of the common tuning systems, or in a user-specified tuning system. In addition, a set of equal-tempered pitch/frequency equivalents is defined.

When you try the examples in this documentation, your computer display may not look exactly the same, since the graphic displays accompanying *Mathematica*'s sound generation vary from platform to platform.

Scale[*ilist*, *freq*, *dur*]	create a Sound object that is a sequence of pitches corresponding to *ilist*, a list of intervals measured in cents, starting at *freq* hertz and lasting *dur* seconds

Creating a scale.

Scale creates a pitch sequence from a predefined interval list or an arbitrary list of numbers interpreted as intervals measured in cents.

This loads the package.

```
In[1]:= << Miscellaneous ` Music `
```

JustMajor is an interval list. This plays a major scale in just intonation that starts at 440 Hz and lasts for 3 seconds.

```
In[2]:= Scale[JustMajor, 440, 3] // Show
Out[2]=        -Sound-
```

The list of intervals does not have to be in ascending or descending order. Here the starting frequncy is 880 Hz.

```
In[3]:= Scale[{100, 950, 350, 1200}, 880, 1] // Show
Out[3]=        -Sound-
```

QuarterTone	SixthTone
PythagoreanMajor	JustMajor
PythagoreanChromatic	JustMinor
MeanMajor	TemperedMajor
MeanMinor	TemperedMinor
MeanChromatic	TemperedChromatic

Predefined interval lists measured in cents.

HertzToCents[*flist*]	convert a list of frequencies measured in hertz to a list of intervals measured in cents
CentsToHertz[*ilist*]	convert a list of intervals measured in cents to a list of frequencies measured in hertz, beginning at frequency 440 hertz
CentsToHertz[*ilist*, *f*]	convert a list of intervals measured in cents to a list of frequencies measured in hertz, beginning at frequency *f*

Converting between hertz and cents.

The two functions HertzToCents and CentsToHertz convert a list of one type to its complementary type.

This takes a list of frequencies in hertz and gives the distance from one frequency to the next in cents.

```
In[4]:= HertzToCents[{400, 450, 525}]
Out[4]= {203.91, 266.871}
```

Here is a list consisting of the frequencies in a one-octave, equal-tempered chromatic scale starting at 440 hertz.

```
In[5]:= alist = Table[ N[440 2^(i/12)], {i, 0, 12}]
Out[5]= {440., 466.164, 493.883, 523.251, 554.365, 587.33, 622.254,
         659.255, 698.456, 739.989, 783.991, 830.609, 880.}
```

This confirms that the distance between adjacent pairs of frequencies in alist is 100 cents.

```
In[6]:= HertzToCents[alist]
Out[6]= {100., 100., 100., 100., 100., 100., 100., 100., 100., 100.,
         100., 100.}
```

This gives the frequency that is 600 cents above the default frequency, 440 hertz, or in musical terminology, one-half octave above the pitch A4.

```
In[7]:= CentsToHertz[{0, 600}]
Out[7]= {440., 622.254}
```

Here is a list of all the frequencies of equal-tempered half-steps between 880 and 1760 hertz.

```
In[8]:= CentsToHertz[Range[0, 1200, 100], 880]
Out[8]= {880., 932.328, 987.767, 1046.5, 1108.73, 1174.66, 1244.51,
         1318.51, 1396.91, 1479.98, 1567.98, 1661.22, 1760.}
```

Here are the frequencies of a 36-tone octave, starting at 660 hertz.

```
In[9]:= CentsToHertz[Range[0, 1200, 33.333333], 660]
Out[9]= {660., 672.831, 685.911, 699.246, 712.839, 726.697, 740.825,
         755.227, 769.909, 784.877, 800.135, 815.69, 831.548,
         847.714, 864.194, 880.994, 898.121, 915.581, 933.381,
         951.526, 970.025, 988.883, 1008.11, 1027.71, 1047.68,
         1068.05, 1088.82, 1109.98, 1131.56, 1153.56, 1175.99,
         1198.85, 1222.15, 1245.91, 1270.14, 1294.83, 1320.}
```

The Miscellaneous'Music' package provides a list of equal-tempered pitch/frequency equivalents. Pitches are named in pitch class/octave notation, where the pitch class is given by a letter from A to G, and the octave is an integer from 0 and 7. Flat notes are designated with the appendage flat (as in `Bflat` for B-flat), and sharp notes are designated with the appendage sharp (as in `Gsharp` for G-sharp).

Most chromatic equivalences are available, for example, C-flat is the same as B, and E-sharp is the same as F. Double-flats and double-sharps are not defined.

The difference between `Aflat4` and `Eflat5` is 700 cents in equal temperament.	`In[10]:= HertzToCents[{Aflat4, Eflat5}]`
	
	`Out[10]= {700.}`

This plays a perfect fifth.	`In[11]:= Play[Sin[2 Pi Aflat4 t] + Sin[2 Pi Eflat5 t],`
	`            {t, 0, 0.2}]`
	
	`Out[11]=        -Sound-`

■ Miscellaneous 'PhysicalConstants'

In addition to providing a comprehensive environment for calculations and a programming language, *Mathematica* is also a system for representing and presenting scientific and technical knowledge. Certain packages are included with *Mathematica* to provide easy access to commonly used scientific data, such as the value of physical constants and conversion factors for various systems of units.

SpeedOfLight	the speed of light is 299792458 meter/second
AvogadroConstant	Avogadro's constant is approximately 6.0221367×10^{23} mole^{-1}
ElectronMass	the mass of an electron is approximately $9.10938797 \times 10^{-31}$ kilograms
FineStructureConstant	the fine structure constant is approximately $1/137.0359895$
EarthMass	the mass of the earth is approximately 5.976×10^{24} kilograms
AccelerationDueToGravity	the acceleration due to gravity is approximately 9.80665 meters/second^2

Some common physical constants.

This loads the package.	`In[1]:= <<Miscellaneous'PhysicalConstants'`
This gives the mass of a proton.	`In[2]:= ProtonMass`
	$Out[2]= 1.67262 \times 10^{-27}$ Kilogram
Here is the distance that light could travel in the age of the universe.	`In[3]:= SpeedOfLight AgeOfUniverse`
	$Out[3]= 1.40902 \times 10^{26}$ Meter

AccelerationDueToGravity   MuonMagneticMoment
AgeOfUniverse   MuonMass
AvogadroConstant   NeutronComptonWavelength
BohrRadius   NeutronMagneticMoment
BoltzmannConstant   NeutronMass
ClassicalElectronRadius   PlanckConstant
CosmicBackgroundTemperature   PlanckConstantReduced
DeuteronMagneticMoment   PlanckMass
DeuteronMass   ProtonComptonWavelength
EarthMass   ProtonMagneticMoment
EarthRadius   ProtonMass
ElectronCharge   QuantizedHallConductance
ElectronComptonWavelength   RydbergConstant
ElectronGFactor   SackurTetrodeConstant
ElectronMagneticMoment   SolarConstant
ElectronMass   SolarLuminosity
FaradayConstant   SolarRadius
FineStructureConstant   SolarSchwarzschildRadius
GalacticUnit   SpeedOfLight
GravitationalConstant   SpeedOfSound
HubbleConstant   StefanConstant
IcePoint   ThomsonCrossSection
MagneticFluxQuantum   VacuumPermeability
MolarGasConstant   VacuumPermittivity
MolarVolume   WeakMixingAngle
MuonGFactor

Physical constants.

◼ Miscellaneous`RealOnly`

In high school algebra, exponents and radicals are taught early, but complex numbers are usually left to more advanced courses. Some algebra teachers have asked for a package that would allow them to avoid complex numbers. *Mathematica* is flexible enough to block out imaginary and complex numbers in a way that is mathematically correct.

Two ideas are implemented in the package `RealOnly`. Odd roots of negative numbers are defined to be negative, and calculations with unavoidable complex numbers are condensed to the symbol `Nonreal`. This is done by redefining the built-in functions `Power` and `$Post`.

Without loading the package, *Mathematica* calculates a cube root of a negative number to be complex. So no points are plotted for negative values of x and warning messages are generated.

```
In[1]:= Plot[x ^ (1/3), {x, -8, 8}];

Plot::plnr:
    1/3
   x    is not a machine-size real number at x = -8..

Plot::plnr:
    1/3
   x    is not a machine-size real number at x = -7.35093.

Plot::plnr:
    1/3
   x    is not a machine-size real number at x = -6.64306.

General::stop:
   Further output of Plot::plnr
     will be suppressed during this calculation.
```

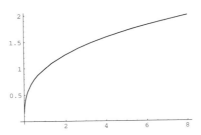

Every cubic equation has three roots, counting multiplicity.

```
In[2]:= Solve[x^3 == -8.0]

Out[2]= {{x → -2.}, {x → 1. - 1.73205 i}, {x → 1. + 1.73205 i}}
```

Any one of these three roots could be taken as the cube root of −8.0. Ordinarily, *Mathematica* chooses the one with the least positive argument (the third solution in this case).

```
In[3]:= (-8.0) ^ (1/3)

Out[3]= 1. + 1.73205 i
```

$b \wedge (m/n)$	gives $(-(-b) \wedge (1/n))\wedge m$ if b is negative and m and n are integers with n odd
$x + y\, I$	if x and y are real, gives x if y is small and gives `Nonreal` otherwise
$f[\ldots, \text{Nonreal}, \ldots]$	gives `Nonreal` for an elementary function or operation f

Automatic transformations caused by the `RealOnly` package.

This loads the package.

```
In[4]:= Needs["Miscellaneous`RealOnly`"]
```

Power has been redefined so that an odd root of a negative number is negative.

```
In[5]:= (-8.0) ^ (1/3)
Out[5]= -2.
```

Now the plot works for negative values of x.

```
In[6]:= Plot[x ^ (1/3), {x, -8, 8}];
```

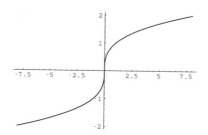

In addition to modifying `Power`, the package suppresses complex numbers. This is now the solution of the cubic equation.

```
In[7]:= Solve[x^3 == -8.0]
Nonreal::warning: Nonreal number encountered.
Out[7]= {{x -> -2.}, {x -> Nonreal}, {x -> Nonreal}}
```

Very small imaginary parts are transformed to 0.

```
In[8]:= {23 + 0. I, Sin[ArcSin[23.]]}
Out[8]= {23, 23.}
```

A number with an imaginary part that is not small is transformed to `Nonreal`.

```
In[9]:= {ArcSin[23.], Sin[23. + I]}
Nonreal::warning: Nonreal number encountered.
Out[9]= {Nonreal, Nonreal}
```

Finally, elementary calculations involving unavoidable complex numbers are transformed to `Nonreal`.

```
In[10]:= Tan[a + 23 / (a + b I)]
Nonreal::warning: Nonreal number encountered.
Out[10]= Nonreal
```

⊞ Miscellaneous`ResonanceAbsorptionLines`

The functions defined in Miscellaneous`ResonanceAbsorptionLines` allow you to efficiently search through an atomic data table for resonance absorption lines. Other functions give absorption maps of particular elements or of a particular wavelength range.

FindIons[*wavelength1*, *wavelenth2*]	give the resonance absorption lines in the wavelength range between *wavelength1* and *wavelength2*

Finding the resonance absorption lines.

This loads the package.

In[1]:= **<<Miscellaneous`ResonanceAbsorptionLines`**

This gives the resonance absorption lines in the wavelength range between 1215 Angstrom and 1220 Angstrom.

In[2]:= **FindIons[1215 Angstrom, 1220 Angstrom]**

Out[2]= {{Hydrogen, I, 1215.67 Angstrom}, {Hydrogen,
  I, 1215.67 Angstrom}, {Hydrogen, I, 1215.67 Angstrom},
  {Deuterium, I, 1215.34 Angstrom}, {Deuterium,
  I, 1215.34 Angstrom}, {Deuterium, I, 1215.34 Angstrom},
  {Oxygen, Vanadium, 1218.34 Angstrom}, {Phosphorus,
  I, 1218.39 Angstrom}, {Phosphorus, I, 1217.84 Angstrom},
  {Sulfur, I, 1218.6 Angstrom}, {Sulfur, I, 1218.57 Angstrom},
  {Sulfur, I, 1218.51 Angstrom}, {Manganese,
  II, 1219.6 Angstrom}, {Manganese, II, 1218.75 Angstrom},
  {Manganese, II, 1218.7 Angstrom}}

AtomicData[*element*]	give the spectral data for the resonance absorption lines produced by the specified element
VacuumWavelength[*element*]	give a list of the wavelength in vacuum for the resonance absorption lines produced by the specified element

Properties of resonance absorption lines.

AtomicData[*element*] gives a list of properties for the lines produced by the specified element. These properties are vacuum wavelength, air wavelength, lower term fine structure energy, statistical weight of the lower level, statistical weight of the upper level, relative strength, transition probability, damping constant, and oscillator strength of the element. Individual properties can be selected using the functions VacuumWavelength, AirWavelength, LowerTermFineStructureEnergy, LowerStatisticalWeight, UpperStatisticalWeight, RelativeStrength, TransitionProbability, DampingConstant, and OscillatorStrength.

AirWavelength[*element*]	give a list of {*wavelength*$_v$, *wavelength*$_a$} pairs, where *wavelength*$_v$ is the wavelength in vacuum and *wavelength*$_a$ is the wavelength in air for the resonance absorption lines produced by the specified element
LowerTermFineStructureEnergy[*element*]	
	give a list of {*wavelength*$_v$, *energy*} pairs, where *energy* is the energy of the fine structure level in the lower term for the lines produced by the specified element
LowerStatisticalWeight[*element*]	
	give a list of {*wavelength*$_v$, *weight*} pairs, where *weight* is the statistical weight of the lower level for the lines produced by the specified element
UpperStatisticalWeight[*element*]	
	give a list of {*wavelength*$_v$, *weight*} pairs, where *weight* is the statistical weight of the upper level for the lines produced by the specified element
RelativeStrength[*element*]	give a list of {*wavelength*$_v$, *strength*} pairs, where *strength* is the relative strength of the lines produced by the specified element
TransitionProbability[*element*]	
	give a list of {*wavelength*$_v$, *probability*} pairs, where *probability* is the spontaneous transition probability of the lines produced by the specified element
DampingConstant[*element*]	give a list of {*wavelength*$_v$, *damping*} pairs, where *damping* is a natural damping constant of the lines produced by the specified element
OscillatorStrength[*element*]	give a list of {*wavelength*$_v$, *strength*} pairs, where *strength* is the absorption oscillator strength of the lines produced by the specified element

Properties of resonance absorption lines paired with associated wavelengths in vacuum.

This gives a list of pairs of vacuum wavelength and oscillator strength for the resonance absorption lines produced by Beryllium.

In[3]:= `OscillatorStrength[Beryllium]`

$$Out[3]= \left\{\left\{1036.3\,\text{Angstrom},\ \frac{1.788\times10^8}{\text{Second}}\right\},\right.$$
$$\left\{1036.31\,\text{Angstrom},\ \frac{1.28\times10^7}{\text{Second}}\right\},\ \left\{1036.32\,\text{Angstrom},\right.$$
$$\left.\frac{1.7879\times10^8}{\text{Second}}\right\},\ \left\{1661.48\,\text{Angstrom},\ \frac{0.}{\text{Second}}\right\},$$
$$\left\{2349.33\,\text{Angstrom},\ \frac{5.4699\times10^8}{\text{Second}}\right\},\ \left\{3131.33\,\text{Angstrom},\right.$$
$$\left.\frac{1.1502\times10^8}{\text{Second}}\right\},\ \left\{3131.54\,\text{Angstrom},\ \frac{0.}{\text{Second}}\right\},$$
$$\left.\left\{3131.97\,\text{Angstrom},\ \frac{1.1495\times10^8}{\text{Second}}\right\}\right\}$$

The ionization level of an element can be specified by giving the quoted roman numeral, "I", "II", "III", "IV", "V", or "VI", as a second argument to a property function.

This gives the paired data for vacuum wavelength and oscillator strength for the lines produced by Beryllium at the ionization level I.

In[4]:= `OscillatorStrength[Beryllium, "I"]`

$$Out[4]= \left\{\left\{1661.48\,\text{Angstrom},\ \frac{0.}{\text{Second}}\right\},\right.$$
$$\left.\left\{2349.33\,\text{Angstrom},\ \frac{5.4699\times10^8}{\text{Second}}\right\}\right\}$$

`WavelengthAbsorptionMap[`*wavelength1*`, `*wavelength2*`]`
give the absorption map in the wavelength range between *wavelength1* and *wavelength2*

`ElementAbsorptionMap[`*element*`]`
give the absorption map of the specified element

`ElementAbsorptionMap[`*element*`, `*ionstage*`]`
give the absorption map of the element at the specified ionization level

Absorption maps.

This gives the absorption map in the range between 1213 Angstrom and 1215 Angstrom.

In[5]:= **WavelengthAbsorptionMap[1213 Angstrom, 1218 Angstrom]**

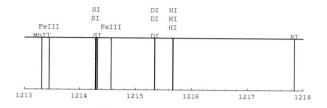

Here is the absorption map of Hydrogen.

In[6]:= **ElementAbsorptionMap[Hydrogen]**

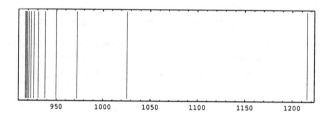

You can zoom in on a particular area of the spectrum.

In[7]:= **ElementAbsorptionMap[Hydrogen, PlotRange->{{915, 950}, All}]**

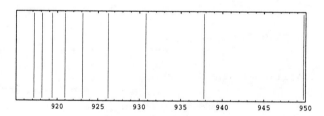

Here is the absorption map of Carbon at the ionization level I.

$In[8]:=$ **ElementAbsorptionMap[Carbon, "I"]**

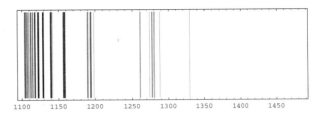

⁺■ Miscellaneous`StandardAtmosphere`

AtmosphericPlot[*property*]	plot the specified property on the horizontal axis versus the altitude on the vertical axis

Plotting an atmospheric property.

This package provides support for plotting how U.S. Standard Atmosphere properties vary with altitude.

This loads the package.   *In[1]:=* **<<Miscellaneous`StandardAtmosphere`**

The speed of sound does not decrease monotonically with increasing altitude.   *In[2]:=* **AtmosphericPlot[SoundSpeed]**

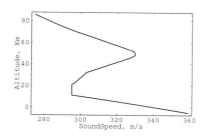

The speed of particles does not increase monotonically with increasing altitude.   *In[3]:=* **AtmosphericPlot[MeanParticleSpeed]**

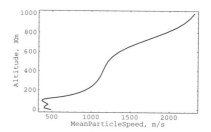

> CollisionFrequency   MeanMolecularWeight
> DynamicViscosity   MeanParticleSpeed
> GravityAcceleration   NumberDensity
> KinematicViscosity   Pressure
> KineticTemperature   PressureScaleHeight
> MeanDensity   SoundSpeed
> MeanFreePath   ThermalConductivityCoefficient

Atmospheric properties.

You can also treat the various atmospheric properties as functions of altitude. These functions understand the units defined in `Miscellaneous`Units``.

This gives the mean particle speed at 5 kilometers.

In[4]:= **MeanParticleSpeed[5000 Meter]**

$$Out[4]= \frac{432.31\,\text{Meter}}{\text{Second}}$$

■ Miscellaneous `Units`

There are many systems of units. The particular set of units that is used depends on factors as various as the field of study and the author's country of origin. The function Convert provides conversion between different units.

Convert[*old*, *newunits*]	convert *old* to a form involving a combination of the *newunits*

Converting units.

This loads the package.	In[1]:= **<<Miscellaneous`Units`**
This converts meters per second into miles per hour.	In[2]:= **Convert[12 Meter/Second, Mile/Hour]**
	Out[2]= $\dfrac{26.8432\,\text{Mile}}{\text{Hour}}$
You have to give prefixes for units as separate words.	In[3]:= **Convert[3 Kilo Meter / Hour, Inch / Minute]**
	Out[3]= $\dfrac{1968.5\,\text{Inch}}{\text{Minute}}$

The conversion of temperature units is different from most other unit conversions, because it is not multiplicative. This is simply because the zeros of various systems are set at different values. For example, zero degrees Centigrade is the same as 32 degrees Fahrenheit.

ConvertTemperature[*temp*, *oldunits*, *newunits*]	
	convert *temp* from the *oldunits* scale to the *newunits* scale

Converting temperatures.

This converts the temperature. Convert only converts the units of temperature.	In[4]:= **ConvertTemperature[20, Fahrenheit, Centigrade]**
	Out[4]= -6.66667

Celsius	Kelvin
Centigrade	Rankine
Fahrenheit	

Temperature scales.

To organize the use of units, certain standardized systems have been developed. These include the International System (SI) and systems using particular metric units, such as the meter/kilogram/second system. The functions SI, MKS, and CGS convert various units into the standard systems.

SI[*expr*]	convert *expr* to SI units (International System)
MKS[*expr*]	convert *expr* to MKS units (meter/kilogram/second)
CGS[*expr*]	convert *expr* to CGS units (centimeter/gram/second)

Conversion of units into standard systems.

The International Standard unit for pressure is the Pascal.

```
In[5]:= SI[3 Atmosphere]
Out[5]= 303975. Pascal
```

You can request information about any unit.

```
In[6]:= ?Pascal
Pascal is the derived SI unit of pressure.
```

Yocto	10^{-24}		Deca	10^{1}
Zepto	10^{-21}		Hecto	10^{2}
Atto	10^{-18}		Kilo	10^{3}
Femto	10^{-15}		Mega	10^{6}
Pico	10^{-12}		Giga	10^{9}
Nano	10^{-9}		Tera	10^{12}
Micro	10^{-6}		Peta	10^{15}
Milli	10^{-3}		Exa	10^{18}
Centi	10^{-2}		Zetta	10^{21}
Deci	10^{-1}		Yotta	10^{24}

SI unit prefixes.

Abampere	Abhenry
Abcoulomb	Abmho
Abfarad	Abohm
	Abvolt

Electrical units.

Amp	Siemens
Biot	Statampere
Coulomb	Statcoulomb
Farad	Statfarad
Gilbert	Stathenry
Henry	Statohm
Mho	Statvolt
Ohm	Volt

Electrical units. (continued)

AU	Meter
Bolt	Micron
Cable	Mil
Caliber	Mile
Centimeter	NauticalMile
Chain	Parsec
Cicero	Perch
Cubit	Pica
Didot	Point
DidotPoint	Pole
Ell	Rod
Fathom	Rope
Feet	Skein
Fermi	Span
Foot	Stadion
Furlong	Stadium
Hand	StatuteMile
Inch	SurveyMile
League	XUnit
LightYear	Yard
Link	

Units of length.

Baud   Byte
Bit   Nibble

Units of information.

Century   Month
Day   Second
Decade   SiderealSecond
Fortnight   SiderealYear
Hour   TropicalYear
Millennium   Week
Minute   Year

Units of time.

AMU   MetricTon
AtomicMassUnit   Quintal
Dalton   Slug
Geepound   SolarMass
Gram   Tonne
Kilogram

Units of mass.

AssayTon   Drachma
AvoirdupoisOunce   Grain
AvoirdupoisPound   GrossHundredweight
Bale   Hundredweight
Carat   Libra
Cental   Mina

Units of weight.

NetHundredweight
Obolos
Ounce
Pennyweight
Pondus
Pound
Shekel

ShortHundredweight
ShortTon
Stone
Talent
Ton
TroyOunce
Wey

Units of weight. (continued)

Dyne
GramWeight
KilogramForce
KilogramWeight
Newton

Poundal
PoundForce
PoundWeight
TonForce

Units of force.

Diopter

Kayser

Units of inverse length.

Bag
Barrel
BoardFoot
Bucket
Bushel
Butt
Cord
Cup

Drop
Ephah
Fifth
Firkin
FluidDram
FluidOunce
Gallon
Gill

Units of volume.

Hogshead	Quart
Jeroboam	RegisterTon
Jigger	Seam
Last	Shot
Liter	Stere
Magnum	Tablespoon
Minim	Teaspoon
Noggin	Tun
Omer	UKGallon
Pint	UKPint
Pony	WineBottle
Puncheon	

Units of volume. (continued)

Poise	Rhes
Reyn	Stokes

Units of viscosity.

Apostilb	Lumerg
Candela	Lux
Candle	Nit
FootCandle	Phot
Hefner	Stilb
Lambert	Talbot
Lumen	

Units of types of luminous energy and intensity.

Becquerel	Roentgen
Curie	Rontgen
Gray	Rutherford
Rad	

Units of radiation.

ArcMinute	Quadrant
ArcSecond	Radian
Circle	RightAngle
Degree	Steradian
Grade	

Angles.

ChevalVapeur	Watt
Horsepower	

Units of power.

Acre	Rood
Are	Section
Barn	Township
Hectare	

Units of area.

Dozen	Mole
Gross	

Amounts of substances.

Gal	Gravity

Acceleration due to gravity.

BohrMagneton	NuclearMagneton
Gauss	Oersted
Gamma	Tesla
Maxwell	Weber

Magnetic units.

ArcSecond	Grade
BakersDozen	Gross
Circle	Percent
Degree	Quadrant
Dozen	RightAngle

Unit multipliers.

Atmosphere	MillimeterMercury
Bar	Pascal
Barye	Torr
InchMercury	

Units of pressure.

```
        BritishThermalUnit          Erg
        BTU                         Joule
        Calorie                     Rydberg
        ElectronVolt                Therm
```

Units of energy.

```
        Hertz
```

Unit of frequency.

```
        Knot
```

Unit of speed.

```
        Denier
```

Unit of fineness for yarn or thread.

■ Miscellaneous `WorldData`

The package `Miscellaneous`WorldData`` is used by the package `Miscellaneous`WorldPlot`` and is automatically loaded when you load `Miscellaneous`WorldPlot``. Most users do not need to be aware of it, but if you want to expand on the list of countries `WorldPlot` knows about you will want to update `Miscellaneous`WorldData`` as well as `Miscellaneous`WorldNames``.

`WorldPlot` works by creating a *Mathematica* graphics object that represents the map. Each country on the map is given as a `Polygon` primitive. To make a map from a list of countries, *Mathematica* must know the vertices of these polygons for each country in your list. These data are contained in the package `Miscellaneous`WorldData``. As noted previously, the vertex data are given as ordered pairs of latitude and longitude expressed in minutes. By convention, latitudes north of the equator are positive while those to the south are negative, and longitudes east of Greenwich are positive and those to the west are negative.

The vertex data for a country is attached to `WorldData` of the name of that country. The data are in the form of a list of lists of points. This is so multiple polygons can be specified for each country.

You can specify your own database of geographic coordinates by setting the `WorldPlot` options `WorldDatabase` and `WorldCountries`. The setting for `WorldDatabase` is the name of the function that is applied to a country name to yield its polygonal vertices. It defaults to `WorldData`. `WorldCountries` is set to a list of accepted country names, and defaults to `World` (from the `Miscellaneous`WorldNames`` package). `Miscellaneous`WorldData`` contains all of the `WorldData["`*countryname*`"]` rules that `WorldPlot` has access to.

This loads the package.	`In[1]:= <<Miscellaneous`WorldData``
Here is the list of the vertices of the polygon that give the map of Ireland.	`In[2]:= WorldData["Ireland"]`
	`Out[2]= {{{3245, -376}, {3131, -382}, {3087, -586}, {3131, -628}, {3160, -524}, {3246, -607}, {3303, -435}, {3266, -489}, {3245, -376}}}`

■ Miscellaneous`WorldNames`

The package Miscellaneous`WorldNames` is used by the package Miscellaneous`WorldPlot` and is automatically loaded when you load Miscellaneous`WorldPlot`. Most users do not need to be aware of it, but if you want to expand on the list of countries WorldPlot knows about, you will want to update Miscellaneous`WorldNames` as well as Miscellaneous`WorldData`.

The names of the countries that WorldPlot recognizes are specified using the option WorldCountries. The setting for this option is the name of the *Mathematica* list that contains the allowable country names. The default value is World, which is a list given in the package Miscellaneous`WorldNames`. This package also defines major geographical areas of the world, such as continents, as *Mathematica* lists containing the country names.

Africa	NorthAmerica
Asia	Oceania
Europe	SouthAmerica
MiddleEast	World

Mathematica lists containing country names.

This loads the package.

Here the symbol NorthAmerica is a list of strings containing the countries of the North American continent.

```
In[1]:= <<Miscellaneous`WorldNames`

In[2]:= NorthAmerica // InputForm

Out[2]//InputForm= {"USA", "Canada", "Mexico", "Greenland",
             "Bermuda", "Cuba", "Jamaica", "Haiti", "Belize",
             "Dominican Republic", "El Salvador", "Guatemala",
             "Honduras", "Nicaragua", "Costa Rica", "Panama",
             "Puerto Rico"}
```

■ Miscellaneous`WorldPlot`

WorldPlot[*countrylist*]	generate a map of the countries named in *countrylist*
WorldPlot[{*countrylist*, RandomColors}]	color the countries with randomly chosen colors
WorldPlot[{*countrylist*, RandomGrays}]	use randomly chosen gray levels

Displaying a map.

To make a map of an entire continent, you can give the name of the continent in place of the list of country names. Thus, for example, WorldPlot[Oceania] is equivalent to WorldPlot[{"Indonesia","Papua New Guinea","Fiji","Australia","New Zealand"}]. The names of the countries that can be mapped are listed at the end of this section. Note that the names of countries are strings. This means they must be surrounded by quotes when you use them in a list of countries. However, the continent names represent lists and therefore are not strings but symbols. They should not be put in quotes.

This loads the package.

In[1]:= <<Miscellaneous`WorldPlot`

This gives a map of Africa with all countries drawn as white with black outlines.

In[2]:= WorldPlot[Africa]

Here is a map of the world with each country colored with a randomly chosen gray level.

In[3]:= WorldPlot[{World, RandomGrays}]

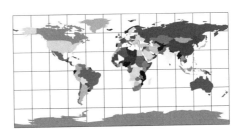

| WorldPlot[{*countrylist*, *colorfunc*}] | color the countries as specified by *colorfunc* |
| WorldPlot[{*countrylist*, *colorlist*}] | color the countries using the list of color directives |

Specifying the color gray level of maps.

When you make a map, you can specify the color of each country in several ways. The first is to give an explicit list of graphics directives such as GrayLevel, RGBColor, or Hue. The nth element in this list specifies the color of the map of the nth element in your list of country names. You can also specify the colors by defining your own color function. This color function must take names of countries as arguments and return a color directive. Perhaps the simplest way to create maps with colors is to specify the color function as RandomColors or RandomGrays. These two functions use random numbers to assign a color or gray level to each country on your list.

Here is a simple color function.

```
In[4]:= shadefunc[country_] :=
            Switch[country, "Canada", GrayLevel[0],
                    "Mexico", GrayLevel[.3],
                    _, GrayLevel[.6]]
```

The color function causes Canada to be drawn black, Mexico dark gray, and other countries a lighter gray.

```
In[5]:= WorldPlot[{NorthAmerica, shadefunc}]
```

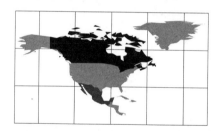

A map is simply the representation of a portion of the Earth's surface on a flat page. Since the Earth is nearly spherical, this representation requires that we adopt some scheme for taking the surface of a spherical object and representing it as a flat two-dimensional image. These schemes are called *projections*. By their very nature, all projections give rise to certain distortions. Various projections have been developed that preserve certain properties of the surface of the Earth while distorting others. An *equal-area* projection has the property that two regions that have the same area on the map have the same area on the globe. A projection is called *conformal* if it preserves angular relationships and therefore directions. An *azimuthal* projection preserves true directions from a central point.

The projection for a map is specified by the option WorldProjection. You can define your own projection by giving a pure function of two arguments. For example, the default setting for WorldProjection is Equirectangular, which as a pure function is given as WorldProjection -> ({#2, #1}&). The parentheses around the pure function ensure that *Mathematica* recognizes it as a single expression. If you define your own projections, it is important to remember that the coordinates in the database are given in minutes. This means that you must convert them to radians before using a built-in *Mathematica* trigonometric function. Also, the coordinates of the boundaries of countries are given as pairs with the latitude first.

Albers	Mercator
Equirectangular	Mollweide
LambertAzimuthal	Orthographic
LambertCylindrical	Sinusoidal

Projections.

You can also give the name of a projection as a value for the option `WorldProjection`. Many of the standard projections are included in this package. These are described below.

The simplest projection is the **equirectangular projection** `Equirectangular`. This projection simply takes the latitude as the y coordinate and the longitude as the x coordinate. This projection does not preserve angles or area. `Equirectangular` is the default setting for `WorldProjection`.

The **Lambert cylindrical projection** `LambertCylindrical` is just an equirectangular projection with the spacing between parallels adjusted so the projection is equal area. This projection is sometimes called the *cylindrical equal-area projection*.

In the **Lambert azimuthal projection** `LambertAzimuthal` the globe is projected onto a plane that is tangential to the globe at one point, and then the spacing of parallel circles around the projection point is adjusted to make it equal area. This projection gives true directions from the center point and is sometimes called the *azimuthal equal-area projection*.

Another azimuthal projection is the orthographic projection. `Orthographic` specifies a projection of the sphere with the projection point at infinity. The result looks like a view of the planet as seen from very far away. The projection preserves neither area nor angles.

The **sinusoidal projection** `Sinusoidal` belongs to the class of pseudo-cylindrical projections, that is, parallels are straight lines, meridians are curved, and their spacing is adjusted to make it equal area.

The most popular equal-area projection for world maps is the **Mollweide projection** `Mollweide`. The adjustment used to achieve equal areas is fairly sophisticated and involves the solution of a trigonometric equation. This projection is sometimes also called *elliptical* or *homolographic*.

The **Mercator projection** `Mercator` is a cylindrical projection that preserves angles but is not equal area. It is produced by adjusting a cylindrical projection that is projected from the center of the Earth. This projection is particularly useful for navigation, as a straight line on the map corresponds to a fixed directional bearing.

A conic projection is produced by projecting the surface of the Earth onto a cone that is tangential to the Earth along a circle. The **Albers conic projection** Albers is a conic projection that is adjusted to make it equal area. Unlike the other projections, Albers requires you to specify additional information. This takes the form of Albers[par_1, par_2]. The two parallels you specify are the parallels along which the scale is correct. A good projection for the United States is Albers[20, 60]. The Albers conic projection is sometimes called the *Albers equal-area projection*.

The sinusoidal projection gives little distortion near the equator and the prime meridian, and is therefore very good for showing Africa.

```
In[6]:= WorldPlot[{Africa, RandomGrays},
            WorldProjection -> Sinusoidal]
```

option name	default value	
WorldBorders	Automatic	style to display borders of countries; with None, no borders are drawn
WorldCountries	World	name of the list of allowable country names
WorldDatabase	WorldData	name of the database containing polygon data for countries
WorldToGraphics	False	whether to return a standard Graphics object

Some options for WorldPlot.

option name	default value	
WorldBackground	None	style to use for the background polygon
WorldClipping	Full	specify what happens to lines or polygons that are partially outside the plot range
WorldFrame	Automatic	style to use for the frame around the map; with None, no boundary is drawn
WorldFrameParts	{1, 1, 1, 1}	what parts of the frame to draw
WorldGrid	Automatic	locations of parallels and meridians to be drawn
WorldGridBehind	True	whether the grid is drawn behind (True) or in front (False) of the countries
WorldGridStyle	Thickness[.001]	style for the grid
WorldPoints	100	number of divisions used in plotting grid lines and clipping polygons
WorldProjection	Equirectangular	function to use for the projection
WorldRange	Automatic	portion of the surface of the Earth to be drawn; specifications must be of form {{minlat, maxlat}, {minlong, maxlong}}
WorldRotatedRange	False	coordinate system to which the range specification is applied; with True, it is applied to the system resulting from WorldRotation
WorldRotation	{0, 0, 0}	rotation to be applied to coordinates before projection

More options for WorldPlot. These options can also be used in WorldGraphics.

To specify how the borders of countries are to be drawn, you set the WorldBorders option. The settings for this option can be None, Automatic, or a style list. With the setting Automatic the borders are drawn with the style {GrayLevel[0], Thickness[.001]} unless a style list for the shading of the countries is given. If this is the case, no borders are drawn.

The style of the frame around the map is controlled by the WorldFrame option. To determine which portion of the frame is to be drawn, specify WorldFrameParts -> $\{s_1, s_2, s_3, s_4\}$. Each s_i is either 0 or 1 and specifies whether a portion of the frame is drawn (1) or not (0). The sides are ordered clockwise, with the eastern side given first.

WorldGrid controls the drawing of parallels and meridians. A setting for this option of the form WorldGrid->{deg_1, deg_2} specifies the spacing of the latitude and longitude lines that are drawn beginning with the equator or a prime meridian. A setting of WorldGrid->*deg* is the same as WorldGrid->{*deg*, *deg*}. You can explicitly specify which latitude and longitude lines you want drawn with WorldGrid->{{lat_1, lat_2, ... }, {lat_1, lat_2, ... }}. The default setting Automatic is equivalent to WorldGrid->30. Note that all settings are given in degrees.

One of the most time-intensive parts of the plot is clipping polygons or lines that are partially outside the plot range. The way this clipping is done is determined by the option WorldClipping. The default setting Full causes these objects to be properly clipped at the edge of the plot range. To save rendering time you can reset this option at Simple, which causes objects outside the plot range to not be rendered, or None, which causes the entire object to be rendered.

In this map of Africa the background is light gray, there are no grid lines, and the frame around the map is somewhat thicker than usual.

```
In[7]:= afmap = WorldPlot[Africa,
            WorldBackground -> GrayLevel[0.7],
            WorldGrid -> None,
            WorldFrame -> Thickness[.012],
            WorldProjection -> LambertCylindrical]
```

As noted previously, a projection is a scheme for transforming latitudes and longitudes on the Earth into x and y coordinates on a flat page. Each projection involves certain fixed geometric choices. For example, the Lambert azimuthal projection projects the surface of the Earth onto a plane that is tangent at one point. When you specify LambertAzimuthal as the projection, this point is fixed at zero degrees latitude and longitude. You can change the choice of this point by setting the WorldRotation option.

A value for WorldRotation must be a list of three numbers {deg_1, deg_2, deg_3} with the first two between 0 and 180 and the last between −180 and 180. To understand the effect of these numbers, you can imagine the globe in a standard (x, y, z) coordinate system with the positive z axis coming out of the North Pole and the x axis through the equator at the Prime Meridian. The three numbers give the amount of rotation (in degrees) of three sequential rotations. The first is about the y axis, the second is about the z axis, and the third is about the North Pole in the position where it is *after* the first two rotations.

This setting for `WorldRotation` causes the Earth to be rotated by 90 degrees before the projection is applied. The result is a view of the Northern Hemisphere centered at the North Pole.

```
In[8]:= WorldPlot[{World, RandomGrays},
            WorldRotation -> {90, 0, 0},
            WorldRange -> {{0, 90}, {-180, 180}},
            WorldProjection -> LambertAzimuthal]
```

`WorldPlot` works by creating a *Mathematica* graphics object that represents the map. Each country on the map is given as a `Polygon` primitive. To make a map from a list of countries, *Mathematica* must know the vertices of these polygons for each country in your list. These data are contained in the package `Miscellaneous`WorldData``, which is automatically loaded when `Miscellaneous`WorldPlot`` is loaded. As noted above, the vertex data are given as ordered pairs of latitude and longitude expressed in minutes. By convention, latitudes north of the equator are positive while those to the south are negative, and longitudes east of Greenwich are positive and those to the west are negative.

You can specify your own database of geographic coordinates by setting the option `WorldDatabase`. The setting for this option is the name of the function that is applied to a country name to yield its polygonal vertices. The names of the countries that appear in your database are specified using the option `WorldCountries`. The setting for this option is the name of the *Mathematica* list that contains the allowable country names. The default value is `World`, which is a list given in the package `Miscellaneous`WorldNames``. This package is also automatically loaded when you load `Miscellaneous`WorldPlot``.

`WorldGraphics[`*primitives*, *options*`]`	a graphics object representing a planetary map
`Show[`*wg*, *options*`]`	display a `WorldGraphics` object using the options specified
`Graphics[WorldGraphics[`*primitives*, *options*`]]`	convert a `WorldGraphics` object to a `Graphics` object

Creating and displaying `WorldGraphics` objects.

Built-in *Mathematica* functions like `Plot` and `ListPlot` work by building up a `Graphics` object, and then displaying it. The resulting `Graphics` object can be manipulated and redisplayed using various options. `WorldPlot` works in a very similar way, creating a `WorldGraphics` object and then displaying it. A `WorldGraphics` object is essentially a `Graphics` object that has been adapted to work with geographic data. All coordinates given in the primitives `Polygon`, `Line`, `Point`, and `Text` are given as *{lat, long}* with the latitude and longitude given in minutes of an arc. You can convert data given in degrees and minutes into minutes using the function `ToMinutes`. Thus `Point[ToMinutes[{{41, 49}, -{87, 37}}]]` represents a point displayed at the location of Chicago, Illinois, which is at latitude 41 degrees, 49 seconds North and longitude 87 degrees, 37 minutes West. Before a `WorldGraphics` object is displayed, it is internally converted to a standard `Graphics` object using the projection specified by the value of `WorldProjection`.

Here is the list of the vertices of the polygon that give the map of Ireland.

```
In[9]:= WorldData["Ireland"]

Out[9]= {{{3245, -376}, {3131, -382}, {3087, -586}, {3131, -628},
         {3160, -524}, {3246, -607}, {3303, -435}, {3266, -489},
         {3245, -376}}}
```

This is a list of the latitude and longitude in minutes of two cities in Africa.

```
In[10]:= {capetown, cairo} = ToMinutes[
          {{{-33, -56}, {18, 22}},
           {{30, 3}, {31, 15}}}]

Out[10]= {{-2036, 1102}, {1803, 1875}}
```

You can combine maps with `WorldGraphics` objects using `Show`. The map of Africa given by afmap was defined above.

```
In[11]:= Show[{afmap,
          WorldGraphics[
          {Dashing[{0.05, 0.03}],
          Line[{capetown, cairo}]}]}]
```

`ToMinutes[`*deg*`]`	convert `deg` into minutes
`ToMinutes[{`*deg, min*`}]`	convert when the argument is in degrees and minutes
`ToMinutes[{`*deg, min, sec*`}]`	convert when the argument is in degrees, minutes, and seconds

Converting into minutes.

Giving the name of the continent is the same as giving the list of names of countries in that continent. `World` gives the list of all the countries in the world. As previously noted, the names of countries are strings and need to be included in quotes. The names of continents are symbols and do not require quotes. The following countries can be given:

Belize	Haiti
Bermuda	Honduras
Canada	Jamaica
Costa Rica	Mexico
Cuba	Nicaragua
Dominican Republic	Panama
El Salvador	Puerto Rico
Greenland	USA
Guatemala	

Countries in the list `NorthAmerica`.

Albania	Liechtenstein
Andorra	Lithuania
Austria	Luxembourg
Belarus	Macedonia
Belgium	Moldova
Bosnia and Herzegovina	Monaco
Bulgaria	Netherlands
Croatia	Norway
Cyprus	Poland
Czech Republic	Portugal
Denmark	Romania
Estonia	Russia
Finland	San Marino
France	Serbia and Montenegro
Germany	Slovakia
Gibraltar	Slovenia
Greece	Spain
Hungary	Sweden
Iceland	Switzerland
Ireland	Turkey
Italy	Ukraine
Latvia	United Kingdom

Countries in the list `Europe`.

Argentina	Guyana
Bolivia	Paraguay
Brazil	Peru
Chile	Suriname
Colombia	Uruguay
Ecuador	Venezuela
French Guiana	

Countries in the list SouthAmerica.

Australia	New Zealand
Fiji	Papua New Guinea
Indonesia	

Countries in the list Oceania.

Afghanistan	Israel
Armenia	Japan
Azerbaijan	Jordan
Bahrain	Kazakhstan
Bangladesh	Kuwait
Bhutan	Kyrgyzstan
Brunei	Laos
Burma	Lebanon
Cambodia	Malaysia
China	Mongolia
Georgia	Nepal
India	North Korea
Indonesia	Oman
Iran	Pakistan
Iraq	Philippines

Countries in the list Asia.

Qatar
Russia
Saudi Arabia
Singapore
South Korea
Sri Lanka
Syria

Taiwan
Tajikistan
Thailand
Turkey
Turkmenistan
Uzbekistan
Vietnam

Countries in the list Asia. (continued)

Bahrain
Egypt
Iran
Iraq
Israel
Jordan
Kuwait
Lebanon

Oman
Qatar
Saudi Arabia
Syria
Turkey
UAE
Yemen

Countries in the list MiddleEast.

Algeria	Malawi
Angola	Mali
Benin	Mauritania
Botswana	Morocco
Burkina	Mozambique
Burundi	Namibia
Cameroon	Niger
CAR	Nigeria
Chad	Rwanda
Congo	Senegal
Cote d'Ivoire	Sierra Leone
Djibouti	Somalia
Egypt	South Africa
Equatorial Guinea	Sudan
Eritrea	Swaziland
Ethiopia	Tanzania
Gabon	The Gambia
Ghana	Togo
Guinea	Tunisia
Guinea-Bissau	Uganda
Kenya	Western Sahara
Lesotho	Zaire
Liberia	Zambia
Libya	Zimbabwe
Madagascar	

Countries in the list Africa.

9. Number Theory

▪ NumberTheory`ContinuedFractions`

The decimal expansion is the most common way to represent a real number. This package supports two alternative representations as follows: (1) the continued fraction expansion of a real number and (2) the arbitrary base expansion of a rational number in terms of preperiodic and periodic parts.

The *continued fraction expansion* of a real number x is a representation of the form

$$a_0 + \cfrac{1}{a_1 + \cfrac{1}{a_2 + \cdots}}$$

The integers a_i are called the *partial quotients*. Rational numbers have a finite number of partial quotients, while irrational numbers have an infinite continued fraction expansion. Continued fractions also find application in the factorization of integers (see, for example, Chapter 10 in [Rosen]).

If the number x has partial quotients $a_0, a_1, \ldots$, the rational number p_n/q_n formed by considering the first n partial quotients $a_0, a_1, \ldots, a_n$, is called the nth *convergent* of x. The convergents of a number provide, in a certain sense, the best rational approximation with a small denominator to the given real number.

In *Mathematica* versions 4.0 and later, the kernel functions `ContinuedFraction` and `RealDigits` can be used to produce continued fraction and periodic representations of rational numbers. `FromContinuedFraction` and `FromDigits` are used to invert these operations. This package enhances these capabilities by providing functions for computing convergents and for nicely typesetting continued fractions and periodic forms.

`ContinuedFractionForm[{`a_0`, `a_1`, ... }]`
  a representation of a continued fraction with partial quotients a_0, a_1, ...

`ContinuedFractionForm[{`a_0`, `a_1`, ... , {`p_0`, `p_1`, ... }}]`
  a representation of a continued fraction with partial quotients a_0, a_1, ... and additional quotients p_0, p_1, ... that repeat periodically

`Normal[ContinuedFractionForm[`*quotients*`]]`
  give the rational number corresponding to the given continued fraction

---

Continued fractions.

This loads the package.

In[1]:= **<<NumberTheory`ContinuedFractions`**

The kernel function
ContinuedFraction generates a list of
the partial quotients of the continued
fraction. Here are the first 10 terms of
the expansion of *pi*.

In[2]:= **cf = ContinuedFraction[Pi, 10]**

Out[2]= {3, 7, 15, 1, 292, 1, 1, 1, 2, 1}

ContinuedFractionForm can be
wrapped around the result of
ContinuedFraction for a much clearer
representation as a sum of nested
fractions.

In[3]:= **ContinuedFractionForm[cf]**

$$Out[3]= 3 + \cfrac{1}{7 + \cfrac{1}{15 + \cfrac{1}{1 + \cfrac{1}{292 + \cfrac{1}{1 + \cfrac{1}{1 + \cfrac{1}{1 + \cfrac{1}{2 + \cfrac{1}{1}}}}}}}}}$$

Quadratic irrational numbers are of the form $\frac{p \pm \sqrt{d}}{q}$, where d, p, and q are integers; d is positive and not a perfect square; and q is nonzero and divides $d - p^2$. Such numbers have a continued fraction expansion that is infinite but periodic. Thus they can be represented finitely in terms of the preperiodic part followed by the periodically repeating part.

This is the continued fraction expansion
of the square root of 7, a quadratic
irrational. Typesetting rules defined for
ContinuedFractionForm put the
repeating block in parenthesis, and add
an ellipse to mark the repetition.

In[4]:= **cf = ContinuedFractionForm[
          ContinuedFraction[Sqrt[7]]
       ]**

$$Out[4]= 2 + \cfrac{1}{\left(1 + \cfrac{1}{1 + \cfrac{1}{1 + \cfrac{1}{4 + \cfrac{1}{\cdots}}}}\right)}$$

A continued fraction can be turned
back into a rational or quadratic
irrational by application of Normal.

In[5]:= **Normal[cf]**

Out[5]= $\sqrt{7}$

Convergents[*rat*]	give the convergents for all terms of the continued fraction corresponding to the rational or quadratic irrational number *rat*
Convergents[*num*, *terms*]	give the convergents for the given number of terms of the continued fraction expansion of *num*
Convergents[*cf*]	give the convergents for the particular continued fraction *cf* returned from ContinuedFractions or ContinuedFractionForm
QuadraticIrrationalQ[*expr*]	whether *expr* is a quadratic irrational

Finding convergents and quadratic irrationals.

The golden ratio has all of its partial quotients equal to one.

```
In[6]:=  cf = ContinuedFractionForm[
             ContinuedFraction[GoldenRatio, 10]
         ]
```

$$Out[6]= 1 + \cfrac{1}{1 + \cfrac{1}{1 + \cfrac{1}{1 + \cfrac{1}{1 + \cfrac{1}{1 + \cfrac{1}{1 + \cfrac{1}{1 + \cfrac{1}{1}}}}}}}}$$

This gives a list of the convergents of the continued fraction. These convergents have the Fibonacci numbers for numerators and denominators.

```
In[7]:= Convergents[cf]
```

$$Out[7]= \left\{1, 2, \frac{3}{2}, \frac{5}{3}, \frac{8}{5}, \frac{13}{8}, \frac{21}{13}, \frac{34}{21}, \frac{55}{34}, \frac{89}{55}\right\}$$

The convergents of a number converge to it while alternating sides.

```
In[8]:= % - N[GoldenRatio]
```

```
Out[8]= {-0.618034, 0.381966, -0.118034, 0.0486327, -0.018034,
         0.00696601, -0.00264937, 0.00101363, -0.00038693,
         0.000147829}
```

Another useful representation of certain types of numbers is the base b expansion. Not all such expansions are finite. An infinite base b expansion $(.c_1 c_2 c_3 \cdots)_b$ is periodic if there are positive integers m and k such that $c_{n+k} = c_n$ for $n \geq m$. It is common to express the base expansion

$$(.c_1 c_2 \cdots c_{m-1} c_m \cdots c_{m+k-1} c_m \cdots c_{m+k-1} c_m \cdots)_b$$

as

$$(.c_1 c_2 \cdots, c_{m-1}, \overline{c_m \cdots c_{m+k-1}})_b$$

The nonrepeating elements constitute the preperiodic part and the repeating elements constitute the periodic part.

  ~   PeriodicForm[{{a_0, ... , {a_m,... }}, *exp*}]

                     a representation of a repeated decimal expansion in terms of preperiodic and periodic parts with a specific exponent as found by RealDigits

  ~   PeriodicForm[{{a_0,... , {a_m,... }}, *exp*}, *b*]

                     a representation of an expansion in base *b*

      Normal[PeriodicForm[*args*]]   give the rational number corresponding to the decimal expansion

Periodic expansions.

This rational number has a finite decimal expansion; the preperiodic part has length two and the periodic part has length zero.

```
In[9]:= PeriodicForm[RealDigits[ 1/20 ]]
Out[9]= 0.05
```

This rational number has an infinite decimal expansion; the preperiodic part has length zero and the periodic part has length 16. The periodic part is highlighted.

```
In[10]:= PeriodicForm[RealDigits[ 1/17 ]]
Out[10]= 0.0588235294117647̄0̄
```

The decimal number 1/10 has an infinite binary expansion. This is the reason that 0.1 cannot be stored in a binary digital computer without representation error.

```
In[11]:= PeriodicForm[RealDigits[ 1/10, 2 ], 2]
```
$Out[11]= 0.0001\overline{1001}_2$

This reconstructs the previous rational number from its binary digit expansion.

```
In[12]:= Normal[ % ]
```
$Out[12]= \dfrac{1}{10}$

The periodic expansion can be found to any base. If the base is under 36, the letters of the alphabet are used for the digits.

```
In[13]:= PeriodicForm[RealDigits[573498753434/13, 16], 16]
```
$Out[13]= 0.A4579E295\overline{B13}_{16} \times 16^9$

Here is a classical example with a lengthy periodic part involving pairs of digits 00 01 $\cdots$ in the decimal digit expansion (see [Glaisher]).

```
In[14]:= PeriodicForm[RealDigits[1/9801]]
Out[14]= 0.0001020304050607080910111213141516171819202122232425262
          7282930313233343536373839404142434445464748495051525354 55
          5657585960616263646566676869707172737475767778798081828 38
          4858687888990919293949596979900̄0̄
```

References

[Rosen] K. H. Rosen, *Elementary Number Theory and Its Applications*, Third edition, Addison Wesley, Reading, MA, 1993.
[Glaisher] J. W. L. Glaisher, *Messenger of Math.* 2, 41, 1873.

■ NumberTheory`FactorIntegerECM`

This package implements Lenstra's Elliptic Curve method of factorization. The package is designed to find prime factors of up to about 18 digits in reasonable time (up to three hours on a workstation). This extends *Mathematica*'s integer factoring to all numbers of 40 digits or less. The program in the package is a fairly direct implementation of the algorithm described in P. L. Montgomery's, "Speeding up the Pollard and Elliptic Curve Methods of Factorization," *Mathematics of Computation* 48 (1987), pages 243–264.

FactorIntegerECM[n]	give a single factor of the composite number n using Lenstra's elliptic curve method

Using FactorIntegerECM.

The algorithm returns a single factor (not necessarily a prime). To obtain a complete factorization, you should use FactorIntegerECM or the built-in FactorInteger on the factor and cofactor. The algorithm is probabilistic, so there could be a large variance in running times, even for similar inputs. SeedRandom[101] is used to generate pseudorandom numbers for the algorithm, so the program will always run exactly the same on the same input.

FactorIntegerECM should be used as an enhancement to the built-in functions PrimeQ and FactorInteger. The algorithm will always fail if the input is a prime. A prime number should never be given as input to FactorIntegerECM. Before using FactorIntegerECM, you should always use PrimeQ to make sure that your number is not prime.

The algorithm is designed with the assumption that the number given was not factored by FactorInteger, and so its smallest prime factor is at least 10^{12}. The algorithm is optimized to find factors of 17 digits or less, so it should factor most numbers of 40 digits or less (and such numbers will probably only have two prime factors if they are hard to factor).

This loads the package.	In[1]:= **<<NumberTheory`FactorIntegerECM`**
FactorIntegerECM returns only one factor.	In[2]:= **FactorIntegerECM[91]** Out[2]= 13
In general, the hardest numbers to factor in a given range are those with two unequal prime factors of about the same size. These numbers can be generated using the built-in function Prime.	In[3]:= **Prime[10^7] Prime[10^7+1]** Out[3]= 32193216510801043
This gives a factor of the previous number.	In[4]:= **FactorIntegerECM[%]** Out[4]= 179424673

Here is a fairly large integer.	*In[5]:=* `2^128 + 1`
	Out[5]= 340282366920938463463374607431768211457
This took about three and a half hours on a workstation.	*In[6]:=* `FactorIntegerECM[%]`
	Out[6]= 59649589127497217

The ECM method was discovered and analyzed by H. W. Lenstra. It first appeared as an announcement, "Elliptic Curve Factorization," dated February 14, 1985, and published in H. W. Lenstra, "Factoring Integers with Elliptic Curves," *Annals of Mathematics* 126 (1987).

This method is a generalization of the $p-1$ factoring algorithm of J. Pollard. The idea is to factor the composite number n by generating a random point P on a random elliptic curve $E \bmod n$, and then use the fact that E has an algebraic group structure to compute $k!\,P$, where k is a relatively small integer chosen during the algorithm. If $k!\,P$ is the identity on the group $E \bmod p$, where p is a prime factor of n, then a factorization of n is achieved (one has to think of $k!\,P$ as being reduced $\bmod p$). This can be detected algorithmically, since an illegal inversion $\bmod n$ must occur (*i.e.*, an illegal use of `PowerMod[a, -1, n]` will occur). This happens exactly when the order of the group $E \bmod p$, where p is a prime divisor of n, is divisible only by primes less than k. This happens in reasonable time because one can choose many curves E and the order of the group $E \bmod p$ as E varies is well distributed around p. This means that it will eventually hit a value that is divisible only by small primes (here p is a fixed prime divisor of n).

The original algorithm of Lenstra was mostly of theoretical interest. Many of the implementation ideas are given in Montgomery's paper. The most important point, first suggested by Pollard as an improvement to his $p-1$ method, is to introduce a second stage to the algorithm. The idea is that instead of looking just for numbers with only small factors, one looks for numbers that have all small factors, except for a single large factor. The second stage of the algorithm, therefore, takes the point $Q = k!\,P$ computed in the first stage and looks to see if any of $p_1 Q, p_2 Q, \ldots, p_k Q$ generate a factorization of n. Here $k < p_1 < p_2 < \ldots < p_k$ are the primes in an interval between k and Bk ($B = 25k$ in the program). Using the second stage represents an important practical improvement.

Montgomery and others discovered many ways to implement the above efficiently, and the program in the package reflects some of these ideas. An introductory text to this material is D. Bressoud, *Factorization and Primality Testing*, Springer-Verlag, 1989.

Since the algorithm is quite involved, it is inefficient to use it on numbers that have small factors. These factors can be found more effectively using other techniques, for example, trial division. For this reason, the function `FactorIntegerECM[n]` does not perform a complete factorization of n but instead returns only a single factor.

The package should therefore be used as a method to find factors of numbers not factored directly by `FactorInteger` or when only one factor at a time is required, as in the function `SquareFreeQ` from the package `NumberTheory`NumberTheoryFunctions`.

FactorIntegerECM[n, FactorSize -> q]

                    optimize the algorithm to find factors of size at most q

FactorIntegerECM[n, CurveNumber -> b]

                    use b curves at a time for each iteration of the algorithm

FactorIntegerECM[n, CurveCountLimit -> c]

                    use a total of c curves in the algorithm

Options for FactorIntegerECM.

The options to FactorIntegerECM allow you to vary parameters in the algorithms and to limit to the number of total steps in the algorithm. This allows one to search large numbers for small factors without having to achieve a complete factorization.

The option FactorSize specifies what size of factor you are looking for. When doing general purpose factoring, you usually only want to find any factor of the number n. The default is therefore to let FactorSize be about $\sqrt{n}$.

The algorithm uses a number of curves in parallel according to the size of the input n. The option CurveNumber allows the user to specify how many curves in parallel are used. A value for this option must be a power of 2. The default value of CurveNumber depends on the size of the given number n. For $n > 10^{30}$, it is 8. For $10^{20} < n \le 10^{30}$, it is 4. And for $n \le 10^{20}$, it is 2.

The advantage of using more curves in parallel is that fewer GCDs are used in stage one of the algorithm and less interpretation overhead occurs in stage two. The disadvantage is that a nontrivial factor found on one curve may have to wait until the algorithm has completed all the curves. The number therefore depends on how many curves one expects to need in total.

The option CurveCountLimit gives an upper bound to the number of curves used in the algorithm. This allows the user to terminate the algorithm before a factor is found. The default is 10^4 curves (essentially an infinite number).

The program has modest memory requirements. A table of $10,000$ binary digits is set up, as well as a table of $30,000$ primes.

■ NumberTheory `NumberTheoryFunctions`

This package contains a variety of functions that are useful for number theory applications. For more information on the mathematics related to these functions, see G. H. Hardy and E. M. Wright, *An Introduction to the Theory of Numbers*, Oxford University Press, 1988, D. E. Knuth, *Seminumerical Algorithms*, Addison-Wesley, 1981, and E. Grosswald, *Representations of Integers as Sums of Squares*, Springer, 1985.

SquareFreeQ[*n*]	give True if *n* contains a squared factor, False otherwise

Testing for a squared factor.

SquareFreeQ[n] checks to see if n has a square prime factor. It is believed that this problem is, in general, as hard as the problem of finding the prime factorization of *n*. However, in many cases one can do much better than simply factoring *n* and seeing if a prime factor occurs with a power equal to two or higher.

To show that *n* is not square-free, one only needs to find a *single* prime factor of *n* whose square divides *n*. In principle then, one could perform the factorization of *n* one prime at a time to see if the square of the prime divides *n*. This method, while simple to describe, is rather inefficient. The actual procedure used by SquareFreeQ[n] is somewhat more complicated to describe, but it is much more efficient computationally.

First, the greatest common divisor of *n* and the product of the primes less than 10,000 is computed. (Call this product of primes *P*.) The next step is to compute the GCD of this result and *P*. If this GCD is not equal to one, then *n* has a square factor. If this GCD is equal to one, then a new quantity *q* is defined to be *n*/GCD[n, P]. If *q* is prime (an easy thing to check), then *n* is square-free. If *q* is not prime, then the process continues with the factorization of *q* (the small factors found with the GCD no longer matter since they occur to power one in the factorization of *n*).

The first thing to check about *q* is whether it is a perfect power of an integer (this can be done easily). If it is not, then the elliptic curve method of factorization is used as implemented in the package NumberTheory `FactorIntegerECM`. FactorIntegerECM is used to find a single factor *p* of *q*. The next step is to check whether *p* and *q*/*p* have no common factor. If they do, then *q* has a square factor. If they don't, then the prime factorizations of *p* and *q*/*p* do not intersect, and the answer can be obtained recursively by applying SquareFreeQ to both *p* and *q*/*p*.

This loads the package.	*In[1]:=* `<<NumberTheory`NumberTheoryFunctions` `
This product of primes contains no squared factors.	*In[2]:=* `SquareFreeQ[2*3*5*7]`
	Out[2]= True
The square number 4 divides 60.	*In[3]:=* `SquareFreeQ[60]`
	Out[3]= False

SquareFreeQ can handle large integers.

```
In[4]:= SquareFreeQ[2^101 - 1]

Out[4]= True
```

SquareFreeQ uses FactorIntegerECM as a subroutine, so it should return a value for numbers less than 40 digits.

NextPrime[n]	give the smallest prime larger than n

Finding the next prime.

NextPrime[n] finds the smallest prime p such that $p > n$. For n less than 20 digits, the algorithm does a direct search using PrimeQ on the odd numbers greater than n. For n with more than 20 digits, the algorithm builds a small sieve and first checks to see whether the candidate prime is divisible by a small prime before using PrimeQ. This seems to be slightly faster than a direct search.

This gives the next prime after 10.

```
In[5]:= NextPrime[10]

Out[5]= 11
```

Even for large numbers, the next prime can be computed rather quickly.

```
In[6]:= NextPrime[10^64]

Out[6]= 10000000000000000000000000000000000000000000000000000000000000000.
          00000057
```

ChineseRemainder[$list_1$, $list_2$]	give the smallest non-negative integer r with Mod[r, $list_2$] == $list_1$

Solving simultaneous congruences.

The *Chinese Remainder Theorem* states that a certain class of simultaneous congruences always has a solution. ChineseRemainder[$list_1$, $list_2$] finds the smallest non-negative integer r such that Mod[r, $list_2$] is $list_1$. The solution is unique modulo the least common multiple of the elements of $list_2$. The code for ChineseRemainder was contributed by Stan Wagon of Macalaster College.

This means that $244 \equiv 0 \bmod 4$, $244 \equiv 1 \bmod 9$, and $244 \equiv 2 \bmod 121$.

```
In[7]:= ChineseRemainder[{0, 1, 2}, {4, 9, 121}]

Out[7]= 244
```

This confirms the result.

```
In[8]:= Mod[244, {4, 9, 121}]

Out[8]= {0, 1, 2}
```

For longer lists the routine is still quite fast.

```
In[9]:= ChineseRemainder[Range[20], Prime[Range[20]]]

Out[9]= 16999109964912512727883514
```

| SqrtMod[d, n] | give the square root of $d \bmod n$, for odd n |

Finding square roots modulo n.

SqrtMod[d, n] computes the square root of $d \bmod n$. In other words, it returns x, where $x^2 \equiv d \bmod n$. The algorithm used by SqrtMod is discussed in *Mathematica in Action*, Section 9.6. It is interesting to note that this method does fewer divisions than Newton's method for extracting square roots, and so is faster by a constant factor.

For given d and n, there may not exist an integer x with $x^2 \equiv d \bmod n$. Clearly d must be a perfect square $\bmod n$, so to have a solution one must have that JacobiSymbol[d, n] be equal to 1. This condition is also sufficient if n is a prime. The algorithm used for the case when n is prime was discovered by Shanks.

If n is not prime, the algorithm that is used requires that n be factored completely. In this case, for d to be a perfect square, every prime factor p of n for which JacobiSymbol[d, p] is -1 must divide n to an even power.

In the special case when n is a prime power $n = p^k$, SqrtMod[d, n] is computed using a variant of the classical Newton iteration

$$x \mapsto \frac{1}{2}\left(x + \frac{d}{x}\right)$$

The Newton iteration sends a $\bmod p^k$ square root to a $\bmod p^{2k}$ solution, but does a modular division at each step.

One can compute the square root by doing modular divisions only at the first step by first computing $x \equiv 1/\sqrt{d} \pmod p$ and then iterating

$$x \mapsto \frac{3x - dx^3}{2}$$

as in Newton's iteration. The answer is recovered by multiplying back by d on the final step.

The method is based on the p–adic identity

$$\sqrt{d} = d\,\frac{x}{\sqrt{1 - (1 - dx^2)}} = d\,x \sum_{k=0}^{\infty} \frac{\binom{2k}{k}}{4^k}(1 - dx^2)^k$$

where $x^2 \equiv 1/d \pmod{p^k}$, $k > 0$.

For a general composite n, n is first factored into primes. The square root modulo primes and prime powers is then computed using the techniques described above. These solutions are then used with the Chinese Remainder Theorem to get the final solution.

This finds an x so that x^2 is equal to 3 mod 11.

```
In[10]:= SqrtMod[3, 11]

Out[10]= 5
```

This verifies the result.

```
In[11]:= Mod[5^2, 11]
Out[11]= 3
```

If *d* does not have a square root modulo *n*, Sqrt[*d*, *n*] will remain unevaluated.

```
In[12]:= SqrtMod[3, 5]
Out[12]= SqrtMod[3, 5]
```

This checks that 3 is not a square modulo 5.

```
In[13]:= Mod[{0, 1, 2, 3, 4}^2, 5]
Out[13]= {0, 1, 4, 4, 1}
```

Even for large modulus, the square root can be computed fairly quickly.

```
In[14]:= SqrtMod[2, 10^64 + 57]
Out[14]= 8765044674966816437359261119965461004010336119767770749091.
         122865
```

SqrtMod[*d*, *n*] also works for composite *n*.

```
In[15]:= SqrtMod[3, 11^3]
Out[15]= 578
```

Since the algorithm factors *n*, SqrtMod[*d*, *n*] may not return a result for very large composite values of *n*.

PrimitiveRoot[*n*]	give the primitive root of *n*, where *n* is a prime power or twice a prime power

Computing primitive roots.

PrimitiveRoot[*n*] returns a generator for the group of numbers relatively prime to *n* under multiplication mod *n*. This has a single generator if and only if *n* is a power of a prime or twice a power of a prime. The algorithm is probabilistic but runs very fast in practice (it does not require one to factor *n*). This implementation was improved by some suggestions of Ferrell S. Wheeler. A variation of this implementation can be used to generate the Pratt primality certificates used in the package NumberTheory`PrimeQ`. A discussion of Pratt certificates can be found in *Mathematica in Action*, Section 8.7.

Here is the primitive root of 5.

```
In[16]:= PrimitiveRoot[5]
Out[16]= 2
```

This confirms that it does generate the group.

```
In[17]:= Sort[Mod[2^Range[4], 5]]
Out[17]= {1, 2, 3, 4}
```

Here is the primitive root of a prime power.

```
In[18]:= PrimitiveRoot[1093^3]
Out[18]= 5
```

Here is the primitive root of twice a prime power.

```
In[19]:= PrimitiveRoot[2*5^5]
Out[19]= 3127
```

If the argument is composite and not a prime power or twice a prime power, the function does not evaluate.

```
In[20]:= PrimitiveRoot[11*13]
Out[20]= PrimitiveRoot[143]
```

`PrimitiveRoot` uses `FactorInteger` as a subroutine, so it may not return a result for very large arguments.

`QuadraticRepresentation[d, n]`	give {x, y} solving $x^2 + dy^2 = n$ (when a solution exists), for odd n and positive d

Finding quadratic representations.

`QuadraticRepresentation[d, n]` returns {x, y} where $x^2 + dy^2 = n$, if such a representation exists. Here d must be a positive integer and n is odd. The algorithm resembles the Euclidean algorithm, and for the case of prime n was discovered by Cornacchia, see S. Wagon, "The Euclidean Algorithm Strikes Again," *American Mathematical Monthly* 97 (1990), pages 124–125. The generalization to all n is given in the paper by K. Hardy, J. B. Muskat, and K. S. Williams, "A Deterministic Algorithm for Solving $n = fu^2 + gv^2$ in Coprime Integers u and v," *Mathematics of Computation* 55 (1990), pages 327–343. This algorithm uses `SqrtMod[-{d}, {n}]` as a subroutine and therefore requires the factorization of n.

`QuadraticRepresentation[d, n]` may not return an answer for two reasons:

(1) $-d$ is not a perfect square mod n, that is, `JacobiSymbol[-d, n]` is -1.

(2) The class number of the extension field $\mathbf{Q}(\sqrt{-d})$ is greater than one, and a prime divisor p of n splits into prime ideals not in the principal class.

The reason that condition (1) can imply the nonexistence of a representation is that the equation $x^2 + dy^2 = n \bmod n$ implies that $x^2 + dy^2 = 0 \bmod n$, so that $-d = (x/y)^2 \bmod n$ is a perfect square mod n (here division is mod n). It follows from this that for such a representation to exist, each prime p that divides n and for which $-d$ is not a perfect square must divide n to an even power.

A complete analysis of condition (2) is given in the book D. A. Cox, *Primes of the Form $x^2 + ny^2$*, Wiley, 1989.

This gives a quadratic representation of 13.

```
In[21]:= QuadraticRepresentation[1, 13]
Out[21]= {3, 2}
```

This verifies the result.

```
In[22]:= (%^2) . {1, 1}
Out[22]= 13
```

The case $d = 1$ is essentially the same as `FactorInteger[n, GaussianIntegers -> True]`.

```
In[23]:= FactorInteger[13, GaussianIntegers -> True]
Out[23]= {{-i, 1}, {2 + 3 i, 1}, {3 + 2 i, 1}}
```

Here is a fairly large composite number.	`In[24]:= 13*31*61*Prime[10^7]` `Out[24]= 4410796736359`
This computes its quadratic representation using $d = 3$.	`In[25]:= QuadraticRepresentation[3, %]` `Out[25]= {1864234, 558399}`
This verifies the result.	`In[26]:= (%^2) . {1, 3}` `Out[26]= 4410796736359`

Even for large numbers, you can get a quadratic representation fairly quickly.	`In[27]:= QuadraticRepresentation[1, 10^64+57]`
	`Out[27]= {84124543127432900917005691375104,`
	`54065342351645956058977745119829}`

`ClassList[d]`	give a list of inequivalent quadratic forms of discriminant d for negative, square-free integers d of the form $4n + 1$
`ClassNumber[d]`	give the number of inequivalent quadratic forms of discriminant d

Using `ClassList`.

`ClassList[d]` gives a set of representatives of the equivalence classes under composition of binary quadratic forms $ax^2 + bxy + cy^2$ of discriminant d. It is assumed that d is a negative square-free integer of the form $d = 4k + 1$. A quadratic form is represented by the list $\{a, b, c\}$. The algorithm is the most straightforward one and is slow for inputs much larger in magnitude than 10^4.

Here are representatives of the three quadratic forms with discriminant -23.	`In[28]:= ClassList[-23]` `Out[28]= {{1, 1, 6}, {2, -1, 3}, {2, 1, 3}}`
The class number is just the number of inequivalent quadratic forms with the given discriminant.	`In[29]:= ClassNumber[-10099]` `Out[29]= 25`
Gauss conjectured and H. Stark proved in 1968 that this is the last negative discriminant of class number one.	`In[30]:= ClassNumber[-163]` `Out[30]= 1`

+	`SumOfSquaresR[d, n]`	give the number of representations of an integer n as a sum of d squares
+	`SumOfSquaresRepresentations[d, n]`	give a list of all representations of an integer n as a sum of d squares, ignoring order and signs

Representing an integer as a sum of squares.

`SumOfSquaresRepresentations[d, n]` gives a set of representations of the integer n as a sum of d squares. `SumOfSquaresR[d, n]` gives $r_d(n)$, the number of representations of the integer n as a sum of d squares. For $d = 2, 4, 6, 8$, `SumOfSquaresR[d, n]` can handle large integer values of n, as long as n can be factored. For other values of d, `SumOfSquaresR[d, n]` uses recursion, thus only modestly sized values of m and d can be used.

Here are the representations of 100 as a sum of 3 squares.	*In[31]:=* `SumOfSquaresRepresentations[3, 100]`
	Out[31]= {{0, 0, 10}, {0, 6, 8}}
This checks that the representations are valid.	*In[32]:=* `Apply[Plus, (%^2), 2]`
	Out[32]= {100, 100}
The asymptotic average value of r_2 is π.	*In[33]:=* `Sum[N[SumOfSquaresR[2, k]], {k, 200}] / 200`
	Out[33]= 3.16

`SumOfSquaresRepresentations` and `SumOfSquaresR` were contributed by Stan Wagon. For more information see "The Magic of Imaginary Factoring," *Mathematica in Education and Research* 5:1 (1996), pages 43–47.

■ NumberTheory`PrimeQ`

This package implements primality proving. If `ProvablePrimeQ[n]` returns `True`, then the number *n* can be mathematically proven to be prime. In addition, `PrimeQCertificate[n]` prints a certificate that can be used to verify that *n* is prime or composite. Note that the built-in primality testing function `PrimeQ` does not actually give a proof that a number is prime. However, as of this writing, there are no known examples where `PrimeQ` fails.

`ProvablePrimeQ[n]`	give `True` if *n* can be proved to be prime, and `False` if *n* can be proved to be composite
`ProvablePrimeQ[n, Certificate -> True]`	print a certificate that can be used to verify the result
`PrimeQCertificate[n]`	print a certificate that *n* is prime or that *n* is composite
`PrimeQCertificateCheck[cert, n]`	verify that the certificate *cert* proves the primality or compositeness of *n*

Proving primality or compositeness.

The functions provided in this package not only prove primality, but they also generate a *certificate* of primality. A certificate of primality is a relatively short set of data that can be easily used to prove primality. The word easily means that using the data to prove primality is much easier and faster than generating the data in the first place. As a simple example of a certificate, the factors of a composite number provide a certificate of compositeness. Multiplying the numbers together to show that they are the factors is much easier than finding the factors. The advantage of providing certificates is that the user does not have to trust the internal mechanism of the algorithm that generated the certificate. It is fairly easy to write a program (in any system) that checks that the certificate provides a proof of primality.

This loads the package.	`In[1]:= <<NumberTheory`PrimeQ``
PrimeQ indicates that the number 1093 is prime.	`In[2]:= PrimeQ[1093]` `Out[2]= True`
ProvablePrimeQ gives the same result, but it has generated a certificate.	`In[3]:= ProvablePrimeQ[1093]` `Out[3]= True`

This prints the certificate.	`In[4]:= PrimeQCertificate[1093]`
	`Out[4]= {1093, 5, {2, {3, 2, {2}}, {7, 3, {2, {3, 2, {2}}}},`
	`      {13, 2, {2, {3, 2, {2}}}}}}`

This prints the certificate directly.	`In[5]:= ProvablePrimeQ[1093, Certificate->True]`
	`Out[5]= {True, {1093, 5, {2, {3, 2, {2}}, {7, 3, {2, {3, 2, {2}}}},`
	`      {13, 2, {2, {3, 2, {2}}}}}}}`

The certificate of primality used in this package for large n is based on the theory of elliptic curves. The basic idea was discovered by S. Goldwasser and J. Kilian, "Almost All Primes Can Be Quickly Certified," in *Proc. 18th STOC*, 1986, pp. 316–329. Their algorithm was only of theoretical significance, however. A. O. L. Atkin found a way to make it practical by using ideas from complex multiplication, which is a branch of number theory that combines the fields of complex analysis, Galois theory and modular forms. This method was implemented very successfully by F. Morain in "Implementation of the Atkin-Goldwasser-Kilian Primality Testing Algorithm," *INRIA Research Report*, # 911, October 1988. In November 1989, Morain was able to give a primality proof for a 1065-digit number, the first titanic prime (> 1000 digits) to be tested without special purpose algorithms. Since that time Atkin and Morain have written an extensive treatise on the algorithm: A. O. L. Atkin and F. Morain, "Elliptic Curves and Primality Proving," *Mathematics of Computation*, 1993, 29–68.

For an introduction to primality testing and elliptic curves, see D. Bressoud, *Factorization and Primality Testing*, Springer-Verlag, 1989.

This package can also be used to generate certificates of compositeness for composite numbers. These certificates are based on showing that simple properties that are true of prime numbers are not true for the given number. For example, `PrimeQCertificate[3837523]` returns the certificate {2, 3837522, 3837523}, which is intended to show that $2^{3837522}$ (mod 3837523) is not equal to 1.

`ProvablePrimeQ[`n`]` returns `True` or `False` depending on whether n is prime or not. The certificate for primality or compositeness is generated by `PrimeQCertificate[`n`]`. `ProvablePrimeQ` calls `PrimeQCertificate` and stores the result, so it does not take any extra time to create a certificate once `ProvablePrimeQ` has returned an answer. The certificate generated by `PrimeQCertificate` can be checked by `PrimeQCertificateCheck`. This function recognizes whether the certificate asserts primality or compositeness and then uses the certificate to verify the assertion.

This prints the certificate of the prime number.

```
In[6]:= ProvablePrimeQ[1093,
            Certificate -> True]
Out[6]= {True, {1093, 5, {2, {3, 2, {2}}}, {7, 3, {2, {3, 2, {2}}}},
            {13, 2, {2, {3, 2, {2}}}}}}}
```

This verifies primality using the certificate.

```
In[7]:= PrimeQCertificateCheck[Last[%], 1093]
Out[7]= True
```

Here is the certificate for a composite number. You can recognize a certificate of compositeness because it will always be a list of three integers.

```
In[8]:= PrimeQCertificate[1093 * 3511]
Out[8]= {2, 3837522, 3837523}
```

This verifies the compositeness.

```
In[9]:= PrimeQCertificateCheck[%, 3837523]
Out[9]= True
```

The built-in function `PrimeQ` first tests for divisibility using small primes, then uses the Miller-Rabin strong pseudoprime test base 2 and base 3, and then uses the Lucas test. As of 1998, this procedure is known to be correct only for $n < 10^{16}$, and it is conceivable that for larger n it could claim a composite number to be prime. However, it is a mathematical theorem that when `PrimeQ[`n`]` returns `False`, the number *n* is genuinely composite. Thus PrimeQ[*n*] can only fail if *n* is composite but PrimeQ declares it to be prime. It is important to note that PrimeQ is deterministic; no computations based on random numbers are involved.

This package is not meant to replace the built-in primality tester PrimeQ but rather to allow one to be completely secure that a number is truly prime. The package should be used only to certify results after all the number theoretical work has been done. For example, it would be a mistake to use ProvablePrimeQ as a primality test for an integer factoring algorithm. Rather, only when the complete factorization has been achieved (using PrimeQ for primality testing) would one use ProvablePrimeQ to certify the primality of the prime factors given by the algorithm. The reason for this is that PrimeQ will be, in general, several orders of magnitude faster than ProvablePrimeQ.

As noted above, there is a possibility that PrimeQ is incorrect, that is, it asserts that a number is prime when it is really composite. It is unclear whether ProvablePrimeQ always detects this; but if it does, a warning message is generated indicating a counterexample to PrimeQ, and False is returned. This behavior can be simulated by artificially setting PrimeQ[*n*] to True for a known composite *n*.

Here PrimeQ is artificially set to give an incorrect answer. ProvablePrimeQ detects that PrimeQ is incorrect, prints a warning message, and returns the correct answer.

```
In[10]:= (Unprotect[PrimeQ];
         PrimeQ[38200901201] = True;
         ProvablePrimeQ[38200901201])

SqrtMod::fail:
   Warning: $IterationLimit exceeded; PrimeQ[38200901201
   ] may be incorrect.

PrimeQCertificate::qrsqrtmod:
   Failure of elliptic curves certificate for p =
   38200901201.  Unable to find quadratic representation
   4*p = u^2 + 7*v^2 due to failure of SqrtMod[-7, p].

PrimeQCertificate::false:
   Warning: PrimeQCertificate has detected a
   counterexample to PrimeQ: PowerMod[3, 38200901200,
   38200901201] != 1.

Out[10]= False
```

option name	*default value*	
`SmallPrime`	`10^10`	lower bound for using the Atkin-Morain primality test
`Certificate`	`False`	whether to print a certificate
`PollardPTest`	`Automatic`	whether to apply the Pollard $p-1$ factoring algorithm in the search for the next prime in the recursive certificate
`PollardRhoTest`	`Automatic`	whether to apply the Pollard ρ factoring algorithm in the search for the next prime in the recursive certificate
`TrialDivisionLimit`	`Automatic`	number of primes to be used in the trial division part of `PrimeQCertificate`
`PrimeQMessages`	`False`	whether to print out the progress of the algorithm

Options for `ProvablePrimeQ` and `PrimeQCertificate`.

When n is larger than the value of the option `SmallPrime`, `ProvablePrimeQ` uses the Atkin-Morain test as described above. This primality proving algorithm is suboptimal if the number is within the range of efficient factoring algorithms. When this is the case, a method of V. Pratt is preferable: V. Pratt, "Every Prime Has a Succinct Certificate," *SIAM Journal of Computation* 4 (1975), pages 214–220. An implementation of this algorithm in *Mathematica* is described in S. Wagon, *Mathematica in Action*, W. H. Freeman, 1991, Section 8.7.

Note that you must use the same value of `SmallPrime` when you check a certificate using `PrimeQCertificate` that you used when you generated it using `ProvablePrimeQ` or `PrimeQCertificate`.

Since the default value of `SmallPrime` is larger than the given number, Pratt's certificate of primality is returned.

```
In[11]:= PrimeQCertificate[3511]

Out[11]= {3511, 7,
            {2, {3, 2, {2}}, {5, 2, {2}}, {13, 2, {2, {3, 2, {2}}}}}}
```

Here, the value of `SmallPrime` has been reset so that it is less than the given number. This causes the Atkin-Goldwasser-Kilian-Morain certificate to be returned.

```
In[12]:= PrimeQCertificate[3511, SmallPrime -> 1000]

Out[12]= {{CertificatePrime → 3511, CertificatePoint →
            PointEC[2, 2467, 1447, 2135, 3511], CertificateK → 32,
            CertificateM → 3424, CertificateNextPrime → 107,
            CertificateDiscriminant → -7}, 107, 2,
            {2, {53, 2, {2, {13, 2, {2, {3, 2, {2}}}}}}}}
```

For large numbers, the certificate can be quite long and involved.

```
In[13]:= PrimeQCertificate[10^20 + 39]

Out[13]= {{CertificatePrime →
            100000000000000000039, CertificatePoint →
            PointEC[2, 1729260293697269439, 64272530717713441964,
              28545061435426883889, 100000000000000000039],
          CertificateK → 1012, CertificateM →
            100000000010180551292, CertificateNextPrime →
            98814229259071691, CertificateDiscriminant → -43},
         {CertificatePrime → 98814229259071691, CertificatePoint →
            PointEC[2, 14775259946196422, 20390237783617966,
              79469644695126438, 98814229259071691],
          CertificateK → 2822600, CertificateM → 98814229876628200,
          CertificateNextPrime → 35008229957,
          CertificateDiscriminant → -7}, {CertificatePrime →
            35008229957, CertificatePoint → PointEC[
             5, 11747318414, 5556861890, 30747969158, 35008229957],
          CertificateK → 4, CertificateM → 35008421452,
          CertificateNextPrime → 8752105363,
          CertificateDiscriminant → -7},
         8752105363, 2, {2, {3, 2, {2}}, {7, 3, {2, {3, 2, {2}}}}},
          {11, 2, {2, {5, 2, {2}}}}, {13, 2, {2, {3, 2, {2}}}}, {43, 3,
           {2, {3, 2, {2}}, {7, 3, {2, {3, 2, {2}}}}}}, {33889, 13, {2,
           {3, 2, {2}}, {353, 3, {2, {11, 2, {2, {5, 2, {2}}}}}}}}}}}
```

■ NumberTheory`PrimitiveElement`

This package provides a function for computing primitive elements of multiple algebraic extensions of rationals.

Given algebraic numbers $a_1, \ldots, a_n$ you can always find a single algebraic number b such that each of $a_1, \ldots, a_n$ can be expressed as a polynomial in b with rational coefficients. The number b is called a primitive element of the field extension $\mathbf{Q}(a_1, \ldots, a_n)/\mathbf{Q}$. In other words, an algebraic number b is a primitive element of $\mathbf{Q}(a_1, \ldots, a_n)/\mathbf{Q}$ iff $\mathbf{Q}(a_1, \ldots, a_n) = \mathbf{Q}(b)$.

The function `PrimitiveElement` takes a variable z and a list of algebraic numbers $a_1, \ldots, a_n$ and returns a primitive element b of $\mathbf{Q}(a_1, \ldots, a_n)/\mathbf{Q}$, and a list of polynomials $f_1(z), \ldots, f_n(z)$ such that $a_i = f_i(b)$ for all i.

`PrimitiveElement[z, {`$a_1, \ldots, a_n$`}]` give a list {b, {$f_1, \ldots, f_n$}} where b is a primitive element for the extension of rationals by algebraic numbers $a_1, \ldots, a_n$, and f_i is a polynomial in the variable z representing a_i in terms of the primitive element

The primitive element of an algebraic extension of the rationals.

This loads the package.

$In[1]:=$ `<<NumberTheory`PrimitiveElement``

Here is a primitive element of $\mathbf{Q}(\text{Sqrt}[2], \text{Sqrt}[3])/\mathbf{Q}$, and a list of polynomials showing how to represent Sqrt[2] and Sqrt[3] in terms of the primitive element.

$In[2]:=$ `PrimitiveElement[z, {Sqrt[2], Sqrt[3]}]`

$Out[2]=$ $\left\{\text{Root}\left[1 - 10\,\#1^2 + \#1^4\,\&, 4\right], \left\{-\dfrac{9z}{2} + \dfrac{z^3}{2}, \dfrac{11z}{2} - \dfrac{z^3}{2}\right\}\right\}$

This checks that the computed polynomials evaluated at the primitive element give Sqrt[2] and Sqrt[3].

$In[3]:=$ `RootReduce[%[[2]] /. z -> %[[1]]]`

$Out[3]=$ $\left\{\sqrt{2}, \sqrt{3}\right\}$

■ NumberTheory'Ramanujan'

The Riemann ζ function

$$\zeta(s) = \sum_{n=1}^{\infty} n^{-s}$$

is the simplest of all Dirichlet series. Ramanujan studied the Dirichlet series

$$f(s) = \sum_{n=1}^{\infty} \tau_n n^{-s}$$

where the τ_n are the coefficients of z^n in the series expansion

$$z \prod_{k=1}^{\infty} (1 - z^k)^{24} = z - 24z^2 + 252z^3 - 1472z^4 + 4830z^5 - 6048z^6 - 16744z^7 +$$
$$84480z^8 - 113643z^9 - 115920z^{10} + 534612z^{11} - 370944z^{12} -$$
$$577738z^{13} + 401856z^{14} + 1217160z^{15} + 987136z^{16} - \cdots$$

Just as there is the Riemann hypothesis that all of the nontrivial zeros of the ζ lie on the critical line $\operatorname{Re} s = 1/2$, there is a conjecture due to Ramanujan that all of the nontrivial zeros of f lie on the critical line $\operatorname{Re} s = 6$. The function f satisfies the functional equation

$$f(s)\Gamma(s)/(2\pi)^s = f(12 - s)\Gamma(12 - s)/(2\pi)^{12-s}$$

Just as ζ can be split into

$$\zeta(1/2 + it) = Z(t)e^{-i\vartheta(t)}$$

where Z is `RiemannSiegelZ` and ϑ is `RiemannSiegelTheta`, f can split into

$$f(6 + it) = z(t)e^{-i\theta(t)}$$

where

$$z(t) = \Gamma(6 + it)f(6 + it)(2\pi)^{-it} \sqrt{\frac{\sinh(\pi t)}{\pi t(1 + t^2)(4 + t^2)(9 + t^2)(16 + t^2)(25 + t^2)}}$$

and

$$\theta(t) = \frac{-i}{2} \log \frac{\Gamma(6 + it)}{\Gamma(6 - it)} - t \log(2\pi)$$

RamanujanTau[n]	n^{th} coefficient of the Ramanujan τ-Dirichlet series τ_n
RamanujanTauGeneratingFunction[z]	generating function of the Ramanujan τ-Dirichlet series, $z \prod_{k=1}^{\infty}(1 - z^k)^{24}$
RamanujanTauDirichletSeries[s]	Ramanujan τ-Dirichlet series $f(s)$
RamanujanTauTheta[t]	Ramanujan τ-Dirichlet function $\theta(t)$
RamanujanTauZ[t]	Ramanujan τ-Dirichlet function $z(t)$

Functions related to the Ramanujan τ-Dirichlet series.

The Ramanujan τ-Dirichlet series is rather difficult to evaluate, especially far up the critical line $\operatorname{Re} s = 6$. It is only within the last few years that even a few of the zeros have been verified to lie on the critical line. This package does not provide any great new method to help with this effort, but it does use the fastest methods known.

This loads the package.	*In[1]:=* **<<NumberTheory'Ramanujan'**
This gives τ_5.	*In[2]:=* **RamanujanTau[5]**
	Out[2]= 4830
This gives the first five terms in the generating function RamanujanTauGeneratingFunction[z].	*In[3]:=* **Sum[RamanujanTau[n] z^n, {n, 5}]**
	Out[3]= $z - 24\,z^2 + 252\,z^3 - 1472\,z^4 + 4830\,z^5$
The generating function can be evaluated numerically.	*In[4]:=* **RamanujanTauGeneratingFunction[.1]**
	Out[4]= 0.00610209
The generating function can be evaluated numerically even at some points outside the radius of convergence. This uses a functional equation to achieve analytic continuation.	*In[5]:=* **RamanujanTauGeneratingFunction[.99]**
	Out[5]= $4.10287803703 \times 10^{-1673}$
Here is the value of the τ-Dirichlet series near the first zero on the critical line.	*In[6]:=* **RamanujanTauDirichletSeries[6 + 9.22I]**
	Out[6]= $0.00040309 - 0.00239013\,i$
This is the value of z near the same zero.	*In[7]:=* **z = RamanujanTauZ[9.22]**
	Out[7]= 0.00242388
This is the value of θ.	*In[8]:=* **theta = RamanujanTauTheta[9.22]**
	Out[8]= 1.40372
Here is the value of the τ-Dirichlet series again.	*In[9]:=* **z Exp[-I theta]**
	Out[9]= $0.00040309 - 0.00239013\,i$

■ NumberTheory`Rationalize`

It is frequently useful to approximate arbitrary real numbers with a nearby rational. The built-in function `Rationalize` gives a rational approximation to a single real number.

In certain situations, such as the computation of gear ratios or the setting of musical scales, one wants to get a list of rational numbers that approximates a given list of real numbers. You could simply apply `Rationalize` to each element in the list, but it is very likely that the elements in the result would not be related to each other in a simple way. To get a simultaneous rational approximation that preserves the relationships among the given numbers, you should use `ProjectiveRationalize` or `AffineRationalize`.

`ProjectiveRationalize[{`x_0`, `x_1`, ... , `x_n`}]`	give a list of integers whose ratios well approximate the corresponding ratios of the real numbers x_i
`ProjectiveRationalize[{`x_0`, `x_1`, ... , `x_n`}, `*prec*`]`	use a tolerance of 10^{-prec} in the approximation
`AffineRationalize[{`x_0`, `x_1`, ... , `x_n`}]`	give a list of rational numbers with a small least common denominator that well approximate the corresponding real numbers x_i
`AffineRationalize[{`x_0`, `x_1`, ... , `x_n`}, `*prec*`]`	use a tolerance of 10^{-prec} in the approximation

Getting a simultaneous rational approximation.

The second argument in `ProjectiveRationalize` and `AffineRationalize` controls the number of digits that are to be considered significant in the numbers given in the first argument. If no second argument is given all digits are considered significant. Note that the convention used for specifying the tolerances in this package differs from the one used in the built-in `Rationalize`.

This loads the package.

```
In[1]:= <<NumberTheory`Rationalize`
```

Here is the ratio of rational approximations. The result is close to $\frac{3}{11}$, but it is a very awkward way to approximate it.

```
In[2]:= Rationalize[N[3 Pi], 6]/
            Rationalize[N[11 Pi], 6]
```

$$Out[2]= \frac{9}{34}$$

This computes a simultaneous rational approximation that preserves the simple relationship between the given numbers.

```
In[3]:= AffineRationalize[{N[3 Pi], N[11 Pi]}, 6]
```

$$Out[3]= \left\{ \frac{1065}{113}, \frac{3905}{113} \right\}$$

This ratio is much simpler.

In[4]:= `%[[1]]/%[[2]]`

Out[4]= $\dfrac{3}{11}$

The ratios of the integers returned by ProjectiveRationalize approximate the ratios of the corresponding irrationals.

In[5]:= `ProjectiveRationalize[{N[3 Pi], N[11 Pi]}]`

Out[5]= `{3, 11}`

■ NumberTheory`Recognize`

This package defines the function Recognize for determining a polynomial with integer coefficients, given an approximate real zero of the polynomial and the degree of the polynomial. The resulting polynomial is normally not unique.

Recognize[x, n, t]	find a polynomial of degree at most n in t such that x is an approximate zero of the polynomial
Recognize[x, n, t, k]	find a polynomial of degree at most n in t such that x is a zero, and with penalty weight k against higher-degree polynomials.

Determining a polynomial from a solution.

This loads the package.

    In[1]:= << NumberTheory`Recognize`

This finds a linear polynomial in t with solution 1.7.

    In[2]:= Recognize[1.7, 1, t]
    Out[2]= -17 + 10 t

NSolve gives the numerical solutions of a cubic equation.

    In[3]:= NSolve[3 x^3 - 2 x + 5 == 0]
    Out[3]= {{x → -1.37174}, {x → 0.68587 - 0.862893 i},
             {x → 0.68587 + 0.862893 i}}

Here is the first solution.

    In[4]:= sol = First[x /. %]
    Out[4]= -1.37174

This result is proportional to the original polynomial used in NSolve.

    In[5]:= Recognize[sol, 3, t]
    Out[5]= -5 + 2 t - 3 t^3

Here is a quadratic polynomial for which sol is an approximate solution.

    In[6]:= Recognize[sol, 2, t]
    Out[6]= -26873 + 86814 t + 77569 t^2

This result is a polynomial of degree 5.

    In[7]:= Recognize[N[Sqrt[3^(2/5)]], 5, t]
    Out[7]= -3 + t^5

If the penalty is large enough, a lower-order polynomial may be returned.

    In[8]:= Recognize[N[Sqrt[3^(2/5)]], 5, t, 10]
    Out[8]= -14625 + 11193 t + 328 t^2 + 88 t^3 + t^4

◼ NumberTheory`SiegelTheta`

The Siegel theta function $\Theta(\mathbf{Z}, \mathbf{s})$ is defined as

$$\Theta(\mathbf{Z}, \mathbf{s}) = \sum_{\mathbf{t}} e^{\pi i \mathbf{t}' \mathbf{Z} \mathbf{t} + 2\pi i \mathbf{t}' \mathbf{s}}$$

where $\mathbf{Z}$ is a $p \times p$ symmetric complex matrix $\mathbf{Z} = \mathbf{X} + i\mathbf{Y}$ with imaginary part $\mathbf{Y}$ positive definite, $\mathbf{s}$ is a complex vector of dimension p, and $\mathbf{t}$ is an integer vector of dimension p that ranges over the entire p-dimensional lattice of integers. This function was initially investigated by Riemann and Weierstrass and further studies were done by Frobenius and Poincaré. These investigations represent some of the most significant accomplishments of nineteenth century mathematics.

`SiegelTheta[z, s]`	Siegel theta function $\Theta(\mathbf{Z}, \mathbf{s})$

The Siegel theta function.

This loads the package.

```
In[1]:= << NumberTheory`SiegelTheta`
```

This evaluates Θ for particular arguments in 2-space.

```
In[2]:= SiegelTheta[{{1+I,2+I}, {2+I,-1+4I}}, {1.2, 2.3+.3I}]
Out[2]= 0.973715 - 0.000297048 i
```

This is a slow, brute force way to get the same answer. (The tails beyond -10 and 10 die off quickly.)

```
In[3]:= Sum[E^(Pi I {t1,t2}.{{1+I,2+I}, {2+I,-1+4I}}.{t1,t2} +
               2 Pi I {t1,t2} . {1.2, 2.3+.3I}),
         {t1, -10, 10}, {t2, -10, 10}]
Out[3]= 0.973715 - 0.000297048 i
```

If the imaginary part of $\mathbf{Z}$ is not positive definite, $\Theta(\mathbf{Z}, \mathbf{s})$ is not defined.

```
In[4]:= SiegelTheta[{{1+I,2+I}, {2+I,-1-4I}}, {1.2, 2.3+.3I}]

SiegelTheta::npd:
   The imaginary part of the matrix
   {{1 + I, 2 + I}, {2 + I, -1 + <<1>>}}
   is not positive definite.

Out[4]= SiegelTheta[{{1 + i, 2 + i}, {2 + i, -1 - 4 i}},
         {1.2, 2.3 + 0.3 i}]
```

10. Numerical Mathematics

■ NumericalMath`Approximations`

A degree (m, k) rational function is the ratio of a degree m polynomial to a degree k polynomial. Because rational functions only use the elementary arithmetic operations, they are very easy to evaluate numerically. The polynomial in the denominator allows one to approximate functions that have rational singularities. For these reasons a rational function is frequently useful in numerical work to approximate a given function.

There are various methods to perform this approximation. The methods differ in how they interpret the notion of the goodness of the approximation. Each method is useful for certain classes of problems. You can use this package to compute general rational interpolations and minimax approximations. The package Calculus`Pade` contains functions that perform Padé approximations and economized rational approximations.

There is a related class of approximation questions that involves the interpolation or fitting of a set of data points by an approximating function. In this type of situation you should use the built-in functions Fit, InterpolatingPolynomial, and Interpolation. For more information, see the section covering numerical operations on data in *The Mathematica Book*.

RationalInterpolation[f, $\{x, m, k\}$, $\{x_1, x_2, \ldots, x_{m+k+1}\}$]
                        give a rational interpolation of degree (m, k) to the points
                        $(x_i, f(x_i))$

RationalInterpolation[f, $\{x, m, k\}$, $\{x, xmin, xmax\}$],
                        give a rational interpolation with the points x_i chosen
                        automatically

Rational interpolations.

One way to approximate a given function by a rational function is to choose a set of values for the independent variable and then construct a rational function that agrees with the given function at this set of values. This is what is done by RationalInterpolation.

There are two ways of using RationalInterpolation. If you just specify a range in the independent variable, then the set of values is chosen automatically in a way that ensures a reasonable approximation for the degree of approximation you have chosen. You can also give an explicit list of the set of values to be used. Note that in this case if you ask for a degree (m, k)-approximation, you must specify a list of $m + k + 1$ values for the independent variable.

This loads the package.   *In[1]:=* **<<NumericalMath`Approximations`**

This gives a rational interpolation of degree $(2, 4)$ to e^x at 7 equally spaced points between 0 and 2.

```
In[2]:= ri1 = RationalInterpolation[
              Exp[x], {x, 2, 4},
              {0, 1/3, 2/3, 1, 4/3, 5/3, 2}]
```

```
Out[2]= (1.000000000000000 +
            0.379961505998214 x + 0.0469527572648759 x^2) /
           (1 - 0.620028516690566 x + 0.1669139144430911 x^2 -
            0.02340576618306169 x^3 + 0.001452790199322340 x^4)
```

This plots the difference between the function and its approximation. Note that the error tends to get larger near the endpoints.

```
In[3]:= Plot[ri1 - Exp[x], {x, 0, 2}]
```

Here *Mathematica* automatically chooses the interpolation points.

```
In[4]:= ri2 =
         RationalInterpolation[Exp[x],
               {x, 2, 4}, {x, 0, 2}]
```

```
Out[4]= (1.000000157557967 +
            0.379826643610590 x + 0.0468693215807399 x^2) /
           (1 - 0.620165730391327 x + 0.1669778816332341 x^2 -
            0.02341189497930664 x^3 + 0.001451916095874726 x^4)
```

The interpolation points are somewhat more bunched at the ends of the interval. This usually results in a smaller maximum error.

```
In[5]:= Plot[ri2 - Exp[x],
             {x, 0, 2}]
```

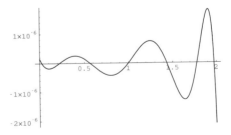

option name	default value	
WorkingPrecision	$MachinePrecision	number of digits of precision to use
Bias	0	bias in the automatic choice of interpolation points

Options for rational approximations.

When you specify a range of x values for RationalInterpolation, the interpolation points are chosen automatically. The option Bias allows you to bias the interpolation points to the right or to the left. Values for Bias must be numbers between -1 and 1. A positive value causes the points to be biased to the right. The default is Bias -> 0, which causes the points to be symmetrically distributed.

When you bias the distribution of the points to the right, you get smaller errors there and larger errors to the left.

```
In[6]:= ri3 = RationalInterpolation[
            Exp[x], {x, 2, 4}, {x, 0, 2},
                Bias -> .25]
```

$$Out[6]= (1.000000680916800 + \\ 0.386185595122318\,x + 0.0491526115537505\,x^2)\,/ \\ (1 - 0.613791918364478\,x + 0.1628204893739067\,x^2 - \\ 0.02234036054893554\,x^3 + 0.001343596942334393\,x^4)$$

This shows the influence of the bias.

```
In[7]:= Plot[ri3 - Exp[x],
            {x, 0, 2}]
```

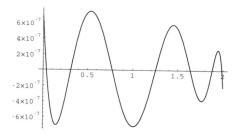

When you use RationalInterpolation, you get a rational function that agrees with the given function at a set of points. This guarantees that the rational function is, in one sense, close to the given function. A stronger requirement for a good rational approximation would be to require that the rational function be close to the given function over the entire interval. This type of rational approximation is produced by MiniMaxApproximation. This approximation is so named because it minimizes the maximum value of the relative error between the approximation and the given function. This means that minimax approximation $r(x)$ to a given function $f(x)$ is the rational function of the given degree that minimizes the maximum value of the quantity $|1 - r(x)/f(x)|$ over the interval under consideration. Note that the term minimax approximation is also sometimes used for the rational function that minimizes the absolute error rather than the relative error used here.

MiniMaxApproximation[*f*, {*x*, {*xmin*, *xmax*}, *m*, *k*}]
                give the minimax approximation to *f* of degree (*m*, *k*) on the
                interval from *xmin* to *xmax*

MiniMaxApproximation[*f*, *approx*, {*x*, {*xmin*, *xmax*}, *m*, *k*}]
                give the minimax approximation starting the iterative
                algorithm with *approx*

The minimax approximation.

MiniMaxApproximation works using an iterative scheme. The first step is to construct a rational approximation using RationalInterpolation. This first approximation is then used to generate a better approximation using a scheme based on Remes's algorithm. Generating the new approximation consists of adjusting the choice of the interpolation points in a way that ensures that the relative error will diminish.

MiniMaxApproximation returns a list with two parts: a list of the points at which the maximum error occurs and a list consisting of the rational approximation and the value of the maximum error. This extra information is provided not so much for the user's information, but to provide the capability of restarting the procedure without having to start back at the beginning. This is useful because the algorithm is iterative, and if convergence does not occur before MaxIterations is reached, the incomplete answer is returned along with a warning.

This gives a list containing the points where the maximum error occurs and the desired interpolation, along with the value of the error.

In[8]:= `mmlist = MiniMaxApproximation[Exp[x],`
            `{x, {0, 2}, 2, 4}]`

Out[8]= {{0, 0.1063486487628711,
       0.400915308296993, 0.816636147978239,
       1.262697793262660, 1.649749456495083, 1.909120496974457,
       2.000000000000000}, {(1.000000206052106 +
          $0.380881473299276\,x + 0.0472394925262197\,x^2$) /
          $(1 - 0.619109229762198\,x + 0.1662828794269402\,x^2 -$
          $0.02323044886214790\,x^3 + 0.001433248923477303\,x^4$),
          $-2.060521062420475 \times 10^{-7}$}}

This extracts the rational approximation.

In[9]:= `mmfunc = mmlist[[2, 1]]`

Out[9]= (1.000000206052106 +
          $0.380881473299276\,x + 0.0472394925262197\,x^2$) /
          $(1 - 0.619109229762198\,x + 0.1662828794269402\,x^2 -$
          $0.02323044886214790\,x^3 + 0.001433248923477303\,x^4$)

Here is a plot of the relative error in the approximation over the interval $0 \le x \le 2$. Reducing the error at any one of the extrema will force the error to increase at one of the others.

$In[10]:=$ **Plot[1 - mmfunc/Exp[x], {x, 0, 2}]**

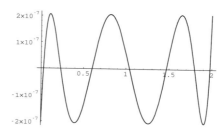

Because `MiniMaxApproximation` tries to minimize the maximum of the *relative* error, it is not possible to find a minimax approximation to a function that has a zero in the interval in question. The rational approximation would have to be *exactly* zero at the zero of the function, or the relative error would be infinite. It is still possible to deal with such functions, but the zero must be divided out of the function and then multiplied back into the rational function.

At $\frac{\pi}{2}$ the relative error is infinite.

$In[11]:=$ **MiniMaxApproximation[**
                  Cos[x], {x, {1, 2}, 2, 4}]

MiniMaxApproximation::van:
    Failed to locate the extrema in 20
        iterations. The function Cos[x]
        may be vanishing on the interval {1, 2}
        or the WorkingPrecision may be insufficient to get
        convergence.

$Out[11]=$ MiniMaxApproximation[Cos[x], {x, {1, 2}, 2, 4}]

Dividing by (x - Pi/2) cancels the zero and there is now no problem computing the approximation.

$In[12]:=$ **MiniMaxApproximation[**
                  Cos[x]/(x-Pi/2),{x,{1,2},2,4}][[2,1]]

$Out[12]=$ $(-0.636482640526357 -$
               $0.2841959632488293\,x + 0.0904595526698534\,x^2\,)\,/$
               $(1 - 0.1913611750941225\,x + 0.0771021866417798\,x^2 -$
               $0.01030585036517800\,x^3 + 0.001640468335757167\,x^4\,)$

Multiplying the approximation by (x - Pi/2) then gives the minimax approximation to Cos[x].

$In[13]:=$ **mmacos = % N[x - Pi/2]**

$Out[13]=$ $((-1.5708 + x)\,(-0.636482640526357 -$
               $0.2841959632488293\,x + 0.0904595526698534\,x^2\,))\,/$
               $(1 - 0.1913611750941225\,x + 0.0771021866417798\,x^2 -$
               $0.01030585036517800\,x^3 + 0.001640468335757167\,x^4\,)$

This plots the relative error.

In[14]:= **Plot[1 - mmacos/Cos[x],**
                     {x, 1, 2}]

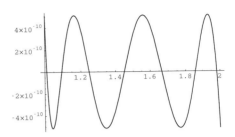

There are several ways in which `MiniMaxApproximation` can fail. In these cases, you will usually get a message indicating what probably went wrong and what you can do to avoid the problem. For example, if you ask for a minimax approximation of degree (m, k), `MiniMaxApproximation` will look for a rational minimax approximation such that the relative error oscillates in sign and the extreme values are achieved $m + k + 2$ times. Sometimes the extreme values occur more times. It may be possible to design a more robust algorithm to deal with this problem, but in practice it is usually quite simple just to ask for a minimax approximation with different degree.

When you try to compute this approximation you get a warning. Notice that there is not a single error, but a list of errors corresponding to the abscissas in the first part.

In[15]:= **MiniMaxApproximation[**
                    Cos[x]/(x - Pi/2), {x, {1, 2}, 2, 2}]

MiniMaxApproximation::extalt:
    The extrema of the error do not alternate in sign. It
    may be that MiniMaxApproximation has lost track of
    the extrema by going too fast. If so try increasing
    the values in the option Brake. It may be that the
    WorkingPrecision is insufficient. Otherwise there is
    an extra extreme value of the error, and
    MiniMaxApproximation cannot deal with this problem.

Out[15]= $\Big\{\{1.000000000000000, 1.091205197185748,$
    $1.330309061116209, 1.624666422133682, 1.854008048144718,$
    $2.000000000000000\}, \dfrac{-0.634342 - 0.324437\,x + 0.103283\,x^2}{1. - 0.141132\,x + 0.0449124\,x^2},$
    $\{4.083 \times 10^{-7}, -3.64006 \times 10^{-7}, 2.53276 \times 10^{-7}, -1.22862 \times 10^{-7},$
    $2.19191 \times 10^{-8}, 3.25618 \times 10^{-8}\}\Big\}$

This extracts the approximation and cancels the factor.

In[16]:= **badmma = %[[2]] N[x - Pi/2]**

Out[16]= $\dfrac{(-1.5708 + x)\,(-0.634342 - 0.324437\,x + 0.103283\,x^2)}{1. - 0.141132\,x + 0.0449124\,x^2}$

Notice that the relative error has seven local extrema rather than the expected six.

`In[17]:= Plot[1 - badmma/Cos[x], {x, 1, 2}]`

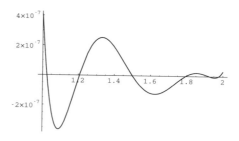

After changing the degree of the requested approximation, you no longer have the problem.

```
In[18]:= MiniMaxApproximation[
            Cos[x]/(x - Pi/2),
              {x, {1, 2}, 2, 3}][[2, 1]]
```

$Out[18]= (-0.634876215933256 - 0.317691489428260\,x + 0.1024524456924874\,x^2)\ /\ (1 - 0.1489630847121669\,x + 0.0477726888266556\,x^2 - 0.000714750253605406\,x^3)$

Another thing that can happen is that the initial rational interpolation can have a zero in the denominator somewhere in the interval. In such cases it is usually easiest to ask for a minimax approximation of different degree. Occasionally, however, this approach does not solve the problem.

A trick that will sometimes work is to start with an approximation that is valid over a shorter interval. Because the minimax approximation will usually change continuously as you lengthen the interval, you can use the approximation for the shorter interval as a starting point for an approximation on a slightly longer interval. By slowly stretching the interval, you may be able to eventually get a minimax approximation that is valid over the interval you desire.

MiniMaxApproximation has several options that give the user control over how it works and two options that help in diagnosing failures.

option name	default value	
WorkingPrecision	$MachinePrecision	number of digits of precision to use
Bias	0	bias in the automatic choice of interpolation points
Brake	{5, 5}	braking to apply on iterative algorithm
MaxIterations	20	maximum number of iterates after braking has ended
Derivatives	Automatic	specifies a function to use for the derivatives
PrintFlag	False	whether to print information about the relative error at each step in the iteration
PlotFlag	False	whether to plot the relative error at each step in the iteration

Options for minimax approximations.

MiniMaxApproximation works by first finding a rational interpolation to the given function and then perturbing the coefficients until the error is equi-oscillatory. The option Bias is used to control the initial rational approximation in exactly the same way it is used in RationalInterpolation.

As MiniMaxApproximation proceeds, it alternately locates the extrema of the relative error and then perturbs the coefficients in an effort to equalize the magnitudes of the extrema. If the extrema move only a small amount from one iteration to the next, their previous positions can be used as starting values in locating their new positions. If they move too much from one iteration to the next, MiniMaxApproximation gets lost. The way MiniMaxApproximation knows it is lost is if the extrema do not alternate in sign, two extrema are the same, or their abscissas are not in sorted order.

The way to prevent MiniMaxApproximation from getting lost is to set the option Brake. Brake acts as a braking mechanism on the changes from one iteration to the next, but its influence eventually dies off to the point where there is no braking effect. When the algorithm has almost converged, there is no need to provide braking, because the changes are very small.

A value for Brake must be a list of two positive integers. The first integer specifies how many iterations are to be affected by the braking, and the second integer specifies how much braking force is to be applied to the first iteration. Brake is much more important for minimax approximations of high degree, because in this case, the abscissas of the extrema are very close together.

To perform its iterative scheme, MiniMaxApproximation must know the first two derivatives of the function being approximated. If *Mathematica* cannot compute the derivatives analytically, you must specify them explicitly. A related situation is when the derivatives can be found, but calculating them involves a lot of work, much of which is redundant. For example, in trying to find a minimax approximation to e^x, *Mathematica* needs to evaluate e^x to find the value of the function, *Mathematica* needs to evaluate e^x to find the value of the first derivative, and *Mathematica* needs to evaluate e^x to find the value of the second derivative. A much simpler way would be for the user to specify a function that returns a list of these three values for each value of x. This is the purpose of the option Derivatives.

There are two things to be aware of when you use this option. First, the function should not be allowed to evaluate until x is actually a number, or the whole purpose of using the option will be defeated. Second, the function must be applicable to lists in the same way that a list of functions is applicable to lists.

This prevents derivs from evaluating unless x is a number.

```
In[19]:= derivs[x_?NumberQ] :=
             Block[{exp = Exp[x]}, {exp, exp, exp}]
```

This makes derivs behave correctly for arguments that are lists of numbers.

```
In[20]:= derivs[x_List] := Transpose[Map[derivs, x]]
```

Here is what happens if the derivatives are evaluated separately.

```
In[21]:= {Exp[x], Exp[x], Exp[x]} /. x-> {1,2,3}
```

$Out[21]= \{\{e, e^2, e^3\}, \{e, e^2, e^3\}, \{e, e^2, e^3\}\}$

We get the same behavior with our function.

```
In[22]:= derivs[x] /. x-> {1,2,3}
```

$Out[22]= \{\{e, e^2, e^3\}, \{e, e^2, e^3\}, \{e, e^2, e^3\}\}$

MiniMaxApproximation works with our definition for the derivatives.

```
In[23]:= MiniMaxApproximation[
              Exp[x], {x, {-1, 1}, 2, 2},
                 Derivatives -> derivs[x]]
```

$Out[23]= \{\{-1.000000000000000,$
$-0.812304291437255, -0.312414594402135,$
$0.312414594402110, 0.812304291437204,$
$1.000000000000000\}, \{(0.999999996233065 +$
$0.499785623826605\,x + 0.0815926963252361\,x^2)\,/$
$(1 - 0.499785625709268\,x + 0.0815926966325922\,x^2),$
$-0.0000867978639860722\}\}$

To prevent infinite iteration, MiniMaxApproximation has the option MaxIterations. If convergence does not occur before the number of iterations after the braking stops reaches MaxIterations, a warning is returned along with the current approximation. If the problem is simply slow convergence, you can restart the iteration from the current approximation by inserting the approximation that was returned as the second argument to MiniMaxApproximation. You may find it useful to begin the new iteration with different options.

To get an example of a poor approximation, you can choose a small value of MaxIterations, a large bias, and no braking.

```
In[24]:= approx =
            MiniMaxApproximation[
               Exp[x], {x, {-1, 1}, 2, 2},
                  Brake -> {0,0},
                  MaxIterations -> 2, Bias -> .4]

MiniMaxApproximation::conv:
   Warning: convergence was not complete.
```

$Out[24]=$ {{-1.000000000000000,
         -0.827819803348445, -0.330480880241506,
         0.421134148525593, 0.884742099970785,
         1.000000000000000}, {(0.999972668569625 +
            0.498526709170391 x + 0.0809720528324210 x^2) /
            (1 - 0.500985708196881 x + 0.0820810105294591 x^2),
         -0.0000692310641567448}}

The result of the previous approximation attempt is used as the starting point of the new iteration by inserting it as a second argument.

```
In[25]:= MiniMaxApproximation[
            Exp[x], approx,
                  {x, {-1, 1}, 2, 2},
                        Brake -> {0,0}]
```

$Out[25]=$ {{-1.000000000000000,
         -0.812304295692391, -0.312414608257099,
         0.312414566520745, 0.812304353494467,
         1.000000000000000}, {(0.999999996223222 +
            0.499785622543369 x + 0.0815926957504196 x^2) /
            (1 - 0.499785627011307 x + 0.0815926972425114 x^2),
         -0.0000867978556026979}}

PrintFlag and PlotFlag are options to MiniMaxApproximation that are useful for diagnosing the reason for failure. Setting either of these options will have no effect on the calculations. If PlotFlag is set to True, a plot of the relative error in each iterated rational approximation will be generated. If these plots change dramatically from one iteration to the next, you should probably increase the braking. If PrintFlag is set to True, two things will happen. First, as the extrema are being located for the first time, lists of the changes in the approximations to the abscissas will be printed out. The numbers in these lists should rapidly decrease once they get reasonably small. After the extrema are located for the first time, lists of ordered pairs are printed consisting of abscissas of the extrema of the relative error and the value of the relative error at each of those abscissas.

GeneralRationalInterpolation[{f_x, f_y}, {t, m, k}, x, {t_1, t_2, ... , t_{n+k+1}}]
  give a rational interpolation of degree (m, k) to a function of x whose graph is given parametrically as a function of t

GeneralRationalInterpolation[{f_x, f_y}, {t, m, k}, x, {t, tmin, tmax}]
  give a rational interpolation with the points t_i chosen automatically

General rational interpolations.

There are certain approximation problems in which you will want to use GeneralRationalInterpolation instead of RationalInterpolation. For example, you should use GeneralRationalInterpolation if you want to find a rational interpolating function to the *inverse* of a function that can only be evaluated by using FindRoot. In such a case, RationalInterpolation would be very slow.

GeneralRationalInterpolation lets you do more general approximation problems by allowing the function that is to be approximated to be given parametrically. For example, the graph of the function $f(x) = \sqrt{1 - x^2}$ is just the upper half of the unit circle. This can also be described parametrically as $(\cos t, \sin t)$ where $0 \le t \le \pi$. Thus you can compute an approximation to $\sqrt{1 - x^2}$ by specifying the function as {Cos[t], Sin[t]}

In the general case, when you specify the functions in RationalInterpolation as $\{f_x, f_y\}$, the expressions f_x and f_y are functions of t. The function that is interpolated is the one whose graph is given parametrically by $(f_x(t), f_y(t))$ for *tmin* $\le t \le$ *tmax*.

Note that you must always specify a symbol for the independent variable; using the parametric variable as the independent variable would be incorrect. GeneralRationalInterpolation takes the same options as RationalInterpolation.

This gives an approximation to the function whose graph is the upper half circle.

In[26]:= **gri1 =**
 GeneralRationalInterpolation[
  {Cos[t], Sin[t]}, {t, 2, 4}, x,
  Table[i Pi/6, {i,0,6}]]

Out[26]= $(1.000000000000000 - 1.000000000000000\, x^2) /$
 $(1 - 1.099543852374659 \times 10^{-16}\, x - 0.470514243960035\, x^2 +$
 $1.466058469832878 \times 10^{-16}\, x^3 - 0.2615365636088429\, x^4)$

The error is quite large near the endpoints.

In[27]:= **Plot[gri1 - Sqrt[1 - x^2],**
  {x, -1, 1}, PlotRange -> All]

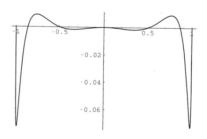

You don't need to specify the interpolation points explicitly.

```
In[28]:= gri2 =
            GeneralRationalInterpolation[
               {Cos[t], Sin[t]},{t, 2, 4}, x,
                        {t, 0, Pi}]
```

$$Out[28]= \left(1.000000000000000 - \right.$$
$$1.285986783597736 \times 10^{-17} x - 0.992219893855438 x^2\left.\right) \Big/$$
$$\left(1 - 6.90658186947699 \times 10^{-18} x - 0.413205048712037 x^2 + \right.$$
$$3.51458146698783 \times 10^{-17} x^3 - 0.351858737735565 x^4\left.\right)$$

As is the case with `RationalInterpolation`, the error is often smaller if the interpolation points are not given explicitly. The points chosen automatically tend to be better distributed.

```
In[29]:= Plot[gri2 - Sqrt[1 - x^2], {x, -1, 1}]
```

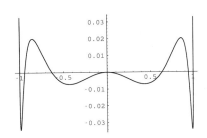

`GeneralMiniMaxApproximation[{`f_x`, `f_y`}, {`*t*`, {`*tmin*`, *tmax*`}, `*m*`, `*k*`}, `*x*`]`	give the rational approximation of degree (m, k) to a function of x whose graph is given parametrically as a function of t
`GeneralMiniMaxApproximation[{`f_x`, `f_y`}, `*approx*`, {`*t*`, {`*tmin*`, *tmax*`}, `*m*`, `*k*`}, `*x*`]`	give the minimax approximation starting the iterative algorithm with *approx*
`GeneralMiniMaxApproximation[{`f_x`, `f_y`, `*g*`}, {`*t*`, {`*tmin*`, *tmax*`}, `*m*`, `*k*`}, `*x*`]`	give the rational approximation computing the error using a factor $g(t)$

General minimax approximations.

The function that is to be approximated is specified in `GeneralMiniMaxApproximation` in the same way as it is in `GeneralRationalInterpolation`. The options for `GeneralMiniMaxApproximation` are the same as for `MiniMaxApproximation`.

This gives a degree (2,4) minimax approximation to the inverse of Exp.

```
In[30]:= gmma1 =
           GeneralMiniMaxApproximation[
             {Exp[t], t},
               {t, {1, 2}, 2, 4}, x]
```

$Out[30]= \{\{1.000000000000000,$
$1.047160165211972, 1.181310737847884, 1.379305047076280,$
$1.603108046914012, 1.807147573858294, 1.949194055056309,$
$2.000000000000000\}, \{(-2.082397791582349 +$
$1.273808774978038\,x + 0.823600244099670\,x^2) /$
$(1 + 1.731869303741129\,x + 0.2459175701326090\,x^2 -$
$0.00309657120420604\,x^3 + 0.0000584282364752244\,x^4),$
$-6.74683885161629 \times 10^{-8}\}\}$

Since there is an easy way to evaluate the inverse of Exp, it is also possible to use MiniMaxApproximation for this problem. The only difference between the solutions is in the abscissas of the extrema.

```
In[31]:= MiniMaxApproximation[
             Log[x],
               {x, {E, E^2}, 2, 4}]
```

$Out[31]= \{\{2.718281828459046,$
$2.84954737301506, 3.25864263093092, 3.97214021752741,$
$4.96845062955420, 6.09304266696276, 7.02302512744650,$
$7.38905609893065\}, \{(-2.082397791601480 +$
$1.273808774972108\,x + 0.823600244123541\,x^2) /$
$(1 + 1.731869303772081\,x + 0.2459175701407112\,x^2 -$
$0.00309657120435831\,x^3 + 0.0000584282364787639\,x^4),$
$-6.74683885227962 \times 10^{-8}\}\}$

This extracts the minimax approximation.

```
In[32]:= log = gmma1[[2,1]];
```

Here is a plot of the relative error in the approximation over the interval $e \le x \le e^2$.

```
In[33]:= Plot[1 - log/Log[x], {x, E, E^2}]
```

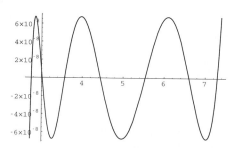

If you use the option Derivatives with GeneralMiniMaxApproximation, you must specify a list of derivatives for both parts of the parametrically defined function.

This prevents gderivs from acting on symbols.

```
In[34]:= gderivs[t_?NumberQ] :=
             Block[{exp = Exp[t]},
                {{exp, exp, exp}, {t,1,0}}
                ]
```

This makes `gderivs` have the correct behavior when a list is given as an argument.

```
In[35]:= gderivs[t_List] := Transpose[
              Map[gderivs, t],{3,1,2}]
```

We get the same result again.

```
In[36]:= GeneralMiniMaxApproximation[
             {Exp[t], t},
                { t, {1,2}, 2, 4}, x,
                Derivatives -> gderivs[t]]
```

$Out[36]= \{\{1.000000000000000,$
$1.047160165211972, 1.181310737847884, 1.379305047076280,$
$1.603108046914012, 1.807147573858294, 1.949194055056309,$
$2.000000000000000\}, \{(-2.082397791582349 +$
$1.273808774978038\,x + 0.823600244099670\,x^2)\, /$
$(1 + 1.731869303741129\,x + 0.2459175701326090\,x^2 -$
$0.00309657120420604\,x^3 + 0.0000584282364752244\,x^4),$
$-6.74683885161629 \times 10^{-8}\}\}$

Another situation in which `GeneralMiniMaxApproximation` is useful is when you want to do an approximation and measure its goodness of fit using the absolute error instead of the relative error that is used by default. If you want to use a different metric for the error, you can specify it as the third part of the parametrically defined function. If the function is given as $\{x(t), y(t), g(t)\}$ and $h(x)$ is the rational minimax approximation to the function that relates $x(t)$ to $y(t)$, then the error that is minimized is $(y(t) - h(x(t)))/g(t)$. If $g(t)$ is not specified, it is taken to be the same as $y(t)$, and it is the maximum relative error that is minimized. If you want to minimize the absolute error, simply use the constant 1 for $g(t)$, which is the default.

This gives a rational minimax approximation to the inverse of Exp with the maximum absolute error minimized.

```
In[37]:= gmma2 =
         GeneralMiniMaxApproximation[
             {Exp[t], t, 1},
                {t, {1, 2}, 2, 4}, x]
```

$Out[37]= \{\{1.000000000000000,$
$1.052667790596414, 1.198145710760290, 1.403433639618959,$
$1.625304663316387, 1.820457892092102, 1.953108843839385,$
$2.000000000000000\}, \{(-2.070176403273674 +$
$1.279157640993006\,x + 0.806683931208878\,x^2)\, /$
$(1 + 1.710829203154739\,x + 0.2400605646862769\,x^2 -$
$0.00297718354749508\,x^3 + 0.0000554613227317537\,x^4),$
$-9.77379379167500 \times 10^{-8}\}\}$

This extracts the approximation.

```
In[38]:= log = gmma2[[2,1]];
```

Now the *absolute* error is equi-oscillatory.

In[39]:= Plot[log - Log[x], {x, E, E^2}]

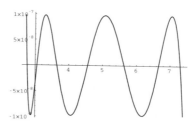

If you get an approximation for which the error is unacceptably large, there are several things you can do. If you increase the degree of the numerator and/or the denominator, the minimax error will usually decrease; it cannot increase. Even shifting a degree from the numerator to the denominator or vice versa can affect the size of the error. If the interval for which the approximation is to be valid is very long, it is probably a good idea to look at the asymptotic behavior of the function and choose degrees for the numerator and denominator that give the correct asymptotic behavior. For example, to get an approximation to $\tan^{-1}(x)$ for large x, the degrees of the numerator and denominator should be the same, since for large x the function has a nearly constant value of $\frac{\pi}{2}$.

Another way to decrease the error is to shorten the interval for which the approximation is to be valid. Often it is better to have several low-degree approximations to cover a long interval than a single high-degree approximation. The extra storage required is not that much, and each of the simpler approximations will evaluate faster.

To get an optimal minimax approximation you need to take into account the numerical behavior of the final approximation. It is usually a good idea to define the function so that the variable appearing in the approximation has values near the origin. Thus, instead of finding a minimax approximation to e^x on the interval $999 \leq x \leq 1001$ it would be better to find a minimax approximation to e^{t+1000} on the interval $-1 \leq t \leq 1$.

In cases where you want to avoid all potential problems associated with loss of digits due to subtractive cancellation, you may even want to do some shifting of the variable after the approximation is found. For example, the rational minimax approximation of degree $(7, 7)$ to e^x on the interval $-1 \leq x \leq 1$ has positive coefficients in the numerator and coefficients with alternating signs in the denominator. The relative error in the approximation is only about 10^{-20}, but using the approximation in the given form could result in a larger relative error, since a few bits could be lost due to cancellation near the endpoints: cancellation occurs in the numerator near -1 and in the denominator near 1. By replacing the x in the numerator by $s - 1$ and the x in the denominator by $1 - t$, all coefficients in both the numerator and the denominator become positive, and the values of s and t will be between 0 and 2; no cancellation can occur. Of course all of this must be done to much higher precision to ensure that the coefficients themselves are correct to the required precision.

It is very important to also consider the zeros of the function and its asymptotic behavior. The simplicity of the resulting minimax approximation is *greatly* affected by the extent to which you can trivially make the function look like a constant function. As an example, to find a minimax approximation to Gamma[1/2, x, Infinity] on the interval $1 \le x \le 3$, you can consider the function Gamma[1/2, x, Infinity] Exp[x] (x + 4/7) (*cf.* Abramowitz and Stegun, *Handbook of Mathematical Functions*, 6.5.31; the 4/7 was chosen empirically). This function only varies a few percent over the interval in question; it will be *much* easier to find a minimax approximation to this function than to the original function.

If you are attempting to minimize the maximum relative error, and there are zeros of the function in the interval in question, you will have to divide out the zeros first. If singularities occur in the interval they will have to be eliminated also, either by multiplying by a zero or subtracting them away.

■ NumericalMath`BesselZeros`

Exact solutions to many partial differential equations can be expressed as infinite sums over the zeros of some Bessel function or functions. For example, the solution $U(r,t)$ to the heat equation in canonical units on the unit disc with initial temperature $U(r,0) = 0$ and boundary condition $U(1,t) = 1$ is given by

$$U(r,t) = 1 - 2 \sum_{n=1}^{\infty} \frac{J_0(\alpha_n r)}{\alpha_n J_1(\alpha_n)} e^{-\alpha_n^2 t}$$

where the α_n are the positive zeros of J_0, $\alpha_1 \approx 2.40483$, $\alpha_2 \approx 5.52008$, $\alpha_3 \approx 8.65373$, etc. Using `FindRoot` it is not difficult to find any single desired zero if you can find a good pair of starting values. This package automatically chooses starting values and uses `FindRoot` to efficiently produce lists of zeros of various Bessel functions.

BesselJZeros[*nu*, *n*]	give a list of the first *n* zeros of $J_\nu(x)$
BesselYZeros[*nu*, *n*]	give a list of the first *n* zeros of $Y_\nu(x)$
BesselJPrimeZeros[*nu*, *n*]	give a list of the first *n* zeros of $J'_\nu(x)$
BesselYPrimeZeros[*nu*, *n*]	give a list of the first *n* zeros of $Y'_\nu(x)$
BesselJYJYZeros[*nu*, *lambda*, *n*]	give a list of the first *n* zeros of $J_\nu(x)Y_\nu(\lambda x) - J_\nu(\lambda x)Y_\nu(x)$
BesselJPrimeYPrimeJPrimeYPrimeZeros[*nu*, *lambda*, *n*]	give a list of *n* zeros of $J'_\nu(x)Y'_\nu(\lambda x) - J'_\nu(\lambda x)Y'_\nu(x)$
BesselJPrimeYJYPrimeZeros[*nu*, *lambda*, *n*]	give a list of *n* zeros of $J'_\nu(x)Y_\nu(\lambda x) - J_\nu(\lambda x)Y'_\nu(x)$
BesselJZeros[*nu*, {*m*, *n*}], BesselYZeros[*nu*, {*m*, *n*}], etc.	give a list containing the mth through the nth zeros

Finding zeros of Bessel functions.

Note that `FindRoot` can be used with a single starting value, in which case the method is based on Newton's method. But the derivative of a Bessel function is usually expressed in terms of two other Bessel functions. In such cases the secant method is more efficient than Newton's method. The secant method requires a pair of starting values, preferably one on each side of the desired zero and sufficiently close to uniquely determine the zero.

Asymptotic formulae exist for approximating the nth zeros as $n \to \infty$, but the approximations are too inaccurate even to be used as starting values to `FindRoot` when n is small and the order ν is large. As a result, the package works by finding an n sufficiently large that a good approximation results. After finding several consecutive zeros it is able to extrapolate backwards to get a starting value for the zero immediately preceding the smallest currently known zero. By proceeding in this manner it is able to find the requested zeros.

option name	default value	
WorkingPrecision	$MachinePrecision	precision of the arithmetic to use in calculations
AccuracyGoal	Automatic	desired accuracy of the function at the zeros

Options for the BesselZero functions.

This loads the package.

```
In[1]:= << NumericalMath`BesselZeros`
```

This gives the first 5 zeros of $J_0(x)$.

```
In[2]:= BesselJZeros[0, 5]
Out[2]= {2.40483, 5.52008, 8.65373, 11.7915, 14.9309}
```

Here are the 17th, 18th, and 19th zeros of $Y'_3(x)$.

```
In[3]:= BesselYPrimeZeros[3, {17, 19}]
Out[3]= {57.2489, 60.3949, 63.5405}
```

This gives high-precision values of the first 3 zeros of $J_2(x)Y_2(6/5x) - J_2(6/5x)Y_2(x)$.

```
In[4]:= BesselJYJYZeros[2, 6/5, 3,
                WorkingPrecision -> 30]
Out[4]= {15.8066224441765790253647015576,
         31.4655600915368446462654024798,
         47.1570167108650317281338335527}
```

■ NumericalMath`Butcher`

Runge-Kutta methods are useful for numerically solving certain types of ordinary differential equations. Deriving high-order Runge-Kutta methods is no easy task, however. There are several reasons for this. The first difficulty is in finding the so-called order conditions. These are nonlinear equations in the coefficients for the method that must be satisfied to make the error in the method of order $O(h^n)$ for some integer n where h is the step size. The second difficulty is in solving these equations. Besides being nonlinear, there is generally no unique solution, and many heuristics and simplifying assumptions are usually made. Finally, there is the problem of combinatorial explosion. For a twelfth-order method there are 7813 order conditions!

This package performs the first task: finding the order conditions that must be satisfied. The result is expressed in terms of unknown coefficients a_{ij}, b_j, and c_i. The s-stage Runge-Kutta method to advance from x to $x + h$ is then

$$Y(x + h) = y(x) + h \sum_{j=1}^{s} b_j f(Y_j(x + h))$$

where

$$Y_i(x + h) = y(x) + h \sum_{j=1}^{s} a_{ij} f(Y_j(x + h)), \quad i = 1, 2, \ldots, s$$

Sums of the elements in the rows of the matrix $[a_{ij}]$ occur repeatedly in the conditions imposed on a_{ij} and b_j. In recognition of this and as a notational convenience it is usual to introduce the coefficients c_i and the definition

$$c_i = \sum_{j=1}^{s} a_{ij}, \quad i = 1, 2, \ldots, s$$

This definition is referred to as the row-sum condition and is the first in a sequence of row-simplifying conditions.

If $a_{ij} = 0$ for all $i <= j$ the method is *explicit*; that is, each of the $Y_i(x + h)$ is defined in terms of previously computed values. If the matrix $[a_{ij}]$ is not strictly lower triangular, the method is *implicit* and requires the solution of a (generally nonlinear) system of equations for each timestep. A diagonally implicit method has $a_{ij} = 0$ for all $i < j$.

There are several ways to express the order conditions. If the number of stages s is specified as a positive integer, the order conditions are expressed in terms of sums of explicit terms. If the number of stages is specified as a symbol, the order conditions will involve symbolic sums. If the number of stages is not specified at all, the order conditions will be expressed in stage-independent tensor notation. In addition to the matrix a and the vectors b and c, this notation involves the vector e, which is composed of all ones. This notation has two distinct advantages: it is independent of the number of stages s and it is independent of the particular Runge-Kutta method.

For further details of the theory see the references.

$a_{i,j}$	the coefficient of $f(Y_j(x))$ in the formula for $Y_i(x)$ of the method
b_j	the coefficient of $f(Y_j(x))$ in the formula for $Y(x)$ of the method
c_i	a notational convenience for $\sum_{j=1}^{s} a_{ij}$
e	a notational convenience for the vector $(1, 1, 1, \ldots)$

Notation used by functions in `NumericalMath'Butcher'`.

`RungeKuttaOrderConditions[`p`, `s`]`	give a list of the order conditions that any s-stage Runge-Kutta method of order p must satisfy
+ `ButcherPrincipalError[`p`, `s`]`	give a list of the order $p + 1$ terms appearing in the Taylor series expansion of the error for an order-p, s-stage Runge-Kutta method
`RungeKuttaOrderConditions[`p`]`, `ButcherPrincipalError[`p`]`	give the result in stage-independent tensor notation

Functions associated with the order conditions of Runge-Kutta methods.

+ `ButcherRowSum`	specify whether the row-sum conditions for the c_i should be explicitly included in the list of order conditions
+ `ButcherSimplify`	specify whether to apply Butcher's row and column simplifying assumptions

Some options for `RungeKuttaOrderConditions`.

This loads the package.

```
In[1]:= << NumericalMath'Butcher'
```

This gives the number of order conditions for each order up through order 10. Notice the combinatorial explosion.

```
In[2]:= Length /@ RungeKuttaOrderConditions[10]

Out[2]= {1, 1, 2, 4, 9, 20, 48, 115, 286, 719}
```

This gives the order conditions that must be satisfied by any first-order, 3-stage Runge-Kutta method, explicitly including the row-sum conditions.

```
In[3]:= RungeKuttaOrderConditions[1, 3,
            ButcherRowSum -> True]

Out[3]= {{b_1 + b_2 + b_3 == 1}, {a_{1,1} + a_{1,2} + a_{1,3} == c_1,
           a_{2,1} + a_{2,2} + a_{2,3} == c_2, a_{3,1} + a_{3,2} + a_{3,3} == c_3}}
```

These are the order conditions that must be satisfied by any second-order, 3-stage Runge-Kutta method. Here the row-sum conditions are not included.

$In[4]:=$ **RungeKuttaOrderConditions[2, 3]**

$Out[4]= \left\{\{b_1 + b_2 + b_3 == 1\}, \left\{b_1\, c_1 + b_2\, c_2 + b_3\, c_3 == \dfrac{1}{2}\right\}\right\}$

It should be noted that the sums involved on the left-hand sides of the order conditions will be left in symbolic form and not expanded if the number of stages is left as a symbolic argument. This will greatly simplify the results for high-order, many-stage methods. An even more compact form results if you do not specify the number of stages at all and the answer is given in tensor form.

These are the order conditions that must be satisfied by any second-order, s-stage method.

$In[5]:=$ **RungeKuttaOrderConditions[2, s]**

$Out[5]= \left\{\left\{\displaystyle\sum_{i=1}^{s} b_i == 1\right\}, \left\{\displaystyle\sum_{i=1}^{s} b_i\, c_i == \dfrac{1}{2}\right\}\right\}$

Replacing s by 3 gives the same result as RungeKuttaOrderConditions[2, 3].

$In[6]:=$ **% /. s -> 3**

$Out[6]= \left\{\{b_1 + b_2 + b_3 == 1\}, \left\{b_1\, c_1 + b_2\, c_2 + b_3\, c_3 == \dfrac{1}{2}\right\}\right\}$

These are the order conditions that must be satisfied by any second-order method. This uses tensor notation. The vector e is a vector of ones whose length is the number of stages.

$In[7]:=$ **RungeKuttaOrderConditions[2]**

$Out[7]= \left\{\{b\,.\,e == 1\}, \left\{b\,.\,c == \dfrac{1}{2}\right\}\right\}$

The tensor notation can likewise be expanded to give the conditions in full.

$In[8]:=$ **% /. {a -> Array[a,{3,3}], b -> Array[b,3],**
                  c -> Array[c,3], e -> {1,1,1}}

$Out[8]= \left\{\{b_1 + b_2 + b_3 == 1\}, \left\{b_1\, c_1 + b_2\, c_2 + b_3\, c_3 == \dfrac{1}{2}\right\}\right\}$

These are the principal error coefficients for any third-order method.

$In[9]:=$ **ButcherPrincipalError[3]**

$Out[9]= \left\{-\dfrac{1}{24} + b\,.\,a\,.\,a\,.\,c,\ \dfrac{1}{2}\left(-\dfrac{1}{12} + b\,.\,a\,.\,c^2\right),\ -\dfrac{1}{8} + b\,.\,(c\,a\,.\,c),\right.$
$\left.\dfrac{1}{6}\left(-\dfrac{1}{4} + b\,.\,c^3\right)\right\}$

This is a bound on the local error of any third-order method in the limit as h approaches 0, normalized to eliminate the effects of the ODE.

$In[10]:=$ **(Plus @@ Abs[%]) h^4**

$Out[10]= h^4\left(\dfrac{1}{6}\,\text{Abs}\left[-\dfrac{1}{4} + b\,.\,c^3\right] + \text{Abs}\left[-\dfrac{1}{8} + b\,.\,(c\,a\,.\,c)\right] +\right.$
$\left.\dfrac{1}{2}\,\text{Abs}\left[-\dfrac{1}{12} + b\,.\,a\,.\,c^2\right] + \text{Abs}\left[-\dfrac{1}{24} + b\,.\,a\,.\,a\,.\,c\right]\right)$

Here are the order conditions that must be satisfied by any fourth-order, 1-stage Runge-Kutta method. Note that there is no possible way for these order conditions to be satisfied; there need to be more stages (the second argument must be larger) for there to be sufficiently many unknowns to satisfy all of the conditions.

$In[11]:=$ **RungeKuttaOrderConditions[4, 1]**

$Out[11]= \left\{\{b_1 == 1\}, \left\{b_1\, c_1 == \dfrac{1}{2}\right\}, \left\{a_{1,1}\, b_1\, c_1 == \dfrac{1}{6},\ b_1\, c_1^2 == \dfrac{1}{3}\right\},\right.$
$\left\{a_{1,1}^2\, b_1\, c_1 == \dfrac{1}{24},\ a_{1,1}\, b_1\, c_1^2 == \dfrac{1}{12},\ a_{1,1}\, b_1\, c_1^2 == \dfrac{1}{8},\right.$
$\left.\left.b_1\, c_1^3 == \dfrac{1}{4}\right\}\right\}$

+	RungeKuttaMethod	specify the type of Runge-Kutta method for which order conditions are being sought
+	Explicit	a setting for the option RungeKuttaMethod specifying that the order conditions are to be for an explicit Runge-Kutta method
+	DiagonallyImplicit	a setting for the option RungeKuttaMethod specifying that the order conditions are to be for a diagonally implicit Runge-Kutta method
+	Implicit	a setting for the option RungeKuttaMethod specifying that the order conditions are to be for an implicit Runge-Kutta method
+	$RungeKuttaMethod	a global variable whose value can be set to Explicit, DiagonallyImplicit, or Implicit

Controlling the type of Runge-Kutta method in RungeKuttaOrderConditions and related functions.

RungeKuttaOrderConditions and certain related functions have the option RungeKuttaMethod with default setting $RungeKuttaMethod. Normally you will want to determine the Runge-Kutta method being considered by setting $RungeKuttaMethod to one of Implicit, DiagonallyImplicit, and Explicit, but you can specify an option setting or even change the default for an individual function.

These are the order conditions that must be satisfied by any second-order, 3-stage diagonally implicit Runge-Kutta method.

```
In[12]:= RungeKuttaOrderConditions[2, 3,
            RungeKuttaMethod -> DiagonallyImplicit]
```

$$Out[12]= \left\{\{b_1 + b_2 + b_3 == 1\}, \left\{b_1 \, c_1 + b_2 \, c_2 + b_3 \, c_3 == \frac{1}{2}\right\}\right\}$$

An alternative (but less efficient) way to get a diagonally implicit method is to force a to be lower triangular by replacing upper-triangular elements with 0.

```
In[13]:= RungeKuttaOrderConditions[2, 3] /.
            a[i_,j_]:>0 /; i<j
```

$$Out[13]= \left\{\{b_1 + b_2 + b_3 == 1\}, \left\{b_1 \, c_1 + b_2 \, c_2 + b_3 \, c_3 == \frac{1}{2}\right\}\right\}$$

These are the order conditions that must be satisfied by any third-order, 2-stage explicit Runge-Kutta method. The contradiction in the order conditions indicates that no such method is possible, a result which holds for any explicit Runge-Kutta method when the number of stages is less than the order.

```
In[14]:= RungeKuttaOrderConditions[3, 2,
            RungeKuttaMethod -> Explicit]
```

$$Out[14]= \left\{\{b_1 + b_2 == 1\}, \left\{b_2 \, c_2 == \frac{1}{2}\right\}, \left\{False, \, b_2 \, c_2^2 == \frac{1}{3}\right\}\right\}$$

+ `ButcherColumnConditions[p, s]`

give the column simplifying conditions up to and including order p for s stages

+ `ButcherRowConditions[p, s]`   give the row simplifying conditions up to and including order p for s stages

+ `ButcherQuadratureConditions[p, s]`

give the quadrature conditions up to and including order p for s stages

+ `ButcherColumnConditions[p]`, `ButcherRowConditions[p]`, etc.

give the result in stage-independent tensor notation

More functions associated with the order conditions of Runge-Kutta methods.

Butcher showed that the number and complexity of the order conditions can be reduced considerably at high orders by the adoption of so-called simplifying assumptions. For example, this reduction can be accomplished by adopting sufficient row and column simplifying assumptions and quadrature-type order conditions. The option `ButcherSimplify` in `RungeKuttaOrderConditions` can be used to determine these automatically.

These are the column simplifying conditions up to order 4.

In[15]:= `ButcherColumnConditions[4]`

$$Out[15]= \left\{ b \cdot a == b\,(-c + e),\ (b\,c) \cdot a == \frac{1}{2}\,b\,(-c^2 + e), \right.$$
$$\left. (b\,c^2) \cdot a == \frac{1}{3}\,b\,(-c^3 + e),\ (b\,c^3) \cdot a == \frac{1}{4}\,b\,(-c^4 + e) \right\}$$

These are the row simplifying conditions up to order 4.

In[16]:= `ButcherRowConditions[4]`

$$Out[16]= \left\{ a \cdot e == c,\ a \cdot c == \frac{c^2}{2},\ a \cdot c^2 == \frac{c^3}{3},\ a \cdot c^3 == \frac{c^4}{4} \right\}$$

These are the quadrature conditions up to order 4.

In[17]:= `ButcherQuadratureConditions[4]`

$$Out[17]= \left\{ \{b \cdot e == 1\},\ \left\{b \cdot c == \frac{1}{2}\right\},\ \left\{b \cdot c^2 == \frac{1}{3}\right\},\ \left\{b \cdot c^3 == \frac{1}{4}\right\} \right\}$$

Trees are fundamental objects in Butcher's formalism. They yield both the derivative in a power series expansion of a Runge-Kutta method *and* the related order constraint on the coefficients. This package provides a number of functions related to Butcher trees.

	f	the elementary symbol used in the representation of Butcher trees
~	ButcherTrees[p]	give a list, partitioned by order, of the trees for any Runge-Kutta method of order p
+	ButcherTreeSimplify[p, η, ξ]	give the set of trees through order p that are not reduced by Butcher's simplifying assumptions, assuming that the quadrature conditions through order p, the row simplifying conditions through order η, and the column simplifying conditions through order ξ all hold. The result is grouped by order, starting with the first nonvanishing trees
+	ButcherTreeCount[p]	give a list of the number of trees through order p
+	ButcherTreeQ[$tree$]	give True if the tree or list of trees $tree$ is valid functional syntax, and False otherwise

Constructing and enumerating Butcher trees.

This gives the trees that are needed for any third-order method. The trees are represented in a functional form in terms of the elementary symbol f.

```
In[18]:= ButcherTrees[3]

Out[18]= {{f}, {f[f]}, {f[f[f]], f[f^2]}}
```

This tests the validity of the syntax of two trees. Butcher trees must be constructed using multiplication, exponentiation or application of the function f.

```
In[19]:= ButcherTreeQ /@ {f[f[f[f] f^2]], f[f f[f+f]]}

Out[19]= {True, False}
```

This evaluates the number of trees at each order through order 10. The result is equivalent to Out[2] but the calculation is much more efficient since it does not actually involve constructing order conditions or trees.

```
In[20]:= ButcherTreeCount[10]

Out[20]= {1, 1, 2, 4, 9, 20, 48, 115, 286, 719}
```

The previous result can be used to calculate the *total* number of trees required at each order through order 10.

```
In[21]:= FoldList[ Plus, First[%], Rest[%] ]

Out[21]= {1, 2, 4, 8, 17, 37, 85, 200, 486, 1205}
```

The number of constraints for a method using row and column simplifying assumptions depends upon the number of stages. ButcherTreeSimplify gives the Butcher trees that are not reduced assuming that these assumptions hold.

This gives the additional trees that are necessary for a fourth-order method assuming that the quadrature conditions through order 4 and the row and column simplifying assumptions of order 1 hold. The result is a single tree of order 4 (which corresponds to a single fourth-order condition).

```
In[22]:= ButcherTreeSimplify[4, 1, 1]
Out[22]= {{f[f f[f]]}}
```

It is often useful to be able to visualize a tree or forest of trees graphically. For example, depicting trees yields insight, which can in turn be used to aid in the construction of Runge-Kutta methods.

+ ButcherPlot[*tree*]	give a plot of the tree *tree*
+ ButcherPlot[{*tree*$_1$, *tree*$_2$, ... }]	give an array of plots of the trees in the forest {*tree*$_1$, *tree*$_2$, ... }

Drawing Butcher trees.

+ ButcherPlotColumns	specify the number of columns in the GraphicsArray plot of a list of trees
+ ButcherPlotLabel	specify a list of plot labels to be used to label the nodes of the plot
+ ButcherPlotNodeSize	specify a scaling factor for the nodes of the trees in the plot
+ ButcherPlotRootSize	specify a scaling factor for the highlighting of the root of each tree in the plot; a zero value does not highlight roots

Options to ButcherPlot.

This plots and labels the trees through order 4.

```
In[23]:= ButcherPlot[ #,
            ButcherPlotLabel -> (InputForm /@ #)]& @
          Flatten[ ButcherTrees[4] ]
```

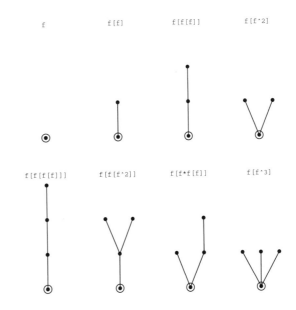

In addition to generating and drawing Butcher trees, many functions are provided for measuring and manipulating them. For a complete description of the importance of these functions, see Butcher [1].

+	ButcherHeight[*tree*]	give the height of the tree *tree*
+	ButcherWidth[*tree*]	give the width of the tree *tree*
~	ButcherOrder[*tree*]	give the order, or number of vertices, of the tree *tree*
+	ButcherAlpha[*tree*]	give the number of ways of labeling the vertices of the tree *tree* with a totally ordered set of labels such that if (m, n) is an edge, then $m < n$
+	ButcherBeta[*tree*]	give the number of ways of labeling the tree *tree* with ButcherOrder[*tree*]-1 distinct labels such that the root is not labeled, but every other vertex is labeled
+	ButcherBeta[*n*, *tree*]	give the number of ways of labeling n of the vertices of the tree with n distinct labels such that every leaf is labeled and the root is not labeled
+	ButcherBetaBar[*tree*]	give the number of ways of labeling the tree *tree* with ButcherOrder[*tree*] distinct labels such that every node, including the root, is labeled
+	ButcherBetaBar[*n*, *tree*]	give the number of ways of labeling n of the vertices of the tree with n distinct labels such that every leaf is labeled
~	ButcherGamma[*tree*]	give the density of the tree *tree*; the reciprocal of the density is the right-hand side of the order condition imposed by *tree*
~	ButcherPhi[*tree*, *s*]	give the weight of the tree *tree*; the weight $\Phi(tree)$ is the left-hand side of the order condition imposed by *tree*
~	ButcherPhi[*tree*]	give $\Phi(tree)$ using tensor notation
+	ButcherSigma[*tree*]	give the order of the symmetry group of isomorphisms of the tree *tree* with itself

Other functions associated with Butcher trees.

This gives the order of the tree f[f[f[f] f^2]].

```
In[24]:= ButcherOrder[f[f[f[f] f^2]]]
Out[24]= 6
```

This gives the density of the tree f[f[f[f] f^2]].

```
In[25]:= ButcherGamma[f[f[f[f] f^2]]]
Out[25]= 60
```

This gives the elementary weight function imposed by f[f[f[f] f^2]] for an *s*-stage method.

```
In[26]:= ButcherPhi[f[f[f[f] f^2]], s]
```

$$Out[26]= \sum_{i=1}^{s} b_i \sum_{j=1}^{s} a_{i,j} \, c_j^2 \sum_{k=1}^{s} a_{j,k} \, c_k$$

The subscript notation is a formatting device and the subscripts are really just the indexed variable `NumericalMath'Butcher'Private'$i`.

```
In[27]:= FullForm[%[[1,1]]]

Out[27]//FullForm= b[NumericalMath'Butcher'Private'$i1]
```

It is also possible to obtain solutions to the order conditions using `Solve` and related functions. Many issues related to the construction Runge-Kutta methods using this package can be found in Sofroniou [6]. The article also contains details concerning algorithms used in `Butcher.m` and discusses applications.[1]

References

[1] *The Numerical Analysis of Ordinary Differential Equations: Runge-Kutta and General Linear Methods*, J. C. Butcher, John Wiley and Sons, New York, 1987.

[2] *A First Course in the Numerical Analysis of Differential Equations* , A. Iserles, Cambridge University Press, Cambridge, England, 1996.

[3] *Numerical Methods for Ordinary Differential Systems, The Initial Value Problem*, J. D. Lambert, John Wiley and Sons, New York, 1991.

[4] *Solving Ordinary Differential Equations I: Nonstiff Problems*, E. Hairer, S. P. Norsett and G. Wanner, Second edition, Springer Verlag, New York, 1993.

[5] *Solving Ordinary Differential Equations II: Stiff and Differential Algebraic Problems*, E. Hairer and G. Wanner, Springer-Verlag, New York, 1991.

[6] "Symbolic Derivation of Runge-Kutta Methods", M. Sofroniou, *Journal of Symbolic Computation*, 18(3), pp. 265–296, 1994.

---

[1]Some of the function names used in [6] have since been changed.

■ NumericalMath`CauchyPrincipalValue`

The *Mathematica* function `NIntegrate` computes a numerical approximation to a definite integral. However, if you want to evaluate the Cauchy principal value of an integral, `NIntegrate` cannot be used directly. To find the Cauchy principal value, you should use instead `CauchyPrincipalValue`.

`CauchyPrincipalValue[f, {x, a, {b}, c}, options]`	
	numerically find the Cauchy principal value of the integral $\int_a^c f\,dx$ which has a nonintegrable singularity at $x = b$
`CauchyPrincipalValue[f, {x, a, {b, eps}, c}, options]`	
	find the Cauchy principal value by integrating from a to $b - \epsilon$ and from $b + \epsilon$ to c and exploiting symmetry on the interval from $b - \epsilon$ to $b + \epsilon$

Finding the Cauchy principal value of an integral.

`CauchyPrincipalValue` works by using `NIntegrate` directly on those regions where there is no difficulty and by pairing values symmetrically about the specified singularities in order to take advantage of the cancellation of the positive and negative values. Thus `CauchyPrincipalValue[f[x], {x, a, {b, eps}, c}]` is evaluated as

$$\int_a^{b-\epsilon} f(x)\,dx + \int_0^{\epsilon} (f(b+t) + f(b-t))\,dt + \int_{b+\epsilon}^c f(x)\,dx$$

where each of the integrals is evaluated using `NIntegrate`. If ϵ is not given explicitly, a value is chosen based upon the differences $b - a$ and $c - b$. The options to `CauchyPrincipalValue` are simply passed directly to `NIntegrate`; `CauchyPrincipalValue` itself does not make any use of them.

This loads the package.	`In[1]:= <<NumericalMath`CauchyPrincipalValue``
This finds the Cauchy principal value of $\int_{-1/2}^1 \frac{1}{x+x^2}\,dx$.	`In[2]:= CauchyPrincipalValue[1/(x+x^2), {x, -1/2,` `{0}, 1}]`
	`Out[2]= -0.693147`
Here is the Cauchy principal value of $\int_{-2}^1 \frac{1}{x+x^2}\,dx$. Note that there are two singularities that need to be specified.	`In[3]:= CauchyPrincipalValue[1/(x+x^2), {x, -2, {-1},` `{0}, 1}]`
	`Out[3]= -1.38629`
This checks the value. The result would be 0 if everything were done exactly.	`In[4]:= % + 2 Log[2.]`
	`Out[4]= 8.04468×10^{-13}`

It should be noted that the singularities must be located exactly. Because the points on both sides of the singularity are paired together in the algorithm, if the singularity is slightly mislocated the cancellation will not be sufficiently good near the pole and the result can be significantly in error if `NIntegrate` converges at all.

■ NumericalMath `ComputerArithmetic`

The arithmetic used by *Mathematica* is a mixture of variable precision software arithmetic and whatever is provided by the manufacturer of the floating-point hardware (or the designer of the compiler, if there is no floating-point hardware). If you want to examine the machine arithmetic on your machine you can use the functions defined in `NumericalMath `Microscope``. If you want to learn about the basic ideas of computer floating-point arithmetic in general you can use `NumericalMath `ComputerArithmetic``. This allows you to examine arithmetic with various bases, precisions, and rounding rules.

`ComputerNumber[x]`	convert the ordinary number x to a computer number in the arithmetic currently in effect
`ComputerNumber[sign, mantissa, exp]`	form the computer number with sign *sign*, mantissa *mantissa*, and exponent *exp*
`ComputerNumber[sign, mantissa, exp, value, x]`	the complete data object that makes up a computer number
`NaN`	a nonrepresentable number in the current arithmetic

Computer numbers and nonnumbers in `NumericalMath `ComputerArithmetic``.

Much of the information carried around in the data object that makes up a computer number is redundant. In particular, the first three arguments contain exactly the same information as the fourth argument. The redundancy exists partly for the sake of efficiency and partly to allow the user access to the various fields. The fifth argument has nothing to do with the computer number itself. It instead represents what the value of the number would be without the cumulative effects of all the roundoff errors that went into the computer number. It is computed using *Mathematica*'s high-precision arithmetic and can generally be regarded as the correct value of the number. Comparing the computer number with this number gives the error in the computer number.

This loads the package.	`In[1]:= <<NumericalMath `ComputerArithmetic``
Here is the computer number representing the ordinary number 2.	`In[2]:= a = ComputerNumber[2]` `Out[2]= 2.000000000000000000`
This gives the computer number representation of π.	`In[3]:= b = ComputerNumber[Pi]` `Out[3]= 3.142000000000000000`
Arithmetic works with computer numbers just as with ordinary numbers.	`In[4]:= c = a + b` `Out[4]= 5.142000000000000000`

Here is the complete structure of c.

```
In[5]:= InputForm[c]
Out[5]//InputForm= ComputerNumber[1, 5142, -3, 2571/500,
                5.14159265358979323846264338327950324]
```

You can also enter just the sign, mantissa, and exponent.

```
In[6]:= ComputerNumber[-1, 1234, -6]
Out[6]= -0.001234000000000000000
```

But if your input doesn't make sense in the arithmetic currently in effect you get NaN. Here the problem is that the mantissa is only three digits long.

```
In[7]:= ComputerNumber[-1, 123, 7]
Out[7]= NaN
```

SetArithmetic[*n*]	set the arithmetic to be *n* digits, base 10
SetArithmetic[*n*, *b*]	set the arithmetic to be *n* digits, base *b*
Arithmetic[ ]	give the parameters of the arithmetic currently in effect

Changing the type of arithmetic to be used.

The default arithmetic is four digits in base 10 with a rounding rule of RoundToEven. Only numbers between 10^{-50} and $.9999 \times 10^{50}$ are allowed. Mixed-mode arithmetic is not allowed and division is not done with correct rounding. (It is performed as two operations: multiplication by the reciprocal. Each operation involves rounding errors.)

```
In[8]:= Arithmetic[ ]
Out[8]= {4, 10, RoundingRule → RoundToEven,
          ExponentRange → {-50, 50}, MixedMode → False,
          IdealDivide → False}
```

Now the arithmetic is set to be six digits in base 8.

```
In[9]:= SetArithmetic[6, 8]
Out[9]= {6, 8, RoundingRule → RoundToEven,
          ExponentRange → {-50, 50}, MixedMode → False,
          IdealDivide → False}
```

The result is displayed in octal (with trailing zeros suppressed).

```
In[10]:= ComputerNumber[Pi]
Out[10]= 3.11040000000000000000₈
```

There are several options that can be used when setting the arithmetic. In addition to changing the precision and the base, you can control the type of rounding used, the magnitude of the numbers allowed, whether mixed-mode arithmetic is to be allowed, and whether division is to be done with a single rounding operation.

option name	default value	
RoundingRule	RoundToEven	the type of rounding to be used
ExponentRange	{-50, 50}	the range of exponents that are to be allowed
MixedMode	False	whether mixed-mode arithmetic is to be allowed
IdealDivide	False	whether correctly rounded division is to be used

Options for `SetArithmetic`.

It should be noted that correctly rounded division is implemented by the function `IdealDivide`. This function can be used whether or not the arithmetic is set to automatically use correct division. It is difficult to get x/y to give correctly rounded division since the x/y is converted to x y^(-1) before the package ever sees it. The way we get around this is to define `$PreRead` to convert x/y into x ~IdealDivide~ y before the parser has a chance to change it to x y^(-1). If you want to use `$PreRead` for your own purposes this will interfere with your definition.

RoundToEven	round to the nearest representable number and, in the case of a tie round, round to the one represented by an even mantissa
RoundToInfinity	round to the nearest representable number and, in the case of a tie round, round away from 0
Truncation	simply discard excess digits, much as `Floor` does for positive numbers

Types of rounding available.

Mixed-mode arithmetic (any arithmetic operation involving an integer and a computer number) is not allowed.

```
In[11]:= 3 ComputerNumber[Pi]
```
$$Out[11]= 3\,3.11040000000000000000_8$$

This turns on mixed-mode arithmetic (and sets the arithmetic to six digits in hexadecimal).

```
In[12]:= SetArithmetic[6, 16, MixedMode -> True]
```
$$Out[12]= \{6, 16, \text{RoundingRule} \to \text{RoundToEven},$$
$$\text{ExponentRange} \to \{-50, 50\}, \text{MixedMode} \to \text{True},$$
$$\text{IdealDivide} \to \text{False}\}$$

Now the product is computed.

```
In[13]:= 3 ComputerNumber[Pi]
```
$$Out[13]= 9.6cbe5000000000_{16}$$

There are many things about computer arithmetic that are very different from ordinary arithmetic. Most of these differences are quite easy to demonstrate.

This sets the arithmetic back to the default.

```
In[14]:= SetArithmetic[4, 10]
Out[14]= {4, 10, RoundingRule → RoundToEven,
         ExponentRange → {-50, 50}, MixedMode → False,
         IdealDivide → False}
```

Expressions are evaluated numerically before they become computer numbers.

```
In[15]:= ComputerNumber[Pi - 22/7]
Out[15]= -0.001264000000000000000
```

If the separate parts are converted to computer numbers first, catastrophic cancellation of digits can occur.

```
In[16]:= ComputerNumber[Pi] - ComputerNumber[22/7]
Out[16]= -0.001000000000000000000
```

Summing the terms from smallest to largest gives one answer.

```
In[17]:= (sum = 0;
         Do[sum += ComputerNumber[i]^(-2),
             {i, 200}];
         FullForm[sum])
Out[17]//FullForm= ComputerNumber[1, 1625, -3, Rational[13, 8],
                   1.6399465460149972679456945528281 67'23.699]
```

As a general rule, it is better to sum from smallest to largest. You can see what the error is by comparing the mantissa (the second argument) to the correct value (the last argument).

```
In[18]:= (sum = 0;
         Do[sum += ComputerNumber[i]^(-2),
             {i, 200, 1, -1}];
         FullForm[sum])
Out[18]//FullForm= ComputerNumber[1, 1640, -3, Rational[41, 25],
                   1.6399465460149972679456945528281 85'23.699]
```

Here is an example where summing from largest to smallest gives the better result.

```
In[19]:= (sum = 0;
         Do[sum += 1/ComputerNumber[i], {i, 300}];
         FullForm[sum])
Out[19]//FullForm= ComputerNumber[1, 6281, -3, Rational[6281, 1000],
                   6.2826638802995034619194855410472 7957972'24]
```

The difference is slight, and such examples are rare.

```
In[20]:= (sum = 0;
         Do[sum += 1/ComputerNumber[i],
             {i, 300, 1, -1}];
         FullForm[sum])
Out[20]//FullForm= ComputerNumber[1, 6280, -3, Rational[157, 25],
                   6.2826638802995034619194855410472 7957972'24]
```

Basic arithmetic is all that is implemented in the package. We could easily extend things to include elementary functions.

```
In[21]:= Sin[ComputerNumber[N[Pi]/7]]
Out[21]= Sin[0.4488000000000000000]
```

Here is the square root of 47.

```
In[22]:= sq = ComputerNumber[Sqrt[47]]
Out[22]= 6.856000000000000000
```

It is a theorem that correctly rounded square roots of small integers will always square back to the original integer if the arithmetic is correct.

```
In[23]:= sq sq
Out[23]= 47.00000000000000000
```

But a similar theorem for cube roots does not exist.

```
In[24]:= cr = ComputerNumber[3^(1/3)]; cr cr cr
Out[24]= 2.998000000000000000
```

This changes the arithmetic to seven digits in base 10 with a rounding rule of RoundToEven and an exponent range of −50 to 50.

```
In[25]:= SetArithmetic[7]
Out[25]= {7, 10, RoundingRule → RoundToEven,
          ExponentRange → {-50, 50}, MixedMode → False,
          IdealDivide → False}
```

This number rounds down.

```
In[26]:= ComputerNumber[.9999999499999999999999999]
Out[26]= 0.9999999000000000000
```

This number rounds up because it rounds toward the mantissa that is even (1000000) rather than the one that is odd (9999999).

```
In[27]:= ComputerNumber[.99999995000000000000000000]
Out[27]= 1.000000000000000000
```

Again it rounds toward the even mantissa (1000000 rather than 1000001).

```
In[28]:= ComputerNumber[1.0000005000000000000000000]
Out[28]= 1.000000000000000000
```

The reciprocal of the reciprocal is not the original number; in fact it may be quite different.

```
In[29]:= (x = ComputerNumber[9010004]; y = 1/x; z = 1/y)
Out[29]= 9.01000700000000000 × 10^6
```

This is multiplication by the reciprocal. It involves two rounding operations.

```
In[30]:= ComputerNumber[2]/x
Out[30]= 2.21975400000000000 × 10^-7
```

This is true division. It uses a single rounding operation. You can get this better type of division to work with "/" by setting the option IdealDivide to True when you use SetArithmetic.

```
In[31]:= IdealDivide[ComputerNumber[2], x]
Out[31]= 2.21975500000000000 × 10^-7
```

Normal converts a computer number back to an ordinary rational number with exactly the same value.

```
In[32]:= Normal[ComputerNumber[Pi]]
Out[32]= 3141593
         -------
         1000000
```

Now we change the arithmetic again.

```
In[33]:= SetArithmetic[3, 2,
            RoundingRule -> Truncation,
            ExponentRange -> {-3,3}]
Out[33]= {3, 2, RoundingRule → Truncation, ExponentRange → {-3, 3},
          MixedMode → False, IdealDivide → False}
```

This suppresses error messages that will result from plotting nonnumeric values in the following examples.

```
In[34]:= Off[ComputerNumber::ovrflw];
         Off[ComputerNumber::undflw];
         Off[Plot::plnr];
```

It is easy to plot the error in the
computer number representation of
each number.

In[37]:= `Plot[Normal[ComputerNumber[x]] - x,`
`{x, -10, 10}, PlotPoints -> 193]`

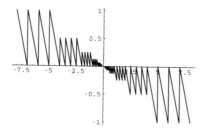

You can zoom in to see the hole at
zero.

In[38]:= `Plot[Normal[ComputerNumber[x]] - x,`
`{x, -1, 1}, PlotPoints -> 47]`

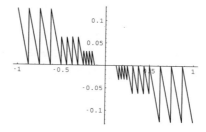

■ NumericalMath`GaussianQuadrature`

As one of its methods, the *Mathematica* function NIntegrate uses a fairly sophisticated Gauss-Kronrod-based algorithm. The package NumericalMath`GaussianQuadrature` allows you to easily study some of the theory behind ordinary Gaussian quadrature which is a little less sophisticated.

The basic idea behind Gaussian quadrature is to approximate the value if an integral as a linear combination of values of the integrand evaluated at specific points:

$$\int_a^b f(x)\, dx = \sum_{i=1}^{n} w_i f(x_i)$$

Since there are $2n$ free parameters to be chosen (both the abscissas x_i and the weights w_i) and since both integration and the sum are linear operations, you can expect to be able to make the formula correct for all polynomials of degree less than about $2n$. In addition to knowing what the optimal abscissas and weights are, it is often desirable to know how large the error in the approximation will be. This package allows you to answer both of these questions.

GaussianQuadratureWeights[*n*, *a*, *b*]	give a list of the pairs (x_i, w_i) to machine precision for quadrature on the interval *a* to *b*
GaussianQuadratureError[*n*, *f*, *a*, *b*]	give the error to machine precision
GaussianQuadratureWeights[*n*, *a*, *b*, *prec*]	give a list of the pairs (x_i, w_i) to precision *prec*
GaussianQuadratureError[*n*, *f*, *a*, *b*, *prec*]	give the error to precision *prec*

Finding formulas for Gaussian quadrature.

This loads the package.

```
In[1]:= <<NumericalMath`GaussianQuadrature`
```

This gives the abscissas and weights for the five-point Gaussian quadrature formula on the interval (−3, 7).

```
In[2]:= GaussianQuadratureWeights[5, -3, 7]

Out[2]= {{-2.5309, 1.18463}, {-0.692347, 2.39314}, {2, 2.84444},
         {4.69235, 2.39314}, {6.5309, 1.18463}}
```

Here is the error in that formula. Unfortunately it involves the tenth derivative of *f* at an unknown point so you don't really know what the error itself is.

```
In[3]:= GaussianQuadratureError[5, f, -3, 7]

Out[3]= -0.0394497 f^{(10)}
```

You can see that the error decreases rapidly with the length of the interval.

```
In[4]:= GaussianQuadratureError[5, f, a, a+h]

Out[4]= -3.94497 × 10^{-13} h^{11} f^{(10)}
```

■ NumericalMath`InterpolateRoot`

The function `FindRoot` is useful for finding a root of a function. It is fairly robust and will almost always find a root if it is given a sufficiently close starting value and the root is simple (or if it is multiple and the option `DampingFactor` is appropriately set). To achieve this robustness `FindRoot` makes compromises and is not particularly conservative about the number of function evaluations it uses. There are cases, however, where you know that the function is very well behaved, but evaluating it is extremely expensive, particularly for very high precision. In such cases `InterpolateRoot` may be more efficient.

`InterpolateRoot` looks at previous evaluations of the function, say $\{a, f(a)\}$, $\{b, f(b)\}$, $\{c, f(c)\}$, and $\{d, f(d)\}$ and forms the interpolating polynomial which passes through the points $\{f(a), a\}$, $\{f(b), b\}$, $\{f(c), c\}$, and $\{f(d), d\}$. The algorithm gets the next approximation for the root of f by evaluating the interpolating polynomial at 0. It turns out that using all of the previous data is not the best strategy. While the convergence rate increases with the use of additional data points, the rate is never greater than quadratic. Further, the more data points used, the less robust the algorithm becomes. `InterpolateRoot` uses only the previous four data points since there is almost no benefit to using more.

`InterpolateRoot[f, {x, a, b}]`	find a root of the function f near the starting points a and b
`InterpolateRoot[eqn, {x, a, b}]`	find a root of the equation *eqn* near the starting points a and b

Root finding with `InterpolateRoot`.

option name	default value	
`AccuracyGoal`	`Automatic`	the desired accuracy in the root being sought
`MaxIterations`	`15`	maximum number of function evaluations before giving up
`WorkingPrecision`	`$MachinePrecision`	the maximum precision to use in the arithmetic calculations
`ShowProgress`	`False`	whether to print intermediate results and other information as the algorithm progresses

Options for `InterpolateRoot`.

The `Automatic` choice for `AccuracyGoal` means that the `AccuracyGoal` will be chosen to be 10 digits less than the `WorkingPrecision`. It should be noted that `AccuracyGoal` as used in `InterpolateRoot` is different from `AccuracyGoal` in `FindRoot`. `FindRoot` is a much more general function that works for systems of equations. Trying to justify an accuracy in the value of the root itself is too difficult. `FindRoot` merely stops when the value of the function is sufficiently small. `InterpolateRoot` is much more specialized. It only works for a single function of a single variable at simple roots and assumes that the function is very well behaved. In such cases it is quite easy to justify an accuracy in the value of the root itself.

This loads the package.	`In[1]:=  <<NumericalMath'InterpolateRoot'`

This uses `FindRoot` to find `Log[2]`.	`In[2]:=  n = 0; FindRoot[n++; Exp[x] == 2, {x, 0, 1},`
	`            WorkingPrecision -> 800,`
	`            AccuracyGoal -> 795]`

```
Out[2]= {x ->
          0.6931471805599453094172321214581765680755001343602552546
          41206800094933936219696947156058633269964186875420014814
          10205706857336855202357581305570326707516350759619307214
          75708283714351903070386238916734711233501153644979552373
          91204751726815749320651555247341395258829504530070953246
          36366426541042391578149520437404303855008019441706416716
          51864471283996817178454695702627163106454615025720740702
          57626520988596932019650585547647033067936544325476372744
          95125040606943814710468994650622016772042452452961126879
          46546193165174681392672504103802546259656869144192871608
          29380317271436778265487756648508567407764845146443994046
          14226031930967354025744460703080960850474866385231381816
          767514386674766478908814371419854942315199735488037516586
          1275352916610007105355824987943
```

The previous operation took 28 function evaluations to get its result.	`In[3]:=  n`
	
	`Out[3]= 28`

Since `InterpolateRoot` is not `HoldFirst` you have to try harder to count the iterations.	`In[4]:=  n = 0; f[x_] := (n++; Exp[x]-2) /; NumberQ[x]`

`InterpolateRoot` requires only 14 function evaluations to get the same result.	`In[5]:=  InterpolateRoot[f[x], {x, 0, 1},`
	`            WorkingPrecision -> 800,`
	`            AccuracyGoal -> 795]; n`
	
	`Out[5]= 13`

You can observe how the
approximations converge to the root.

```
In[6]:= InterpolateRoot[Exp[x] == 2, {x, 0, 1},
            ShowProgress -> True,
            WorkingPrecision -> 40]
```

{0, 0.581976706869326424385}

{21, 0, -0.122463963520395240998}

{1, 0.70193530378827640144433707646495898853943}

{21, 20, 0.013012162957540438912093039225}

{3, 0.6932065772065262316528998579372055577282372}

{21, 20, 0.0000624807887477135488047731120288}

{6, 0.6931471932603933841618726058237293497975889}

$$\{21, 20, 1.264434836935848880384603824201 0^{-8} \}$$

{12, 0.6931471805599451194578224469559025922230084521279\
    09527498873}

$$\{40, 20, -1.899537670481520869100141764591 0^{-16} \}$$

{24, 0.6931471805599453094172321214578625715711811717337249\
    0767409687}

Out[6]= {x → 0.6931471805599453094172321}

+■ NumericalMath`IntervalRoots`

Interval methods in numerical computation provide a mechanism for verified calculation. With ordinary computer arithmetic you almost never know how much error is in the final result. With *Mathematica*'s variable-precision arithmetic this issue is addressed somewhat for basic arithmetic and the elementary functions, but no claim is made to rigor. With interval arithmetic absolute rigor is possible: the correct value is always maintained between two numbers, which are hopefully not too far apart.

In addition to basic arithmetic, there are interval analogs of many of the standard algorithms of numerical analysis. The package `NumericalMath`IntervalRoots`` provides three interval root-finding methods: bisection, secant, and Newton's method. A nice feature of interval root-finding methods is that they find *all* roots of the given function on a given interval. More precisely, they start with the given interval and discard parts of it that cannot possibly contain any roots. What you end up with are some subintervals of the given interval that are guaranteed to contain all of the roots that are contained in the the given interval. If the roots of the given interval are well separated then the result consists of short subintervals, each of which contains exactly one root.

`IntervalBisection[f, x, int, eps]`	finds the roots of the function f of the variable x on the interval *int* to within tolerance *eps* using the interval bisection method
`IntervalSecant[f, x, int, eps]`	finds the roots using the interval secant method
`IntervalNewton[f, x, int, eps]`	finds the roots using the interval Newton method

Interval root-finding methods.

`MaxRecursion`	specifies the maximum level of recursion allowed
`WorkingPrecision`	specifies the precision to use in the calculations

Options for interval root-finding methods.

This loads the package.

```
In[1]:= <<NumericalMath`IntervalRoots`
```

This finds the roots of $\sin x$ on the interval $[2, 8]$ and stops recursing when the subintervals have decreased to less than 0.1

```
In[2]:= IntervalBisection[Sin[x], x, Interval[{2., 8.}], .1]
Out[2]= Interval[{3.125, 3.21875}, {6.21875, 6.3125}]
```

This attempts to find the roots with a smaller error tolerance. For each of the two roots `MaxRecursion` is exceeded before the tolerance is achieved.

```
In[3]:= IntervalBisection[Sin[x], x, Interval[{2., 8.}], .01]
IntervalBisection::rec: MaxRecursion exceeded.
IntervalBisection::rec: MaxRecursion exceeded.
Out[3]= Interval[{3.125, 3.17188}, {6.26563, 6.3125}]
```

We can increase MaxRecursion to achieve the smaller tolerance.

```
In[4]:=  IntervalBisection[Sin[x], x, Interval[{2., 8.}], .01,
               MaxRecursion -> 10]

Out[4]=  Interval[{3.13672, 3.14258}, {6.27734, 6.2832}]
```

The interval secant method converges more rapidly and does not need the extra recursion to achieve the same tolerance.

```
In[5]:=  IntervalSecant[Sin[x], x, Interval[{2., 8.}], .01]

Out[5]=  Interval[{3.14159, 3.1416}, {6.28316, 6.28321}]
```

The interval Newton's method is used in the same way.

```
In[6]:=  IntervalSecant[Sin[x], x, Interval[{2., 8.}], .01]

Out[6]=  Interval[{3.14159, 3.1416}, {6.28316, 6.28321}]
```

The working precision can be infinite.

```
In[7]:=  IntervalBisection[Sin[x], x, Interval[{2, 8}], .1,
               WorkingPrecision -> Infinity]
```

$$Out[7]= \text{Interval}\left[\left\{\frac{25}{8}, \frac{103}{32}\right\}, \left\{\frac{199}{32}, \frac{101}{16}\right\}\right]$$

Infinite precision with Newton's method gives rather complicated results.

```
In[8]:=  IntervalNewton[Sin[x], x, Interval[{2, 8}], .1,
               MaxRecursion -> 2,
               WorkingPrecision -> Infinity]

IntervalNewton::rec: MaxRecursion exceeded.

IntervalNewton::rec: MaxRecursion exceeded.
```

$$Out[8]= \text{Interval}\left[\left\{\frac{1}{2}(7+\text{Sin}[5]) + \text{Sin}\left[\frac{1}{2}(7+\text{Sin}[5])\right],\right.\right.$$
$$\left.\frac{1}{2}(7+\text{Sin}[5]) - \text{Sec}[2]\,\text{Sin}\left[\frac{1}{2}(7+\text{Sin}[5])\right]\right\},$$
$$\left.\left\{5-\text{Sin}[5], \frac{1}{2}(13-\text{Sin}[5]) - \text{Sin}\left[\frac{1}{2}(13-\text{Sin}[5])\right]\right\}\right]$$

◾ NumericalMath`ListIntegrate`

The *Mathematica* function NIntegrate computes a numerical approximation to a definite integral. To use NIntegrate you must enter a symbolic expression for the function you want to integrate. There are many situations that arise in experimental and numerical work in which all you have is a list of values of the function to be integrated. The function ListIntegrate given in this package will compute an approximation to the integral in this case.

ListIntegrate[$\{y_1, y_2, \ldots, y_n\}$, h]
  give an approximation to the integral of the function having values $\{y_1, y_2, \ldots, y_n\}$ using constant step size h in x

ListIntegrate[$\{y_1, y_2, \ldots, y_n\}$, h, k]
  do the approximation using the nearest k points for each subinterval

ListIntegrate[$\{\{x_1, y_1\}, \ldots, \{x_n, y_n\}\}$, k]
  do the approximation for variable step-size data

Approximating a definite integral from a list of function values.

ListIntegrate works by using Interpolation to construct an InterpolatingFunction object to approximate the function that produced the data with a collection of interpolating polynomials. The InterpolatingFunction is integrated to obtain the result. You can specify the degree of the polynomial used in the InterpolatingFunction object by giving a value for k. k is the number of points used to construct each polynomial and the degree of each polynomial is $k-1$ (InterpolationOrder->$k-1$). The default value for k is 4.

This loads the package.

```
In[1]:= <<NumericalMath`ListIntegrate`
```

This gives a list of function values for x^2.

```
In[2]:= data = Table[ n^2, {n, 0, 7}]
Out[2]= {0, 1, 4, 9, 16, 25, 36, 49}
```

This gives an approximation to the integral of the function that produced the list of data. The step size of 1 means that the values in the list come from x values that are 1 unit apart.

```
In[3]:= ListIntegrate[data, 1]
```

$$Out[3]= \frac{343}{3}$$

Because the data were created by a degree two polynomial, the approximation is exact.

```
In[4]:= Integrate[x^2, {x, 0, 7}]
```

$$Out[4]= \frac{343}{3}$$

This gives the integral derived from the same data with a small random perturbation added.

```
In[5]:= ListIntegrate[
            Table[ n^2 + .1 Random[ ],
                {n, 0, 7}], 1]
Out[5]= 114.785
```

| If the data are a little noisy, the approximation is still fairly good. | `In[6]:= % - %%` |
| | `Out[6]= 0.451207` |

| By giving a list of pairs you can work with variable step-size data. The approximation is not as good as before, because the degree of the approximation has been reduced to 1, that is, linear interpolation. | `In[7]:= ListIntegrate[` `{{0,0},{1,1},{2,4},{5,25},{7,49}},2]` |
| | `Out[7]= ` $\dfrac{241}{2}$ |

If you know that there is significant error in your data, that is, it differs a great deal from the true function, it is better to smooth the error using `Fit` and then use `NIntegrate` to compute the integral of the fit.

Integration Using Interpolation

This package has been included for compatibility with previous versions of *Mathematica*. The functionality of this package has been superseded by improvements made to `InterpolatingFunction`. For example, the first and last examples can just as easily be done directly.

| This makes an `InterpolatingFunction` approximation. | `In[8]:= app = ListInterpolation[data,{{0,7}}]` |
| | `Out[8]= InterpolatingFunction[{{0, 7}}, <>]` |

| This integrates the approximation. | `In[9]:= Integrate[app[x],{x,0,7}]` |
| | `Out[9]= ` $\dfrac{343}{3}$ |

| Here approximation and integration are performed in one step. | `In[10]:= Integrate[Interpolation[{{0,0},{1,1},{2,4},{5,25},{7,49}},` `InterpolationOrder->1][x],{x,0,7}]` |
| | `Out[10]= ` $\dfrac{241}{2}$ |

It is advantageous to use the direct construction because it can be used to find the integral over part of the interval between the points, an approximate indefinite integral function, or the approximate integral for multidimensional data on tensor product grids.

■ NumericalMath`Microscope`

Mathematica uses both the machine arithmetic that is provided by the machine and its own arbitrary-precision arithmetic, which is the same on all machines (except for the variations in the size of the largest representable number and the amount of memory on the machine). This package deals with the floating-point arithmetic provided by the machine, not the arbitrary-precision arithmetic of *Mathematica*.

Numbers on a computer comprise a discrete set. There are gaps between the numbers and when you do arithmetic the result often is not representable. When the result falls between two representable numbers the best that can be done is to use the closest representable number as the result instead of the correct result. The set of numbers that can be represented on a computer in floating-point format are commonly referred to as the set of machine numbers. If you want to investigate how arithmetic is done on computers in a general sense you should use the package `NumericalMath`ComputerArithmetic``. That package allows you to vary certain fundamental parameters that control the arithmetic.

The difference between two consecutive machine numbers is called an ulp (<u>u</u>nit in the <u>l</u>ast <u>p</u>lace, *i.e.*, one digit in the least significant place). The size of an ulp varies depending on where you are in the set of machine numbers. Between 1 and 2 an ulp is equal to `$MachineEpsilon`. Between 2 and 4 it is equal to 2 `$MachineEpsilon`. Ideally no function should ever return a result with error exceeding half of an ulp since the distance from the true result to the nearest machine number is always less than half of an ulp, the worst case being when it is exactly halfway between two machine numbers. It is relatively easy to achieve this ideal for the four arithmetic operations and for the square root function. For the elementary transcendental functions it becomes more difficult due to the fact that they cannot be evaluated in a single operation and the combined effects of all the rounding errors would have to be made less than half an ulp. Nevertheless, it is quite possible to design algorithms for these functions such that the error is never more than one ulp.

The package `NumericalMath`Microscope`` provides four functions that are useful in examining the machine floating-point arithmetic on your machine.

`Ulp[a]`	give the size of an ulp near *a*
`MachineError[f, x -> a]`	give the error in evaluating *f* at *x* = *a* using machine arithmetic
`Microscope[f, {x, a}]`	plot *f* near *x* = *a* using machine arithmetic
`MicroscopicError[f, {x, a}]`	plot the error in evaluating *f* near *x* = *a* using machine arithmetic

Functions for examining machine floating-point arithmetic.

The default neighborhood of the point *x* = *a* used in `Microscope` and `MicroscopicError` is from 30 ulps to the left of *a* to 30 ulps to the right of *a*, where the ulp used is that defined at *x* = *a*, that is, Ulp[*a*]. Near powers of 2 and near 0 it is not clear what should be done since the size of an ulp changes. Near powers of 2 it is not much of a problem in the abscissa since an ulp is chosen to be the smaller of the two values and the resulting machine numbers just get included multiple times due to rounding effects. You can change the default size of the neighborhood by including a third value in the neighborhood specification.

A problem arises with Microscope and MicroscopicError near places where the function value becomes infinite. Since the function is changing by orders of magnitude very rapidly it is difficult to choose a good scale that displays the information in which you are interested. In such cases you may have to examine the function several hundreds of ulps away from the point you really want.

Microscope[*f*, {*x*, *a*, *n*}]	plot *f* from $x = a - n$ Ulp[*a*] to $x = a + n$ Ulp[*a*] using machine arithmetic
MicroscopicError[*f*, {*x*, *a*, *n*}]	plot the error in evaluating *f* from $x = a - n$ Ulp[*a*] to $x = a + n$ Ulp[*a*] using machine arithmetic

Controlling the size of the neighborhood.

The option PlotJoined controls the way the plot is drawn. It cannot be overemphasized that the functions that we are examining map the machine numbers to the machine numbers. For our purposes the real numbers in between do not even exist. Thus the plots produced by Microscope and MicroscopicError should be nothing but a set of plotted points. However, it is easier to see what is happening if the points are joined with straight line segments. Finally, if you want to see what a function does as a map from the real numbers to the real numbers, that is, rounding the real argument to the nearest machine number and applying the function to this result, you can do so, but when you see large errors, don't conclude that the function is to blame; it can't do any better than deal with the machine numbers that it gets as arguments.

option name	default value	
PlotJoined	True	the way the points are to be connected; either True, False, or Real

Options for Microscope and MicroscopicError.

This loads the package.	*In[1]:=* <<NumericalMath`Microscope`
Here is the size of an ulp at 1.	*In[2]:=* Ulp[1]
	Out[2]= 1.11022×10^{-16}
The size of an ulp changes at powers of 2.	*In[3]:=* {Ulp[7.999999], Ulp[8], Ulp[8.000001]}
	Out[3]= $\{8.88178 \times 10^{-16}, 8.88178 \times 10^{-16}, 1.77636 \times 10^{-15}\}$

There is a large hole near 0.

In[4]:= {Ulp[0], Ulp[$MinMachineNumber]}

Out[4]= $\{2.22507 \times 10^{-308}, 4.94065645841247 \times 10^{-324}\}$

Here are the combined errors of rounding $49\pi/50$ to the nearest machine number and then taking the square root.

In[5]:= MachineError[Sqrt[x], x -> 49 Pi/50]

Out[5]= -1.22219 Ulps

Here is the error of just the square root.

In[6]:= MachineError[Sqrt[x], x -> N[49 Pi/50]]

Out[6]= 0.0458162 Ulps

For another number close to N[49 Pi/50], the error in the square root function is less than half an ulp.

In[7]:= MachineError[Sqrt[x],
          x -> N[49 Pi/50] - 6 Ulp[49 Pi/50]]

Out[7]= 0.465321 Ulps

The function $\tan(\sqrt{e^{\sin(\log x)}})$ is not provided by the computer manufacturer so it is evaluated as a nested sequence of operations that are provided. This shows how much error is involved in the sequence, but this information is rarely useful. For testing purposes you normally want to look at an individual function evaluated at a machine number to avoid the effect of an ill-conditioned function magnifying prior error.

In[8]:= MachineError[Tan[Sqrt[Exp[Sin[Log[x]]]]],
          x -> N[Pi]]

Out[8]= -26.8911 Ulps

Here is the log function evaluated at machine numbers near 7.

In[9]:= Microscope[Log[x], {x, 7},
          PlotJoined -> False]

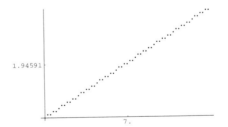

Here is the log function evaluated at $10 + 1 + 10$ machine numbers near 7 with the points joined by straight lines.

In[10]:= **Microscope[Log[x], {x, 7, 10}]**

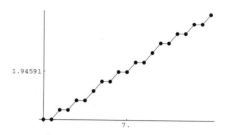

And here are the combined effects of rounding real numbers to the nearest machine number and taking the log of the result. This is *not* a valid test of the log function.

In[11]:= **Microscope[Log[x], {x, 7, 10},**
      PlotJoined -> Real]

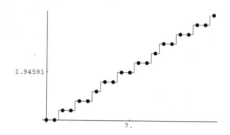

This shows the error in evaluating the sine function at 31 machine numbers near 16. Note how the size of an ulp changes at 16. Note also that rounding has moved some points to coincide so that there appear to be fewer than 31 points. The scale on the vertical axis represents ulps.

In[12]:= **MicroscopicError[Sin[x], {x, 16, 15},**
      PlotJoined -> False]

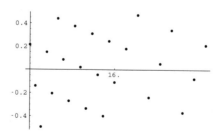

Here is the error in evaluating sine at 21 machine numbers near 31 with the points joined by straight lines.

In[13]:= `MicroscopicError[Sin[x], {x, 31, 10},`
`PlotJoined -> True]`

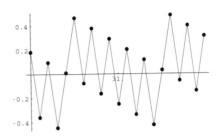

And here are the combined effects of rounding real numbers to the nearest machine number and taking the sine of the result. This is *not* a valid test of the sine function. The error in evaluating the sine function at a machine number near 31 is much smaller than the combination of errors resulting from first rounding a real number to the nearest machine number and then taking the sine of that machine number.

In[14]:= `MicroscopicError[Sin[x], {x, 31, 10},`
`PlotJoined -> Real]`

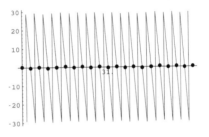

Here you see how bad the square root function really is. It appears that near 3.3 its error is bounded by about 1.0 ulps.

In[15]:= `MicroscopicError[Sqrt[x], {x, 3.3, 100}]`

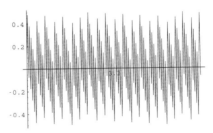

You cannot examine this function exactly at 1 since it is singular there. You can, however, examine it near 1. The label for 1 + 300 Ulp[1] is printed as 1. because the label is limited to 6 characters.

```
In[16]:= MicroscopicError[1/(x - 1) - 1/(x + 1),
             {x, 1 + 300 Ulp[1]}]
```

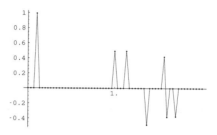

One point needs to be made clear here since rounding errors are often misunderstood and blame is incorrectly placed on an algorithm that has nothing to do with the error. Algorithms are designed to map the set of machine numbers into the set of machine numbers. To consider other numbers does not make sense. As far as the computer is concerned there *are* no other numbers. So, for example, if you want to find the square root of $49\pi/50$, you might do it as follows.

Start with a good numerical approximation to $49\pi/50$.

```
In[17]:= a = N[49 Pi/50, 30]
Out[17]= 3.078760800517997373693339051561
```

This finds the nearest machine number to a.

```
In[18]:= b = N[a]
Out[18]= 3.07876
```

This finds the square root of the machine number b using the machine-precision algorithm for square root.

```
In[19]:= c = Sqrt[b]
Out[19]= 1.75464
```

Here the error in c is measured in ulps. This result gives the error for the particular machine on which this example was run. Your machine may give a very different result.

```
In[20]:= (SetPrecision[c,30]-Sqrt[a])/$MachineEpsilon
Out[20]= -0.222188
```

Here the error is less than half an ulp. However, this error is due to both the square root function and the rounding error incurred in converting the number a to the machine number b. In fact, the square root function has an error of less than 0.1 ulps.

Here is the correct value for the square root of b.

```
In[21]:= d = Sqrt[SetPrecision[b, 30]]
Out[21]= 1.7546397922417002921821754735 2
```

This shows the error in the square root function.

```
In[22]:= (SetPrecision[c, 30] - d)/$MachineEpsilon
Out[22]= 0.0458162
```

⁺■ **NumericalMath`NIntegrateInterpolatingFunct`**

The *Mathematica* function NIntegrate uses algorithms that assume that the integrand is smooth to at least several orders. InterpolatingFunction objects typically do not satisfy this assumption; they are continuous, but only piecewise smooth. The algorithms used by NIntegrate converge very slowly when applied to InterpolatingFunction objects, especially in several dimensions. NIntegrate allows the domain of integration to be broken up into several pieces and the integral evaluated over each piece. If the pieces of the domain correspond to the pieces over which the InterpolatingFunction is smooth, NIntegrate will converge much more rapidly. NIntegrateInterpolatingFunction automatically breaks up the domain of integration.

NIntegrateInterpolatingFunction[*expr*, {*x, xmin, xmax*}]
        find a numerical approximation to an integral with
        InterpolatingFunction objects in the integrand

NIntegrateInterpolatingFunction[*expr*, {*x, xmin, xmax*}, {*y, ymin, ymax*}, ...]
        find a numerical approximation to a multidimensional
        integral with InterpolatingFunction objects in the
        integrand

Numerical approximations to integrals with InterpolatingFunction objects in the integrand.

NIntegrateInterpolatingFunction uses the function NIntegrate, but it breaks up the domain into sections where the InterpolatingFunction object is smooth.

This loads the package.	`In[1]:= <<NumericalMath`NIntegrateInterpolatingFunct``
This creates an InterpolatingFunction object approximating the sine function.	`In[2]:= sin = Interpolation[Table[{x,Sin[x]},{x,0,4,.5}]]` `Out[2]= InterpolatingFunction[{{0., 4.}}, <>]`

This list gives the time used to evaluate the integral plus the result of the integral.	`In[3]:= NIntegrateInterpolatingFunction[sin[x^2]^2,`
	            `{x,0,2}] // Timing`
	`Out[3]= {0.16 Second, 0.715792}`

NIntegrate produces almost exactly the same result, but takes much longer because the convergence is poor if the domain is not properly broken up.	`In[4]:= NIntegrate[sin[x^2]^2, {x,0,2}] // Timing` `Out[4]= {0.11 Second, 0.715792}`

If you simply need to find the integral of an InterpolatingFunction object (as opposed to a function of one), it is better to use Integrate because this gives you the result which is exact for the polynomial approximation used in the InterpolatingFunction object.

~■ NumericalMath`NLimit`

The built-in function `Limit` computes limits using symbolic and analytic methods. The function `NLimit` contained in this package works by numerically evaluating a short sequence of function values as the argument approaches the specified point. The result of this calculation is passed to a routine that uses either Wynn's ϵ-algorithm or a generalized Euler transformation to find an approximation to the limit.

`NLimit[`*expr*`, x -> `x_0`]`	numerically find the limit as x approaches x_0

Computing numerical limits.

This loads the package.	`In[1]:= <<NumericalMath`NLimit``
Here is the numerical computation of a limit.	`In[2]:= NLimit[Zeta[s] - 1/(s-1), s->1]` `Out[2]= 0.577216`
The limit gives the irrational number known as Euler's gamma.	`In[3]:= N[EulerGamma]` `Out[3]= 0.577216`

You can also compute limits as x approaches infinity.	`In[4]:= NLimit[(2 x^3 + Sin[x])/(5 x^3 + Log[x]),`
	`            x->Infinity]`
	`Out[4]= 0.4`

option name	default value	
`WorkingPrecision`	`$MachinePrecision`	number of digits of precision to be used
`Scale`	1	initial step size
`Terms`	7	total number of terms generated in the sequence
`Method`	EulerSum	method of evaluation, either `EulerSum` or `SequenceLimit`
`WynnDegree`	1	degree to use in the Wynn method

Options for `NLimit`.

There are many specialized techniques for accelerating the convergence of a series. Faster convergence means that in a numerical evaluation fewer terms are needed to give a result of the desired accuracy. One such technique, Euler's transformation, is used by `EulerSum`.

EulerSum is particularly good for working with alternating series and series whose terms have the form $p(n)r^n$ where $p(n)$ is a polynomial in n. It is a useful adjunct to the built-in NSum, which is designed to be an effective general case algorithm.

EulerSum[f, {i, $imin$, Infinity}]	use Euler's transformation to numerically evaluate $\sum_{imin}^{\infty} f$

Numerical evaluation of sums using Euler's transformation.

option name	default value	
WorkingPrecision	$MachinePrecision	number of digits of precision to be used
Terms	5	total number of terms generated before extrapolation
ExtraTerms	7	number of terms to be used in the extrapolation process; must be at least 2
EulerRatio	Automatic	the fixed ratio to be used in the transformation

Options for EulerSum.

This uses EulerSum to compute a numerical approximation to the sum of an alternating series.

```
In[5]:= EulerSum[(-1)^k/(2k + 1), {k, 0, Infinity}]
Out[5]= 0.785398
```

Increasing the precision and the number of terms does not change the answer in the first six decimal places. This provides a check on the accuracy of the numerically computed result.

```
In[6]:= EulerSum[(-1)^k/(2k + 1), {k, 0, Infinity},
            WorkingPrecision->40, Terms->30,
            ExtraTerms->30]
Out[6]= 0.7853981633974483096156608455791303225540
```

The result is also in good agreement with the known exact result.

```
In[7]:= % - N[Pi/4, 40]
Out[7]= -2.857249565 × 10^{-29}
```

There are occasionally instances in which it is difficult or impossible to analytically compute the derivative of a function. In these cases you can compute the derivative using the function ND instead of the built-in function D.

ND[f, x, x_0]	give a numerical approximation to $\frac{\partial f}{\partial x}$ evaluated at the point x_0
ND[f, {x, n}, x_0]	give the nth derivative

Numerical computation of derivatives.

Here is a numerical approximation of the derivative of $e^{\sin(x)}$ at $x = 2$.

```
In[8]:= ND[Exp[Sin[x]], x, 2]
Out[8]= -1.03312
```

After increasing the setting of the option Terms, the difference between the symbolically computed result and the numerical result for a third derivative is quite small.

```
In[9]:= ND[Exp[Sin[x]], {x, 3}, 2, Terms->10] -
          N[D[Exp[Sin[x]], {x, 3}] /. x->2]
Out[9]= 2.23989 × 10^-7
```

This is the error in the numerical derivative using Cauchy's integral formula.

```
In[10]:= ND[Exp[Sin[x]], {x, 3}, 2, Method -> NIntegrate] -
           N[D[Exp[Sin[x]], {x, 3}] /. x->2]
Out[10]= -1.30118 × 10^-13 + 1.70697 × 10^-15 i
```

option name	default value	
WorkingPrecision	$MachinePrecision	number of digits of precision to be used
Scale	1	size of steps in the evaluation
Terms	7	total number of terms generated in the sequence
+ Method	EulerSum	method of evaluation, either EulerSum (numerical limit of difference quotients) or NIntegrate (Cauchy's integral formula)

Options for ND.

You should realize that with sufficiently pathological examples, the algorithms used for EulerSum, NLimit, or ND can give wrong answers. In most cases, you can test your answer by looking at the sensitivity to changes in the setting of options.

+■ NumericalMath`NResidue`

The *Mathematica* function `Residue` symbolically finds the residue of an expression at a point in the complex plane. Because it is symbolic in nature it is sometimes unable to get a result.

`NResidue` is the numerical version of `Residue`. It works by numerically integrating around a small circle centered at the point at which the residue is being sought. The obvious problem with this approach is that it in fact finds the sum of the residues at all of the points contained within the circle. By making the radius of the circle sufficiently small you can exclude all singularities but the one in question.

`NResidue[`*expr*`, {`*x*`, `*x₀*`}]`	numerically find the residue of *expr* at the point $x = x_0$

Numerical evaluation of residues.

`Radius`	specifies the radius of the circle around which the integration is performed
`PrecisionGoal`	the `PrecisionGoal` to be used by `NIntegrate`
`WorkingPrecision`	the `WorkingPrecision` to be used by `NIntegrate`

Options for `NResidue`.

This loads the package.

`In[1]:= <<NumericalMath`NResidue``

Find the residue of 1/z at the origin.

`In[2]:= NResidue[1/z, {z, 0}]`

`Out[2]= 1.`

Define an expression whose residue you will find.

`In[3]:= f = 1/Expand[(z-1.7)(z+.2+.5 I)(z+.2-.5 I)]`

$$Out[3]= \frac{1}{\left(-0.493 - 7.20994 \times 10^{-18} \, i\right) - (0.39 + 0. \, i) \, z - (1.3 + 0. \, i) \, z^2 + z^3}$$

Find the residue. Strictly speaking, f has no singularity at $z = 1.7$, but it has one very near to 1.7.

`In[4]:= Residue[f, {z, 1.7}]`

`Out[4]= 0`

Numerically find the residue.

`In[5]:= NResidue[f, {z, 1.7}]`

$Out[5]= 0.259067 - 2.39067 \times 10^{-17} \, i$

This is another way to find the residue.

`In[6]:= 1/((z+.2+.5 I)(z+.2-.5 I)) /. z -> 1.7`

`Out[6]= 0.259067 + 0. i`

+■ NumericalMath`NSeries`

The *Mathematica* function `Series` finds a power series expansion of a function about a point by evaluating derivatives. However, sometimes you only want a numerical approximation to a series and the derivatives are difficult to evaluate. You could use `ND` to evaluate the derivatives, but that would involve repeating most of the work (*i.e.*, evaluating the function itself at several points) for each derivative. If the function is analytic and can be evaluated in the complex plane, the solution is to use the `NSeries`.

`NSeries[f, {x, x_0, n}]`	give a numerical approximation to the series expansion of f about $x = x_0$ including the terms $(x - x_0)^{-n}$ through $(x - x_0)^n$

Numerically finding series expansions.

    NSeries works by evaluating the function at discrete points on a circle centered at the expansion point. It then uses `InverseFourier` to express the function as a sum of orthogonal basis functions, each of which is trivial to integrate around the circle. By Cauchy's integral formula it is seen that `InverseFourier` essentially gives us the required series coefficients; very little additional work is required and `NSeries` does it all for you. Because it is based on Cauchy's integral formula, care should be taken to ensure that no singularities of the function occur inside the circle of sample points.

option name	default value	
`WorkingPrecision`	`$MachinePrecision`	precision of the arithmetic to use in calculations
`Radius`	1	radius of the circle on which the function is sampled

Options for NSeries.

This loads the package.

`In[1]:= << NumericalMath`NSeries``

This gives an approximation to the series expansion of e^x about the origin. Note that NSeries is unable to recognize small numbers that should in fact be zero.

`In[2]:= NSeries[Exp[x], {x, 0, 3}]`

$$Out[2]= \frac{1.6059 \times 10^{-10} + 9.70427 \times 10^{-17} \, i}{x^3} +$$
$$\frac{1.14706 \times 10^{-11} - 4.22939 \times 10^{-17} \, i}{x^2} +$$
$$\frac{7.647 \times 10^{-13} - 6.37716 \times 10^{-17} \, i}{x} + (1. - 1.62663 \times 10^{-17} \, i) +$$
$$(1. - 1.61858 \times 10^{-16} \, i) \, x + (0.5 - 9.77 \times 10^{-17} \, i) \, x^2 +$$
$$(0.166667 - 4.49268 \times 10^{-17} \, i) \, x^3 + O[x]^4$$

Chop and Rationalize can often clean up the result.

`In[3]:= Rationalize[Chop[%]]`

$$Out[3]= \frac{1.6059 \times 10^{-10}}{x^3} + \frac{20946975011026}{20946975011025} + \frac{375299968947542\,x}{375299968947541} +$$
$$\frac{1125899906842625\,x^2}{2251799813685249} + \frac{600479950316068\,x^3}{3602879701896407} + O[x]^4$$

If the radius is too small, cancellation becomes a problem.

`In[4]:= Rationalize[Chop[NSeries[Exp[x], {x, 0, 5},`
`              Radius -> 1/8]]]`

$$Out[4]= \frac{4503599627370497}{4503599627370496} + \frac{4503599627370497\,x}{4503599627370496} +$$
$$\frac{173215370283481\,x^2}{346430740566961} + \frac{12254692863593\,x^3}{73528157181557} + \frac{61956247453\,x^4}{1486949938873} +$$
$$\frac{1700662020\,x^5}{204079442401} + O[x]^6$$

Increasing the WorkingPrecision will usually solve this problem.

`In[5]:= Rationalize[Chop[NSeries[Exp[x], {x, 0, 5},`
`              WorkingPrecision -> 40, Radius -> 1/8]]]`

$$Out[5]= 1 + x + \frac{x^2}{2} + \frac{x^3}{6} + \frac{x^4}{24} + \frac{x^5}{120} + O[x]^6$$

If the radius is too large, the sample points become too scattered and it starts looking like poles exist.

`In[6]:= Rationalize[Chop[NSeries[Exp[x], {x, 0, 5},`
`              Radius -> 4]]]`

$$Out[6]= \frac{1.69285 \times 10^{-9}}{x^5} + \frac{219687786700998}{219687786700999} + \frac{900719925474099\,x}{900719925474100} +$$
$$\frac{1125899906842624\,x^2}{2251799813685249} + \frac{428914250225754\,x^3}{2573485501354525} + \frac{x^4}{24} + \frac{x^5}{120} + O[x]^6$$

NSeries also recognizes poles.

`In[7]:= Chop[NSeries[Zeta[s], {s, 1, 5}]]`

$$Out[7]= \frac{1}{s-1} + 0.577216 + 0.0728158\,(s-1) - 0.00484518\,(s-1)^2 -$$
$$0.000342306\,(s-1)^3 + 0.0000968904\,(s-1)^4 -$$
$$6.61103 \times 10^{-6}\,(s-1)^5 + O[s-1]^6$$

■ NumericalMath`NewtonCotes`

As one of its methods, the *Mathematica* function NIntegrate uses a fairly sophisticated Gauss-Kronrod based algorithm. Other types of quadrature formulas exist, each with their own advantages. For example, Gaussian quadrature uses values of the integrand at oddly spaced abscissas. If you want to integrate a function presented in tabular form at equally spaced abscissas, it won't work very well. An alternative is to use Newton-Cotes quadrature.

The basic idea behind Newton-Cotes quadrature is to approximate the value of an integral as a linear combination of values of the integrand evaluated at equally spaced points:

$$\int_a^b f(x)\,dx = \sum_{i=1}^n w_i f(x_i)$$

In addition, there is the question of whether or not to include the end points in the sum. If they are included, the quadrature formula is referred to as a closed formula. If not, it is an open formula. If the formula is open there is some ambiguity as to where the first abscissa is to be placed. The open formulas given in this package have the first abscissa one half step from the lower end point.

Since there are n free parameters to be chosen (the weights) and since both integration and the sum are linear operations, you can expect to be able to make the formula correct for all polynomials of degree less than about n. In addition to knowing what the weights are, it is often desirable to know how large the error in the approximation will be. This package allows you to answer both of these questions.

NewtonCotesWeights[n, a, b]	give a list of the n pairs (w_i, x_i) for quadrature on the interval a to b
NewtonCotesError[n, f, a, b]	give the error in the formula

Finding formulas for Newton-Cotes quadrature.

option name	default value	
QuadratureType	Closed	the type of quadrature, Open or Closed

Option for NewtonCotesWeights and NewtonCotesError.

This loads the package.

In[1]:= <<NumericalMath`NewtonCotes`

Here are the weights and abscissas for the five-point closed Newton-Cotes quadrature formula on the interval (−3, 7).

In[2]:= NewtonCotesWeights[5, -3, 7]

$Out[2]= \left\{\left\{-3, \frac{7}{9}\right\}, \left\{-\frac{1}{2}, \frac{32}{9}\right\}, \left\{2, \frac{4}{3}\right\}, \left\{\frac{9}{2}, \frac{32}{9}\right\}, \left\{7, \frac{7}{9}\right\}\right\}$

Here is the error in that formula. Unfortunately it involves the sixth derivative of f at an unknown point so you don't really know what the error itself is.

In[3]:= **NewtonCotesError[5, f, -3, 7]**

Out[3]= $\dfrac{15625\ f^{(6)}}{3024}$

You can see that the error decreases rapidly with the length of the interval.

In[4]:= **NewtonCotesError[5, f, a, a+h]**

Out[4]= $\dfrac{h^7\ f^{(6)}}{1935360}$

This gives the weights and abscissas for the five-point open Newton-Cotes quadrature formula on the interval $(-3, 7)$.

In[5]:= **NewtonCotesWeights[5, -3, 7, QuadratureType -> Open]**

Out[5]= $\left\{\left\{-2, \dfrac{1375}{576}\right\}, \left\{0, \dfrac{125}{144}\right\}, \left\{2, \dfrac{335}{96}\right\}, \left\{4, \dfrac{125}{144}\right\}, \left\{6, \dfrac{1375}{576}\right\}\right\}$

Here is the error in that formula.

In[6]:= **NewtonCotesError[5, f, -3, 7, QuadratureType -> Open]**

Out[6]= $-\dfrac{5575\ f^{(6)}}{1512}$

⁺■ NumericalMath ' OrderStar '

Analysis of the stability of numerical methods for solving differential equations is a considerably more difficult task than finding the order of approximation. This difficulty is reflected in the fact that there are many different ways of defining stability. This package assists in the determination of stability regions for numerical methods.

Stability regions are important because they reflect the rate at which errors are propagated in the approximate solution. Just as there are absolute and relative errors in numerical analysis, there are also absolute and relative measures of stability. This package renders order stars, which are useful in examining the relative stability of a method. Furthermore, by specifying the comparison function to be identically 1, you can also draw regions of absolute stability.

A given numerical method for a problem can be recast into the framework of approximation theory. The goal is then to study how well this approximant behaves when compared with the solution. There is a kind of paradox here, for if the solution were known then you would have no need to resort to a numerical approximation. However, you want to establish a framework which applies to any problem in a given class. Since generically analytic solutions to problems cannot be found, it is common to study how a numerical method behaves when it is applied to a linearized system. In the area of ordinary differential equations, for example, you might be interested in solutions to the system of equations:

$$\mathbf{y}'(t) = \mathbf{f}(\mathbf{y}(t), t)$$

for a generally nonlinear $\mathbf{f}$. It is common to replace this system by a scalar linear problem that you can solve, namely,

$$y'(t) = \lambda y(t), \quad y(t_0) = y_0 \tag{1}$$

where λ is considered to be a complex constant and you have fixed an initial condition so that the equation is uniquely determined. Stability analysis is now a study of how well a numerical solution behaves when applied to the simplified differential equation (1). Equation (1) is often referred to as the scalar linear test problem, or Dahlquist's equation.

The discussion which follows concentrates on how to use the package. You should keep in mind that although the focus is on the behavior of an approximant, our underlying interest is in the numerical method from which the approximant arose when applied to some problem. For more information on this correspondence, stability analysis, and the theory of order stars, see the references at the end of this section.

`OrderStar[r, f]`	draw the order star depicting the region where $|r/f| < 1$, for the functions r and f
`OrderStar[r, f, z]`	draw the region in the complex z-plane where $|r/f| < 1$, where r and f are functions of z
`OrderStar[r, f, OrderStarKind -> Second]`	draw the order star depicting the region where $\operatorname{Re}(r - f) < 0$

Drawing order stars.

Padé approximations are rational polynomial approximants where all parameters are chosen to maximize order at some local expansion point. Certain numerical methods such as Runge-Kutta methods are related to Padé approximants to the exponential.

This loads the package.

In[1]:= `<<NumericalMath`OrderStar``

This constructs a Padé approximant to exp(z). The package for doing this is loaded automatically. This approximant corresponds to the forward Euler method.

In[2]:= `approx = Pade[ Exp[z], {z, 0, 1, 0} ]`

Out[2]= `1 + z`

This is the relative stability region, or order star of the first kind, for the forward Euler method. The pole of the approximant is highlighted.

In[3]:= `OrderStar[ approx, E^z ]`

```
OrderStar::sols:
    Warning: No finite zeros of function
      found using NSolve. Either inverse functions or
      transcendental dependencies were involved. Try
      specifying omitted points using options.
```

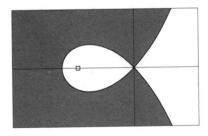

This is the absolute stability region for the forward Euler method, obtained as a relative comparison with 1.

In[4]:= **OrderStar[approx, 1]**

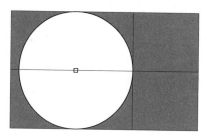

OrderStarInterpolation	specifies whether to display points where r and f are equal
OrderStarKind	specifies which kind (First or Second) of order star to draw
OrderStarLegend	specifies whether to include a plot legend containing the various symbols used
OrderStarPoles	specifies whether to indicate the poles of the approximant and/or the function
OrderStarZeros	specifies whether to indicate the zeros of the approximant and/or the function
OrderStarSubPlots	specifies subplot ranges and the number of points to be used in subplots
OrderStarSymbolSize	specifies the size of the symbols used to indicate zeros, poles, and interpolation points
OrderStarSymbolThickness	specifies the line thickness for the symbols used to indicate zeros, poles, and interpolation points

Options unique to OrderStar.

When you ask for certain features to be displayed and *Mathematica* is unable to find these features, you will obtain the message OrderStar::sols containing more specific information relating to the problem. Solve may also issue messages such as when inverse functions are being used.

OrderStar uses heuristics in order to determine what the independent variable is. You can save time in a very complicated expression by specifying the variable to use explicitly. If there is any ambiguity in the variable choice, then input returns unevaluated and an appropriate warning message is issued, since the function will not evaluate numerically.

This indicates the variable to use and highlights points where $1 + z = \exp(z)$. This may not be possible in general if the relationship is nonalgebraic.

```
In[5]:= OrderStar[approx, Exp[z], z,
                 OrderStarInterpolation->True]
```

```
OrderStar::sols:
    Warning: No finite zeros of function
        found using NSolve. Either inverse functions or
        transcendental dependencies were involved. Try
        specifying omitted points using options.
```

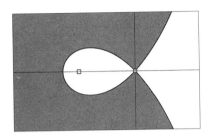

In addition to `True` and `False`, the options `OrderStarInterpolation`, `OrderStarLegend`, `OrderStarPoles`, and `OrderStarZeros` can take on lists of coordinate pairs to specify points that cannot be found automatically. As well as resizing the plot legend by specifying scaled coordinates, you can specify information to the legend such as the style and size of the font to use.

The position of the legend is given in scaled coordinates using the same syntax as that of `Rectangle`. Font style and size information is also specified and the symbols used to represent zeros and poles are increased in size.

```
In[6]:= OrderStar[ Pade[ Sinh[z-1], {z, 0, 3, 3}], Sinh[z-1],
            OrderStarLegend -> {{.6, .6}, {.98, .98}},
            DefaultFont -> { "Courier", 6.5},
            OrderStarSymbolSize -> 0.02 ]
```

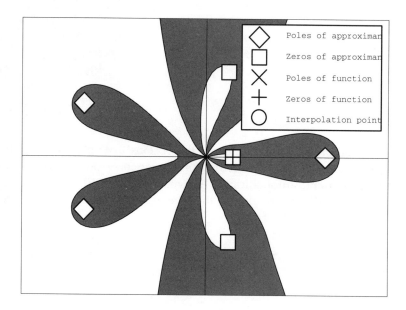

In addition to the many options unique to `OrderStar`, there are several that are simply passed to `ContourPlot` and used to produce the plot.

AspectRatio	specifies the aspect ratio of the plot
Axes	specifies whether to draw axes
AxesOrigin	specifies the intersection of the axes
ColorFunction	specifies a function to apply to color the stability and instability regions
FrameTicks	specifies whether or where to place tick marks around the frame
PlotPoints	specifies the number of sample points to use in constructing the contour plot
PlotRange	specifies the plot range to be used in the plot
Ticks	specifies whether or where to place tick marks along the axes

Options common to many graphics functions.

An important issue is whether an order star crosses the imaginary axis. Additionally, it may be interesting to illustrate symmetry around the real axis. In order to facilitate these comparisons OrderStar uses graphics options to render axes which pass through the origin.

The default plot region and subdivision are determined from essential features of the order star. However, this default can be overridden using standard Graphics options.

This defines a function.	*In[7]:=* **fun = Exp[Cos[z]+ I Cosh[z]];**
This constructs a Padé approximant to the function.	*In[8]:=* **approx = Pade[fun, {z, 0, 2, 3}];**

You can change the default plot region and plot density using standard options. However, in doing so you can make the plot quite jagged. Increasing PlotPoints can resolve this issue.

```
In[9]:= OrderStar[approx, fun,
                PlotRange -> {{-5, 5},{-5, 5}},
                PlotPoints -> 40 ]
```

```
OrderStar::sols:
    Warning: No poles of function
        found using NSolve. Either inverse functions or
        transcendental dependencies were involved. Try
        specifying omitted points using options.
```

```
OrderStar::sols:
    Warning: No zeros of function
        found using NSolve. Either inverse functions or
        transcendental dependencies were involved. Try
        specifying omitted points using options.
```

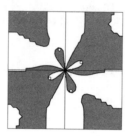

Order stars of the second kind are useful in the study of stability for linear multistep methods.

You can also plot the order star of the second kind. Note the poor resolution near the point of expansion $(1, 0)$. There is not a similar problem near the origin because extra work is done there by default.

```
In[10]:= OrderStar[ Pade[ Log[1+z], {z, 1, 3, 2}], Log[1+z],
                OrderStarKind -> Second,
                PlotPoints -> 50,
                    PlotRange -> {{-.5, 2},{-1, 1}} ]
```

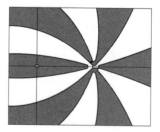

By default OrderStar resolves fine features at the origin by overlaying a subplot. However, there may be times when you wish to disable this feature, or to resolve fine features in other specified regions. Increasing the overall PlotPoints setting is an inefficient solution to this problem. The option OrderStarSubPlots provides a mechanism for doing this.

By overlaying smaller contour plots in regions of poor resolution the figure is much improved. If no `PlotPoints` option is specified for a particular subplot, a fraction of the value for the main plot is used.

```
In[11]:=  OrderStar[ Pade[ Log[1+z], {z, 1, 3, 2}], Log[1+z],
                OrderStarKind -> Second,
                PlotPoints -> 50,
                    PlotRange -> {{-.5, 2},{-1, 1}},
                OrderStarSubPlots ->
                  {{PlotRange ->  {{0.9, 1.1},{-0.1, 0.1}},
                      PlotPoints -> {20, 20}}} ]
```

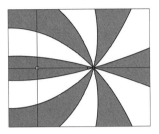

Order stars provide a means of determining, at a glance, many important features of interest such as A-stability. Furthermore, by considering a relative comparison with a function, order stars manage to encrypt the order of accuracy of a numerical scheme into the stability region.

Here are only the zeros and poles of the approximant, since there are no finite zeros or poles of exp(z). The numerical method corresponding to this approximant is A-stable since the approximant has no poles in the left half-plane. Furthermore a count of the sectors adjoining the origin tells you that the order of approximation is 5 (one less than the number of sectors).

```
In[12]:=  OrderStar[ Pade[ Exp[z], {z, 0, 2, 3}], Exp[z],
                OrderStarPoles -> {True, False},
                OrderStarZeros -> {True, False} ]
```

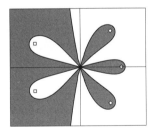

Expositions of the theory of stability of numerical methods can be found in [1], [2], and [3]. More examples of applications of the package are provided in [4].

References

[1] E. Hairer and G. Wanner, *Solving Ordinary Differential Equations II: Stiff and Differential-Algebraic Problems*, Springer, Berlin, 1991.
[2] A. Iserles and S. P. Nørsett, *Order Stars*, Chapman and Hall, London, 1991.
[3] J. D. Lambert, *Numerical Methods for Ordinary Differential Equations: The Initial Value Problem*, John Wiley and Sons, Chichester, 1991.

[4] M. Sofroniou, "Order Stars and Linear Stability Theory", *Journal of Symbolic Computation*, 1996, **11**, pp. 1–31.

■ NumericalMath`PolynomialFit`

The *Mathematica* function Fit does linear least squares fitting to data. It allows any combination of basis functions. However, it is often the case that you want to do polynomial fitting and it would be easier if you did not have to explicitly list the basis functions. In addition, for high-degree fitting, things often get rather unstable numerically if you give simple powers of a variable as basis functions. PolynomialFit avoids these problems.

PolynomialFit[*data*, *n*]	give the least squares n^{th} degree polynomial fit to *data*

Fitting polynomials to data.

PolynomialFit uses the function Fit, but it chooses a more appropriate set of basis functions than simple powers of a variable. It also returns a pure function rather than an expression and evaluates the function in a numerically stable way. If you want, you can evaluate the function at a symbolic point and expand the result to get an ordinary looking polynomial, but this is *not* advised; doing so will result in something that could be numerically very unstable. That is, extreme loss of accuracy could result due to cancellation of digits.

This loads the package.	*In[1]:=* **<<NumericalMath`PolynomialFit`**
Here is the cubic polynomial that fits the data.	*In[2]:=* **p = PolynomialFit[{1,4,9,16,25,36,49},3]**
	Out[2]= FittingPolynomial[<>, 3]
This evaluates the polynomial at 10.	*In[3]:=* **p[10]**
	Out[3]= 100.
This gives the ordinary form of the polynomial. Doing this and then replacing x by some numerical value is not advised, especially for high-degree polynomials.	*In[4]:=* **Expand[p[x]]**
	Out[4]= $-4.61853 \times 10^{-14} + 5.54556 \times 10^{-14}\, x + 1.\, x^2 + 1.39395 \times 10^{-15}\, x^3$

■ NumericalMath`SplineFit`

Most methods of fitting curves to data assume that the fit is one-to-one; that is, for each value of *x*, there is only one value of *y*. For some data, you may want to find a general curve in the plane. This is in general a difficult problem, so the approach of making piecewise fits is useful. These are generally referred to as splines. Note that not all splines interpolate points; some splines use a subset of the points to control the shape of the curve, as in specifying a convex hull using Bezier splines.

SplineFit[*points*, *type*]   generate a SplineFunction object of the specified type

Generating a spline.

The SplineFit routine currently supports three types of splines: Cubic, Bezier, and CompositeBezier. A cubic spline as currently implemented is made of piecewise third-order polynomials, with C^1 continuity, where the second derivative of each polynomial is zero at the endpoints. This curve interpolates each of the points it is created from.

A Bezier spline, on the other hand, interpolates only the endpoints; the other points control the spline, forming a convex hull.

Finally, a composite Bezier spline is made up of a series of third-order Bezier curves with C^1 continuity. It alternates interpolating points and control points.

SplineFit returns a SplineFunction object that represents the piecewise spline. It is a parametric function of one argument, representing a spline curve in the plane. Giving it one numeric argument within the range of the parameterization will evaluate to the (x, y) pair at that point.

This loads the package.	`In[1]:= <<NumericalMath`SplineFit``
Here is a list of points.	`In[2]:= pts = {{0,0},{1,2},{-1,3},{0,1},{3,0}};`
This generates a cubic spline from pts.	`In[3]:= spline = SplineFit[pts, Cubic]`
	`Out[3]= SplineFunction[Cubic, {0., 4.}, <>]`
We can evaluate the function at any point on the curve.	`In[4]:= spline[1.4]`
	`Out[4]= {0.265143, 2.70171}`

Here is a graph of the curve.

```
In[5]:= ParametricPlot[spline[u], {u, 0, 4},
              PlotRange -> All, Compiled -> False]
```

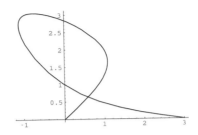

SplineFunction[*type*, *range*, *internal*]	spline function object of type *type* defined over the parameter range *range*

Object returned by SplineFit.

Note that the spline function object returned by SplineFit indicates the type of the spline, and the valid range of the parameter to which the function can be applied. The various internal arguments differ for each type of spline, and are hidden in the standard output format. In the cubic spline, for instance, these internal arguments cache the coefficients of the polynomials that make up the spline.

Here is the internal form of the cubic spline function generated from pts.

```
In[6]:= InputForm[spline]

Out[6]//InputForm= SplineFunction[Cubic, {0., 4.},
            {{0, 0}, {1, 2}, {-1, 3}, {0, 1}, {3, 0}},
            {{{0, 111/56, 0, -55/56}, {0, 57/28, 0, -1/28}},
             {{1, -27/28, -165/56, 107/56},
              {2, 27/14, -3/28, -23/28}},
             {{-1, -9/8, 39/14, -37/56}, {3, -3/4, -18/7, 37/28}},
             {{0, 69/28, 45/56, -15/56},
              {1, -27/14, 39/28, -13/28}}}]
```

◼ NumericalMath`TrigFit`

The *Mathematica* function Fit does linear least-squares fitting to data. It allows any combination of basis functions. However, it is often the case that you want to do trigonometric fitting and it would be easier if you did not have to explicitly list the basis functions 1, $\cos(x)$, $\sin(x)$, $\cos(2x)$, $\sin(2x)$, ... TrigFit does this for you.

TrigFit[*data*, *n*, *x*]	give the least-squares trigonometric fit to *data* up to $\cos(nx)$ and $\sin(nx)$, with fundamental period 2π
TrigFit[*data*, *n*, {*x*, *L*}]	give the least-squares trigonometric fit to *data* up to $\cos(2\pi nx/L)$ and $\sin(2\pi nx/L)$, with fundamental period L
TrigFit[*data*, *n*, {*x*, x_0, x_1}]	give the least-squares trigonometric fit to *data* up to $\cos(2\pi n(x-x_0)/(x_1-x_0))$ and $\sin(2\pi n(x-x_0)/(x_1-x_0))$, with fundamental period x_1-x_0

Fitting trigonometric series to data.

TrigFit uses the function Fourier to quickly find a least-squares trigonometric fit to the data. In doing so it completely avoids casting the problem in terms of an overdetermined linear system and instead directly constructs the solution. It should be pointed out, however, that because TrigFit is based on Fourier, it must assume that the data come from equally spaced sample points and that the data cover exactly one period of a periodic function. Because of this restriction it was decided that TrigFit should not accept data in the form of ordered pairs. It thus only accepts a list of numbers, which are assumed to be sampled with spacing *period/n* where *period* is the period of the function and *n* is the number of elements in *data*. Note that the first datum corresponds to x_0 (default value 0). Because the function in question is assumed to be periodic, the first datum also corresponds to x_1 (or L if x_0 is not specified) and the last datum corresponds to $x_1 - period/n$.

This loads the package.

```
In[1]:= <<NumericalMath`TrigFit`
```

Start with some data. Note that the last datum is given by the $2\pi - 2\pi/7$, not 2π.

```
In[2]:= data = Table[1+2Sin[x]+3Cos[2x]+4 Sin[3x],
            {x, 0, 2Pi-2Pi/7, 2Pi/7}];
```

Find the constant term.

```
In[3]:= TrigFit[data, 0, x]
Out[3]= 1.
```

This gives the least-squares fit including only the fundamental frequency. Here you specify the period to be L rather than the default of 2π.

```
In[4]:= TrigFit[data, 1, {x, L}]
```

$$Out[4]= 1. + 0. \, \text{Cos}\left[\frac{2\pi x}{L}\right] + 2. \, \text{Sin}\left[\frac{2\pi x}{L}\right]$$

You can use Fit to do the fitting, but it is slower and less convenient.

```
In[5]:= Fit[Transpose[{Range[0, 2Pi-2Pi/7, 2Pi/7], data}],
            {1, Cos[x], Sin[x]}, x]
```

$$Out[5]= 1. + 1.02457 \times 10^{-17} \, \text{Cos}[x] + 2. \, \text{Sin}[x]$$

This gives the least-squares fit including the first 3 overtones. In this case you have specified that the interval (x_0, x_1) is the interval covered by the data.

In[6]:= **TrigFit[data, 3, {x, x0, x1}]**

Out[6]= $1. + 0. \cos\left[\frac{2\pi(x-x0)}{-x0+x1}\right] + 3. \cos\left[\frac{4\pi(x-x0)}{-x0+x1}\right] -$

$4.44089 \times 10^{-16} \cos\left[\frac{6\pi(x-x0)}{-x0+x1}\right] + 2. \sin\left[\frac{2\pi(x-x0)}{-x0+x1}\right] +$

$0. \sin\left[\frac{4\pi(x-x0)}{-x0+x1}\right] + 4. \sin\left[\frac{6\pi(x-x0)}{-x0+x1}\right]$

As with Fit, it is often useful to discard the small terms using Chop.

In[7]:= **Chop[%]**

Out[7]= $1. + 3. \cos\left[\frac{4\pi(x-x0)}{-x0+x1}\right] + 2. \sin\left[\frac{2\pi(x-x0)}{-x0+x1}\right] +$

$4. \sin\left[\frac{6\pi(x-x0)}{-x0+x1}\right]$

11. Statistics

■ Statistics `ConfidenceIntervals`

A confidence interval gives a bound within which a parameter is expected to lie with a certain probability. Interval estimation of a parameter is often useful in observing the accuracy of an estimator as well as in making statistical inferences about the parameter in question. With this package, you can find confidence intervals for various parameters such as means, differences between two population means, variances, and ratios of the variance of two populations. The functions in this package calculate sample estimates and return bounds for intervals using the specified confidence level. The confidence intervals computed in this package assume that the univariate data are normally distributed.

MeanCI[*data*]	give the confidence interval for the population mean of *data* based on the Student *t* distribution
MeanCI[*data*, KnownVariance -> *var*]	give the confidence interval for the population mean of *data* based on the normal distribution

Confidence interval for the mean.

A confidence interval for the mean of a distribution is centered at $\bar{x}$ and has a half length proportional to the standard deviation σ of the estimator. If the variance of the underlying distribution is known, and given by the option KnownVariance -> *var*, then the interval is calculated using the appropriate quantile z_c of the standard normal distribution. The resulting interval is $(\bar{x} - z_c\sigma, \bar{x} + z_c\sigma)$, where c is (1 + ConfidenceLevel)/2 and σ^2 = *var*.

If the variance is unknown, the standard deviation must be estimated, and the confidence interval takes the form $(\bar{x} - t_c s, \bar{x} + t_c s)$, where t_c is the cth quantile of the Student *t* distribution and s is the standard error of the mean. The confidence level used in computing the interval is specified by the option ConfidenceLevel, which has a default value of .95.

This loads the package.	`In[1]:= <<Statistics`ConfidenceIntervals``
Here is a list of sample values. The data are assumed to be a random sample from the normally distributed population with unknown variance.	`In[2]:= data1 = {2.1, 1.2, 0.7, 1.0, 1.1, 3.2, 3.2,` `    3.3, 2.1, 0.3};`
The confidence bounds that are computed are based on the Student *t* distribution with confidence level .95.	`In[3]:= MeanCI[data1]` `Out[3]= {1.01857, 2.62143}`

option name	default value	
ConfidenceLevel	.95	confidence level

Option for all confidence interval functions.

You can calculate confidence intervals for the difference in means of two populations using MeanDifferenceCI.

MeanDifferenceCI[$data_1$, $data_2$]
    give the confidence interval for the difference between the population mean of $data_1$ and the population mean of $data_2$ based on the Student t distribution

MeanDifferenceCI[$data_1$, $data_2$, KnownVariance -> {var_1, var_2}]
    give the confidence interval for the difference between the population mean of $data_1$ and the population mean of $data_2$ based on the normal distribution

Confidence intervals for difference in means.

If variances are unknown, you can specify that the population variances are equal with EqualVariances -> True. In this case the Student t distribution is used with $n_1 + n_2 - 2$ degrees of freedom, where n_1 and n_2 are the sample sizes from the first and the second populations, respectively. If the unknown variances are not specified as equal, a more conservative interval is computed using Welch's approximate t-statistic.

Here is a second list of sample values from a population whose variance is unknown.

```
In[4]:= data2 = {1.8, 0.2, 1.5, 1.9, 1.1, 3.0, 2.3,
                 0.9, 2.4, 1.0};
```

This is the interval for the difference in the two means, assuming equal variances.

```
In[5]:= MeanDifferenceCI[data1, data2,
              EqualVariances -> True]

Out[5]= {-0.718667, 1.13867}
```

If equal variances cannot be assumed, the computed interval is larger, or more conservative.

```
In[6]:= MeanDifferenceCI[data1, data2]

Out[6]= {-0.724093, 1.14409}
```

option name	default value	
EqualVariances	False	whether the unknown population variances are assumed equal
KnownVariance	None	value of the known population variance
KnownStandardDeviation	None	value of the known population standard deviation

Options for the confidence interval for difference in means.

You can also compute intervals for population variance and ratio of population variances. The bounds for these intervals are determined by the sample standard deviations and the appropriate quantiles from the chi-square or the F-ratio distributions. Note that the ConfidenceLevel option is available for all confidence interval functions provided in this package.

VarianceCI[*data*]	give the confidence interval for the population variance of data based on the chi-square distribution
VarianceRatioCI[*data*$_1$, *data*$_2$]	give the confidence interval for the ratio of the population variance of *data*$_1$ to the population variance of *data*$_2$ based on the F-ratio distribution

Confidence intervals for variances.

Here is the interval for the population variance of the first sample.

```
In[7]:= VarianceCI[data1]
Out[7]= {0.593815, 4.1831}
```

This gives the 90 percent confidence interval for the ratio of two variances whose populations are represented by the two samples.

```
In[8]:= VarianceRatioCI[data1, data2,
            ConfidenceLevel -> .9]
Out[8]= {0.565024, 5.70978}
```

The package also provides functions for calculating confidence intervals from derived statistics rather than sample data. This may be useful when parameter estimates are available, in which case you do not have to input any data. You can use functions from the Statistics`DescriptiveStatistics` package to get the necessary derived statistics of your sample data. This package is automatically loaded when you load Statistics`ConfidenceIntervals`.

NormalCI[*mean*, *sd*]	give the confidence interval centered at *mean* with standard deviation sd
StudentTCI[*mean*, *se*, *dof*]	give the confidence interval centered at *mean* with specified standard error *se* and *dof* degrees of freedom
ChiSquareCI[*variance*, *dof*]	give the confidence interval for the population variance, given sample variance *variance* and *dof* degrees of freedom
FRatioCI[*ratio*, *numdof*, *dendof*]	give the confidence interval for the ratio of population variances, given the ratio of sample variances *ratio* and where the sample variances in the numerator and denominator have *numdof* and *dendof* degrees of freedom, respectively

Confidence intervals given sample estimates.

This calculates the mean of the sample data that were given at the beginning of this section.

```
In[9]:= mean = Mean[data1]
Out[9]= 1.82
```

This estimates the standard error of the mean using a function from the package Statistics`DescriptiveStatistics` which is automatically loaded with this one.

```
In[10]:= se = StandardErrorOfSampleMean[data1]
Out[10]= 0.354275
```

The same interval is computed using the estimated standard error as was found by using MeanCI above.

```
In[11]:= StudentTCI[mean, se, Length[data1] - 1,
            ConfidenceLevel -> 0.9]
Out[11]= {1.17057, 2.46943}
```

■ Statistics`ContinuousDistributions`

This package gives you access to the most commonly used continuous statistical distributions. You can compute their densities, means, variances, and other related properties. The distributions themselves are represented in the symbolic form *name*[*param*$_1$, *param*$_2$, ...]. Functions such as Mean, which give properties of statistical distributions, take the symbolic representation of the distribution as an argument.

Several of the most commonly used distributions are derived from the normal or Gaussian distribution. These distributions can also be found in the NormalDistribution package. You should use NormalDistribution instead of this package when you need only the normal, Student *t*, chi-square, or *F*-ratio distributions. Descriptions of these four distributions are given in more detail in the NormalDistribution section. The package DiscreteDistributions contains many discrete statistical distributions.

ChiSquareDistribution[*n*]	chi-square distribution with *n* degrees of freedom
FRatioDistribution[*n*$_1$, *n*$_2$]	*F*-ratio distribution with *n*$_1$ numerator and *n*$_2$ denominator degrees of freedom
NormalDistribution[*μ*, *σ*]	normal (Gaussian) distribution with mean *μ* and standard deviation *σ*
StudentTDistribution[*n*]	Student *t* distribution with *n* degrees of freedom

Common distributions derived from the normal distribution.

BetaDistribution[*alpha, beta*]	continuous beta distribution with shape parameters α and β
CauchyDistribution[*a, b*]	Cauchy distribution with location parameter a and scale parameter b
ChiDistribution[*n*]	chi distribution with n degrees of freedom
ExponentialDistribution[*lambda*]	exponential distribution with scale inversely proportional to parameter λ
ExtremeValueDistribution[*alpha, beta*]	extreme value (Fisher-Tippett) distribution with location parameter α and scale parameter β
GammaDistribution[*alpha, lambda*]	gamma distribution with shape parameter α and scale parameter λ
HalfNormalDistribution[*theta*]	half-normal distribution with scale inversely proportional to parameter θ
LaplaceDistribution[*mu, beta*]	Laplace (double exponential) distribution with mean μ and scale parameter β
LogisticDistribution[*mu, beta*]	logistic distribution with mean μ and scale parameter β
LogNormalDistribution[*mu, sigma*]	lognormal distribution based on a normal distribution with mean μ and standard deviation σ
ParetoDistribution[*k, alpha*]	Pareto distribution with minimum value parameter k and shape parameter α
RayleighDistribution[*sigma*]	Rayleigh distribution with scale parameter σ
UniformDistribution[*min, max*]	uniform distribution on the interval {*min, max*}
WeibullDistribution[*alpha, beta*]	Weibull distribution with shape parameter α and scale parameter β

Continuous statistical distributions.

The **uniform distribution** UniformDistribution[*min, max*], commonly referred to as the rectangular distribution, characterizes a random variable whose value is everywhere equally likely. An example of a uniformly distributed random variable is the location of a point chosen randomly on a line from min to max. If X is uniformly distributed on $[-\pi, \pi]$, then the random variable $\tan X$ follows a **Cauchy distribution** CauchyDistribution[*a, b*], with $a = 0$ and $b = 1$.

The **lognormal distribution** LogNormalDistribution[*mu*, *sigma*] is the distribution followed by the exponential of a normally distributed random variable. This distribution arises when many independent random variables are combined in a multiplicative fashion. The **halfnormal distribution** HalfNormalDistribution[*theta*] is proportional to the distribution NormalDistribution[0, 1/(*theta* Sqrt[2/Pi])] limited to the domain [0, ∞).

When $\alpha = n/2$ and $\lambda = 2$, the **gamma distribution** GammaDistribution[*alpha*, *lambda*] describes the distribution of a sum of squares of n unit normal random variables. This form of the gamma distribution is called a **chi-square distribution** with n degrees of freedom. When $\alpha = 1$, the gamma distribution takes on the form of the **exponential distribution** ExponentialDistribution[*lambda*], often used in describing the waiting time between events.

The **chi distribution** ChiDistribution[*n*] is followed by the square root of a chi-square random variable. For $n = 1$, the chi distribution is identical to HalfNormalDistribution[*theta*] with $\theta = 1$. For $n = 2$, the chi distribution is identical to the **Rayleigh distribution** RayleighDistribution[*sigma*] with $\sigma = 1$.

When X_1 and X_2 have independent gamma distributions with equal scale parameters, the random variable $\frac{X_1}{X_1 + X_2}$ follows the **beta distribution** BetaDistribution[*alpha*, *beta*], where α and β are the shape parameters of the gamma variables.

The **Weibull distribution** WeibullDistribution[*alpha*, *beta*] is commonly used in engineering to describe the lifetime of an object. The **extreme value distribution** ExtremeValueDistribution[*alpha*, *beta*] is the limiting distribution for the smallest or largest values in large samples drawn from a variety of distributions, including the normal distribution. The extreme value distribution is sometimes referred to as the log-Weibull distribution because it describes the distribution of the log of a Weibull distributed random variable.

The **Laplace distribution** LaplaceDistribution[*mu*, *beta*] is the distribution of the difference of two independent random variables with identical exponential distributions. The **logistic distribution** LogisticDistribution[*mu*, *beta*] is frequently used in place of the normal distribution when a distribution with longer tails is desired.

The **Pareto distribution** ParetoDistribution[*k*, *alpha*] may be used to describe income, k representing the minimum income possible.

NoncentralChiSquareDistribution[n, *lambda*]
> noncentral chi-square distribution with n degrees of freedom and noncentrality parameter λ

NoncentralStudentTDistribution[n, *lambda*]
> noncentral Student t distribution with n degrees of freedom and noncentrality parameter λ

NoncentralFRatioDistribution[n_1, n_2, *lambda*]
> noncentral F-ratio distribution with n_1 numerator degrees of freedom and n_2 denominator degrees of freedom and numerator noncentrality parameter λ

Distributions with noncentrality parameters.

Distributions that are derived from normal distributions with nonzero means are called *noncentral distributions*.

The sum of the squares of n normally distributed random variables with variance $\sigma^2 = 1$ and nonzero means follows a **noncentral chi-square distribution** NoncentralChiSquareDistribution[n, *lambda*]. The noncentrality parameter λ is the sum of the squares of the means of the random variables in the sum. Note that in various places in the literature, $\lambda/2$ or $\sqrt{\lambda}$ is used as the noncentrality parameter.

The **noncentral Student t distribution** NoncentralStudentTDistribution[n, *lambda*] describes the ratio $X/\sqrt{\chi_n^2/n}$ where χ_n^2 is a central chi-square random variable with n degrees of freedom, and X is an independent normally distributed random variable with variance $\sigma^2 = 1$ and mean λ.

The **noncentral F-ratio distribution** NoncentralFRatioDistribution[n_1, n_2, *lambda*] is the distribution of the ratio of a noncentral chi-square random variable with noncentrality parameter λ and n_1 degrees of freedom to a central chi-square random variable with n_2 degrees of freedom.

PDF[*dist*, *x*]	probability density function at *x*
CDF[*dist*, *x*]	cumulative distribution function at *x*
Quantile[*dist*, *q*]	q^{th} quantile
Domain[*dist*]	range of values of the variable (support)
Mean[*dist*]	mean
Variance[*dist*]	variance
StandardDeviation[*dist*]	standard deviation
Skewness[*dist*]	coefficient of skewness
Kurtosis[*dist*]	coefficient of kurtosis
KurtosisExcess[*dist*]	kurtosis excess
CharacteristicFunction[*dist*, *t*]	characteristic function $\phi(t)$
ExpectedValue[*f*, *dist*]	expected value of pure function *f* with respect to the specified distribution
ExpectedValue[*f*, *dist*, *x*]	expected value of function *f* of *x* with respect to the specified distribution
Random[*dist*]	pseudorandom number with specified distribution
RandomArray[*dist*, *dims*]	pseudorandom array with dimensionality *dims*, and elements from the specified distribution

Functions of statistical distributions.

The **cumulative distribution function** (cdf) at *x* is given by the integral of the **probability density function** (pdf) up to *x*. The pdf can therefore be obtained by differentiating the cdf (perhaps in a generalized sense). In this package the distributions are represented in symbolic form. PDF[*dist*, *x*] evaluates the density at *x* if *x* is a numerical value, and otherwise leaves the function in symbolic form. Similarly, CDF[*dist*, *x*] gives the cumulative distribution. Domain[*dist*] gives the domain of PDF[*dist*, *x*] and CDF[*dist*, *x*].

The quantile Quantile[*dist*, *q*] is effectively the inverse of the cdf. It gives the value of *x* at which CDF[*dist*, *x*] reaches *q*. The median is given by Quantile[*dist*, 1/2]; quartiles, deciles and percentiles can also be expressed as quantiles. Quantiles are used in constructing confidence intervals for statistical parameters.

The mean Mean[*dist*] is the expectation of the random variable distributed according to *dist* and is usually denoted by μ. The mean is given by $\int x f(x)\, dx$, where $f(x)$ is the pdf of the distribution.

The variance `Variance[dist]` is given by $\int (x-\mu)^2 f(x)\, dx$. The square root of the variance is called the standard deviation, and is usually denoted by σ.

The `Skewness[dist]` and `Kurtosis[dist]` functions give shape statistics summarizing the asymmetry and the peakedness of a distribution, respectively. Skewness is given by $\dfrac{\int (x-\mu)^3 f(x)\, dx}{\sigma^3}$ and kurtosis is given by $\dfrac{\int (x-\mu)^4 f(x)\, dx}{\sigma^4}$.

The characteristic function `CharacteristicFunction[dist, t]` is given by $\phi(t) = \int f(x)\exp(itx)\, dx$. In the discrete case, $\phi(t) = \sum f(x)\exp(itx)$. Each distribution has a unique characteristic function, which is sometimes used instead of the pdf to define a distribution.

`Random[dist]` gives pseudorandom numbers from the specified distribution. It can be used with a seed like other built-in forms of `Random`, as described in the section on pseudorandom numbers in *The Mathematica Book*.

This loads the package.	`In[1]:= <<Statistics`ContinuousDistributions``
This gives a symbolic representation of the gamma distribution with 3 as the shape parameter and 1 as the scale parameter.	`In[2]:= gdist = GammaDistribution[3, 1]` `Out[2]= GammaDistribution[3, 1]`
Here is the cumulative distribution function evaluated at 10.	`In[3]:= CDF[gdist, 10]` `Out[3]= GammaRegularized[3, 0, 10]`
This is the cumulative distribution function. It is given in terms of the built-in function `GammaRegularized`.	`In[4]:= cdfunction = CDF[gdist, x]` `Out[4]= GammaRegularized[3, 0, x]`
Here is a plot of the cumulative distribution function.	`In[5]:= Plot[cdfunction, {x, 0, 10}]`

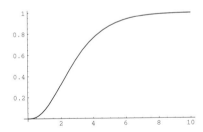

This is a pseudorandom array with elements distributed according to the gamma distribution.	`In[6]:= RandomArray[gdist, 5]` `Out[6]= {3.1281, 2.43083, 1.99986, 5.31523, 5.20405}`

■ Statistics`DataManipulation`

The usual form of input for most statistical functions is a list of data. If the data points are read in from a file using ReadList, it is often necessary to change the format or content of the output to create the required list. The functions described below are an extension of the large number of built-in list manipulation functions found in *The Mathematica Book*.

Column[*data*, *n*]	give the nth column of *data*
Column[*data*, {n_1, n_2, ... }]	give a list of the columns n_i
ColumnTake[*data*, *spec*]	take columns specified by *spec*
ColumnDrop[*data*, *spec*]	drop columns specified by *spec*
ColumnJoin[*data*$_1$, *data*$_2$, ...]	join elements in corresponding columns in *data*$_i$
RowJoin[*data*$_1$, *data*$_2$, ...]	join elements in corresponding rows in *data*$_i$
DropNonNumeric[*list*]	drop nonnumeric elements in *list*
DropNonNumeric[*data*]	drop rows with nonnumeric elements in the matrix *data*
DropNonNumericColumn[*data*]	drop columns with nonnumeric elements in *data*

Data manipulation functions.

This loads the package.

In[1]:= **<<Statistics`DataManipulation`**

Each data point is paired with a letter. There is also a missing value noted by i.

In[2]:= **data = {{a, 3}, {b, 6}, {c, 4}, {d, i}, {e, 5}, {f, 4}}**

Out[2]= {{a, 3}, {b, 6}, {c, 4}, {d, i}, {e, 5}, {f, 4}}

The second column of the data is extracted.

In[3]:= **col2 = Column[data, 2]**

Out[3]= {3, 6, 4, i, 5, 4}

Here is the data with all the nonnumeric elements dropped. Most of the available statistical functions can now use newdata.

In[4]:= **newdata = DropNonNumeric[col2]**

Out[4]= {3, 6, 4, 5, 4}

It is frequently useful to define requirements for extracting or dropping particular elements from a list. BooleanSelect and TakeWhile augment the built-in Select by providing alternative ways to apply criteria for selection.

`BooleanSelect[`*list*`, `*sel*`]`	keep elements in *list* for which the corresponding element in *sel* is `True`
`TakeWhile[`*list*`, `*pred*`]`	take elements from beginning of *list* while *pred* is `True`
`LengthWhile[`*list*`, `*pred*`]`	give the number of contiguous elements for which *pred* is `True`, starting from the beginning of *list*

Functions to extract or describe data.

If you want to extract only the first sequence of elements for which a predicate is `True`, you can use `TakeWhile`.

```
In[5]:= TakeWhile[col2, NumberQ]
Out[5]= {3, 6, 4}
```

Here is the length of the sequence.

```
In[6]:= LengthWhile[col2, NumberQ]
Out[6]= 3
```

`Frequencies[`*list*`]`	give the distinct elements in *list* paired with their frequencies
`QuantileForm[`*list*`]`	give the sorted elements in *list* paired with their quantile positions
`CumulativeSums[`*list*`]`	give the cumulative sums of *list*

Functions that summarize data.

Once you have your data in the correct list format, you can use `Frequencies` to observe the distribution of the data. The output of this function, as well as that of `QuantileForm`, is a list in the correct format for use in various plotting functions. This provides a simple way to observe your sample.

This gives a list of the elements of `newdata` along with their frequency of occurrence.

```
In[7]:= freq = Frequencies[newdata]
Out[7]= {{1, 3}, {2, 4}, {1, 5}, {1, 6}}
```

This loads another package, which contains assorted graphics functions.

```
In[8]:= <<Graphics`Graphics`
```

Here is a histogram of the data.   *In[9]:=* **BarChart[freq]**

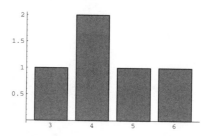

If your sample size is fairly large, it may be difficult to clearly summarize your data using Frequencies. In this case it is better to count the frequency of data points contained in a collection of intervals. BinCounts and RangeCounts do this for the cases of constant and variable length intervals, respectively. You can also use CategoryCounts to count frequencies of particular types of data.

For each of the three count functions, there is also a corresponding list function that gives the elements themselves that fall in the specified intervals or match specified types of data.

`BinCounts[{$x_1$, $x_2$, ... }, {$xmin$, $xmax$, $dx$}]`
> list the number of elements in the data x_1, x_2, ... that lie in bins from $xmin$ to $xmax$ in steps of dx

`RangeCounts[{$x_1$, $x_2$, ... }, {$c_1$, $c_2$, ... }]`
> list the number of elements in the data x_1, x_2, ... that lie between successive cutoffs c_i

`CategoryCounts[{$x_1$, $x_2$, ... }, {$e_1$, $e_2$, ... }]`
> list the number of elements in the data x_1, x_2, ... that match each of the e_i

`CategoryCounts[{$x_1$, $x_2$, ... }, {{$e_{11}$, $e_{12}$, ... }, {$e_{21}$, $e_{22}$, ... }, ... }]`
> list the number of elements that match any of the elements in each list {e_{i1}, e_{i2}, ... }

`BinLists[{$x_1$, $x_2$, ... }, {$xmin$, $xmax$, $dx$}]`
> list the elements that lie in bins from $xmin$ to $xmax$ in steps of dx

`RangeLists[{$x_1$, $x_2$, ... }, {$c_1$, $c_2$, ... }]`
> list the elements that lie between successive cutoffs c_i

`CategoryLists[{$x_1$, $x_2$, ... }, {$e_1$, $e_2$, ... }]`
> list the elements that match each of the e_i

`CategoryLists[{$x_1$, $x_2$, ... }, {{$e_{11}$, $e_{12}$, ... }, {$e_{21}$, $e_{22}$, ... }, ... }]`
> list the elements that match any of the elements in each list {e_{i1}, e_{i2}, ... }

Functions that categorize data.

This gives a list of randomly generated values of the sine function.

```
In[10]:= sindata = N[Table[Sin[Pi Random[]],{100}]];
```

These are the frequencies of data for intervals between 0 and 1 of length 0.2.

```
In[11]:= freq = BinCounts[sindata, {0, 1, 0.2}]

Out[11]= {8, 14, 23, 14, 41}
```

This is a list of the midpoints of the five intervals.

```
In[12]:= midpoints = {0.1, 0.3, 0.5, 0.7, 0.9}

Out[12]= {0.1, 0.3, 0.5, 0.7, 0.9}
```

This is the histogram for the data set using a function from the Graphics`Graphics` package that was previously loaded.

In[13]:= **BarChart[Transpose[{freq, midpoints}]]**

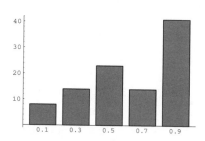

The count and list functions can be used to categorize bivariate and general p-variate data, by an obvious extension of the syntax. A two-dimensional array is generated for bivariate data and a p-dimensional array is generated for p-variate data. The following table describes the syntax for bivariate data for the count functions, but the same syntax applies to the list functions.

BinCounts[{{x_1, y_1}, {x_2, y_2}, ... }, {$xmin$, $xmax$, dx}, {$ymin$, $ymax$, dy}]
list the number of elements in the bivariate data that lie in the two-dimensional bins specified by steps in the x and y dimensions

RangeCounts[{{x_1, y_1}, {x_2, y_2}, ... }, {xc_1, xc_2, ... }, {yc_1, yc_2, ... }]
list the number of elements in the bivariate data that lie between successive cutoffs in the x and y dimensions

CategoryCounts[{{x_1, y_1}, {x_2, y_2}, ... }, {xe_1, xe_2, ... }, {ye_1, ye_2, ... }]
list the number of elements in the bivariate data that match {xe_i, ye_j}, $i = 1, 2, ..., j = 1, 2, ...$

CategoryCounts[{{x_1, y_1}, {x_2, y_2}, ... }, {{xe_{11}, xe_{12}, ... }, {xe_{21}, xe_{22}, ... }, ... }, {{ye_{11}, ye_{12}, ... }, {ye_{21}, ye_{22}, ... }, ... }]
list the number of elements in the bivariate data that match {xe_i, ye_j}, where xe_i is any member of {xe_{i1}, xe_{i2}, ... } and ye_j is any member of {ye_{j1}, ye_{j2}, ... }

Categorizing bivariate data.

+■ Statistics`DataSmoothing`

A series of raw data $\{x_1, x_2, \ldots, x_n\}$ is sometimes transformed to a new series of data before it is analyzed. The purpose of this transformation is to smooth out local fluctuations in the raw data, so the transformation is called data smoothing or a smoother. One common type of smoother employs a linear transformation and is called a linear filter. A linear filter with weights $\{c_0, c_1, \ldots, c_{r-1}\}$ transforms the given data to weighted averages $\sum_{j=0}^{r-1} c_j x_{t-j}$ for $t = r, r+1, \ldots, n$. Notice that the new data set has length $n - r + 1$. If $\sum_{j=0}^{r-1} c_j = 1$ the linear filter is also called an r-term moving average. If all the weights are equal and they sum to unity, the linear filter is called a simple moving average.

If the median of r data points is substituted in place of the average, we obtain a moving median smoother of span r. Repeated application of a moving median smoother can quickly lead to convergence for odd r. Since the values at the ends of the data series are lost with each application of the smoother, we maintain the length of the series by adding on the end values from the original data at all the intermediate steps of repeated moving median smoothing.

Exponential smoothing corresponds to a weighted average with exponentially decreasing weights. Let y_t be the smoothed value at time t, then y_{t+1} can be obtained efficiently by using $y_{t+1} = y_t + a(x_{t+1} - y_t)$ where a is the smoothing constant ($0 < a < 1$). An initial value y_0 is needed to start the iteration and it is commonly chosen to be x_1. For multivariate data the smoothing constant can be a matrix.

`MovingAverage[`*data*`, r]`	smooth *data* using a simple r-term moving average
`MovingMedian[`*data*`, r]`	smooth *data* using a moving median of span r
`MovingMedian[`*data*`, r, RepeatedSmoothing -> True]`	smooth *data* by repeatedly applying a moving median of span r
`LinearFilter[`*data*`, {c`$_0$`, c`$_1$`, ... , c`$_{r-1}$`}]`	pass the data $x_1, x_2, \ldots, x_n$ through the linear filter and give $\sum_{j=0}^{r-1} c_j x_{t-j}$ for $t = r, r+1, \ldots, n$
`ExponentialSmoothing[`*data*`, a]`	smooth *data* using an exponentially weighted average with a smoothing constant a and a starting value set to the first entry in *data*
`ExponentialSmoothing[`*data*`, a, y`$_0$`]`	smooth *data* using an exponentially weighted average with a smoothing constant a and a starting value y_0

Data smoothing functions.

The functions in this package work for both univariate and multivariate data. Data should be entered as a list in the univariate case, and a list of length-m lists in the m-variate case.

This loads the package.

```
In[1]:= <<Statistics`DataSmoothing`
```

Data must be entered as a list.

```
In[2]:= data1 = {7.,4.,5.,3.,8.,5.,2.,3.,6.,8.};
```

Here is a simple 2-term moving average.

```
In[3]:= MovingAverage[data1, 2]
Out[3]= {5.5, 4.5, 4., 5.5, 6.5, 3.5, 2.5, 4.5, 7.}
```

In the case of multivariate data, each entry in a data list is itself a list.

```
In[4]:= data2 = {{a,b}, {c,d}, {e,f}, {g,h}};
```

This gives a simple 3-term moving average of the two-dimensional data. The moving average is done for each dimension (or column) of the data separately.

```
In[5]:= MovingAverage[data2, 3]
```

$$Out[5]= \left\{\left\{\frac{1}{3}(a+c+e), \frac{1}{3}(b+d+f)\right\}, \left\{\frac{1}{3}(c+e+g), \frac{1}{3}(d+f+h)\right\}\right\}$$

A moving median is an example of nonlinear smoothing. It is often used to preserve edges while eliminating noisy spikes in the data. This smooths the data using a moving median of span 3.

```
In[6]:= MovingMedian[data1, 3]
Out[6]= {5., 4., 5., 5., 5., 3., 3., 6.}
```

Here smoothing is repeated until the result no longer changes. Only odd-numbered spans are allowed in repeated smoothing to ensure convergence.

```
In[7]:= MovingMedian[data1, 3, RepeatedSmoothing->True]
Out[7]= {5., 5., 5., 5., 5., 3., 3., 6.}
```

Here is an example of smoothing multivariate data by a moving median. The moving median is done for each dimension (or column) of the data separately.

```
In[8]:= MovingMedian[{{3,4},{9,2},{1,5},{2,6},{2,3}}, 4]
```

$$Out[8]= \left\{\left\{\frac{5}{2}, \frac{9}{2}\right\}, \{2, 4\}\right\}$$

A simple moving average is a special case of a linear filter where all the weights are equal and their sum is unity.

```
In[9]:= LinearFilter[data1, {1/2, 1/2}]
Out[9]= {5.5, 4.5, 4., 5.5, 6.5, 3.5, 2.5, 4.5, 7.}
```

This linear filter has weights $c_0 = 1, c_1 = 2, c_2 = 3$ and gives $x_t + 2x_{t-1} + 3x_{t-2}$. Notice the order in which the weights are entered.

```
In[10]:= LinearFilter[data1, {1, 2, 3}]
Out[10]= {34., 25., 29., 30., 36., 22., 18., 29.}
```

For multivariate data you can include matrix weights for the linear filter. Here the weights are $c_0 = \{\{1, 0.5\}, \{0.5, 1\}\}$, and $c_1 = \{\{1, 0\}, \{0, 1\}\}$.

```
In[11]:= LinearFilter[data2, {{{1,0.5},{0.5,1}},{{1,0},{0,1}}}]
Out[11]= {{a+c+0.5d, b+0.5c+d}, {c+e+0.5f, d+0.5e+f},
          {e+g+0.5h, f+0.5g+h}}
```

Here exponential smoothing is done with the smoothing constant 0.8 and starting value 0.5.

```
In[12]:= ExponentialSmoothing[data1, 0.8, 0.5]
Out[12]= {5.7, 4.34, 4.868, 3.3736, 7.07472, 5.41494, 2.68299,
          2.9366, 5.38732, 7.47746}
```

This time the starting value is taken to be the first entry in the data list, which is 7.

In[13]:= **ExponentialSmoothing[data1, 0.8]**

Out[13]= {7., 4.6, 4.92, 3.384, 7.0768, 5.41536, 2.68307, 2.93661, 5.38732, 7.47746}

~■ Statistics`DescriptiveStatistics`

Descriptive statistics refers to properties of distributions, such as location, dispersion, and shape. The functions in this package compute descriptive statistics of lists of data. You can calculate some of the standard descriptive statistics for various known distributions by using the `Statistics`ContinuousDistributions`` and `Statistics`DiscreteDistributions`` packages. This package also provides some commonly used data transformations.

Note that this package is automatically loaded when most other statistical packages are used. For example, all the functions described below are available for use with the package `Statistics`HypothesisTests``.

The statistics are calculated assuming that each value of data x_i has probability equal to $\frac{1}{n}$, where n is the number of elements in the data.

Mean[*data*]	average value $\frac{1}{n}\sum_i x_i$
Median[*data*]	median (central value)
Mode[*data*]	mode
GeometricMean[*data*]	geometric mean $\prod_i x_i^{\frac{1}{n}}$
HarmonicMean[*data*]	harmonic mean $n/\sum_i \frac{1}{x_i}$
RootMeanSquare[*data*]	root mean square $\sqrt{\frac{1}{n}\sum_i x_i^2}$
TrimmedMean[*data*, *f*]	mean of remaining entries, when a fraction f is removed from each end of the sorted list of data
TrimmedMean[*data*, {f_1, f_2}]	mean of remaining entries, when fractions f_1 and f_2 are dropped from each end of the sorted data
Quantile[*data*, *q*]	q^{th} quantile
InterpolatedQuantile[*data*, *q*]	q^{th} quantile of the distribution inferred by linear interpolation of the entries in the list of data
Quartiles[*data*]	list of quartiles
LocationReport[*data*]	list of location statistics including Mean, HarmonicMean, and Median

Location statistics.

Location statistics describe where the data are located. The most common functions include measures of central tendency like the mean, median, and mode. Quantile[*data*, *q*] gives the location before which (100*q*) percent of the data lie. In other words, Quantile gives a value z such that the probability that ($x_i < z$) is less than or equal to q and the probability that ($x_i \leq z$) is greater than or equal to q. The quantile values at $q = 0.25$, 0.5 and 0.75 are called the quartiles, and you can obtain them using Quartiles.

This loads the package.	In[1]:= **<<Statistics`DescriptiveStatistics`**
Here is a data set.	In[2]:= **data = {6.5, 3.8, 6.6, 5.7, 6.0, 6.4, 5.3}**
	Out[2]= {6.5, 3.8, 6.6, 5.7, 6., 6.4, 5.3}
This gives some general location information about the data.	In[3]:= **LocationReport[data]**
	Out[3]= {Mean → 5.75714, HarmonicMean → 5.57523, Median → 6.}
You can use the replacement operator /. to extract a particular statistic from the report.	In[4]:= **m = Mean /. %**
	Out[4]= 5.75714
This is the mean when the smallest entry in the list is excluded. TrimmedMean allows you to describe the data with removed outliers.	In[5]:= **TrimmedMean[data, {1/7, 0}]**
	Out[5]= 6.08333

SampleRange[*data*]	range
Variance[*data*]	unbiased estimate of variance, $\frac{1}{n-1}\sum_i(x_i-\overline{x})^2$
VarianceMLE[*data*]	maximum likelihood estimate of variance, $\frac{1}{n}\sum_i(x_i-\overline{x})^2$
VarianceOfSampleMean[*data*]	unbiased estimate of variance of sample mean, $\frac{1}{n}$Variance[*data*]
StandardDeviation[*data*]	unbiased estimate of standard deviation
StandardDeviationMLE[*data*]	maximum likelihood estimate of standard deviation
StandardErrorOfSampleMean[*data*]	unbiased estimate of standard error (standard deviation) of sample mean
CoefficientOfVariation[*data*]	coefficient of variation (ratio of standard deviation to mean)
MeanDeviation[*data*]	mean absolute deviation, $\frac{1}{n}\sum_i|x_i-\overline{x}|$
MedianDeviation[*data*]	median absolute deviation, median of $|x_i-median|$ values
InterquartileRange[*data*]	interquartile range
QuartileDeviation[*data*]	quartile deviation
DispersionReport[*data*]	list of dispersion statistics including Variance, StandardDeviation, SampleRange, MeanDeviation, MedianDeviation, and QuartileDeviation

Dispersion statistics.

Dispersion statistics summarize the scatter or spread of the data. Most of these functions describe deviation from a particular location. For instance, variance is a measure of deviation from the mean, and standard deviation is just the square root of the variance.

The range is a value describing the total spread of the data. SampleRange gives the difference between the largest and smallest value in data, while InterquartileRange gives the difference between the 0.75th and the 0.25th quartiles.

This gives an unbiased estimate for the variance of the data with $n-1$ as the divisor.

```
In[6]:= var1 = Variance[data]
Out[6]= 0.962857
```

Here is the maximum likelihood estimate with division by n.

```
In[7]:= var2 = VarianceMLE[data]
Out[7]= 0.825306
```

We can check the relationship between the two estimators.

```
In[8]:= var1 (Length[data] - 1) == var2 Length[data]
Out[8]= True
```

CentralMoment[*data*, *r*]	r^{th} central moment $\frac{1}{n}\sum_i(x_i - \overline{x})^r$
Skewness[*data*]	coefficient of skewness
PearsonSkewness1[*data*]	Pearson's first coefficient of skewness
PearsonSkewness2[*data*]	Pearson's second coefficient of skewness
QuartileSkewness[*data*]	quartile coefficient of skewness
Kurtosis[*data*]	kurtosis coefficient
KurtosisExcess[*data*]	kurtosis excess
ShapeReport[*data*]	list of shape statistics including Skewness, QuartileSkewness, and KurtosisExcess

Shape statistics.

You can get some information about the shape of a distribution using shape statistics. Skewness describes the amount of asymmetry. Kurtosis measures the concentration of data around the peak and in the tails versus the concentration in the flanks.

Skewness is calculated by dividing the third central moment by the cube of the standard deviation. Pearson's two coefficients provide two other well-known measures of skewness. PearsonSkewness1 and PearsonSkewness2 are found by multiplying three times the difference between the mean and either the mode or the median, respectively, and dividing this quantity by the standard deviation of the sample. Quartile skewness gives a measure of asymmetry within the first and third quartiles.

Kurtosis is calculated by dividing the fourth central moment by the square of the variance of the data. KurtosisExcess is shifted so that it is zero for the normal distribution, positive for distributions with a prominent peak and heavy tails, and negative for distributions with prominent flanks.

Here is the second central moment, which is the same as the maximum likelihood estimate of variance.

```
In[9]:= CentralMoment[data, 2]
Out[9]= 0.825306
```

A negative value for skewness indicates that the distribution underlying the data has a long left-sided tail.

```
In[10]:= Skewness[data]
Out[10]= -1.20108
```

+	ExpectedValue[*f*, *data*]	expected value of the pure function *f* with respect to the sample distribution of the data
+	ExpectedValue[*f*, *data*, *x*]	expected value of the function *f* of *x* with respect to the sample distribution of the data

Expected value.

Other location, dispersion, and shape statistics can be computed by taking the expected value of a function with respect to the sample distribution of the data.

This gives the average square root of the data.

In[11]:= **ExpectedValue[Sqrt[#]&, data]**

Out[11]= 2.39098

+	ZeroMean[*data*]	transform the data so that the mean of the result is zero
+	Standardize[*data*]	transform the data so that the mean is zero and the unbiased estimate of variance is unity
+	Standardize[*data*, MLE -> True]	transform the data so that the mean is zero and the maximum likelihood estimate of variance is unity

Data transformations.

Occasionally it is useful to apply transformations to the data using descriptive statistics. ZeroMean shifts the data to have zero mean and Standardize both shifts and scales the data to have unity variance. The default is to standardize using the unbiased estimate of variance; the maximum likelihood estimate is selected using the option MLE -> True.

The mean of the shifted data is approximately 0.

In[12]:= **Mean[ZeroMean[data]]**

Out[12]= 0.

After standardizing, the variance is approximately 1.

In[13]:= **Variance[Standardize[data]]**

Out[13]= 1.

■ Statistics`DiscreteDistributions`

This package gives you access to the most commonly used discrete statistical distributions. You can compute their densities, means, variances, and other related properties. The distributions themselves are represented in the symbolic form *name[param$_1$, param$_2$, ...]*. Functions such as `Mean`, which give properties of statistical distributions, take the symbolic representation of the distribution as an argument. The package `ContinuousDistributions` contains many continuous statistical distributions.

`BernoulliDistribution[`*p*`]`	Bernoulli distribution with mean p
`BinomialDistribution[`*n*`, `*p*`]`	binomial distribution for the number of successes that occur in n trials, where the probability of success in a trial is p
`DiscreteUniformDistribution[`*n*`]`	discrete uniform distribution with n states
`GeometricDistribution[`*p*`]`	geometric distribution for the number of trials before the first success, where the probability of success in a trial is p
`HypergeometricDistribution[`*n*`, `n_{succ}`, `n_{tot}`]`	hypergeometric distribution for the number of successes out of a sample of size n, from a population of size n_{tot} containing n_{succ} successes
`LogSeriesDistribution[`*theta*`]`	logarithmic series distribution with parameter θ
`NegativeBinomialDistribution[`*n*`, `*p*`]`	negative binomial distribution for the number of failures that occur before achieving n successes, where the probability of success in a trial is p
`PoissonDistribution[`*mu*`]`	Poisson distribution with mean μ

Statistical distributions from the package `DiscreteDistributions`.

Most of the common discrete statistical distributions can be understood by considering a sequence of trials, each with two possible outcomes, for example, success and failure.

The **Bernoulli distribution** `BernoulliDistribution[`*p*`]` is the probability distribution for a single trial in which success, corresponding to value 1, occurs with probability p, and failure, corresponding to value 0, occurs with probability $1 - p$.

The **binomial distribution** `BinomialDistribution[`*n*`, `*p*`]` is the distribution of the number of successes that occur in n independent trials, where the probability of success in each trial is p.

The **negative binomial distribution** `NegativeBinomialDistribution[n, p]` is the distribution of the number of failures that occur in a sequence of trials before n successes have occurred, where the probability of success in each trial is p.

The terms in the series expansion of $log(1-\theta)$ about $\theta = 0$ are proportional to the probabilities of a discrete random variable following the **logarithmic series distribution** `LogSeriesDistribution[theta]`. The distribution of the number of items of a product purchased by a buyer in a specified interval is sometimes modeled by this distribution.

The **geometric distribution** `GeometricDistribution[p]` is the distribution of the total number of trials before the first success occurs, where the probability of success in each trial is p.

The **hypergeometric distribution** `HypergeometricDistribution[n, `n_{succ}`, `n_{tot}`]` is used in place of the binomial distribution for experiments in which the n trials correspond to sampling without replacement from a population of size n_{tot} with n_{succ} potential successes.

The **discrete uniform distribution** `DiscreteUniformDistribution[n]` represents an experiment with n outcomes that occur with equal probabilities.

The **Poisson distribution** `PoissonDistribution[mu]` describes the number of points in a unit interval, where points are distributed with uniform density μ.

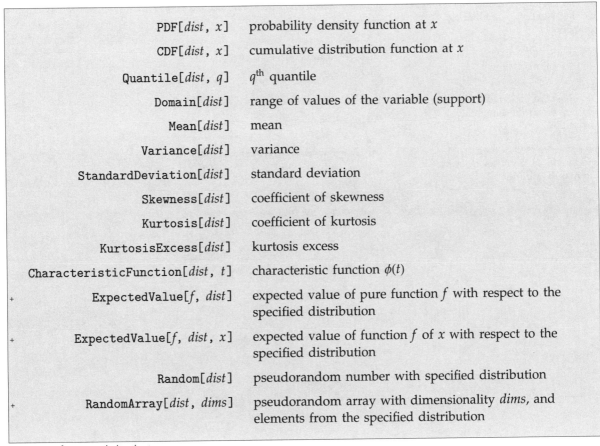

PDF[*dist*, *x*]	probability density function at *x*
CDF[*dist*, *x*]	cumulative distribution function at *x*
Quantile[*dist*, *q*]	*q*th quantile
Domain[*dist*]	range of values of the variable (support)
Mean[*dist*]	mean
Variance[*dist*]	variance
StandardDeviation[*dist*]	standard deviation
Skewness[*dist*]	coefficient of skewness
Kurtosis[*dist*]	coefficient of kurtosis
KurtosisExcess[*dist*]	kurtosis excess
CharacteristicFunction[*dist*, *t*]	characteristic function $\phi(t)$
ExpectedValue[*f*, *dist*]	expected value of pure function *f* with respect to the specified distribution
ExpectedValue[*f*, *dist*, *x*]	expected value of function *f* of *x* with respect to the specified distribution
Random[*dist*]	pseudorandom number with specified distribution
RandomArray[*dist*, *dims*]	pseudorandom array with dimensionality *dims*, and elements from the specified distribution

Functions of statistical distributions.

In this package distributions are represented in symbolic form. PDF[*dist*, *x*] evaluates the density at *x* if *x* is a numerical value, and otherwise leaves the function in symbolic form whenever possible. Similarly, CDF[*dist*, *x*] gives the cumulative distribution and Mean[*dist*] gives the mean of the specified distribution. For a more complete description of the various functions of a statistical distribution, see the description of their continuous analogues in the section concerning the package Statistics`ContinuousDistributions`.

This loads the package.	*In[1]:=* **<<Statistics`DiscreteDistributions`**
Here is a symbolic representation of the binomial distribution for 34 trials, each having probability 0.3 of success.	*In[2]:=* **bdist = BinomialDistribution[34, 0.3]**
	Out[2]= BinomialDistribution[34, 0.3]
This is the mean of the distribution.	*In[3]:=* **Mean[bdist]**
	Out[3]= 10.2

You can get the equation for the mean by using symbolic variables as arguments.

```
In[4]:= Mean[BinomialDistribution[n, p]]
Out[4]= n p
```

Here is the 50% quantile, which is equal to the median.

```
In[5]:= Quantile[bdist, 0.5]
Out[5]= 10
```

This gives the expected value of x^3 with respect to the binomial distribution.

```
In[6]:= ExpectedValue[x^3, bdist, x]
Out[6]= 1282.55
```

The elements of this matrix are pseudorandom numbers from the binomial distribution.

```
In[7]:= RandomArray[bdist, {2, 3}]
Out[7]= {{8, 10, 7}, {12, 9, 6}}
```

◾ Statistics`HypothesisTests`

A test of a statistical hypothesis is a test of assumption about the distribution of a variable. Given sample data, you test whether the population from which the sample came has a certain characteristic. You can use functions in this package to test hypotheses concerning the mean, the variance, the difference in two population means, or the ratio of their variances.

The data that is given as an argument in a test function is assumed to be normally distributed. As a consequence of the Central Limit Theorem, you can disregard this normality assumption in the case of tests for the mean when the sample size, n, is large and the data is unimodal. The test functions accept as arguments the list of univariate data, a hypothesized parameter and relevant options.

MeanTest[*data*, *mu*]	give the p-value for the test that the population mean is equal to μ based on the Student t distribution
MeanTest[*data*, *mu*, KnownVariance -> *var*]	give the p-value for the test that the population mean is equal to μ based on the normal distribution

Hypothesis tests for the mean.

Hypothesis tests for the mean are based on the normal distribution when the population variance is known, and the Student t distribution with $n - 1$ degrees of freedom when the variance has to be estimated. If you know the standard deviation instead of the variance, you can also specify KnownStandardDeviation -> *std*.

The output of a hypothesis test is a p-value, which is the probability of the sample estimate being as extreme as it is given that the hypothesized population parameter is true. A two-sided test can be requested using TwoSided -> True. For more detailed information about a test use FullReport -> True. This causes the parameter estimate and the test statistic to be included in the output. You can also specify a significance level using SignificanceLevel -> *siglev*, which yields a conclusion of the test, stating acceptance or rejection of the hypothesis.

option name	default value	
SignificanceLevel	None	significance level of the test
TwoSided	False	whether to perform a two-sided test
FullReport	False	whether to include the estimate, test statistic and distribution in output

Options for all hypothesis test functions.

This loads the package.

```
In[1]:= <<Statistics`HypothesisTests`
```

Here is a list of data sampled from a normal population whose variance is known to be 8.

```
In[2]:= data1 = {34, 37, 44, 31, 41, 42, 38, 45,
            42, 38};
```

This tests whether the population mean is equal to 34. It is very unlikely that data1 came from a normal population having variance 8 and a mean as low as 34.

```
In[3]:= MeanTest[data1, 34, KnownVariance -> 8]

Out[3]= OneSidedPValue → 3.05394 × 10⁻⁹
```

MeanDifferenceTest[$data_1$, $data_2$, $diff$]
    give the p-value for Welch's approximate *t*-test that the difference in population means is *diff*

MeanDifferenceTest[$data_1$, $data_2$, $diff$, EqualVariances -> True]
    give the p-value for the test that the difference in population means is *diff* based on the Student *t* distribution

MeanDifferenceTest[$data_1$, $data_2$, $diff$, KnownVariance -> {var_1, var_2}]
    give the p-value for the test that the difference in population means is *diff* based on the normal distribution

Hypothesis tests for mean and difference in means.

To test the similarity between two populations, you can test whether their means are equal, or equivalently, you can test whether the difference between their means is zero. If the variances of the populations are known and specified as a value of KnownVariance, the test is based on the normal distribution. Usually, however, the variances are unknown and the test uses quantiles from the Student *t* distribution to evaluate the hypothesis.

option name	default value	
EqualVariances	False	equal unknown population variances
KnownVariance	None	known population variance
KnownStandardDeviation	None	known population standard deviation

Additional options for tests concerning difference in means.

This is a second list of sample data whose population variance is also 8.

```
In[4]:= data2 = {39, 40, 34, 45, 44, 38, 42, 39,
            47, 41};
```

This tests whether the difference between the means of the two populations is 0.

```
In[5]:= MeanDifferenceTest[data1, data2, 0,
        KnownVariance -> {8, 8}]

Out[5]= OneSidedPValue → 0.0894794
```

This is the result of the same test but with a specified significance level and a request for a full report. The output now includes the estimator, test statistic, and the conclusion of the test. At this level of significance, it is not unlikely that data1 and data2 came from the same normal population having variance 8.

```
In[6]:= MeanDifferenceTest[data1, data2, 0,
        KnownVariance -> {8, 8},
        SignificanceLevel -> .05, FullReport -> True]

Out[6]= {FullReport →

           MeanDiff       TestStat       Distribution
           -1.7           -1.34397       NormalDistribution[] '
           OneSidedPValue → 0.0894794,

           Fail to reject null hypothesis at significance level → 0.05}
```

You can also test for variance and the ratio of two variances using `VarianceTest` and `VarianceRatioTest`. These use the chi-square and F-ratio distributions respectively. The same output options, `SignificanceLevel`, `TwoSided`, and `FullReport`, are available for these tests.

`VarianceTest[data, var, options]`	give the p-value for the test that the population variance is *var*
`VarianceRatioTest[data`$_1$`, data`$_2$`, ratio, options]`	give the p-value for the test that the ratio of population variances is *ratio*

Hypothesis tests for variance and ratio of two variances.

Here is another set of data.

```
In[7]:= data = {41.0, 42.4, 42.5, 40.6, 45.6, 34.4};
```

This is a test to see whether the variance of the population from which these data were sampled is 8.

```
In[8]:= VarianceTest[data, 8, TwoSided -> True,
        FullReport -> True]

Out[8]= {FullReport →

           Variance       TestStat       Distribution
           13.8097        8.63104        ChiSquareDistribution[5] '

           TwoSidedPValue → 0.249434}
```

If you have already calculated a test statistic in terms of the normal, chi-square, Student t, or F-ratio distribution, you can get its p-value using the appropriate p-value function. For example, `NormalPValue` computes a p-value for a test statistic using a normal distribution with mean zero and unit variance. A two-sided p-value is obtained by giving `TwoSided -> True`.

NormalPValue[*teststat*]	give the p-value for *teststat* in terms of the normal distribution with mean 0 and unit variance
StudentTPValue[*teststat, dof*]	give the p-value for *teststat* in terms of the Student *t* distribution with *dof* degrees of freedom
ChiSquarePValue[*teststat, dof*]	give the p-value for *teststat* in terms of the chi-square distribution with *dof* degrees of freedom
FRatioPValue[*teststat, numdof, dendof*]	give the p-value for *teststat* in terms of the *F*-ratio distribution with *numdof* numerator degrees of freedom and *dendof* denominator degrees of freedom

Functions providing p-values of test statistics.

This is the tail probability of the normal distribution with mean 0 and unit variance at point −1.96.

```
In[9]:=  NormalPValue[-1.96]
Out[9]=  OneSidedPValue → 0.0249979
```

A TwoSidedPValue gives the probability of the test statistic being at least as extreme as 1.96 at either tail of the distribution.

```
In[10]:=  NormalPValue[-1.96, TwoSided -> True]
Out[10]=  TwoSidedPValue → 0.0499958
```

Note that a p-value for a statistical distribution is not equivalent to the cumulative distribution function (CDF) for that distribution.

```
In[11]:=  Plot[CDF[ChiSquareDistribution[5], x],
          {x, 1, 10}, PlotRange->{0, 1}]
```

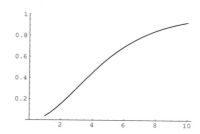

A one-sided p-value has a maximum value of 0.5 because it represents a one-sided tail probability. The maximum occurs at the median for the underlying statistical distribution.

In[12]:= `Plot[OneSidedPValue /. ChiSquarePValue[x, 5],`
`{x, 1, 10}, PlotRange->{0, 1}]`

A two-sided p-value is twice the one-sided p-value.

In[13]:= `Plot[TwoSidedPValue /. ChiSquarePValue[x, 5,`
`TwoSided -> True], {x, 1, 10}, PlotRange->{0, 1}]`

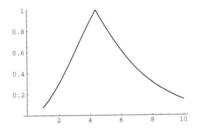

■ Statistics`LinearRegression`

The built-in function `Fit` finds a least-squares fit to a list of data as a linear combination of the specified basis functions. The functions `Regress` and `DesignedRegress` provided in this package augment `Fit` by giving a list of commonly required diagnostics such as the coefficient of determination `RSquared`, the analysis of variance table `ANOVATable`, and the mean squared error `EstimatedVariance`. The output of regression functions can be controlled so that only needed information is produced.

The basis functions f_j specify the predictors as functions of the independent variables. The resulting model for the response variable is $y_i = \beta_1 f_{1i} + \beta_2 f_{2i} + \ldots + \beta_p f_{pi} + e_i$, where y_i is the ith response, f_{ji} is the jth basis function evaluated at the ith observation, and e_i is the ith statistical error.

Estimates of the coefficients $\beta_1, \ldots, \beta_p$ are calculated to minimize $\sum_i e_i^2$, the error or residual sum of squares. For example, simple linear regression is accomplished by defining the basis functions as $f_1 = 1$ and $f_2 = x$, in which case β_1 and β_2 are found to minimize $\sum_i [y_i - (\beta_1 + \beta_2 x_i)]^2$.

`Regress[data, {1, x, x^2}, x]`	fit a list of data points *data* to a quadratic model
`Regress[data,{1, x_1, x_2, x_1 x_2}, {x_1, x_2}]`	fit *data* to a model that includes interaction between independent variables x_1 and x_2
`Regress[data, {f_1, f_2, ... }, vars]`	fit *data* to a model composed of a linear combination of the functions f_i of the variables *vars*

Using `Regress`.

The arguments of `Regress` are of the same form as those of `Fit`. The data can be a list of vectors, each vector consisting of the observed values of the independent variables and the associated response. The basis functions f_j must be functions of the symbols given as variables. These symbols correspond to the independent variables represented in the data.

The data can also be a vector of data points. In this case, `Regress` assumes that this vector represents the values of a response variable with the independent variable having values 1, 2, ...

$\{y_1, y_2, \ldots \}$	data points specified by a list of response values, where a single independent variable is assumed to take the values 1, 2, ...
$\{\{x_{11}, x_{12}, \ldots, y_1\}, \{x_{21}, x_{22}, \ldots, y_2\}, \ldots \}$	data points specified by a matrix, where x_{ik} is the value of the ith case of the kth independent variable, and y_i is the ith response

Ways of specifying data in Regress.

This loads the package.

In[1]:= **<<Statistics`LinearRegression`**

In this data, the first element in each pair gives the value of the independent variable, while the second gives the observed response.

In[2]:= **data = {{0.055, 90}, {0.091, 97}, {0.138, 107},
{0.167, 124}, {0.182, 142}, {0.211, 150},
{0.232, 172}, {0.248, 189}, {0.284, 209},
{0.351, 253}};**

This is a plot of the data.

In[3]:= **dplot = ListPlot[data]**

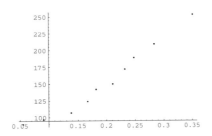

This is the regression output for fitting the model $y_i = \beta_0 + \beta_1 x_i^2 + e_i$. Chop replaces the p-values below 10^{-6} with 0.

In[4]:= **(regress = Regress[data, {1, x^2}, x];
Chop[regress, 10^(-6)])**

Out[4]= {ParameterTable →

	Estimate	SE	TStat	PValue
1	88.194	4.21167	20.9404	0
x^2	1430.68	73.6951	19.4136	0

RSquared → 0.979215, AdjustedRSquared → 0.976616,
EstimatedVariance → 64.9129, ANOVATable →

	DF	SumOfSq	MeanSq	FRatio	PValue
Model	1	24464.8	24464.8	376.887	0
Error	8	519.303	64.9129		
Total	9	24984.1			

}

You can use Fit if you only want the fit function.

In[5]:= **func = Fit[data, {1, x^2}, x]**

Out[5]= $88.194 + 1430.68 \, x^2$

option name	default value	
IncludeConstant	True	constant automatically included in model
Weights	Automatic	list of weights for each data point or pure function
+ RegressionReport	SummaryReport	objects to be included in output
BasisNames	Automatic	names of basis elements for table headings

Options for Regress.

Two of the options of Regress influence the method of calculation. IncludeConstant has a default setting True, which causes a constant term to be added to the model even if it is not specified in the basis functions. To fit a model without this constant term, specify IncludeConstant -> False and do not include a constant in the basis functions.

The Weights option allows you to implement weighted least squares by specifying a list of weights, one for each data point; the default Weights -> Automatic implies a weight of unity for each data point. When Weights -> $\{w_1, \ldots, w_n\}$, the parameter estimates are chosen to minimize the weighted sum of squared residuals $\sum_{i=1}^{n} w_i e_i^2$.

Weights can also specify a pure function of the response. For example, to choose parameter estimates to minimize $\sum_{i=1}^{n} \sqrt{y_i} e_i^2$, set Weights -> (Sqrt[#] &).

The options RegressionReport and BasisNames affect the form and content of the output. If RegressionReport is not specified, Regress automatically gives a list including values for ParameterTable, RSquared, AdjustedRSquared, EstimatedVariance, and ANOVATable. This set of objects comprises the default SummaryReport. The option RegressionReport can be used to specify a single object or a list of objects so that more (or less) than the default set of results is included in the output. RegressionReportValues[Regress] gives the objects that may be included in the RegressionReport list for the Regress function.

With the option BasisNames, you can label the headings of predictors in tables such as Parameter·. Table and ParameterCITable.

The regression functions will also accept any option that can be specified for SingularValues or StudentTCI. In particular, the numerical tolerance for the internal singular value decomposition is specified using Tolerance, and the confidence level for hypothesis testing and confidence intervals is specified using ConfidenceLevel.

	BestFit	best fit function
~	BestFitParameters	best fit parameters
	ANOVATable	analysis of variance table
	EstimatedVariance	estimated error variance
	ParameterTable	table of parameter information including standard errors and test statistics
~	ParameterCITable	table of confidence intervals for the fit parameters
+	ParameterConfidenceRegion	ellipsoidal joint confidence region for the fit parameters
+	ParameterConfidenceRegion[{f_{i1}, f_{i2}, ... }]	ellipsoidal conditional joint confidence region for the fit parameters corresponding to the basis functions {f_{i1}, f_{i2}, ... }
	FitResiduals	differences between the observed responses and the predicted responses
	PredictedResponse	fitted values obtained by evaluating the best fit function at the observed values of the independent variables
+	SinglePredictionCITable	table of confidence intervals for predicting a single observation of the response variable
+	MeanPredictionCITable	table of confidence intervals for predicting the expected value of the response variable
	RSquared	coefficient of determination
	AdjustedRSquared	adjusted coefficient of determination
+	CoefficientOfVariation	coefficient of variation
+	CovarianceMatrix	covariance matrix of the fit parameters
+	CorrelationMatrix	correlation matrix of the fit parameters

Some option settings for `RegressionReport` or objects that may be included in a list specified by `RegressionReport`.

`ANOVATable`, a table for analysis of variance, provides a comparison of the given model to a smaller one including only a constant term. If `IncludeConstant -> False` is specified, then the smaller model is reduced to the data. The table includes the degrees of freedom, the sum of squares and the mean squares due to the model (in the row labeled `Model`) and due to the residuals (in the row labeled `Error`). The residual mean square is also available in `EstimatedVariance`, and is calculated by dividing the residual sum of squares by its degrees of freedom. The F-test compares the two models using the ratio of their mean squares. If the value of F is large, the null hypothesis supporting the smaller model is rejected.

To evaluate the importance of each basis function, you can get information about the parameter estimates from the parameter table obtained by setting `RegressionReport` to `ParameterTable`, or by including `ParameterTable` in the list specified by `RegressionReport`. This table includes the estimates, their standard errors, and t-statistics for testing whether each parameter is zero. The p-values are calculated by comparing the obtained statistic to the t distribution with $n - p$ degrees of freedom, where n is the sample size and p is the number of predictors. Confidence intervals for the parameter estimates, also based on the t distribution, can be found by specifying `ParameterCITable`. `ParameterConfidenceRegion` specifies the ellipsoidal joint confidence region of all fit parameters. `ParameterConfidenceRegion[{`f_{i1}`, `f_{i2}`, ... }]` specifies the joint conditional confidence region of the fit parameters associated with basis functions $\{f_{i1}, f_{i2}, \dots \}$, a subset of the complete set of basis functions.

The square of the multiple correlation coefficient is called the coefficient of determination R^2, and is given by the ratio of the model sum of squares to the total sum of squares. It is a summary statistic that describes the relationship between the predictors and the response variable. `AdjustedRSquared` is defined as $\overline{R}^2 = 1 - (\frac{n-1}{n-p})(1 - R^2)$, and gives an adjusted value that you can use to compare subsequent subsets of models. The coefficient of variation is given by the ratio of the residual root mean square to the mean of the response variable. If the response is strictly positive, this is sometimes used to measure the relative magnitude of error variation.

Each row in `MeanPredictionCITable` gives the confidence interval for the mean response at each of the values of the independent variables. Each row in `SinglePredictionCITable` gives the confidence interval for a single observed response at each of the values of the independent variables. `MeanPredictionCITable` gives a region likely to contain the regression curve, while `SinglePredictionCITable` gives a region likely to contain all possible observations.

In this example, only the residuals, the confidence interval table for the predicted response of single observations, and the parameter joint confidence region are produced.

```
In[6]:= regress = Regress[data, {1, x^2}, x,
            RegressionReport ->
                {FitResiduals, SinglePredictionCITable,
                ParameterConfidenceRegion}]
Out[6]:=
    {FitResiduals → {-2.52183, -3.04151, -8.43996, -4.09436,
        6.41601, -1.88949, 6.80086, 12.8132, 5.41275, -11.4557},
      SinglePredictionCITable →
```

Observed	Predicted	SE	CI
90.	92.5218	9.01141	{71.7415, 113.302}
97.	100.042	8.88427	{79.5543, 120.529}
107.	115.44	8.67222	{95.4418, 135.438}
124.	128.094	8.54926	{108.38, 147.809}
142.	135.584	8.49923	{115.985, 155.183},
150.	151.889	8.45041	{132.403, 171.376}
172.	165.199	8.4723	{145.662, 184.736}
189.	176.187	8.53194	{156.512, 195.861}
209.	203.587	8.83821	{183.206, 223.968}
253.	264.456	10.2072	{240.918, 287.994}

```
      ParameterConfidenceRegion →
        Ellipsoid[{88.194, 1430.68}, {220.303, 7.6006},
          {{0.045514, -0.998964}, {-0.998964, -0.045514}}]]}
```

This is a list of the residuals extracted from the output.

```
In[7]:= errors = FitResiduals /. regress
Out[7]= {-2.52183, -3.04151, -8.43996, -4.09436, 6.41601, -1.88949,
          6.80086, 12.8132, 5.41275, -11.4557}
```

The observed response, the predicted response, the standard errors of the predicted response, and the confidence intervals may also be extracted.

```
In[8]:= {observed, predicted, se, ci} =
            Transpose[(SinglePredictionCITable /. regress)[[1]]];
```

You can now plot the predicted responses against the residuals for diagnostic purposes.

```
In[9]:= ListPlot[Transpose[{predicted, errors}]]
```

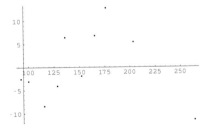

Here the predicted responses and lower and upper confidence limits are paired with the corresponding *x* values.

```
In[10]:= (xval = Map[First, data];
          predicted = Transpose[{xval, predicted}];
          lowerCI = Transpose[{xval, Map[First, ci]}];
          upperCI = Transpose[{xval, Map[Last, ci]}]);
```

This loads the function MultipleListPlot.

```
In[11]:= <<Graphics`MultipleListPlot`
```

This displays the raw data, fitted curve, and the 95% confidence intervals for the predicted responses of single observations.

```
In[12]:= MultipleListPlot[
            data, predicted, lowerCI, upperCI,
            SymbolShape -> {PlotSymbol[Diamond], None, None,
                None},
            PlotJoined -> {False, True, True, True},
            PlotStyle -> {Automatic, Automatic,
                Dashing[{.05, .05}], Dashing[{.05, .05}]}]
        ]
```

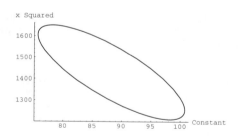

The functions Show and Graphics may be used to display an Ellipsoid object. This is the joint 95% confidence region of the regression parameters.

```
In[13]:= Show[Graphics[ParameterConfidenceRegion /. regress],
            Axes -> True, AxesLabel -> {"Constant","x Squared"}]
```

This package provides numerous diagnostics for evaluating the data and the fit. The HatDiagonal gives the leverage of each point, measuring whether each observation of the independent variables is unusual. CookD and PredictedResponseDelta are influence diagnostics, simultaneously measuring whether the independent variables and the response variable are unusual. Unfortunately, these diagnostics are primarily useful in detecting single outliers. In particular, the diagnostics may indicate a single outlier, but deleting that observation and recomputing the diagnostics may indicate others. All of these diagnostics are subject to this masking effect. They are described in greater detail in *Regression Diagnostics: Identifying Influential Data and Sources of Collinearity*, by D. A. Belsley, E. Kuh, and R. E.

Welsch (John Wiley & Sons, 1980), and "Detection of influential observations in linear regression", by R. D. Cook, *Technometrics*, 19, 1977.

+	HatDiagonal	diagonal of the hat matrix $X(X^T X)^{-1} X^T$, where X is the n by p (weighted) design matrix
+	JackknifedVariance	$\{v_1, \dots, v_n\}$, where v_i is the estimated error variance computed using the data with the ith case deleted
+	StandardizedResiduals	fit residuals scaled by their standard errors, computed using the estimated error variance
+	StudentizedResiduals	fit residuals scaled by their standard errors, computed using the jackknifed estimated error variances
+	CookD	$\{d_1, \dots, d_n\}$, where d_i is Cook's squared distance diagnostic for evaluating whether the ith case is an outlier
+	PredictedResponseDelta	$\{d_1, \dots, d_n\}$, where d_i is Kuh and Welsch's DFFITS diagnostic giving the standardized signed difference in the ith predicted response, between using all the data and the data with the ith case deleted
+	BestFitParametersDelta	$\{\{d_{11}, \dots, d_{1p}\}, \dots, \{d_{n1}, \dots, d_{np}\}\}$, where d_{ij} is Kuh and Welsch's DFBETAS diagnostic giving the standardized signed difference in the jth parameter estimate, between using all the data and the data with the ith case deleted
+	CovarianceMatrixDetRatio	$\{r_1, \dots, r_n\}$, where r_i is Kuh and Welsch's COVRATIO diagnostic giving the ratio of the determinant of the parameter covariance matrix computed using the data with the ith case deleted, to the determinant of the parameter covariance matrix computed using the original data

Diagnostics for detecting outliers.

Some diagnostics indicate the degree to which individual basis functions contribute to the fit, or whether the basis functions are involved in a collinear relationship. The sum of the elements in the SequentialSumOfSquares vector gives the model sum of squares listed in the ANOVATable. Each element corresponds to the increment in the model sum of squares obtained by sequentially adding each (nonconstant) basis function to the model. Each element in the PartialSumOfSquares vector gives the increase in the model sum of squares due to adding the corresponding (nonconstant) basis function to a model consisting of all other basis functions. SequentialSumOfSquares is useful in determining the degree of a univariate polynomial model, while PartialSumOfSquares is useful in trimming a large set of predictors. `VarianceInflation` or `EigenstructureTable` may also be used for predictor set trimming.

+	PartialSumOfSquares	a list giving the increase in the model sum of squares due to adding each nonconstant basis function to the model consisting of the remaining basis functions
+	SequentialSumOfSquares	a list giving a partitioning of the model sum of squares, one element for each nonconstant basis function added sequentially to the model
+	VarianceInflation	$\{v_1, \ldots, v_p\}$, where v_j is the variance inflation factor associated with the jth parameter
+	EigenstructureTable	table giving the eigenstructure of the correlation matrix of the nonconstant basis functions

Diagnostics for evaluating basis functions and detecting collinearity.

The Durbin-Watson d statistic is used for testing the existence of a first-order autoregressive process. A value close to 2 indicates uncorrelated errors, an underlying assumption of the regression model.

+	DurbinWatsonD	Durbin-Watson d statistic

Correlated errors diagnostic.

Other statistics not mentioned here can be computed with the help of the catcher matrix. This matrix catches all the information the predictors have about the parameter vector. This matrix can be exported from `Regress` by specifying `CatcherMatrix` with the `RegressionReport` option.

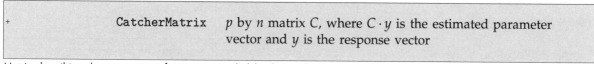

+	CatcherMatrix	p by n matrix C, where $C \cdot y$ is the estimated parameter vector and y is the response vector

Matrix describing the parameter information provided by the predictors.

Frequently, linear regression is applied to an existing design matrix rather than the original data. A design matrix is a list containing the basis functions evaluated at the observed values of the independent variable. If your data are already in the form of a design matrix with a corresponding vector of response data, you can use `DesignedRegress` for the same analyses as provided by `Regress`. `DesignMatrix` puts your data in the form of a design matrix.

`DesignedRegress[`*designmatrix*, *response*`]`	fit the model represented by *designmatrix* given the vector *response* of response data
`DesignMatrix[`*data*, {f_1, f_2, ... }, *vars*`]`	give the design matrix for modeling the data as a linear combination of the functions f_i of variables *vars*

Functions for linear regression using a design matrix.

`DesignMatrix` takes the same arguments as `Regress`. It can be used to get the necessary arguments for `DesignedRegress`, or to check whether you correctly specified your basis functions. When you use `DesignMatrix`, the constant term is always included in the model unless `IncludeConstant -> False` is specified. Every option of `Regress` except `IncludeConstant` is accepted by `DesignedRegress`. `RegressionReportValues[DesignedRegress]` gives the values that may be included in the `RegressionReport` list for the `DesignedRegress` function.

<table>
<tr><td>This is the design matrix used in the previous regression analysis.</td><td><code>In[14]:= mat = DesignMatrix[data, {1, x^2}, x]</code></td></tr>
<tr><td></td><td><code>Out[14]= {{1, 0.003025}, {1, 0.008281}, {1, 0.019044}, {1, 0.027889}, {1, 0.033124}, {1, 0.044521}, {1, 0.053824}, {1, 0.061504}, {1, 0.080656}, {1, 0.123201}}</code></td></tr>
</table>

<table>
<tr><td>Here is the vector of observed responses.</td><td><code>In[15]:= response = Map[Last, data]</code></td></tr>
<tr><td></td><td><code>Out[15]= {90, 97, 107, 124, 142, 150, 172, 189, 209, 253}</code></td></tr>
</table>

The result of `DesignedRegress` is identical to that of `Regress`. Note that the predictor names that were specified for the output appear in the `ParameterTable`.

```
In[16]:= DesignedRegress[mat, response, BasisNames ->
          {"Constant","x Squared"}] // Chop[#, 10^(-6)]&
```

`Out[16]=` {ParameterTable →

	Estimate	SE	TStat	PValue
Constant	88.194	4.21167	20.9404	0
x Squared	1430.68	73.6951	19.4136	0

RSquared → 0.979215,
AdjustedRSquared → 0.976616, EstimatedVariance → 64.9129, ANOVATable →

	DF	SumOfSq	MeanSq	FRatio	PValue
Model	1	24464.8	24464.8	376.887	0
Error	8	519.303	64.9129		
Total	9	24984.1			

}

`DesignedRegress[`*svd*, *response*`]`	fit the model represented by *svd*, the singular value decomposition of the design matrix, given the vector *response* of response data

Linear regression using the singular value decomposition of the design matrix.

`DesignedRegress` will also accept the singular value decomposition of the design matrix. If the regression is not weighted, this approach will save recomputing the design matrix decomposition.

This is the singular value decomposition of the design matrix.

`In[17]:= svd = SingularValues[mat];`

When several responses are of interest, this will save recomputing the design matrix decomposition.

`In[18]:= DesignedRegress[svd, response,`
`              RegressionReport -> BestFitParameters]`

`Out[18]= {BestFitParameters → {88.194, 1430.68}}`

⊞ Statistics`MultiDescriptiveStatistics`

Multivariate data consist of observations on two or more variables measured on a set of objects. Descriptive statistics of multivariate data must not only measure properties such as location, dispersion, and shape, but also the interdependence between variables. The functions in this package compute descriptive statistics of data arranged in a $n \times p$ *data matrix*. Specifically, the n rows of a data matrix are treated as independent identically distributed p-variate observations. If your data (vector- or scalar-valued) are ordered or you suspect the data exhibit a trend, then you should consider describing and analyzing your data using the functions provided by the Time Series Pack, an application available through Wolfram Research.

You can calculate some of the standard descriptive statistics for distributions based on the multivariate normal distribution by using the `Statistics`MultinormalDistribution`` package.

The first effect of loading `MultiDescriptiveStatistics` is to trivially extend most of the univariate descriptive statistics made available in the package `Statistics`DescriptiveStatistics``, by applying them to the columns of the data matrix.

Mean	RootMeanSquare
Median	TrimmedMean
Mode	Quantile
GeometricMean	InterpolatedQuantile
HarmonicMean	Quartiles

Univariate location statistics applied to columns of a data matrix.

This loads the package.

```
In[1]:=  <<Statistics`MultiDescriptiveStatistics`
```

Here is a bivariate data set consisting of measurements of stiffness (modulus of elasticity) and bending strength in *pounds/(inches)*^{2} for a sample of 30 pieces of a particular grade of lumber (courtesy of United States Forest Products Laboratory).

```
In[2]:=  data = {{1232, 4175}, {1115, 6652}, {2205, 7612},
         {1897, 10914}, {1932, 10850}, {1612, 7627}, {1598, 6954},
         {1804, 8365}, {1752, 9469}, {2067, 6410}, {2365, 10327},
         {1646, 7320}, {1579, 8196}, {1880, 9709}, {1773, 10370},
         {1712, 7749}, {1932, 6818}, {1820, 9307}, {1900, 6457},
         {2426, 10102}, {1558, 7414}, {1470, 7556}, {1858, 7833},
         {1587, 8309}, {2208, 9559}, {1487, 6255}, {2206, 10723},
         {2332, 5430}, {2540, 12090}, {2322, 10072}} // N;
```

This gives the mean of the data.

```
In[3]:=  M = Mean[data]

Out[3]= {1860.5, 8354.13}
```

This gives the median for each coordinate of the data.

```
In[4]:=  m = Median[data]

Out[4]= {1839., 8014.5}
```

```
        SampleRange                          StandardErrorOfSampleMean
        Variance                             MeanDeviation
        VarianceMLE                          MedianDeviation
        VarianceOfSampleMean                 InterquartileRange
        StandardDeviation                    QuartileDeviation
        StandardDeviationMLE
```

Univariate dispersion statistics applied to columns of a data matrix.

This gives the variances of the stiffness and bending strength variables.

$In[5]:=$ **Variance[data]**

$Out[5]=$ $\{124055., 3.48633 \times 10^6\}$

```
        CentralMoment                        QuartileSkewness
        Skewness                             Kurtosis
        PearsonSkewness1                     KurtosisExcess
        PearsonSkewness2
```

Univariate shape statistics applied to columns of a data matrix.

The univariate shape statistics can be checked to determine whether the marginal distributions are normal. Since the marginal distributions must be normal for the data to be multinormal, univariate shape statistics can be instrumental in ruling out multinormality.

This gives skewness for the stiffness and bending strength variables. These values should be close to zero for symmetrically distributed data.

$In[6]:=$ **skewness = Skewness[data]**

$Out[6]=$ {0.0532835, -0.0312599}

As $n \to \infty$, the distribution of $n/6\beta_1$ (where β_1 is univariate skewness squared) approaches χ_1^2. At a 5% level of significance, the hypothesis that each marginal distribution is symmetrical is not rejected.

$In[7]:=$ **Map[(30/6 #^2 > Quantile[ChiSquareDistribution[1], .95])&, skewness]**

$Out[7]=$ {False, False}

This gives kurtosis excess for the two variables. These values should be close to zero for normally distributed data.

$In[8]:=$ **kurtosisExcess = KurtosisExcess[data]**

$Out[8]=$ {-0.545181, -0.618941}

As $n \to \infty$, the distribution of $\sqrt{n/24}\,\gamma_2$ (where γ_2 is univariate kurtosis excess) approaches $N(0, 1)$. At a 5% level of significance, the hypothesis that each marginal distribution has a normal shape is not rejected.

```
In[9]:= Map[(Abs[Sqrt[30/24] #] >
            Quantile[NormalDistribution[0, 1], .975])&,
            kurtosisExcess]

Out[9]= {False, False}
```

According to the univariate shape statistics, the lumber data may follow a binormal distribution.

The coordinate-wise multivariate extensions of univariate descriptive statistics are provided to simplify the transition between univariate and multivariate data analysis. However, much more information about the multivariate data structure can be learned from statistics that have no analogues in the univariate case. These statistics can be classified as estimating location, dispersion, association, and shape, and are discussed in the following sections.

Multivariate Location

The coordinate-wise mean is identical to the mean obtained when considering all variates simultaneously. Unfortunately, the coordinate-wise definition is not the best multivariate generalization for other location measures such as the median, mode, and quantiles. This section describes various location measures requiring special definitions in the multivariate case.

It is well known that the mean has the disadvantage of being sensitive to outliers and other deviations from multinormality. The median is resistant to such deviations. Multivariate definitions of the median often make use of geometric ideas, such as minimizing the sum of simplex volumes or peeling convex hulls. The package `DiscreteMath`ComputationalGeometry`` is automatically loaded to take advantage of some geometric functions defined therein.

SpatialMedian[*data*]	multivariate median equal to the *p*-vector minimizing the sum of Euclidean distances between the vector and rows from the data matrix
SimplexMedian[*data*]	multivariate median equal to the *p*-vector minimizing the sum of volumes of *p* dimensional simplices the vector forms with all possible combinations of *p* rows from the data matrix
ConvexHullMedian[*data*]	multivariate median computed by ordering the data according to the convex hull layer on which they lie, and taking the median to be the mean of the data lying on the innermost layer
MultivariateTrimmedMean[*data*, *f*]	mean of remaining data when a fraction *f* is removed, outermost points first
MultivariateMode[*data*]	mode considering all variates simultaneously

Multivariate location statistics.

The L_1 median or SpatialMedian gives the *p* dimensional point that minimizes the sum of the Euclidean distances between the point and the data. This estimator is orthogonally equivariant, but not affinely equivariant.

The SimplexMedian gives the *p* dimensional point that, when joined with all possible combinations of *p* points to form *p* dimensional simplices, yields the smallest total simplex volume. In the case of the lumber data, $n = 30$ and $p = 2$, so there are $n!/((n - p)!p!) = 435$ simplices to consider. Ordering points according to the convex hull on which they lie is the basis for ConvexHullMedian. Both SimplexMedian and ConvexHullMedian are affinely equivariant estimators.

This vector minimizes the sum of the Euclidean distances between the vector and the data.

```
In[10]:= s = SpatialMedian[data]
Out[10]= {1757.53, 8062.87}
```

This vector minimizes the sum of the volumes of all possible simplices having the vector as a vertex.

```
In[11]:= v = SimplexMedian[data]
Out[11]= {1803.99, 8364.76}
```

This gives the median formed by peeling the convex layers of the data and taking the mean of the data lying on the innermost layer.

```
In[12]:= c = ConvexHullMedian[data]
Out[12]= {1791.33, 7982.33}
```

This loads the TextListPlot function.

```
In[13]:= <<Graphics`Graphics`
```

Here is a plot comparing the mean (M), the coordinate-wise median (m), the median computed by minimizing the sum of Euclidean distances (s), the median computed by minimizing the sum of simplex volumes (v), the median computed by peeling convex hulls (c), and the data. If the data is contaminated with outliers, the mean will be a poor estimate of location. Here the data is well approximated by a binormal distribution, so all the location estimates are quite similar.

```
In[14]:= (labeled1 = Transpose[Append[Transpose[{M, m, s, v, c}],
                {"M", "m", "s", "v", "c"}]];
       Show[
         TextListPlot[labeled1, DisplayFunction :> Identity],
         ListPlot[data, DisplayFunction :> Identity],
         DisplayFunction :> $DisplayFunction, AspectRatio -> 1,
         Ticks -> {{1200, 1600, 2000, 2400}, Automatic}])
```

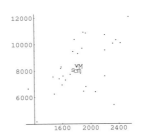

MultivariateTrimmedMean gives an array of estimates ranging from the mean (no trimming) to the convex hull median (all outer convex layers trimmed). This plot shows trims of 20, 40, 60, and 80 percent, in comparison with the mean (M) and the convex hull median (c).

```
In[15]:= (labeled2 = Join[ labeled1[[{1, 5}]],
            Map[Append[MultivariateTrimmedMean[data, #/10],
              ToString[#]]&, {2, 4, 6, 8}] ];
        TextListPlot[labeled2, AspectRatio -> 1])
```

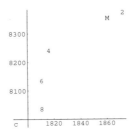

`Ellipsoid[{`x_1`, ... , `x_p`}, {`r_1`, ... , `r_p`}, {`d_1`, ... , `d_p`}]`
  a p-dimensional ellipsoid, centered at {x_1, ... , x_p}, with radii {r_1, ... , r_p}, where r_i is the radius in direction d_i

`Polytope[{{`x_{11}`, ... , `x_{1p}`}, ... , {`x_{m1}`, ... , `x_{mp}`}}, `*conn*`]`
  a p-dimensional polytope with m vertices, where the vertex connectivity is specified by *conn*

Geometric primitives.

In the case of a univariate sample, the qth quantile is that number below which a fraction q of the sample lies. In the case of a multivariate sample and an associated estimate of the underlying population location, we can take the qth quantile to be that locus, centered on the location estimate, within which a fraction q of the sample lies. This leads to different definitions of a multivariate quantile, depending on how the location estimate and the quantile locus are defined. For example, the locus can be an ellipsoid centered on the mean, or a convex polytope centered on the median.

This package defines geometric primitives for representing multidimensional ellipsoids and polytopes. The Ellipsoid and Polytope primitives can be plotted using Graphics and Show for $p = 2$. The results of the location statistics EllipsoidQuantile and EllipsoidQuartiles are expressed in terms of Ellipsoid. The results of the location statistics PolytopeQuantile and PolytopeQuartiles are expressed in terms of Polytope.

The third argument of Ellipsoid, specifying the directions of the semi-axes, is automatically dropped when the semi-axes lie along the coordinate axes. The radii are reordered if necessary.	`In[16]:= Ellipsoid[{1, 2, 3}, {4, 5, 6},`
	`            {{0, 1, 0}, {1, 0, 0}, {0, 0, 1}}]`
	
	`Out[16]= Ellipsoid[{1, 2, 3}, {5, 4, 6}]`

EllipsoidQuantile[*data*, *q*]	$p - 1$ dimensional locus of the qth quantile of the p-variate data, where the data have been ordered using ellipsoids centered on the mean
EllipsoidQuartiles[*data*]	list of the $p - 1$ dimensional loci of the quartiles of the p-variate data, where the data have been ordered using ellipsoids centered on the mean
PolytopeQuantile[*data*, *q*]	$p - 1$ dimensional locus of the qth quantile of the p-variate data, where the data have been ordered using convex hulls centered on the median
PolytopeQuartiles[*data*]	list of the $p - 1$ dimensional loci of the quartiles of the p-variate data, where the data have been ordered using convex hulls centered on the median

More multivariate location statistics.

This gives the minimum and maximum values for the individual stiffness and strength variables.	`In[17]:= ({stiffness, strength} = Transpose[data];`
	`          {{minx, maxx}, {miny, maxy}} =`
	`          Map[{Min[#], Max[#]}&, {stiffness, strength}])`
	
	`Out[17]= {{1115., 2540.}, {4175., 12090.}}`

Here is a plot of the quartile contours of the data, assuming the distribution is elliptically contoured.

```
In[18]:= (q = EllipsoidQuartiles[data];
          Show[Graphics[q], Frame->True, AspectRatio->1,
               PlotRange -> {{minx, maxx}, {miny, maxy}},
               FrameTicks -> {{1200, 1600, 2000, 2400},
               Automatic}])
```

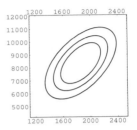

Here is a plot of the quartile contours of the data, found by linear interpolation between convex layers of the data.

```
In[19]:= (q = PolytopeQuartiles[data];
          Show[Graphics[q], Frame->True, AspectRatio->1,
               PlotRange -> {{minx, maxx}, {miny, maxy}},
               FrameTicks -> {{1200, 1600, 2000, 2400},
               Automatic}])
```

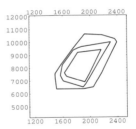

Multivariate Dispersion

While measures of location of p-variate data have p components, measures of dispersion of p-variate data may be matrix-, vector-, or scalar-valued. We have already seen vector-valued dispersion measures in the coordinate-wise extensions of the univariate dispersion measures. This section describes bivariate dispersion measures, matrix-valued measures of the dispersion of all variable pairs, and finally scalar-valued multivariate dispersion measures.

Covariance[*xlist*, *ylist*]	unbiased estimate of covariance between x and y, $\frac{1}{n-1}\sum_i(x_i-\overline{x})(y_i-\overline{y})$
CovarianceMLE[*xlist*, *ylist*]	maximum likelihood estimate of covariance between x and y, $\frac{1}{n}\sum_i(x_i-\overline{x})(y_i-\overline{y})$
Covariance[*xlist*, *ylist*, ScaleMethod -> *method*]	alternative estimate of covariance between x and y, $\sigma_x\sigma_y(\sigma_+^2-\sigma_-^2)/(\sigma_+^2+\sigma_-^2)$, where σ_+ is the scale of $(x/\sigma_x+y/\sigma_y)$, σ_- is the scale of $(x/\sigma_x-y/\sigma_y)$, σ_x is the scale of x, σ_y is the scale of y, and scale is estimated using *method*

Bivariate dispersion statistics.

Covariance and CovarianceMLE consider only a pair of variables at a time. These scalar-valued measures of dispersion are generalizations of Variance and VarianceMLE, respectively. Covariance gives a robust measure of covariance if a robust measure of scale (*i.e.*, MeanDeviation, MedianDeviation, or QuartileDeviation) is selected using the option ScaleMethod.

This gives the value of the off-diagonal elements in CovarianceMatrix[data].

```
In[20]:= cov = Covariance[stiffness, strength]
Out[20]= 361620.
```

The autocovariance of the stiffness is identical to the variance of the stiffness.

```
In[21]:= Covariance[stiffness, stiffness]
Out[21]= 124055.
```

These are alternatives to the usual measure of covariance, employing measures of scale other than StandardDeviation.

```
In[22]:= Map[Covariance[stiffness, strength, ScaleMethod -> #]&,
            {MeanDeviation, MedianDeviation, QuartileDeviation}]
Out[22]= {395846., 300860., 751303.}
```

CovarianceMatrix[*xdata*]	unbiased estimate of $p \times p$ covariance matrix of the vector x based on $n \times p$ data matrix *xdata*, $\frac{1}{n-1}\sum_i(x_i - \overline{x})(x_i - \overline{x})'$
CovarianceMatrix[*xdata*, *ydata*]	unbiased estimate of $p \times q$ covariance matrix between the vectors x and y based on the $n \times p$ data matrix *xdata* and the $n \times q$ data matrix *ydata*, $\frac{1}{n-1}\sum_i(x_i - \overline{x})(y_i - \overline{y})'$
CovarianceMatrix[*xdata*, ScaleMethod -> *method*]	alternative estimate of the covariance matrix, using the specified method of estimating scale
CovarianceMatrixMLE[*xdata*]	maximum likelihood estimate of $p \times p$ covariance matrix of the vector x based on $n \times p$ data matrix *xdata*, $\frac{1}{n}\sum_i(x_i - \overline{x})(x_i - \overline{x})'$
CovarianceMatrixMLE[*xdata*, *ydata*]	maximum likelihood estimate of $p \times q$ covariance matrix between the vectors x and y based on the $n \times p$ data matrix *xdata* and the $n \times q$ matrix *ydata*, $\frac{1}{n}\sum_i(x_i - \overline{x})(y_i - \overline{y})'$
CovarianceMatrixOfSampleMean[*xdata*]	estimate of covariance matrix of sample mean vector $\overline{x}$, $\frac{1}{n}$CovarianceMatrix[*data*]
DispersionMatrix[*xdata*]	estimate of $p \times p$ dispersion matrix of the vector x based on the p-variate points inside the convex hull of *xdata*

Matrix-valued multivariate dispersion statistics.

A dispersion measure such as CovarianceMatrix (using the default option setting ScaleMethod -> StandardDeviation) is sensitive to outliers and other deviations from multinormality. One way to reduce this sensitivity is to replace each element of the covariance matrix with a robust measure of dispersion using an option setting such as ScaleMethod -> MedianDeviation. When this does not result in a positive definite matrix, CovarianceMatrix returns unevaluated. A robust alternative that is guaranteed positive-definite is DispersionMatrix. This function computes a covariance matrix using only those points inside the convex hull of the data. Like CovarianceMatrix with the default setting ScaleMethod -> StandardDeviation, it is affinely equivariant. It is scaled so that the determinant of the matrix is an unbiased estimate of the determinant of the population covariance matrix, when the population distribution is multinormal.

This gives an unbiased estimate for the covariance of the data with $n-1$ as the divisor. Note that the diagonal agrees with Variance[data] and the off-diagonal elements agree with Covariance[stiffness, strength].

```
In[23]:= CovarianceMatrix[data]

Out[23]= {{124055., 361620.}, {361620., 3.48633×10^6}}
```

Here the off-diagonal elements agree with the result obtained for the covariance of stiffness and strength using ScaleMethod -> MedianDeviation.

```
In[24]:= CovarianceMatrix[data, ScaleMethod -> MedianDeviation]

Out[24]= {{133562., 300860.}, {300860., 4.94245×10^6}}
```

This estimate of the dispersion of the data is resistant to outliers that fall on the convex hull of the data.

```
In[25]:= DispersionMatrix[data]

Out[25]= {{149354., 444400.}, {444400., 3.6374×10^6}}
```

GeneralizedVariance[*data*]	determinant of the covariance matrix
TotalVariation[*data*]	trace of the covariance matrix
ConvexHullArea[*data*]	area of region enclosed by convex hull of the bivariate data
MultivariateMeanDeviation[*data*]	scalar mean of the Euclidean distances between the p-variate mean and the p-variate data
MultivariateMedianDeviation[*data*]	scalar median of the Euclidean distances between the p-variate median and the p-variate data

Scalar-valued multivariate dispersion statistics.

These scalar-valued measures of dispersion consider all p variates simultaneously. GeneralizedVariance gives the product of the variances of the principal components of the data, while TotalVariation gives the sum of the variances of the principal components of the data. MultivariateMedianDeviation accepts the option MedianMethod for selecting the coordinate-wise median Median, the total distance minimizing median SpatialMedian, the total simplex volume minimizing median SimplexMedian, or the peeled convex hull median ConvexHullMedian.

The GeneralizedVariance of the data gives the product of the variances of the principal components of the data.

```
In[26]:= GeneralizedVariance[data]

Out[26]= 3.01727×10^11
```

The TotalVariation of the data gives the sum of the variances of the principal components of the data.

```
In[27]:= TotalVariation[data]

Out[27]= 3.61039×10^6
```

This gives the ratio of the area of the convex hull of the data to the area of the smallest box that will enclose the data.

```
In[28]:= ConvexHullArea[data] / Apply[Times,
             SampleRange[data]]

Out[28]= 0.583163
```

Multivariate Association

The scalar measures of association introduced by this package are constrained to lie between −1 and 1. Variables are said to be either negatively correlated, uncorrelated, or positively correlated. Pearson's correlation coefficient is given by `Correlation` and is useful for measuring linear correlation. A value close to zero indicates there is little linear correlation between the variables, but does not rule out significant nonlinear correlation. The default measure of scale is `StandardDeviation`, but alternative measures of scale can be chosen using the option `ScaleMethod`.

`SpearmanRankCorrelation` and `KendallRankCorrelation` are useful when dealing with imprecise numerical or ordinal data. A value close to zero indicates there is not a significant *monotonic* relationship (linear or nonlinear) between the variables.

`Correlation[`*xlist*`, `*ylist*`]`	Pearson's correlation coefficient between x and y, $\sum_i (x_i - \bar{x})(y_i - \bar{y})/(\sqrt{\sum_i (x_i - \bar{x})^2}\sqrt{\sum_i (y_i - \bar{y})^2})$
`Correlation[`*xlist*`, `*ylist*`, ScaleMethod -> ` *method*`]`	alternative estimate of correlation between x and y, $(\sigma_+^2 - \sigma_-^2)/(\sigma_+^2 + \sigma_-^2)$, where σ_+ is the scale of $(x/\sigma_x + y/\sigma_y)$, σ_- is the scale of $(x/\sigma_x - y/\sigma_y)$, σ_x is the scale of x, σ_y is the scale of y, and scale is estimated using *method*
`SpearmanRankCorrelation[`*xlist*`, `*ylist*`]`	Spearman's rank correlation coefficient between x and y, $((n^3 - n)/6 - T_x - T_y - \sum_i r_i^2)/\sqrt{((n^3 - n)/6 - 2T_x)((n^3 - n)/6 - 2T_y)}$ where n is the length of the lists, r_i is the rank difference between x_i and y_i, T_x is the correction term for ties in *xlist*, and T_y is the correction term for ties in *ylist*
`KendallRankCorrelation[`*xlist*`, `*ylist*`]`	Kendall's rank correlation coefficient between x and y, $(n_c - n_d)/\sqrt{(n_c + n_d + n_x)(n_c + n_d + n_y)}$ where n_c is the number of concordant pairs of observations, n_d is the number of discordant pairs, n_x is the number of ties involving only the x variable, and n_y is the number of ties involving only the y variable

Scalar-valued association statistics.

This measures a positive linear correlation between stiffness and strength.

```
In[29]:= r = Correlation[stiffness, strength]
Out[29]= 0.549872
```

Correlation can be used to construct a *t* statistic with *n* − 2 degrees of freedom, where *n* is the sample size. At a 5% level, there is significant nonzero linear correlation between stiffness and strength.

```
In[30]:= Abs[r] Sqrt[(30-2)/(1-r^2)] >
              Quantile[StudentTDistribution[30-2], .975]
Out[30]= True
```

These are alternatives to the Pearson correlation coefficient employing measures of scale other than StandardDeviation.

```
In[31]:= Map[Correlation[stiffness, strength, ScaleMethod -> #]&,
            {MeanDeviation, MedianDeviation, QuartileDeviation}]
Out[31]= {0.585451, 0.370298, 0.722372}
```

These rank measures indicate that there is a positive correlation (possibly nonlinear) between stiffness and strength.

```
In[32]:= {SpearmanRankCorrelation[stiffness, strength],
          KendallRankCorrelation[stiffness, strength]} // N
Out[32]= {0.482367, 0.372843}
```

As DispersionMatrix is a robust alternative to CovarianceMatrix, so is AssociationMatrix a robust alternative to CorrelationMatrix. In the case of the lumber data, the off-diagonal elements of AssociationMatrix are greater than the off-diagonal elements of CorrelationMatrix, indicating that the correlation between stiffness and strength is weaker for the outlying observations.

CorrelationMatrix[*xdata*]	estimate of $p \times p$ correlation matrix of vector *x*, based on $n \times p$ data matrix *xdata*
CorrelationMatrix[*xdata*, *ydata*]	estimate of $p \times q$ correlation matrix between vectors *x* and *y*, based on $n \times p$ data matrix *xdata* and $n \times q$ data matrix *ydata*
CorrelationMatrix[*xdata*, ScaleMethod -> *method*]	alternative estimate of the correlation matrix, using the specified method of estimating scale
AssociationMatrix[*xdata*]	estimate of $p \times p$ association matrix of the vector *x* based on the *p*-variate points inside the convex hull of *xdata*

Matrix-valued association statistics.

The off-diagonal elements of this matrix correspond to Correlation[stiffness, strength].

```
In[33]:= CorrelationMatrix[data]
Out[33]= {{1., 0.549872}, {0.549872, 1.}}
```

Here the off-diagonal elements agree with the result obtained for the correlation of stiffness and strength using ScaleMethod -> MedianDeviation.

```
In[34]:= CorrelationMatrix[data, ScaleMethod -> MedianDeviation]

Out[34]= {{1., 0.370298}, {0.370298, 1.}}
```

This estimate of the association of the data is resistant to outliers that fall on the convex hull of the data.

```
In[35]:= AssociationMatrix[data]

Out[35]= {{1., 0.602933}, {0.602933, 1.}}
```

Multivariate Shape

Multivariate shape statistics consider all variables of the data simultaneously. The functions MultivariateSkewness and MultivariateKurtosisExcess can be used to test for elliptical symmetry or multinormal shape, respectively. MultivariatePearsonSkewness1 measures the skew between the multivariate mean and the multivariate mode, while MultivariatePearsonSkewness2 measures the skew between the multivariate mean and the multivariate median. Note that MultivariateMode is not an interpolated mode and yields {} when all points in the sample are unique. Thus, unless there are many replications in the data, MultivariatePearsonSkewness1 is not recommended. MultivariatePearsonSkewness2 accepts the option MedianMethod for choosing the median.

CentralMoment[$data$, $\{r_1, r_2, \ldots, r_p\}$]	r^{th} central moment $\frac{1}{n} \sum_i (x_{i1} - \overline{x}_1)^{r_1} (x_{i2} - \overline{x}_2)^{r_2} \ldots (x_{ip} - \overline{x}_p)^{r_p}$ where $data$ is an $n \times p$ data matrix and $r = r_1 + r_2 + \ldots + r_p$
MultivariatePearsonSkewness1[$data$]	multivariate Pearson's first coefficient of skewness, $9(\mu_{mean} - \mu_{mode})' \Sigma^{-1} (\mu_{mean} - \mu_{mode})$, where Σ is an unbiased estimate of the population covariance
MultivariatePearsonSkewness2[$data$]	multivariate Pearson's second coefficient of skewness, $9(\mu_{mean} - \mu_{median})' \Sigma^{-1} (\mu_{mean} - \mu_{median})$, where Σ is an unbiased estimate of the population covariance
MultivariateSkewness[$data$]	multivariate coefficient of skewness, $\frac{1}{n^2} \sum_i \sum_j ((x_i - \overline{x})' \Sigma^{-1} (x_j - \overline{x}))^3$, where Σ is the maximum likelihood estimate of the population covariance
MultivariateKurtosis[$data$]	multivariate kurtosis coefficient, $\frac{1}{n} \sum_i ((x_i - \overline{x})' \Sigma^{-1} (x_i - \overline{x}))^2$, where Σ is the maximum likelihood estimate of the population covariance
MultivariateKurtosisExcess[$data$]	multivariate kurtosis excess, MultivariateKurtosis[$data$] $- p(p + 2)$

Multivariate shape statistics.

This list of second-order central moments gives VarianceMLE[data].

```
In[36]:= {CentralMoment[data, {2, 0}],
          CentralMoment[data, {0, 2}]}

Out[36]= {119920., 3.37012 × 10^6}
```

Here is a measure of the skew between the mean and the median computed by peeling the convex hulls.

```
In[37]:= MultivariatePearsonSkewness2[data,
              MedianMethod -> ConvexHullMedian]

Out[37]= 0.45424
```

This gives a single value for skewness for the stiffness and bending strength variables. It should be close to zero for elliptically symmetrical data.

```
In[38]:= multiskewness = MultivariateSkewness[data]

Out[38]= 1.02628
```

As $n \to \infty$, the distribution of $\beta_1 n/6$ (where β_1 is multivariate skewness) approaches χ^2_f, $f = \frac{1}{6}p(p+1)(p+2)$. At a 5% level of significance, the hypothesis of elliptical symmetry is not rejected.

```
In[39]:= multiskewness 30/6 >
          Quantile[ChiSquareDistribution[4], .95]

Out[39]= False
```

This gives a single value for kurtosis excess for the two variables. It should be close to zero for multinormally distributed data.

```
In[40]:= multikurtosisExcess = MultivariateKurtosisExcess[data]

Out[40]= 0.0172012
```

As $n \to \infty$, the distribution of $\gamma_2/\sqrt{8p(p+2)/n}$ (where γ_2 is multivariate kurtosis excess) approaches $N(0, 1)$. At a 5% level of significance, the hypothesis of multinormal shape is not rejected.

```
In[41]:= Abs[ multikurtosisExcess / Sqrt[ 8 2 (2+2)/30 ] ] >
          Quantile[NormalDistribution[0, 1], .975]

Out[41]= False
```

The bivariate shape statistics support the hypothesis that the lumber data follows a binormal distribution.

Multivariate Expected Value

ExpectedValue[f, *data*]	expected value of the pure function *f* with respect to the sample distribution of the data
ExpectedValue[f, *data*, x]	expected value of the function *f* of *x* with respect to the sample distribution of the data, where *x* is scalar-, vector-, or matrix-valued depending on the data

Expected value.

Other location, dispersion, and shape statistics can be computed by taking the expected values of functions with respect to the sample distribution of the data.

Multivariate Data Transformations

As with univariate descriptive statistics, univariate data transformations are applied to columns of the data matrix. ZeroMean[*data*] and Standardize[*data*] do not affect the correlation structure of the data. The package MultiDescriptiveStatistics extends Standardize to accept the option Decorrelate and provides the data transformation PrincipalComponents. Both of these transformations decorrelate the data.

ZeroMean	Standardize

Univariate data transformations applied to columns of a data matrix.

Standardize[*data*, Decorrelate -> True]	transform the data so that the covariance matrix of the result is the identity matrix
PrincipalComponents[*data*]	transform the data so that the covariance matrix of the result is a diagonal matrix with variables ordered from largest variance to smallest

Multivariate data transformations.

Changing the location of the data does not affect the covariance.

```
In[42]:= CovarianceMatrix[ZeroMean[data]]
```
$$Out[42]= \{\{124055., 361620.\}, \{361620., 3.48633 \times 10^6\}\}$$

Standardizing the data coordinate-wise yields unit variances, but does not decorrelate the data.

```
In[43]:= CovarianceMatrix[Standardize[data]]
```
$$Out[43]= \{\{1., 0.549872\}, \{0.549872, 1.\}\}$$

Standardizing the data with Decorrelate -> True gives a new data set with a sample covariance matrix equal to the identity matrix.

```
In[44]:= CovarianceMatrix[Standardize[data, Decorrelate -> True]]
```
$$Out[44]= \{\{1., 0.\}, \{0., 1.\}\}$$

The principal component transformation yields decorrelated variables ordered from largest variance to smallest.

```
In[45]:= CovarianceMatrix[PrincipalComponents[data]]
```
$$Out[45]= \{\{3.52479 \times 10^6, 4.61647 \times 10^{-11}\}, \{4.61647 \times 10^{-11}, 85601.4\}\}$$

If you wish to approximate a multivariate data set by a univariate set, you can take the first column of PrincipalComponents[*data*] and still retain a significant portion of the information conveyed by the original multivariate set. For a data set with $p > 2$, a scatter plot of the first two principal components can sometimes be more informative than scatterplots of all possible variable pairs. Also, some nonparametric procedures that are prohibitively time consuming for higher-dimensional data, can be applied to the first two or three principal components in reasonable time.

◾ Statistics `MultiDiscreteDistributions`

This package provides support for several important multivariate discrete distributions: the multinomial, negative multinomial, and multiple Poisson distributions.

Distributions are usually represented in the symbolic form $name[param_1, param_2, ...]$. When there are many parameters, they may be organized into a list; an example of this is the probability vector parameterizing the multinomial and negative multinomial distributions. Functions such as `Mean`, which give properties of statistical distributions, take the symbolic representation of the distribution as an argument.

`MultinomialDistribution[n, p]`	multinomial distribution with index n and probability vector p
`NegativeMultinomialDistribution[n, p]`	
	negative multinomial distribution with success count n and failure probability vector p
`MultiPoissonDistribution[`μ_0`, `μ`]`	multiple Poisson distribution with mean vector $\{\mu_0 + \mu_1, \mu_0 + \mu_2, ...\}$.

Discrete multivariate probability distributions.

A k-variate **multinomial distribution** with index n and probability vector p may be used to describe a series of n independent trials, in each of which just one of k mutually exclusive events is observed with probability p_i, $i = 1, ..., k$.

A k-variate **negative multinomial distribution** with success count n and failure probability vector p may be used to describe a series of independent trials, in each of which there may be a success or one of k mutually exclusive modes of failure. The ith failure mode is observed with probability p_i, $i = 1, ..., k$, and the trials are discontinued when n successes are observed.

A k-variate **multiple Poisson distribution** with mean vector $\{\mu_0 + \mu_1, ..., \mu_0 + \mu_k\}$ is a common way to generalize the univariate Poisson distribution. Here the random k-vector $\{X_1, ..., X_k\}$ following this distribution is equivalent to $\{Y_1 + Y_0, ..., Y_k + Y_0\}$, where Y_i is a Poisson random variable with mean μ_i, $i = 0, ..., k$.

PDF[*dist*, *x*]	probability density function at *x*, where *x* is vector-valued
CDF[*dist*, *x*]	cumulative distribution function at *x*
Domain[*dist*]	range of values or support of the random vector
Mean[*dist*]	mean
Variance[*dist*]	variance
StandardDeviation[*dist*]	standard deviation
Skewness[*dist*]	coefficient of skewness
Kurtosis[*dist*]	coefficient of kurtosis
KurtosisExcess[*dist*]	kurtosis excess
CharacteristicFunction[*dist*, *t*]	characteristic function $\phi(t)$, where *t* is vector-valued
ExpectedValue[*f*, *dist*]	expected value of pure function *f* with respect to the specified distribution
ExpectedValue[*f*, *dist*, *x*]	expected value of function *f* of *x* with respect to the specified distribution, where *x* is vector-valued
Random[*dist*]	pseudorandom vector with specified distribution
RandomArray[*dist*, *dims*]	pseudorandom array with dimensionality *dims*, and elements from the specified distribution

Functions of univariate statistical distributions applicable to multivariate distributions.

In this package distributions are represented in symbolic form. Generally, PDF[*dist*, *x*] evaluates the density at *x* if *x* is a vector, and otherwise leaves the function in symbolic form. Similarly, CDF[*dist*, *x*] gives the cumulative density and CharacteristicFunction[*dist*, *t*] gives the characteristic function of the specified distribution.

Note that for a vector-valued distribution, functions like Mean, Variance, and Kurtosis give a vector-valued result since they are applied to each coordinate of the vector.

This loads the package.	*In[1]:=* `<<Statistics`MultiDiscreteDistributions``
Here is a symbolic representation of a bivariate multinomial distribution.	*In[2]:=* `(p = {.4, .6};` `mdist = MultinomialDistribution[10, p])`
	Out[2]= `MultinomialDistribution[10, {0.4, 0.6}]`
This gives its probability density function.	*In[3]:=* `pdf = PDF[mdist, {x1, x2}]`
	Out[3]= `If[x1 + x2 == 10, 0.4`^{x1}` 0.6`^{x2}` Multinomial[x1, x2], 0]`

You can make a plot of the density to observe its distribution.

```
In[4]:= (r = Range[0, 10];  t = Transpose[{r + .5, r}];
        ListDensityPlot[
            Table[pdf, {x1, 0, 10}, {x2, 0, 10}],
            FrameTicks -> {t, t}])
```

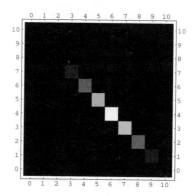

Here is the probability of the distribution in the region $x_1 < 6 \cap x_2 < 7$.

```
In[5]:= CDF[mdist, {6, 7}]
Out[5]= 0.777948
```

This gives the mean vectors of the trivariate versions of the three distributions.

```
In[6]:= {Mean[MultinomialDistribution[n, {p1, p2, p3}]],
        Mean[NegativeMultinomialDistribution[n, {p1, p2, p3}]],
        Mean[MultiPoissonDistribution[mu0, {mu1, mu2, mu3}]]}
```

$$Out[6]= \left\{ \{n\,p1,\, n\,p2,\, n\,p3\},\right.$$
$$\left\{ \frac{n\,p1}{1 - p1 - p2 - p3},\ \frac{n\,p2}{1 - p1 - p2 - p3},\ \frac{n\,p3}{1 - p1 - p2 - p3} \right\},$$
$$\left. \{mu0 + mu1,\, mu0 + mu2,\, mu0 + mu3\} \right\}$$

Here is a sample from each of the distributions.

```
In[7]:= {Random[MultinomialDistribution[10, {.2, .3, .5}]],
        Random[NegativeMultinomialDistribution[5, {2/15, 1/5, 1/3}]],
        Random[MultiPoissonDistribution[1, {1, 2, 4}]]}
Out[7]= {{1, 4, 5}, {0, 0, 1}, {3, 3, 9}}
```

CovarianceMatrix[*dist*]	covariance matrix of the specified distribution
CorrelationMatrix[*dist*]	correlation matrix of the specified distribution
MultivariateSkewness[*dist*]	multivariate coefficient of skewness
MultivariateKurtosis[*dist*]	multivariate kurtosis coefficient
MultivariateKurtosisExcess[*dist*]	multivariate kurtosis excess

Functions of vector-valued multivariate statistical distributions.

The covariance for the bivariate form of the distributions is given here. The covariance is negative for the multinomial distribution, but positive for the negative multinomial and multiple Poisson.

```
In[8]:= {CovarianceMatrix[MultinomialDistribution[n, {p1, p2}]][[1, 2]],
         CovarianceMatrix[NegativeMultinomialDistribution[n, {p1, p2}]][[1,
         2]],
         CovarianceMatrix[MultiPoissonDistribution[mu0, {mu1, mu2}]][[1, 2]]}
```

$$Out[8]= \left\{-n\, p1\, p2,\ \frac{n\, p1\, p2}{(1-p1-p2)^2},\ mu0\right\}$$

+■ Statistics ` MultinormalDistribution `

The most commonly used probability distributions for multivariate data analysis are those derived from the multinormal (multivariate Gaussian) distribution. This package contains multinormal, multivariate Student t, Wishart, Hotelling T^2, and quadratic form distributions.

   Distributions are usually represented in the symbolic form *name*[*param*$_1$, *param*$_2$, ...]. When there are many parameters, they may be organized into lists, as in the case of `QuadraticFormDistribution`. Functions such as `Mean`, which give properties of statistical distributions, take the symbolic representation of the distribution as an argument.

`MultinormalDistribution[`*mu*, *sigma*`]`	multinormal (multivariate Gaussian) distribution with mean vector μ and covariance matrix Σ
`MultivariateTDistribution[`*r*, *m*`]`	multivariate Student t distribution with correlation matrix **R** and m degrees of freedom
`WishartDistribution[`*sigma*, *m*`]`	Wishart distribution with scale matrix Σ and m degrees of freedom
`HotellingTSquareDistribution[`*p*, *m*`]`	Hotelling T^2 distribution with dimensionality parameter p and m degrees of freedom
`QuadraticFormDistribution[{`*A*, *b*, *c*`}, {`*mu*, *sigma*`}]`	distribution of the quadratic form of a multinormal, where A, b, and c are the parameters of the quadratic form $z'Az + b'z + c$, and z is distributed multinormally, with mean vector μ and covariance matrix Σ

Standard probability distributions derived from the multivariate Gaussian distribution.

   A p-variate **multinormal distribution** with mean vector μ and covariance matrix Σ is denoted $N_p(\mu, \Sigma)$. If X_i, $i = 1,...,m$, is distributed $N_p(\vec{0}, \Sigma)$ (where $\vec{0}$ is the zero vector), and $\mathbf{X}$ denotes the $m \times p$ data matrix composed of the m row vectors X_i, then the $p \times p$ matrix $\mathbf{X}'\mathbf{X}$ has a **Wishart distribution** with scale matrix Σ and degrees of freedom parameter m, denoted $W_p(\Sigma, m)$. The Wishart distribution is most typically used when describing the covariance matrix of multinormal samples.

   A vector that has a **multivariate Student t distribution** can also be written as a function of a multinormal random vector. Let X be a standardized multinormal vector with covariance matrix **R** and let S^2 be a chi-square variable with m degrees of freedom. (Note that since X is standardized, $\vec{0}$ is the mean vector of X and **R** is also the correlation matrix of X.) Then $X/S/\sqrt{m}$ has a multivariate t distribution with correlation matrix **R** and m degrees of freedom, denoted $t(\mathbf{R}, m)$. The multivariate Student t distribution is elliptically contoured like the multinormal distribution, and characterizes the ratio of a multinormal vector to the standard deviation common to each variate. When $\mathbf{R} = \mathbf{I}$ and

$m = 1$, the multivariate t distribution is the same as the multivariate Cauchy distribution (here $\mathbf{I}$ denotes the identity matrix).

The **Hotelling T^2 distribution** is a univariate distribution proportional to the F-ratio distribution. If vector d and matrix $\mathbf{M}$ are independently distributed $N_p(\vec{0}, \mathbf{I})$ and $W_p(\mathbf{I}, m)$, then $md'\mathbf{M}^{-1}d$ has the Hotelling T^2 distribution with parameters p and m, denoted $T^2(p, m)$. This distribution is commonly used to describe the sample Mahalanobis distance between two populations.

A **quadratic form** in a multinormal vector X distributed $N_p(\mu, \Sigma)$ is given by $X'AX + b'X + c$, where A is a symmetric $p \times p$ matrix, b is a p-vector, and c is a scalar. This univariate distribution can be useful in discriminant analysis of multinormal samples.

PDF[*dist*, *x*]	probability density function at x, where x is scalar-, vector-, or matrix-valued depending on *dist*
CDF[*dist*, *x*]	cumulative distribution function at x
Domain[*dist*]	range of values or support of the random variable, vector, or matrix
Mean[*dist*]	mean
Variance[*dist*]	variance
StandardDeviation[*dist*]	standard deviation
Skewness[*dist*]	coefficient of skewness
Kurtosis[*dist*]	coefficient of kurtosis
KurtosisExcess[*dist*]	kurtosis excess
CharacteristicFunction[*dist*, *t*]	characteristic function $\phi(t)$, where t is scalar-, vector-, or matrix-valued depending on *dist*
ExpectedValue[*f*, *dist*]	expected value of pure function f with respect to the specified distribution
ExpectedValue[*f*, *dist*, *x*]	expected value of function f of x with respect to the specified distribution, where x is scalar-, vector-, or matrix-valued depending on *dist*
Random[*dist*]	pseudorandom number, vector, or matrix with specified distribution
RandomArray[*dist*, *dims*]	pseudorandom array with dimensionality *dims*, and elements from the specified distribution

Functions of univariate statistical distributions applicable to multivariate distributions.

In this package distributions are represented in symbolic form. Generally, PDF[*dist*, *x*] evaluates the density at *x* if *x* is a numerical value, vector, or matrix, and otherwise leaves the function in symbolic form. Similarly, CDF[*dist*, *x*] gives the cumulative density and CharacteristicFunction[*dist*, *t*] gives the characteristic function of the specified distribution.

In some cases explicit forms of these expressions are not available. For example, PDF[QuadraticFormDistribution[{A, b, c}, {*mu, sigma*}], *x*] does not evaluate, but a Series expansion of the PDF about the lower support point of the domain (for a positive definite quadratic form) does evaluate. The CDF of MultinormalDistribution and StudentTDistribution is available for numerical vector arguments, but not for symbolic vector arguments. In the case of MultivariateTDistribution, the CharacteristicFunction is expressed in terms of an integral.

There are limitations on the covariance matrix Σ in CDF[MultinormalDistribution[*mu, sigma*], *x*] and the correlation matrix **R** in CDF[MultivariateTDistribution[*r*, *m*], *x*]. The matrix $\Sigma = (\sigma_{ij})$ must be of the form $\sigma_{ij} = \sigma_i^2$ for $i = j$ and $\sigma_{ij} = \sigma_i \sigma_j \lambda_i \lambda_j$ for $i \neq j$, where $\lambda_i \in [-1, 1]$. Similarly, the matrix **R** $= (\rho_{ij})$ must be of the form $\rho_{ij} = 1$ for $i = j$ and $\rho_{ij} = \lambda_i \lambda_j$ for $i \neq j$, where $\lambda_i \in [-1, 1]$. A reference for this method of calculating the cumulative distribution function may be found in Y. L. Tong, *The Multivariate Normal Distribution*, Springer-Verlag, 1990.

Note that for a vector-valued distribution such as MultinormalDistribution or MultivariateTDistribution, functions like Mean, Variance, and Kurtosis give a vector-valued result since they are applied to each coordinate of the vector. Similarly, for a matrix-valued distribution, such as WishartDistribution, these functions give a matrix-valued result.

This loads the package.	*In[1]:=* **<<Statistics`MultinormalDistribution`**
Here is a symbolic representation of a standardized binormal distribution. A standardized random vector has a zero mean vector and a covariance matrix equal to its correlation matrix.	*In[2]:=* **(r = {{1, 1/Sqrt[3]}, {1/Sqrt[3], 1}};** **ndist = MultinormalDistribution[{0, 0}, r])** *Out[2]=* MultinormalDistribution$\left[\{0, 0\}, \left\{\left\{1, \frac{1}{\sqrt{3}}\right\}, \left\{\frac{1}{\sqrt{3}}, 1\right\}\right\}\right]$
This gives its probability density function.	*In[3]:=* **pdf = PDF[ndist, {x1, x2}]** *Out[3]=* $\dfrac{\sqrt{\frac{3}{2}}\; \mathbb{e}^{\frac{1}{2}\left(-x2\left(-\frac{\sqrt{3}\,x1}{2}+\frac{3\,x2}{2}\right)-x1\left(\frac{3\,x1}{2}-\frac{\sqrt{3}\,x2}{2}\right)\right)}}{2\,\pi}$

You can make a plot of the density to observe its distribution.

```
In[4]:= Plot3D[pdf, {x1, -3, 3}, {x2, -3, 3},
            PlotRange->All]
```

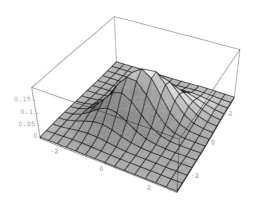

Here is the probability of the distribution in the region $x_1 < -1 \cap x_2 < 1$.

```
In[5]:= CDF[ndist, {-1, 1}]
Out[5]= 0.156544
```

This gives the domain of the quadratic form distribution qdist.

```
In[6]:= (qdist = QuadraticFormDistribution[{{8, -4}, {-4, 3}},
            {-2, 1}, 6}, {{-1, 1}, {{1, 1}, {1, 2}}}];
         Domain[qdist])
```

$$Out[6]= \text{Interval}\left[\left\{\frac{47}{8}, \infty\right\}\right]$$

The series expansion of the PDF of the quadratic form distribution can be plotted. A 20-term expansion is clearly poor for $x > 45$.

```
In[7]:= (polynomial = Normal[Series[PDF[qdist, x],
            {x, 47/8, 20}]];
         Plot[polynomial, {x, 47/8, 50}])
```

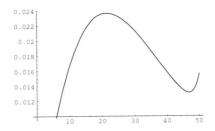

Many of the multivariate distributions have hidden arguments that are evaluated when the distribution is first entered. Random variate generation will be more efficient if these arguments are evaluated only once.

This is an inefficient means of computing 20 multinormal variates because the Cholesky decomposition of the covariance matrix is computed for each variate.

```
In[8]:= (mu = {1, 2, 3, 4};
         sigma = {{1, 1/2, 1/3, 1/4}, {1/2, 1/3, 1/4, 1/5},
                  {1/3, 1/4, 1/5, 1/6}, {1/4, 1/5, 1/6, 1/7}};
         Timing[Table[Random[MultinormalDistribution[mu, sigma]],
                  {20}]][[1]])

Out[8]= 0.52 Second
```

This method of generating 20 variates is more efficient because the Cholesky decomposition is computed once.

```
In[9]:= Timing[RandomArray[
              MultinormalDistribution[mu, sigma],
              20]][[1]]

Out[9]= 0.07 Second
```

Quantile[*dist*, *q*]	q^{th} quantile of the univariate distribution *dist*

Functions of univariate statistical distributions not applicable to multivariate distributions.

In the multivariate case, it is difficult to define Quantile as the inverse of the CDF function, since many values of the random vector (or random matrix) correspond to a single probability value. This package defines Quantile only for the univariate distributions HotellingTSquareDistribution and QuadraticFormDistribution. The elliptically-contoured distributions MultinormalDistribution and MultivariateTDistribution support EllipsoidQuantile and its inverse RegionProbability.

RegionProbability[*dist*, *domain*]	cumulative probability within the specified domain
EllipsoidQuantile[*dist*, *q*]	q^{th} elliptically contoured quantile
CovarianceMatrix[*dist*]	covariance matrix of the specified distribution
CorrelationMatrix[*dist*]	correlation matrix of the specified distribution
MultivariateSkewness[*dist*]	multivariate coefficient of skewness
MultivariateKurtosis[*dist*]	multivariate kurtosis coefficient
MultivariateKurtosisExcess[*dist*]	multivariate kurtosis excess

Functions of vector-valued multivariate statistical distributions.

This gives the ellipse centered on the mean that encloses 50% of the ndist distribution.

```
In[10]:= ellipse = EllipsoidQuantile[ndist, .5]

Out[10]= Ellipsoid[{0, 0}, {1.47874, 0.765452},
             {{0.707107, 0.707107}, {-0.707107, 0.707107}}]
```

This gives the probability of the distribution within the ellipse. Note that the ellipse must correspond to a constant-probability contour of the prescribed distribution.

```
In[11]:= RegionProbability[ndist, ellipse]

Out[11]= 0.5
```

As $m \to \infty$, the qth elliptical contour of MultivariateTDistribution[m, r] approaches the qth elliptical contour of a multinormal distribution with zero mean vector and covariance matrix r.

```
In[12]:= Show[Graphics[{ellipse,
            {Dashing[{.04, .02}], EllipsoidQuantile[
             MultivariateTDistribution[r, 2], .5]},
            {Dashing[{.02, .04}], EllipsoidQuantile[
             MultivariateTDistribution[r, 1], .5]}}
        ], Axes->True]
```

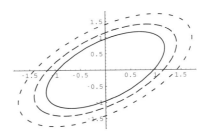

◼ Statistics ' NonlinearFit '

The built-in function `Fit` finds a least-squares fit to a list of data for a model that is a linear combination of the given basis functions; the coefficients of the linear combination are the parameters of the fit. Often a more sophisticated model is desired, where the model is not linear in the parameters. The function `NonlinearFit` allows you to perform this kind of least-squares fit. `NonlinearFit` gives an expression for the model, similar to the output of the built-in function `Fit`. The function `NonlinearRegress` gives a number of regression diagnostics and allows you to specify exactly what will be included in the output, as does the package function `Regress`.

~ `NonlinearFit[`*data, model, variables, parameters*`]`	fit the data to the model with the named variables and parameters, returning the model evaluated at the parameter estimates achieving the least-squares fit
`NonlinearRegress[`*data, model, variables, parameters*`]`	fit the data to the model with the named variables and parameters, returning a list of rules expressing the fit parameter estimates and fit diagnostics

The `NonlinearFit` and `NonlinearRegress` functions.

The model argument of `NonlinearFit` and `NonlinearRegress` must be completely specified by the symbols in the variables argument and the symbols in the parameters argument. The variables argument specifies the independent variables represented in the data. The parameters argument specifies the model parameters for which you would like estimates.

The data argument can be a list of vectors, each vector consisting of the values of the independent variables x_1, x_2, ... , followed by the observed value of the associated response y. The data argument can also be a vector, in which case it is assumed that the vector represents the observed values of the response variable, with the independent variable(s) for the ith response equal to i.

$\{y_1, y_2, \ldots\}$	data points specified by a list of response values, where i is the value of the independent variable associated with the ith response, y_i
$\{\{x_{11}, x_{12}, \ldots, y_1\}, \{x_{21}, x_{22}, \ldots, y_2\}, \ldots\}$	data points specified by a matrix, where x_{ik} is the value of the ith case of the kth independent variable, and y_i is the ith response

Ways of specifying data in `NonlinearFit` and `NonlinearRegress`.

The estimates of the model parameters are chosen to minimize the χ^2 merit function given by the sum of squared residuals $\sum_i e_i^2$. The optimization methods used by `NonlinearFit` and `NonlinearRegress` are iterative so starting values are required for the parameter estimate search. Careful choice of starting values may be necessary, as the parameter estimates found by `NonlinearFit` and `NonlinearRegress` may represent a local minimum in the χ^2 merit function.

The simplest way to specify a parameter is as a symbol, assuming a starting point of 1.0, or as a *{symbol, start}* pair. A parameter can be specified to lie within a prescribed range using *{symbol, start, min, max}* or *{symbol, min, max}*. When elements in the parameter are specified as *{symbol, min, max}*, the starting parameter values are taken to be those minimizing the χ^2 merit function out of the set forming a 2^p factorial design based on the parameter ranges, where p is the number of parameters. For example, if the parameter list is specified as *{{a, 0, 1}, {b, 0, 3}}*, then the value of *{a, b}* in *{{1/3, 1}, {1/3, 2}, {2/3, 1}, {2/3, 2}}* that yields the minimum χ^2 gives starting values for parameters *a* and *b*. When the parameter range is given, the search for the parameter terminates if the search goes outside the specified range.

If a parameter is specified as *{symbol, {start$_0$, start$_1$}}* or *{symbol, {start$_0$, start$_1$}, min, max}*, then the search for parameter estimates uses *start$_0$* and *start$_1$* as the first two values of *symbol*. This form must be used if symbolic derivatives of χ^2 with respect to the parameters cannot be found.

This loads the package.	`In[1]:= << Statistics`NonlinearFit``
This data set [Meyer and Roth, 1972] gives five values for x_1, x_2, and y, describing a reaction involving the catalytic dehydration of n-hexyl alcohol. Here x_1 is partial pressure of alchohol, x_2 is olefin, and y is the rate of reaction.	`In[2]:= data = {{1.0, 1.0, .126}, {2.0, 1.0, .219},` `{1.0, 2.0, .076}, {2.0, 2.0, .126}, {.1, .0, .186}};`

This finds the values of the parameters θ_1, θ_2, and θ_3, such that the model $y = \theta_1\theta_3 x_1/(1 + \theta_1 x_1 + \theta_2 x_2)$ best fits the (x_1, x_2, y) data triples in a least-squares sense. The least-squares parameters are substituted into the model, just as in Fit.

```
In[3]:= NonlinearFit[data,
          theta1 theta3 x1 / (1 + theta1 x1 + theta2 x2),
          {x1, x2}, {theta1, theta2, theta3}]
```

$$Out[3]= \frac{2.44277\, x1}{1 + 3.13151\, x1 + 15.1594\, x2}$$

NonlinearRegress can be used to produce a list of replacement rules for the parameters.

```
In[4]:= BestFitParameters /. NonlinearRegress[data,
          theta1 theta3 x1 / (1 + theta1 x1 + theta2 x2),
          {x1, x2}, {theta1, theta2, theta3},
          RegressionReport -> BestFitParameters]
```

$Out[4]= \{theta1 \to 3.13151, theta2 \to 15.1594, theta3 \to 0.780062\}$

option name	default value	
AccuracyGoal	Automatic	accuracy desired for the χ^2 merit function
Compiled	True	whether the merit function should be compiled
Gradient	Automatic	list of gradient functions
MaxIterations	30	maximum number of iterations in search
Method	LevenbergMarquardt	method used in fit
PrecisionGoal	Automatic	precision desired for the χ^2 merit function
Tolerance	Automatic	numerical tolerance for matrix operations
Weights	Automatic	list of weights for each data point or pure function
WorkingPrecision	$MachinePrecision	precision of the arithmetic to use in calculations

Options for NonlinearFit and NonlinearRegress.

NonlinearFit and NonlinearRegress use FindMinimum to find parameter estimates, thus both functions accept the FindMinimum options AccuracyGoal, Compiled, Gradient, MaxIterations, Method, PrecisionGoal, and WorkingPrecision. The Method option allows you to choose between algorithms for performing the minimization of the χ^2 merit function. The LevenbergMarquardt method gradually shifts the search for the minimum of χ^2 from steepest descent to quadratic minimization. Other possible settings for Method are Gradient (steepest descent), Newton, QuasiNewton, and Automatic. The Automatic method does linear fitting for linear models and LevenbergMarquardt search for nonlinear models, thus the meaning of the automatic method differs between NonlinearFit (or NonlinearRegress) and FindMinimum.

The Weights option allows you to implement weighted least squares by specifying a list of weights, one for each data point; the default Weights -> Automatic implies a weight of unity for each data point. When Weights -> $\{w_1, \ldots, w_n\}$, the parameter estimates are chosen to minimize the weighted sum of squared residuals $\sum_{i=1}^{n} w_i e_i^2$.

Weights can also specify a pure function of the response. For example, to choose parameter estimates to minimize $\sum_{i=1}^{n} \sqrt{y_i} e_i^2$, set Weights -> (Sqrt[#] &).

option name	default value	
RegressionReport	SummaryReport	objects to be included in output

Options unique to NonlinearRegress.

The option `RegressionReport` is accepted by `NonlinearRegress`, but not `NonlinearFit`. If `RegressionReport` is not specified, `NonlinearRegress` automatically gives a list including values for `BestFitParameters`, `ParameterCITable`, `EstimatedVariance`, `ANOVATable`, `Asymptotic`. `CorrelationMatrix`, and `FitCurvatureTable`. This set of objects comprises the default `Summary`. `Report`. The option `RegressionReport` can be used to specify a single object or a list of objects so that more (or less) than the default set of results is included in the output. `RegressionReport`. `Values[NonlinearRegress]` gives the objects that may be included in the `RegressionReport` list for the `NonlinearRegress` function.

`NonlinearRegress` will also accept any option that can be specified for `StudentTCI`. In particular, `ConfidenceLevel` specifies the reference parameter confidence region (the relative curvature of which is given in `FitCurvatureTable`) and the individual parameter confidence intervals given in `ParameterCITable`.

If the `RegressionReport` option is not specified, the default regression output is produced. Note that the `AsymptoticCorrelationMatrix` indicates that the parameters θ_1 and θ_3 are highly correlated, a negative aspect of this model.

```
In[5]:= NonlinearRegress[data,
            theta1 theta3 x1 / (1 + theta1 x1 + theta2 x2),
        {x1, x2}, {theta1, theta2, theta3}]
```

$Out[5]:=$ {BestFitParameters → {theta1 → 3.13151,
         theta2 → 15.1594, theta3 → 0.780062}, ParameterCITable →

	Estimate	Asymptotic SE	CI
theta1	3.13151	0.808417	{-0.346832, 6.60985}
theta2	15.1594	0.631224	{12.4434, 17.8753}
theta3	0.780062	0.151797	{0.126932, 1.43319}

EstimatedVariance → 0.0000217763, ANOVATable →

	DF	SumOfSq	MeanSq
Model	3	0.120041	0.0400138
Error	2	0.0000435527	0.0000217763,
Uncorrected Total	5	0.120085	
Corrected Total	4	0.0126272	

$$\text{AsymptoticCorrelationMatrix} \rightarrow \begin{pmatrix} 1. & 0.287015 & -0.99183 \\ 0.287015 & 1. & -0.182021 \\ -0.99183 & -0.182021 & 1. \end{pmatrix},$$

		Curvature
FitCurvatureTable →	Max Intrinsic	0.037467
	Max Parameter-Effects	12.8161
	95. % Confidence Region	0.22843

BestFit	best fit function
BestFitParameters	best fit parameter estimates
ANOVATable	analysis of variance table
EstimatedVariance	estimated error variance
ParameterTable	table of parameter information including asymptotic standard errors and test statistics
ParameterCITable	table of asymptotic confidence intervals for the parameters
ParameterConfidenceRegion	asymptotic ellipsoidal joint confidence region for the parameters
ParameterConfidenceRegion[{$parm_{i1}$, $parm_{i2}$, ... }]	asymptotic ellipsoidal conditional joint confidence region for the parameters {$parm_{i1}$, $parm_{i2}$, ... }
FitResiduals	differences between the observed responses and the predicted responses
PredictedResponse	fitted values obtained by evaluating the best fit function at the observed values of the independent variables
SinglePredictionCITable	table of asymptotic confidence intervals for predicting a single observation of the response variable
MeanPredictionCITable	table of asymptotic confidence intervals for predicting the expected value of the response variable
AsymptoticCovarianceMatrix	asymptotic covariance matrix of the parameters
AsymptoticCorrelationMatrix	asymptotic correlation matrix of the parameters

Some option settings for `RegressionReport` or objects that may be included in a list specified by `RegressionReport`.

`ANOVATable` provides a partitioning of the sum of squares. Both the uncorrected total sum of squares (without intercept term) and the corrected total sum of squares (with intercept term) are included. The corrected total sum of squares is useful for calculating a value for R^2 comparable to that produced by `Regress`, so that the fit of a nonlinear model can be compared to the fit of a linear model. For example, one possible definition of R^2 for a nonlinear regression is the ratio of the difference between the corrected total sum of squares and the residual sum of squares to the corrected total sum of squares. The other objects in this table have meanings similar to what they would have if specified by the `RegressionReport` option of the linear regression function `Regress`.

StartingParameters	starting values for the parameters

Objects describing the search for the least-squares fit.

Including `StartingParameters` in the list of objects requested by `RegressionReport` is helpful if the search for a least-squares fit is unsuccessful and it is necessary to restart the search at a new point.

HatDiagonal	diagonal of the hat matrix $X(X^T X)^{-1} X^T$, where X is the design matrix for the approximate linear model at the least-squares parameter estimates
StandardizedResiduals	fit residuals scaled by their asymptotic standard errors, computed using the estimated error variance

Diagnostics for detecting outliers.

If the nonlinear model is approximately linear at the least-squares fit, `HatDiagonal` and `StandardizedResiduals` are useful for detecting outliers in the data. `HatDiagonal` gives the leverage of each point, measuring whether each observation of the predictor variables is unusual; a leverage of zero indicates no influence, while a leverage of one indicates that a degree of freedom has been lost to fitting that point.

FitCurvatureTable	maximum relative intrinsic curvature, maximum relative parameter-effects curvature, and relative curvature of the least-squares solution confidence region (where confidence level is given by `ConfidenceLevel`)
ParameterBias	bias in the least-squares estimates of the parameters in a nonlinear model

Diagnostics for evaluating the validity of a linear model approximation to the nonlinear model.

`FitCurvatureTable` expresses the relative curvature of the solution locus at the least-squares estimate in terms of two components, intrinsic and parameter-effects. For the combination of data and model given above, $p = 3$ and $n = 5$. The solution locus is a 3-dimensional subspace of R_5 given by $\{1.0\,\theta_1\theta_3/(1+1.0\,\theta_1+1.0\,\theta_2),\ 2.0\,\theta_1\theta_3/(1+2.0\,\theta_1+1.0\,\theta_2),\ 1.0\,\theta_1\theta_3/(1+1.0\,\theta_1+2.0\,\theta_2),\ 2.0\,\theta_1\theta_3/(1+2.0\,\theta_1+2.0\,\theta_2),\ 0.1\,\theta_1\theta_3/(1+0.1\,\theta_1)\},\ \{\theta_1,\theta_2,\theta_3\} \in R_3$.

Intrinsic curvature describes the normal component of the solution locus curvature at the least-squares estimate. Parameter-effects curvature describes the tangential component of the solution locus curvature at the least-squares estimate. Standardizing curvature to be response-invariant gives relative curvature. Maximizing the relative intrinsic curvature over the $(n-p)$-dimensional subspace normal to the locus gives the maximum relative intrinsic curvature. Similarly, maximizing the relative parameter-effects curvature over the p-dimensional subspace tangential to the locus gives the maximum relative parameter-effects curvature.

Both of these quantities can be compared to the relative curvature of the confidence region centered on the least-squares parameter estimates. If the maximum relative intrinsic curvature is small compared to the confidence region relative curvature, the solution locus is approximately planar over the confidence region. If the maximum relative parameter-effects curvature is small compared to the confidence region relative curvature, the parameter coordinates projected onto the tangential plane are approximately parallel and uniformly spaced over the confidence region.

`ParameterBias` is based on the average curvature of the solution locus tangential to the least-squares estimate.

Here the same data is fit to a reparametrized model, $y = x_1/(\phi_0 + \phi_1 x_1 + \phi_2 x_2)$. Only the BestFit, AsymptoticCorrelationMatrix, and FitCurvatureTable are calculated.

```
In[6]:= NonlinearRegress[data,
          x1 / (phi0 + phi1 x1 + phi2 x2),
          {x1, x2}, {phi0, phi1, phi2},
          RegressionReport -> {BestFit,
                AsymptoticCorrelationMatrix, FitCurvatureTable}]
```

$$Out[6]= \left\{ BestFit \rightarrow \frac{x1}{0.409371 + 1.28195\,x1 + 6.20581\,x2} \right.,$$

AsymptoticCorrelationMatrix $\rightarrow$

$$\begin{pmatrix} 1. & -0.881408 & 0.802639 \\ -0.881408 & 1. & -0.927465 \\ 0.802639 & -0.927465 & 1. \end{pmatrix}, \text{FitCurvatureTable} \rightarrow$$

	Curvature
Max Intrinsic	0.0374669
Max Parameter-Effects	0.0893205
95. % Confidence Region	0.22843

Note that reparametrizing the model does not affect the intrinsic curvature. However, here reparametrization has reduced the parameter-effects curvature below the critical value of 0.22843. This indicates that the least-squares estimates of the parameters ϕ_0, ϕ_1, and ϕ_2 have nearly linear behavior. This could not be said about the least-squares estimates of the parameters θ_1, θ_2, and θ_3 in the original model [Ratkowsky, 1983]. Unfortunately, now the asymptotic correlation between parameters is high for all pairs; a model with fewer parameters should be considered.

The maximum relative curvature diagnostics are useful if you wish to make inferences based on the linear approximation to the nonlinear model. For example, diagnostics based on the asymptotic standard errors of the parameters, such as `ParameterCITable` and `ParameterConfidenceRegion`, are of questionable validity when the linear approximation to the model is poor at the least-squares parameter estimates. The linear approximation is based on the planar assumption, tested by maximum relative intrinsic curvature, and the uniform coordinate assumption, tested by maximum relative parameter-effects curvature. It is usually the uniform coordinate assumption that is invalid [Bates and Watts, 1988].

References

Bates, D. M. and Watts, D. G. (1988). *Nonlinear Regression Analysis and Its Applications*, John Wiley & Sons, New York.

Meyer, R. R. and Roth, P. M. (1972). "Modified Damped Least Squares: An Algorithm for Nonlinear Estimation," *J. Inst. Math. Appl.* 9, 218–233.

Ratkowsky, David A. (1983). *Nonlinear Regression Modeling, A Unified Practical Approach*, Marcel Dekker, New York.

■ Statistics`NormalDistribution`

The most commonly used probability distributions for univariate data analysis are those derived from the normal (Gaussian) distribution. This package contains normal, Student t, chi-square, and F-ratio distributions, which are also included in the package `Statistics`ContinuousDistributions``. If these distributions are all you need, you can save time by loading the `Statistics`Normal`. Distribution`` package instead of the larger `Statistics`ContinuousDistributions``.

The distributions are represented in the symbolic form $name[param_1, param_2, \ldots]$. Functions such as `Mean`, which give properties of statistical distributions, take the symbolic representation of the distribution as an argument.

`NormalDistribution[`*mu, sigma*`]`	normal (Gaussian) distribution with mean μ and standard deviation σ
`StudentTDistribution[`*r*`]`	Student t distribution with r degrees of freedom
`ChiSquareDistribution[`*r*`]`	chi-square distribution with r degrees of freedom
`FRatioDistribution[`r_1, r_2`]`	F-ratio distribution with r_1 numerator and r_2 denominator degrees of freedom

Standard probability distributions derived from the Gaussian distribution.

If each X_i is a normal random variable with unit variance and mean zero, then $\sum_{i=1}^{r} X_i^2$ has a **chi-square distribution** with r degrees of freedom. If a normal variable is standardized by subtracting its mean and dividing by its standard deviation, then the sum of squares of such quantities follows this distribution. The chi-square distribution is most typically used when describing the variance of normal samples.

A variable that has a **Student t distribution** can also be written as a function of normal random variables. Let X be a normal variable with unit variance and zero mean and Z be a chi-square variable with r degrees of freedom. In this case, $X/\sqrt{Z/r}$ has a t distribution with r degrees of freedom. The Student t distribution is symmetric about the vertical axis, and characterizes the ratio of a normal variable to its standard deviation. When $r = 1$, the t distribution is the same as the Cauchy distribution.

The **F-ratio distribution** is the distribution of the ratio of two chi-square variables divided by their respective degrees of freedom. It is commonly used when comparing the variances of two populations in hypothesis testing.

PDF[*dist*, *x*]	probability density function at *x*	
CDF[*dist*, *x*]	cumulative distribution function at *x*	
Quantile[*dist*, *q*]	*q*th quantile	
Domain[*dist*]	range of values of the variable (support)	
Mean[*dist*]	mean	
Variance[*dist*]	variance	
StandardDeviation[*dist*]	standard deviation	
Skewness[*dist*]	coefficient of skewness	
Kurtosis[*dist*]	coefficient of kurtosis	
KurtosisExcess[*dist*]	kurtosis excess	
CharacteristicFunction[*dist*, *t*]	characteristic function $\phi(t)$	
ExpectedValue[*f*, *dist*]	expected value of pure function *f* with respect to the specified distribution	
ExpectedValue[*f*, *dist*, *x*]	expected value of function *f* of *x* with respect to the specified distribution	
Random[*dist*]	pseudorandom number with specified distribution	
RandomArray[*dist*, *dims*]	pseudorandom array with dimensionality *dims*, and elements from the specified distribution	

Functions of statistical distributions.

In this package distributions are represented in symbolic form. PDF[*dist*, *x*] evaluates the distribution at *x* if *x* is a numerical value, and otherwise leaves the function in symbolic form. Similarly, CDF[*dist*, *x*] gives the cumulative distribution and Mean[*dist*] gives the mean of the specified distribution. For a more complete description of the various functions of statistical distributions, see the section that describes the package Statistics`ContinuousDistributions`.

This loads the package.	*In[1]:=* **<<Statistics`NormalDistribution`**
Here is a symbolic representation of the normal distribution with zero mean and unit variance.	*In[2]:=* **ndist = NormalDistribution[0, 1]**
	Out[2]= NormalDistribution[0, 1]
This gives its probability density function.	*In[3]:=* **pdf = PDF[ndist, x]**
	Out[3]= $\dfrac{e^{-\frac{x^2}{2}}}{\sqrt{2\pi}}$

You can make a plot of the density to observe its distribution.

In[4]:= **Plot[pdf,{x, -3, 3}]**

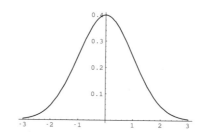

Here is the probability of the lower tail of the distribution, to the left of −2.

In[5]:= **CDF[ndist, -2]**

Out[5]= $\frac{1}{2}\left(1 - \text{Erf}\left[\sqrt{2}\,\right]\right)$

This is the domain.

In[6]:= **Domain[ndist]**

Out[6]= Interval[{-∞, ∞}]

This gives the expected value of a pure function with respect to the chi-square distribution with 5 degrees of freedom.

In[7]:= **ExpectedValue[#^2&, ChiSquareDistribution[5]]**

Out[7]= 35

Here the function is expressed in terms of *x*.

In[8]:= **ExpectedValue[x^2, ChiSquareDistribution[5], x]**

Out[8]= 35

■ Statistics`Common`

The Statistics`Common` subdirectory includes several packages that are used by the primary Statistics packages to share common symbols. These common packages are not meant to be loaded individually. Most users do not need to be aware of them, but if you are writing your own packages using functions defined by a Statistics package, it is wise to check whether symbols you need are introduced via one of the Common packages. The definitions for such symbols are given in the documentation for the primary package that loads the respective Common package. The Statistics`Common` packages are DistributionsCommon`, MultivariateCommon`, PopulationsCommon`, and RegressionCommon`.

CDF	ParameterQ
CharacteristicFunction	PDF
Domain	RandomArray
DomainQ	RegionProbability

Public symbols introduced by Statistics`Common`DistributionsCommon`.

CorrelationMatrix	Ellipsoid
CovarianceMatrix	Polytope

Public symbols introduced by Statistics`Common`MultivariateCommon`.

EqualVariances	KnownVariance
KnownStandardDeviation	

Public symbols introduced by Statistics`Common`PopulationsCommon`.

AdjustedRSquared	ParameterCITable
ANOVATable	ParameterConfidenceRegion
BasisNames	ParameterTable
BestFit	PartialSumOfSquares
BestFitParameters	PredictedResponse
BestFitParametersDelta	PredictedResponseDelta
CatcherMatrix	RegressionReport
CookD	RegressionReportValues
CovarianceMatrixDetRatio	RSquared
DurbinWatsonD	SequentialSumOfSquares
EigenstructureTable	SinglePredictionCITable
EstimatedVariance	StandardizedResiduals
FitResiduals	StudentizedResiduals
HatDiagonal	SummaryReport
JackknifedVariance	VarianceInflation
MeanPredictionCITable	Weights

Public symbols introduced by `Statistics`Common`RegressionCommon``.

12. Utilities

■ Utilities ` BinaryFiles `

This package provides special functions for opening, reading from, and writing to a binary data file. The standard *Mathematica* functions can be used for this purpose, but the functions provided by this package automatically set the relevent options to values suited to binary files. For example, the functions provided for opening a binary file use the option `PageWidth -> Infinity` for setting the output format. *Mathematica* Version 4 provides experimental functionality that may be much more efficient at handling binary files than this package, in the functions `Experimental`BinaryImport` and `Experimental`BinaryExport`.

`OpenReadBinary["`*filename*`"]`	open a file for a binary read
`OpenWriteBinary["`*filename*`"]`	open a new file for a binary write
`OpenAppendBinary["`*filename*`"]`	open a file for appending binary information to the end
`ReadBinary[`*stream*`, `*type*`]`	read the named type of binary data from the stream
`ReadBinary[`*stream*`, `*expr*`]`	read the named types of binary data contained in *expr* from the stream
`ReadListBinary[`*filename*`, `*type*`]`	read all instances of the named type of binary data in the file and place them in a list
`ReadListBinary[`*stream*`, `*type*`, `*n*`]`	read *n* instances of the named type of binary data from the stream and place them in a list
`ReadListBinary[`*stream*`, `*expr*`]`	read the named types of binary data contained in *expr* from the stream and place the resulting expressions in a list
`WriteBinary[`*stream*`, `*data*`]`	write the data to the stream in binary form

Operations involving binary files.

The open file functions return the appropriate `InputStream` or `OutputStream` object. As with the corresponding built-in functions `OpenWrite` and `OpenAppend`, if the file exists, `OpenWriteBinary` overwrites the file, while `OpenAppendBinary` appends to the end of the file. If one of the read or write functions is used on a filename, rather than an opened stream, a stream to that file is opened and left at the position current at the end of the operation. Streams opened for binary operations can be closed using the built-in function `Close`.

The binary read functions `ReadBinary` and `ReadListBinary` behave much as their standard counterparts, `Read` and `ReadList`. The primary difference is that the second argument is held until after the read has occurred. This is important when the second argument is an expression involving binary types. In this case, the types are filled in the order of evaluation.

`WriteBinary` uses a conversion function to convert data into a binary form. This binary form is a list of bytes, each byte represented as an integer between 0 and 255. The conversion function is specified by the `ByteConversion` option, which has a default of `ToBytes`. The list generated by the conversion function is flattened out and written as a stream of bytes.

This loads the package.	*In[1]:=* `<< Utilities`BinaryFiles``
Here is a list of sample data.	*In[2]:=* `data = N[Table[10^n, {n, -10, 10}]]`

Out[2]= $\{1. \times 10^{-10}, 1. \times 10^{-9}, 1. \times 10^{-8}, 1. \times 10^{-7}, 1. \times 10^{-6}, 0.00001,$
$0.0001, 0.001, 0.01, 0.1, 1., 10., 100., 1000., 10000.,$
$100000., 1. \times 10^6, 1. \times 10^7, 1. \times 10^8, 1. \times 10^9, 1. \times 10^{10}\}$

This opens an output stream to the file binarytest.	*In[3]:=* `stream = OpenWriteBinary["binarytest"]`
	Out[3]= `OutputStream[binarytest, 7]`
The list data is written to the file in the default format.	*In[4]:=* `WriteBinary[stream, data]`
This closes the stream.	*In[5]:=* `Close[stream]`
	Out[5]= `binarytest`

This reads in the file binarytest as a list of bytes, giving the binary format of this sequence of numbers.

In[6]:= `ReadListBinary["binarytest", Byte]`

Out[6]= {61, 219, 124, 223,
217, 215, 189, 187, 62, 17, 46, 11, 232, 38, 214,
149, 62, 69, 121, 142, 226, 48, 140, 58, 62, 122, 215, 242,
154, 188, 175, 72, 62, 176, 198, 247, 160, 181, 237, 141, 62,
228, 248, 181, 136, 227, 104, 241, 63, 26, 54, 226, 235, 28,
67, 45, 63, 80, 98, 77, 210, 241, 169, 252, 63, 132, 122, 225,
71, 174, 20, 123, 63, 185, 153, 153, 153, 153, 154, 63,
240, 0, 0, 0, 0, 0, 0, 64, 36, 0, 0, 0, 0, 0, 0, 64, 89, 0, 0,
0, 0, 0, 0, 64, 143, 64, 0, 0, 0, 0, 0, 64, 195, 136, 0, 0, 0,
0, 0, 64, 248, 106, 0, 0, 0, 0, 0, 65, 46, 132, 128, 0, 0, 0, 0,
65, 99, 18, 208, 0, 0, 0, 0, 65, 151, 215, 132, 0, 0, 0, 0, 65,
205, 205, 101, 0, 0, 0, 0, 66, 2, 160, 95, 32, 0, 0, 0}

Note that you can retrieve the original data by reading the file in the same format that it was written.

In[7]:= `ReadListBinary["binarytest", Double]`

Out[7]= $\{1. \times 10^{-10}, 1. \times 10^{-9}, 1. \times 10^{-8}, 1. \times 10^{-7}, 1. \times 10^{-6}, 0.00001,$
$0.0001, 0.001, 0.01, 0.1, 1., 10., 100., 1000., 10000.,$
$100000., 1. \times 10^6, 1. \times 10^7, 1. \times 10^8, 1. \times 10^9, 1. \times 10^{10}\}$

`Byte`	an 8-bit integer
`SignedByte`	an 8-bit signed integer
`Int8`	same as `Byte`
`SignedInt8`	same as `SignedByte`
`Int16`	a 16-bit integer
`SignedInt16`	a signed 16-bit integer
`Int32`	a 32-bit integer
`SignedInt32`	a signed 32-bit integer
`Single`	low-precision real number (32-bits)
`Double`	double-precision real number (64-bits)
`CString`	null-terminated string

Types of binary objects that can be read.

The types of binary objects listed represent the types that can be read and converted. The floating-point formats `Single` and `Double` follow the IEEE specification, used by most C libraries. Once in *Mathematica*, both of these formats are classified as machine precision.

Here the data in binarytest is treated as integers and read in the first five.

In[8]:= `ReadListBinary["binarytest", SignedInt16, 5]`

Out[8]= {15835, 31967, -9769, -16965, 15889}

Unlike Read and ReadList, ReadBinary and ReadListBinary do not evaluate their second argument until after the read has occurred.

In[9]:= `ReadListBinary["binarytest", Double + Double]`

Out[9]= $\{1.1 \times 10^{-9},\ 1.1 \times 10^{-7},\ 0.000011,\ 0.0011,\ 0.11,\ 11.,\ 1100.,$
$110000.,\ 1.1 \times 10^{7},\ 1.1 \times 10^{9},\ 1. \times 10^{10} + \text{EndOfFile}\}$

`ByteOrder -> LeastSignificantByteFirst`	integers are read in order of least significant byte first, as opposed to the default most significant byte first

Option for `ReadBinary` and `ReadListBinary`.

The format in which integers are read is controlled by the `ByteOrder` option. Integers can be treated as least significant byte first or little-endian (a format most often found on machines based on Intel processors, *e.g.*, 386 and 486 MS-DOS, or on DEC VAX) instead of the default most significant byte first or big-endian (a format found on Motorola-based machines, *e.g.*, Macintosh and many RISC-based machines such as SPARC). This option is also available when converting to binary form using `ToBytes`.

ToBytes[*expr*]	Map across the leaves of *expr*, converting the leaves to byte form
ToBytes[*expr*, *type*]	force conversion of the leaves of *expr* to *type*

Utility to convert to byte form.

The ToBytes function converts some kinds of expressions to their byte form (*i.e.*, a list of integers between 0 and 255). ToBytes also works across nested lists of objects of type Integer, Real, or String, converting them to the byte form of one of the binary types listed above. An Integer object is converted to the byte form of the binary type given by the option IntegerConvert. The same may be said for Real objects and the option RealConvert and String objects and the option StringConvert. However, if a type is explicitly specified as a second argument to ToBytes, then conversion is made to that type, overriding any options.

This gives the byte form of the real
number -34.3421435.

In[10]:= **ToBytes[-34.3421435]**

Out[10]= {192, 65, 43, 203, 91, 179, 132, 253}

This converts -34.3421435 to a string of
digits. A warning message is issued.

In[11]:= **ToBytes[-34.3421435, CString]**

ToBytes::cast:
    Warning: converting object of type Real to type CString.

Out[11]= {45, 51, 52, 46, 51, 52, 50, 49, 0}

option name	default value	
ByteOrder	MostSignificantByteFirst	whether to use most-significant-byte-first format for integer conversion
IntegerConvert	Int16	binary type that integers are converted to
RealConvert	Double	binary type that reals are converted to
StringConvert	CString	binary type that strings are converted to

Options for ToBytes.

The ToBytes options control how ToBytes performs type conversion. All of the binary types can be used here. Note that negative integers written as integers (*e.g.*, Int8) will always be automatically written as signed numbers, even if the conversion type does not explicitly specify signed numbers (*e.g.*, SignedInt8).

When using WriteBinary, it may be advantageous to use a conversion function other than ToBytes, for example when writing symbolic expressions in a binary format. If your data are already in byte form, ByteConversion -> Identity tells WriteBinary to perform no conversion.

This opens an output stream to the file binarytest2.

In[12]:= **stream = OpenWriteBinary["binarytest2"]**

Out[12]= OutputStream[binarytest2, 19]

The data are written to the file in single precision real format.

In[13]:= **WriteBinary[stream, data,**
        ByteConversion ->
          (ToBytes[#, RealConvert -> Single]&)]

This closes the stream.

In[14]:= **Close[stream]**

Out[14]= binarytest2

Reading the file assuming a double precision real format yields nonsense.

In[15]:= **ReadListBinary["binarytest2", Double]**

Out[15]= $\{5.74515 \times 10^{-83}, 5.15555 \times 10^{-67}, 7.42285 \times 10^{-51},$
$5.33097 \times 10^{-35}, 5.37764 \times 10^{-19}, 0.0078125, 5.27766 \times 10^{13},$
$5.59549 \times 10^{29}, 7.18642 \times 10^{45}, 4.9389 \times 10^{61}\}$

Of course, the file can be read using the format in which it was written, single precision real format.

In[16]:= **ReadListBinary["binarytest2", Single]**

Out[16]= $\{1. \times 10^{-10}, 1. \times 10^{-9}, 1. \times 10^{-8}, 1. \times 10^{-7}, 1. \times 10^{-6}, 0.00001,$
$0.0001, 0.001, 0.01, 0.1, 1., 10., 100., 1000., 10000.,$
$100000., 1. \times 10^{6}, 1. \times 10^{7}, 1. \times 10^{8}, 1. \times 10^{9}, 1. \times 10^{10}\}$

■ Utilities`DXF`

DXF is a graphics interchange format in plain text form created by AutoDesk, the makers of Auto-CAD. This format can be used for the transfer of graphics to AutoCAD and many other programs, including ray tracers and other three-dimensional rendering packages. The package allows the export of `Graphics3D` objects to a file in the DXF format.

`WriteDXF["`*filename*`", `*graphic*`]`	write a three-dimensional graphic to the named file in DXF format

Using the DXF format.

WriteDXF does not allow writing to an `OutputStream`; it only writes to an unopened file. Note that the graphic must be a `Graphics3D` object. To export a `SurfaceGraphics` or other type of object, the object must first be converted to a `Graphics3D` object.

This loads the package.

```
In[1]:= <<Utilities`DXF`
```

This defines a three-dimensional graphic.

```
In[2]:= gr = Graphics3D[
            {Point[{0, 0, 0}], Point[{0, 1, 0}]}];
```

This creates a DXF file for gr.

```
In[3]:= WriteDXF["test.dxf", gr]

Out[3]= test.dxf
```

Here is what the file looks like.

```
In[4]:= !!test.dxf
  0
SECTION
  2
ENTITIES
  0
POINT
  8
0
  10
0
  20
0
  30
0
  0
POINT
  8
0
  10
0
  20
1
  30
0
  0
ENDSEC
  0
EOF
```

| PolygonsOnly -> False | export all graphics primitives |
| PolygonsOnly -> True | export polygons only |

Options for WriteDXF.

In some cases (*e.g.*, export to ray-tracing software), you may wish to output polygons only. The PolygonsOnly option allows you to do this.

Note: The package currently writes out only certain graphics primitives (Line, Point, Polygon, and Cuboid). Any style information is lost, as are axes, boxes, and so on. This results in a DXF file equivalent to one created by the entities only option from AutoCAD. Cuboids and polygons with more than four sides are subdivided into triangular polygons. (This process creates a temporary file; be sure you have enough disk space to accommodate it. This will consume as much disk space as a *Mathematica* PostScript file for the same objects.)

■ Utilities ` FilterOptions `

The function `FilterOptions` is used to select valid options when passing options from one function to another.

`FilterOptions[`*symbol*`, `*opt*$_1$`, `*opt*$_2$`, ... ]`
                                        return a sequence of options from *opt*$_1$, *opt*$_2$, ... that are valid options for *symbol*

A utility function for passing options.

As an application of `FilterOptions`, consider writing a new function `PlotIntegrate` that calls the functions `Plot` and `NIntegrate` and plots the numerical integral of a function. Although the function `PlotIntegrate` does not use options directly, it passes options along to `Plot` and `NIntegrate`. Options that are valid for `NIntegrate`, however, are not valid for `Plot`, and options that are valid for `Plot` are not valid for `NIntegrate`. The function `FilterOptions` is used to select a valid set of options for each function.

This loads the package.

```
In[1]:= << Utilities`FilterOptions`
```

Here is a simple program that uses the `FilterOptions` function. Valid options are selected using `FilterOptions` before passing the option sequence to `Plot` or `NIntegrate`.

```
In[2]:= PlotIntegrate[f_, {x_, a_, b_}, opts___] :=
          With[{
            optPlot = FilterOptions[Plot, opts],
            optNInt = FilterOptions[NIntegrate,
                                         opts]},
              Plot[
                NIntegrate[f, {x, a, t}, optNInt],
              {t, a, b}, optPlot] ]
```

In this example, the `Frame -> True` and `GridLines -> Automatic` options are passed to `Plot` but not to `NIntegrate`. An error would occur if these options were passed to both functions.

```
In[3]:= PlotIntegrate[Sin[x], {x, 0, 3},
          Frame -> True, GridLines -> Automatic]
```

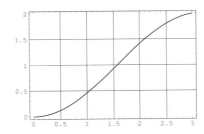

■ Utilities`MemoryConserve`

On computers that have small amounts of installed memory, *Mathematica*'s performance will begin to suffer after carrying out many memory-intensive calculations. This package optimizes *Mathematica*'s use of memory by automatically executing the kernel command Share[ ] whenever memory usage increases by a specified amount.

Share[ ] tries to minimize the memory used to store all expressions by sharing the storage of common subexpressions between different parts of an expression, or different expressions. Using Share[ ] will never affect the results you get from *Mathematica*. It may, however, reduce the amount of memory used, and in many cases also the amount of time taken. Note, however, that the Share[ ] command itself may take some time to run.

On[MemoryConserve]	enable automatic memory conservation
Off[MemoryConserve]	halt automatic memory conservation

Commands for memory conservation.

This loads the package.

```
In[1]:= <<Utilities`MemoryConserve`
```

When memory usage has increased by $MemoryIncrement bytes Share[ ] will be run automatically.

```
In[2]:= $MemoryIncrement
Out[2]= 100000
```

This generates a large list containing multiple copies of the same expression.

```
In[3]:= Table[ ToString[0], {2^15} ];
```

As you do subsequent calculations, Share[ ] is called and a significant amount of memory is freed up. The amount freed will vary from one computer system to another.

```
In[4]:= Length[ % ]
MemoryConserve::start: Running Share[] to conserve memory.
MemoryConserve::end:
    Finished running Share[]; 602156 bytes of memory freed.
Out[4]= 32768
```

This stops automatic memory conservation.

```
In[5]:= Off[ MemoryConserve ]
```

This restarts automatic memory conservation.

```
In[6]:= On[ MemoryConserve ]
```

■ Utilities`Package`

FindPackages[*path*]	give a list of files ending in ".m" for each directory in *path* (*path* may be a single directory of a list of directories)
FindPackages[*path*, *pattern*]	give a list of packages containing the given string pattern (the string pattern should not look for the ".m")

The FindPackages function.

The functions in this package are for searching and maintaining *Mathematica* packages. FindPackages will give a list of the packages available, in their context form (*e.g.*, "Utilities`Package`") or in a full path name form (*e.g.*, "/usr/local/Mathematica/Packages/Standard/Utilities/Package.m".) You can specify a list of directories to search. You can also specify a string pattern, or a list of patterns, to be matched. Note that a pattern should not try to match the ".m"; the function handles this.

This loads the package.

```
In[1]:= <<Utilities`Package`
```

This gives all packages whose names end in "ca" for each directory in $Path. Directories containing no packages fitting the pattern give empty lists.

```
In[2]:= FindPackages[$Path, "*ca"]
Out[2]= {{}, {}, {}, {DiscreteMath`Combinatorica`}, {}}
```

FullPath -> True	return full path names

Option for FindPackages.

Here the same search is performed, but full path names are returned.

```
In[3]:= FindPackages[$Path, "*ca",
            FullPath -> True]
Out[3]= {{}, {}, {},
          {/usr/local/mathematica/AddOns/StandardPackages/
              DiscreteMath/Combinatorica.m},
          {}}
```

Annotation[*package*]	return a list of the keywords (as strings) in the annotation comment fields of the given package
Annotation[*package*, *keyword*]	return the annotation comments that are tagged by *keyword*

The Annotation function.

Mathematica packages contain various annotative comments tagged with keywords. The Annotation function allows you to discover what keywords are present in a package (or list of packages), then retrieve the actual annotation comments containing the keywords. This function recognizes a package name in either context form or as an explicit file name.

This finds the annotative keywords in the `Statistics`NonlinearFit`` package.

```
In[4]:=  Annotation["Statistics`NonlinearFit`"]

Out[4]=  {Title, Context, Name, Author, Summary, Copyright,
            Package Version, Mathematica Version, History, Keywords,
            Sources, Discussion, Warning, Example, Example, Example}
```

The string "Mathematica Version" is a useful keyword; it generally indicates the minimum release of *Mathematica* required for a particular package.

```
In[5]:=  Annotation["Statistics`NonlinearFit`",
            "Mathematica Version"]

Out[5]=  {(* :Mathematica Version: 4.0 *)}
```

■ Utilities `ShowTime`

The function ShowTime uses the built-in function Timing to print timing information for each evaluation. After the package is loaded, ShowTime is automatically applied to every evaluation. Automatic printing of timing information can be turned off using Off[ShowTime] and turned back on using On[ShowTime].

ShowTime[*expr*]	print the time required for evaluation of *expr*
On[ShowTime]	print timing information for subsequent evaluations
Off[ShowTime]	turn off automatic printing of timing information

Automatic printing of timing information.

This loads the package.

```
In[1]:= << Utilities`ShowTime`
```

The time required to evaluate this numerical integral is printed before returning the result.

```
In[2]:= NIntegrate[x Exp[-x] Sin[x],
            {x, 0, Infinity}]
```

0.06 Second

```
Out[2]= 0.5
```

This turns automatic timing off.

```
In[3]:= Off[ShowTime]
```

0. Second

Timing information is printed if ShowTime is entered explicitly.

```
In[4]:= ShowTime[Sum[1/n, {n, 1, 99}]]
```

0. Second

$$Out[4]= \frac{360968703235711654233892612988250163157207}{6972037522971247716453380893535312303556800}$$

Appendix: Functions Moved to the Kernel

As *Mathematica* continues to be enhanced, it is sometimes useful to move functionality previously implemented as add-on packages to the kernel. This allows a function to take advantage of internal features of the kernel. In Version 4, several packages and functions became kernel functions.

Calculus`DiracDelta`	DiscreteMath`KroneckerDelta`
Calculus`FourierTransform`	DiscreteMath`ZTransform`
Calculus`LaplaceTransform`	NumberTheory`ContinuedFractions`

Packages with functionality moved into the kernel.

The following is a summary of the changes involved. Detailed information about the use of the kernel versions of these functions can be found in *The Mathematica Book*.

■ From the `Calculus` Directory

The Laplace transform functionality (from the packages `LaplaceTransform.m` and `DiracDelta.m`) were moved entirely to the kernel. The symbolic Fourier transforms from `FourierTransform.m` were made part of the kernel, although the numeric transforms remain in the add-on.

In `DiracDelta.m`, the functions `UnitStep` and `DiracDelta` were moved directly into the kernel. The simplification functions `SimplifyUnitStep` and `SimplifyDiracDelta` were converted into an internal `Developer`` context function named `Developer`PseudoFunctionsSimplify`. You will not normally need to call this directly, as `Simplify` takes advantage of its functionality. Also note that the `ZeroValue` option of `UnitStep` is no longer applicable; `UnitStep[0]` is defined as 1.

The Laplace and inverse Laplace functions from `LaplaceTransform.m` were moved directly into the kernel. The main change is that, because the kernel implementation is based on enhancements to integration, the old `DefiniteIntegral` option to these functions is no longer appropriate. `LaplaceTransform` also now inherits the options of `Integrate`.

For `FourierTransform.m`, only the symbolic functions were moved. This includes `FourierTransform`, `FourierCosTransform`, `FourierSinTransform`, and their inverses. As with the Laplace transform, the `DefiniteIntegral` option is no longer used. In addition, the `FourierFrequencyConstant` and `FourierOverallConstant` options were combined into the option `FourierParameters`. A similar change was made to the numeric transforms that remain in the modified add-on.

■ From the `DiscreteMath` Directory

As with the continuous transforms, so with the discrete transforms; the `ZTransform.m` and `Kronecker` `Delta.m` packages were moved into the kernel, with the exception of the `DiscreteStep` function.

In the case of `KroneckerDelta.m`, the `KroneckerDelta` pseudo-function became a kernel function. However, it should be noted that the multi-dimensional definition changed; `KroneckerDelta[`i, j, k, ... `]` is defined as 1 where $i == j == k == \ldots$. This was formerly defined as 1 only where $i == j == k == \ldots == 0$. The old definition can be found in the new function `DiscreteDelta`. The simplfication capabilities of `SimplifyKroneckerDelta` are now automatic or part of `Simplify`; there is no separate function for this purpose. The functions `DiscreteStep` and `SimplifyDiscreteStep` are now found in the add-on `DiscreteStep.m`.

The `ZTransform` and `InverseZTransform` functions from `ZTransform.m` were moved entirely to the kernel. As a result, transforms that the package was not able to perform can now be computed. The syntax is entirely as before.

■ From the `NumberTheory` Directory

Several pieces of functionality were moved from the `ContinuedFractions.m` add-on to the kernel. The most significant was `ContinuedFraction` itself. In the process, it was enhanced to handle periodic continued fractions; but it no longer returns the `ContinuedFractionForm` data type, instead returning a list structure. As a result of the new return type, the kernel also includes `FromContinuedFraction`, which performs the same operation as `Normal` on a `ContinuedFractionForm` data object. `Continued` `FractionForm` itself is still found in the package, and is used primarily to nicely typeset the continued fraction.

Also in the same package, the capabilities of `ToPeriodicForm` were used to enhance the kernel function `RealDigits`. `PeriodicForm` remains in `ContinuedFractions.m` for formatting.

■ Additional Changes

A number of packages had been made obsolete in Version 3, but remained as a stub package warning of the change. Those stub packages have now been removed completely.

The `DiracDelta`, `LaplaceTransform`, `KroneckerDelta`, and `ZTransform` packages described above now exist only as stubs to emit a warning that the file is obsolete.

Also, note that the package `Horner.m` has been moved from the `NumericalMath` to the `Algebra` directory, with the corresponding change in context name.

Appendix: How *Mathematica* Packages Are Set Up

This appendix discusses package contexts, loading packages, autoloading packages, and naming packages. Contexts in *Mathematica* allow you to use the same symbol names for several different functions and to load and autoload packages in a system-independent way. The discussion is illustrated using the standard add-on packages, but it also applies to the *Mathematica* Applications Library packages and *Mathematica* packages you write and share with colleagues. The appendix concludes with a discussion of how to use the standard add-on packages as building blocks for your own packages.

■ Contexts

In *Mathematica* the mechanism of contexts is used to keep package symbols separate from symbols in the main session. The basic idea is that the *full name* of any symbol is broken into two parts: a *context* and a *short name*. The full name is written as *context`short*, where ` is the backquote or grave accent character, called a context mark in *Mathematica*.

Contexts in *Mathematica* work somewhat like file directories in many operating systems. You can always specify a particular file by giving its complete name, including its directory. But at any given point, there is usually a current working directory, analogous to the current *Mathematica* context. Variables that are in the current context can be specified just by giving their short names in the same way that files in the current working directory can be specified by just giving their short names. The global variable $Context gives the current *Mathematica* context.

As is also the case with directories, contexts in *Mathematica* can be hierarchical. For example, the full name of a symbol can involve a sequence of context names, as in c_1`$c_2$`c_3`*name*. By convention, the symbols that are created by loading a standard *Mathematica* package have a context whose name is related to the name of the package. As an example, loading the package Statistics`Descriptive`. Statistics` defines the symbol Statistics`DescriptiveStatistics`Mean, which you can then use to compute the mean of a list of data.

`<<`*context*`	read in a *Mathematica* package corresponding to the specified context
`<<`c_1`$c_2$` ... `$c_n$`	read in a *Mathematica* package corresponding to a hierarchical context

Using contexts to specify a *Mathematica* package.

This loads a package for calculating descriptive statistics.

     In[1]:=   `<<Statistics`DescriptiveStatistics``

The symbol `Mean` is in the context set up by the package.	`In[2]:=` **`Context[Mean]`**
	`Out[2]=` `Statistics`DescriptiveStatistics``
You can refer to the symbol using its short name.	`In[3]:=` **`Mean[{1., 2., 3., 4.}]`**
	`Out[3]=` `2.5`

The full names of symbols defined in packages can be quite long. In most cases, you will only need to use their short names. However, if two symbols with the same short name appear in two different packages, *Mathematica* must decide which symbol to use. The decision is made using a list of contexts called the *context search path*. The global variable `$ContextPath` gives this list of contexts.

When you type in a short name for a symbol, *Mathematica* assumes that you want the symbol with that name whose context appears earliest in the context search path. As a result, symbols with the same short name whose contexts appear later in the context search path are effectively shadowed. To refer to these symbols, you need to use their full names. In such a case, *Mathematica* will warn you when you read in the package that creates the overlap in short names. It will tell you which symbols will be shadowed by the new symbols that are being introduced.

This reads in a package that contains specifications for various colors.	`In[4]:=` **`<<Graphics`Colors`**
A warning is generated because a symbol with the short name `Gray` occurs in both packages we have loaded.	`In[5]:=` **`<<Miscellaneous`Units`**

```
Gray::shdw:
    Symbol Gray appears in multiple contexts
    {Miscellaneous`SIUnits`, Graphics`Colors`}
    ; definitions in context Miscellaneous`SIUnits`
    may shadow or be shadowed by other definitions.
```

You can use the full name to distinguish between the two uses of `Gray`. This gives a color specification.	`In[6]:=` **`?Graphics`Colors`Gray`**
	`Gray is a color given in the RGBColor system.`
This gives a unit of radiation.	`In[7]:=` **`?Miscellaneous`SIUnits`Gray`**
	`Gray is the derived SI unit of absorbed dose of radiation.`

Conflicts can occur not only between symbols in different packages, but also between symbols in packages and symbols that you introduce directly in your *Mathematica* session. If you define a symbol in your current context, then this symbol will shadow any other symbol with the same short name in packages that you read in. The reason for this is that *Mathematica* always searches for symbols in the current context before looking in contexts on the context search path.

`$Context` is a global variable that gives the current context. The default context for *Mathematica* sessions is `Global``.	`In[8]:=` **`$Context`**
	`Out[8]=` `Global``
This defines a function `Div` in the current context `Global``.	`In[9]:=` **`Div[f_] := 1/f`**

Any other functions with the short name Div will be shadowed by the one in your current context.	`In[10]:= <<Calculus`VectorAnalysis``  `Div::shdw: Symbol Div appears in multiple contexts` `   {Calculus`VectorAnalysis`, Global`}` `   ; definitions in context Calculus`VectorAnalysis`` `    may shadow or be shadowed by other definitions.`
This removes Div completely from the current context.	`In[11]:= Remove[Div]`

Now the Div from the package is used. It computes the divergence of a given vector field in the Cartesian coordinate system.	`In[12]:= Div[{x, y^2, x}, Cartesian[x, y, z]]`
	
	`Out[12]= 1 + 2 y`

Many *Mathematica* users choose to load their favorite packages automatically at start-up, and autoloading is discussed later in this section. If you autoload your packages at start-up, you will not need to be concerned about using a package function in a *Mathematica* session before actually reading in the package. If you mistakenly introduce a package function and do not apply Remove to the function before loading the package, *Mathematica* will warn you that the package function is being shadowed. *Mathematica* will use your version of the function, rather than the one from the package. Applying Remove after the package is loaded will remove your version of the function and allow you to use the package definition for the function.

Remove["*name*"]	remove a function that has been introduced in error

Making sure that *Mathematica* uses correct definitions from packages.

■ Loading Packages

Contexts in *Mathematica* are used to specify packages in a way that is independent of the particular computer system being used. From this point of view, loading a package is simply a way of making a particular context available. The global variable $Packages gives a list of the contexts corresponding to all the packages that have been loaded in your current *Mathematica* session.

<<*context*` or Get["*context*`"]	read in a *Mathematica* package corresponding to the specified context
Needs["*context*`"]	read in the package if the specified context is not already in $Packages
DeclarePackage["*context*`", {"*name₁*", "*name₂*", ... }]	
	declare that Needs["*context*`"] should be automatically executed if a symbol with any of the names *nameᵢ* is used

Ways to load packages.

You have already seen how to explicitly read in a package using the command <<*context*`, or equivalently, Get["*context*`"]. Often, however, you will want to read in a particular package only if it is needed. The command Needs["*context*`"] tells *Mathematica* to read in a package if the context associated with that package is not already in the list $Packages.

Some packages are not designed to be loaded twice and large packages may take a while to load. You should use Needs if you are unsure whether you have loaded a particular package in your current session. Some packages are set up so that when they are loaded, other related packages are automatically loaded at the same time. Packages may have been loaded that you haven't explicitly read in, so it is best to let *Mathematica* decide which packages need loading.

When you set up a large collection of *Mathematica* packages, it is a good idea to create an initialization package or names file that contains a sequence of DeclarePackage commands, specifying packages to load when particular names are used. Within a particular *Mathematica* session, you then need to load explicitly only the initialization package. When you have done this, all the other packages will automatically be loaded if and when they are needed. Initialization packages and autoloading packages via the Autoload directory are discussed in detail in the next section.

The package context list initially contains only the Global` and System` contexts. Usually new symbols are introduced in the context Global`. Built-in symbols are in the context System`.

```
In[1]:= $Packages
Out[1]= {Global`, System`}
```

This specifies that the symbols Div, Grad, and Curl are defined in Calculus`VectorAnalysis`. Now Needs["Calculus`VectorAnalysis`"] will be executed if any of these symbols are used.

```
In[2]:= DeclarePackage["Calculus`VectorAnalysis`",
            {"Div", "Grad", "Curl"}]
Out[2]= Calculus`VectorAnalysis`
```

When you first use Grad, *Mathematica* automatically loads the package Calculus`VectorAnalysis`.

```
In[3]:= Grad[x^2 + y^2, Cartesian[x, y, z]]
Out[3]= {2 x, 2 y, 0}
```

The package's context has been prepended to $Packages.

```
In[4]:= $Packages
Out[4]= {Calculus`VectorAnalysis`, Global`, System`}
```

■ Autoloading Packages

Explicit loading of packages is useful if you are trying to minimize the amount of memory used by your *Mathematica* session or if you are in an early stage of package development. However, most users find that they use a particular set of packages often, and they want those packages to load automatically.

Initialization Packages

<<dir`	read in the initialization package from the directory dir

Initializing all packages in a directory.

If you frequently use many functions from different packages in the same standard package directory, you will find it convenient to load the initialization package from that directory. After you load the initialization package you can use any of the functions contained in packages included in the directory. You will not need to load each package separately.

For example, **<<Graphics`** loads the initialization package **Graphics`Kernel`init`** and makes all the functions provided in the **Graphics** packages available in your current session. Using one of these functions will cause the appropriate package to be loaded if it has not been loaded already. An initialization package really consists of nothing more than a sequence of **DeclarePackage** commands.

This loads the **Graphics`Kernel`init`** package. All the functions contained in **Graphics** packages are now available for use.

In[1]:= **<<Graphics`**

Since the **Graphics`Graphics`** package defining **BarChart** has not yet been loaded, using **BarChart** will cause the package to load.

In[2]:= **BarChart[{1.2, 3.4, 2.2, 1.8}]**

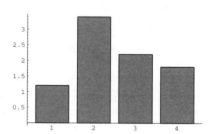

Autoload Directory

The main *Mathematica* distribution CD-ROM typically includes the standard add-on packages described in this book, placed in the **AddOns/StandardPackages/** subdirectory of your main *Mathematica* directory. *Mathematica* application packages, such as *Electrical Engineering*, are usually installed in the **AddOns/Applications/** subdirectory. The **AddOns/Autoload/** subdirectory provides another way to autoload packages.

+	AddOns/StandardPackages/*name*/	directory for a named category within the standard add-on packages
+	AddOns/Applications/*name*/	directory for a named application within the *Mathematica* Applications Library
+	AddOns/Autoload/*name*/	directory in which to place an initialization file so that it is loaded when *Mathematica* is started

Directories for *Mathematica* packages.

If you would like *Mathematica* to automatically load the initialization file for a directory of packages whenever you start the kernel, then you should copy the initialization file into the appropriate place in the AddOns/Autoload/ directory. For example, you might copy AddOns/Standard·Packages/Graphics/Kernel/init.m into AddOns/Autoload/Graphics/Kernel/init.m so that all graphics packages will load as needed. If you have the *Electrical Engineering* application, you might copy AddOns/Applications/EE/Kernel/init.m into AddOns/Autoload/EE/Kernel/init.m so that the *Electrical Engineering* application will load as needed. Effective use of the Autoload directory allows you to create a version of *Mathematica* tailored to your needs.

■ Advanced Topic: Package File Names

+	*name*.mx	file in DumpSave format
	name.m	file in *Mathematica* source format
+	*name*/Kernel/init.m	kernel initialization file for a particular directory
+	*name*/init.m	default initialization file for a particular directory

The typical sequence of files looked for by <<*name*`.

To take advantage of loading packages using contexts, you should know how Get and related *Mathematica* functions translate names of the form *name*` into particular file names. <<*name*` first tries to load *name*.mx, the preferred name for a *Mathematica* expression dump. If there is no *name*.mx, <<*name*` tries to load *name*.m, the preferred name for a *Mathematica* source file or package. If there is no *name*.m, <<*name*` tries to load the file *name*/Kernel/init.m, the preferred name for a kernel initialization package for the directory *name*. If there is no *name*/Kernel/init.m, <<*name*` tries to load the file *name*/init.m, the default initialization package for the directory *name*.

The names of the source files for the standard packages have the .m extension, and you are encouraged to name your package source files using this extension as well.

■ Advanced Topic: Basing New Packages on the Standard *Mathematica* Packages

There is a standard sequence of *Mathematica* commands that is typically used to set up the contexts in a package. These commands set the values of $Context and $ContextPath so that the new symbols which are introduced are created in the appropriate contexts.

BeginPackage["*Package*`"]	set *Package*` to be the current context, and put only System` on the context search path
f::usage = "*text*", ...	introduce the objects intended for export (and no others)
Begin["`Private`"]	set the current context to *Package*`Private`
f[*args*] = *value*, ...	give the main body of definitions in the package
End[ ]	revert to the previous context (here *Package*`)
EndPackage[ ]	end the package, prepending the *Package*` to the context search path

The standard sequence of context control commands in a package.

When you write a package that uses symbols provided by one of the standard packages, you need to be aware of auxiliary packages automatically loaded via a multiargument BeginPackage. A few directories have a Common subdirectory for auxiliary packages containing shared symbols. For example, the package Statistics`ConfidenceIntervals` automatically loads Statistics`Common`PopulationsCommon` using the BeginPackage function.

BeginPackage["*Package*`", "*Needed*$_1$`", ...]	begin a package, specifying that contexts in addition to System` are needed

Specifying interdependence of packages using BeginPackage.

$ContextPath is a global variable that gives a list of contexts to search in trying to find a symbol.

```
In[1]:= $ContextPath
Out[1]= {Global`, System`}
```

This loads the standard package Statistics`ConfidenceIntervals`.

```
In[2]:= <<Statistics`ConfidenceIntervals`
```

The context for the auxiliary package PopulationsCommon was automatically added to $ContextPath when the package ConfidenceIntervals was loaded.

```
In[3]:=  $ContextPath
Out[3]=  {Statistics`ConfidenceIntervals`,
             Statistics`Common`PopulationsCommon`,
             Statistics`NormalDistribution`,
             Statistics`Common`DistributionsCommon`,
             Statistics`DescriptiveStatistics`, Global`, System`}
```

You can request all symbols from the Statistics`Common`PopulationsCommon` context.

```
In[4]:=  Names["Statistics`Common`PopulationsCommon`*"]
Out[4]=  {EqualVariances, KnownStandardDeviation, KnownVariance}
```

You can determine the context of a particular symbol by applying the Context function or by locating the symbol in the index of this book.

```
In[5]:=  {Context[MeanCI], Context[KnownVariance]}
Out[5]=  {Statistics`ConfidenceIntervals`,
             Statistics`Common`PopulationsCommon`}
```

Here is the confidence interval for the mean of the data set {-1., 0., 1.}, where the default option setting KnownVariance -> None specifies that the population variance is to be estimated from the data.

```
In[6]:=  MeanCI[{-1., 0., 1.}]
Out[6]=  {-2.48414, 2.48414}
```

Here is the confidence interval for the mean of the data when the population variance is known to be 1., a machine-precision number. Both symbols MeanCI and KnownVariance are recognized because their contexts are on $ContextPath.

```
In[7]:=  MeanCI[{-1., 0., 1.}, KnownVariance -> 1.]
Out[7]=  {-1.13159, 1.13159}
```

When loading a standard package into a session, there is no need to be concerned about the existence of an auxiliary package, or the specific contexts of the symbols introduced by the load. However, if you would like to use BeginPackage to base a package of your own on symbols from a standard package, then the contexts of the symbols are important. Consider the example packages myPackage1.m and myPackage2.m.

```
BeginPackage["myPackage1`", "Statistics`ConfidenceIntervals`"]

myMeanCI::usage = "myMeanCI[list] gives my value for MeanCI."

Begin["`Private`"]

myMeanCI[list_] := MeanCI[list, KnownVariance -> 1.]

End[ ]

EndPackage[ ]
```

The sample package myPackage1.m.

In the first example package `myPackage1.m`, the `BeginPackage` statement calls `Needs` on the standard package `ConfidenceIntervals`. The function `myMeanCI` is defined in terms of the package symbols `MeanCI` and `KnownVariance`. You probably won't want to create a package solely for the sake of hardwiring an option value for a function, but this example illustrates the general situation of using symbols defined in other packages in your own package definitions.

This loads the package.	`In[1]:= <<myPackage1\``
This applies the package function `myMeanCI` to the data set.	`In[2]:= myMeanCI[{-1., 0., 1.}]` `Out[2]= {-2.48414, 2.48414}`

Unfortunately, since the auxiliary package was not specified in `BeginPackage`, the symbol `KnownVariance` in the definition for `myMeanCI` has context `myPackage1\`Private\`` rather than context `Statistics\`Common\`PopulationsCommon\``. The context `myPackage1\`Private\`` is not on `$ContextPath` after the package is loaded, so the option setting `myPackage1\`Private\`KnownVariance -> 1.` is not recognized and the default `KnownVariance -> None` is used. Rather than the interval obtained using the option setting `KnownVariance -> 1.`, `myMeanCI` gives the same confidence interval as the default `MeanCI`.

This example shows that when you want to use symbols from the standard packages in your own package, you should determine the specific context for each symbol you need, and include those contexts in the `BeginPackage` statement of your package. The second example package does just that.

```
BeginPackage["myPackage2`", "Statistics`ConfidenceIntervals`",
            "Statistics`Common`PopulationsCommon`"]

myMeanCI::usage = "myMeanCI[list] gives my value for MeanCI."

Begin["`Private`"]

myMeanCI[list_] := MeanCI[list, KnownVariance -> 1.]

End[ ]

EndPackage[ ]
```

The sample package `myPackage2.m`.

In the second example package `myPackage2.m`, the `BeginPackage` statement calls `Needs` on both the `ConfidenceIntervals` package and the auxiliary package `PopulationsCommon`. This is necessary for *Mathematica* to correctly interpret all the standard package symbols used in the `myPackage2.m`.

This loads the package.	`In[1]:= <<myPackage2\``
Now `myMeanCI` implements `KnownVariance -> 1.` as desired.	`In[2]:= myMeanCI[{-1., 0., 1.}]` `Out[2]= {-1.13159, 1.13159}`

Auxiliary packages are usually employed to allow two or more packages to share symbols without shadowing. Symbol shadowing can be useful when it warns you that two symbols with the same name, but different purposes, occur in your session. However, in the case of standard packages from a single subdirectory (such as `Statistics`), the packages are meant to work together and shadowing is undesirable.

In this book, symbols introduced by an auxiliary package are documented both with the standard packages that load the auxiliary package and in a separate section devoted to the auxiliary package.

Index